ROYAL HISTORICAL SOCIETY

# ANNUAL
# BIBLIOGRAPHY
# OF
# BRITISH AND IRISH
# HISTORY

ROYAL HISTORICAL SOCIETY

# ANNUAL
# BIBLIOGRAPHY
# OF
# BRITISH AND IRISH
# HISTORY

## PUBLICATIONS OF 1990

GENERAL EDITORS:

### BARBARA ENGLISH & J.J.N. PALMER

J.S.A. Adamson   Andrew Ayton   Jeremy Black   Virginia Davis
C.C. Eldridge   Barbara English   M.W.C. Hassall   A.C. Howe
James Kirk   V.J. Morris   Mary O'Dowd
D.J. Orton   D.M. Palliser   Michael S. Partridge
Huw Pryce   John Turner   A. Williams

For the Royal Historical Society and
in association with the Institute of
Historical Research

OXFORD UNIVERSITY PRESS

1991

*Oxford University Press, Walton Street, Oxford* OX2 6DP

*Oxford New York Toronto*
*Delhi Bombay Calcutta Madras Karachi*
*Petaling Jaya Singapore Hong Kong Tokyo*
*Nairobi Dar es Salaam Cape Town*
*Melbourne Auckland*
*and associated companies in*
*Berlin Ibadan*

*Oxford is a trade mark of Oxford University Press*

*Published in the United States*
*by Oxford University Press, New York*

*British Library Cataloguing in Publication Data*
(data available)
*ISBN 0–19–820294–6*

*Library of Congress Cataloging in Publication Data*
*(data available)*
*ISBN 0–19–820294–6*

*Typeset by Pentacor* PLC, *High Wycombe, Bucks*
*Printed and bound in*
*Great Britain by Biddles Ltd.*
*Guildford and King's Lynn*

# CONTENTS

# Contents

# Contents

# Contents

# PREFACE

The Annual Bibliography of the Royal Historical Society is designed in the first place to serve the urgent needs of scholars, which has meant subordinating total coverage and refinements of arrangement to speed of production. Nevertheless, it aims to be as comprehensive as possible: this year's volume includes 1221 books and 2948 articles by 3608 authors. There is some variety in the subdivisions of sections, which are those approved by section editors. Searchers are advised to use these subdivisions in conjunction with the four indices. The indices form an important part of the work and cover, as far as is practicable, all major subjects of the book and articles listed, whether or not they figure in the titles. The counties used in identifying places are, in general, the pre-1974 counties. A list of the county abbreviations employed is given at the head of the Index of Places.

Within each subsection (except Bc) the items are arranged in alphabetical order of authors. All collective works by a number of authors (such as *Festschriften* and Conference Proceedings) are placed in section Bc. Articles contained in these collective works are individually listed in the appropriate subsection and there referred to by their Bc numbers in lieu of the usual publication details. In this year's volume, these Bc references are the only abbreviated form of publication details. Items in the section 'Empire and Commonwealth post 1783' are included only if they contribute substantially to British or Irish history: for example, 'British teaplanters in Ceylon' would be included, whereas 'The social structure of Ceylon' would not.

Works that extend over two sections appear as a rule in the earlier and are cross-referenced at the head of the later section. Items covering more than two sections are listd in Ba or Bb.

The general editors regret that the name of A.C. Howe, co-editor of Section H, was inadvertently omitted from the list of section editors in the volume published in 1990.

The editors are especially indebted to the Director and the library staff of the Institute of Historical Research for undertaking searches without which the compilation of this Bibliography would not be practicable. The editors also wish to express their particular gratitude to their colleague George Slater of the Computer Centre for important programming assistance.

This is the first Annual Bibliography since the foundation of the project that has not been edited, in whole or part, by Professor Sir Geoffrey Elton; he has decided to 'retire', although he continues to supply many items for other editors. A short history of the Annual Bibliography is included overleaf. In recognition of his contribution over the years, this volume is dedicated to its founder, Professor Sir Geoffrey Elton.

University of Hull

# THE ANNUAL BIBLIOGRAPHY

I had been aware of the need for an annual bibliography of British history for quite a few years, especially since the series called *Writings on British History*, published by the Institute of Historical Research, was running years behind current dates. In the second year of my presidency of the Royal Historical Society I therefore persuaded the Council of the Society that such an enterprise would make sense. Two problems arose. One concerned the planning and production of annual volumes; the other their publication and distribution. I knew that the Society would have to undertake the first and hoped that it would also look after the second (if only to keep the price low), but I could not raise any money for the purpose and thus came to an arrangement with Harvester Press which proved efficient enough but put up the price of each volume considerably.

We first set up a trial committee to plan a satisfactory scheme, and on the strength of that experiment we organised things along lines which have proved enduring. In 1975 we collected the material for the first volume which appeared, as I had stipulated from the first, in September the following year. Of the gallant twelve adventurers then setting sail five were still in the crew in 1989.

I had from the first worked on the supposition that one could not expect section editors to do their own searching and collecting; instead they were asked to process cards sent out every quarter, though they were to add any items they knew ought to be included that failed to reach them. The cards were obtained by the Institute of Historical Research for books (using mostly the BNB) and the International Medieval Bibliography at Leeds for articles, with additional searches by myself made possible by the open access to periodicals and new books offered by the Cambridge University Library. For ten years the AB was thus put together in my office in the History Faculty at Cambridge where I kept the material and indexes in boxes and in February each year typed the copy for the printer. I was aware that the whole thing ought to be handled by computerisation but postponed that move for two reasons: I had no knowledge or skill in that area, and I reckoned that we should first arrive experimentally at the right way of presenting the results. In the early years I constantly took some pretty chancy decisions at speed, hoping that a correct and usable product would emerge from much trial and little error. I kept in touch with the section editors – most of whom obligingly observed the rules and times set – by fairly regular circulars, and the volumes continued to appear never later than October in the following year.

Ten years of this somewhat primitive method of working produced a standardized form for the Bibliography which seemed to satisfy the profession. The only trouble was that I spent a lot of time on the work – something like two to three hours a day throughout the year if one averaged it out. By the spring of 1984 I had decided that the time had come to find a successor, and by the end of that year David Palliser had bravely agreed to take over. Even discovering how much of the operation existed only in my head did not put him off. Soon after he accepted the chair at Hull where he found a team well versed in the use of a computer, and the outcome was the present excellent organisation in the truly competent hands of Barbara English and John Palmer. There have been other changes, not only in the editorial team. In 1984 the Leeds enterprise had to cease its assistance, and before that the BNB cards had ceased to be useful, but between them the Hull editorial team and the IHR have devised highly effective ways of getting the information to the section editors. So, when Harvester in effect bowed out, a well matured product could be handed on to Oxford University Press. *Writings on British History* was in the end completed down to 1974, so we now possess an effective bibliographical analysis of everything published in the twentieth century on British and Irish history. The next step, I suppose, should be an amalgamated index to the Annual Bibliography to help us find items of whose date of publication we are not quite sure!

Geoffrey Elton

| | |
|---|---|
| Arch. | Archaeological |
| B. | Bulletin |
| BAR | British Archaeological Reports |
| c. | circa |
| (comp.) | compiler(s) |
| CBA | Council for British Archaeology |
| (ed.) | editor(s) |
| edn. | edition |
| fl. | floruit |
| HMSO | Her Majesty's Stationery Office |
| Inst. | Institute |
| J. | Journal |
| ns | new series |
| no. | number |
| P. | Proceedings |
| Q. | Quarterly |
| R. | Review |
| rev. | revised |
| ser. | series |
| Soc. | Society |
| T. | Transactions |
| UP | University Press |

# A. AUXILIARY

*See also* Bc65; Fd27.

(a) *Archives and Bibliography*

1. Anon. 'List of publications of the history of the book trade in the north', Bc139, 193–98.
2. Anon. 'Periodical literature in Wales, 1987', *Archaeologia Cambrensis* 137 (1989 for 1988), 152–56.
3. Anon. 'Select annotated bibliography' [arts, literature and society], Bc61, 320–24.
4. Anon. 'The *Innes Review*, 1950–1990', *Innes R.* 41 (1990), 3–6.
5. Anon. 'The publications of Asa Briggs', Bc104, 249–57.
6. Anon. *Archives of the British Conservative Party, 1867–1986: a detailed guide to the microform collections.* Reading; Research Publications; 1989. Pp 153.
7. Anon. *Archives of the British Labour Party: a detailed guide to the microform collections.* Reading; Research Publications; 1990. Pp 180.
8. Anon. *Archives of the Independent Labour Party, 1856–1975: a detailed guide to the microform collections.* Reading; Research Publications; 1990. Pp 260.
9. Anon. *Archives of the Settlement movement; series 1: the archives of the National Federation of Settlements and Successors, c.1899–1958, listing and guide to parts one to five.* Reading; Research Publications; 1990. Pp 145.
10. Anon. *British biographical index.* London; Saur for Glasgow University (Humanities Reference Systems Unit); 1990. 4 vols. Pp 1600.
11. Anon. *Chancery patent rolls calendar (C66: 20–23 Jas. 1).* Richmond; List & Index Soc. vol. 233; 1989. Unpaginated.
12. Anon. *Chatham papers: correspondence of William Pitt the Younger, 1783–1806.* Richmond; List & Index Soc. vol. 237; 1989. Pp 526.
13. Anon. *Foreign Office general correspondence: political, 1953 (FO 371/102561–108094).* Richmond; List & Index Soc. vol. 235; 1989. Pp 400.
14. Anon. *Kirklees archives, 1959–1989: an illustrated guide to Kirklees District Archives.* Wakefield; West Yorkshire Archives & Archaeology Joint Committee; 1989. Pp 80.
15. Anon. *Records of the Information Departments (INF), 1915–1982.* Richmond; List & Index Soc. vol. 236; 1989. Pp 644.
16. Anon. *Records of the Royal Mint, 1446-C20th (MINT 1–29).* Richmond; List & Index Soc. vol. 234; 1989. Pp 489.
17. Anon. *The condition of the English working class: the papers of the Reverend Henry Solby, 1813–1903: a listing and guide to the Research Publications microfilm collections.* Reading; Research Publications; 1989. Pp 160.

18. Bell, Peter (comp.). *Victorian women: an index to biographies and memoirs.* Edinburgh; Bell; 1989. Pp 134.

19. Bellinger, Aidan; Eggleston, Paul. 'Downside Abbey architectural drawings collection', *Catholic Archives* 10 (1990), 26–31.

20. Bennett, John (comp.). 'British labour history publications, 1989', *Labour History R.* 55/2 (1990), 28–63.

21. Bennett, Scott. 'The Golden Stain of Time: preserving Victorian periodicals', Bc87, 166–83.

22. Bentley, Michael (ed.). *International review of periodical literature: British history, 1988.* Cambridge; Chadwyck-Healey; 1989. Pp 100.

23. Bicknell, Peter. *The picturesque scenery of the Lake District, 1752–1855: a bibliographical study.* Winchester; St Paul's Bibliographies; 1990. Pp 208.

24. Bird, Stephen (comp.). 'Classified list of archive deposits, 1988', *Labour History R.* 55/2 (1990), 21–27.

25. Blom, F.J.M. 'The publications of Charles Leslie', *Edinburgh Bibliographical Soc. T.* 6/1 (1990), 10–36.

26. Blyth, Joan. 'Records for the primary school', Bc132, 157–61.

27. Bogan, Peter Paul. 'The archival heritage of Dr Milner and Archbishop King of St Peter's parish, Winchester', *Catholic Archives* 10 (1990), 8–16.

28. Camp, Anthony J. 'The genealogist's use of probate records', Bc132, 287–98.

29. Coates, Richard. *A bibliography of place-names in Hampshire and the Isle of Wight: with a section on Hampshire dialect.* Brighton; Younsmere; 1988. Pp iv, 65.

30. Colwell, Stella. 'A genealogist's view of the public records—ideals and reality', Bc132, 151–56.

31. Cooter, Roger. *Phrenology in the British Isles: an annotated historical biobibliography and index.* Metuchen (NJ); Scarecrow; 1990. Pp xviii, 431.

32. Cox, Nicholas. 'The thirty-year rule and freedom of information: access to government records', Bc132, 75–88.

33. Cox, Richard William. *History of sport in Britain: a bibliography of historical publications, 1800–1987.* Manchester; Manchester UP; 1990. Pp 272.

34. Dixon, Diana; Costa, Pierre; Goose, Nigel. 'Current bibliography of urban history', *Urban History Yearbook* 17 (1990), 264–321.

35. Dyer, Christopher C.; *et al.* (comp.). 'Review of periodical literature in economic and social history, 1988', *Economic History R.* 2nd ser. 43 (1990), 104–36.

36. Dyson, Brian. 'Business archives in the library at the university of Hull', *Business Archives* 60 (1990), 14–23.

37. Egan, Geoff. 'Post-medieval Britain and Ireland in 1988', *Post-Medieval Archaeology* 23 (1989), 25–67.

38. English, Barbara; Palmer, J.J.N. (ed.). *Annual bibliography of British and Irish history: publications of 1989.* Oxford; Oxford UP for the Royal Historical Soc.; 1990. Pp x, 244.

39. English, Richard (comp.). 'Select bibliography of writings on Irish economic and social history published in 1989', *Irish Economic & Social History* 17 (1990), 101–16.

40. Erickson, Amy Louise. 'An introduction to probate accounts', Bc132, 273–86.

41. Everitt, Alan. 'Joan Thirsk: a personal appreciation', Bc77, 17–26.

42. Forsythe, John. 'Clogher diocesan papers, 2', *Archivium Hibernicum* 44 (1989), 5–70.

43. Foster, Meryl. 'Copyright and the business archivist', *Business Archives* 59 (1990), 1–18.

44. Frere, S.S. 'Roman Britain in 1989, i: sites explored', *Britannia* 21 (1990), 304–64.

45. Frow, Edmund; Frow, Ruth. 'The Irish collection in the Working Class Movement Library', *Labour History R.* 55/2 (1990), 75–78.

46. George, E.; George, S. *Guide to the probate inventories of the Bristol deanery of the diocese of Bristol (1542–1804)*. Bristol; Bristol Record Soc.; 1988. Pp xxiv, 292.

47. Gibson, Jeremy S.W. *Poll books, c.1692–1872: a directory to holdings in Great Britain*. Birmingham; Federation of Family History Societies; 1989. Pp 69.

48. Gibson, Jeremy S.W.; Rogers, Colin D. *Electoral registers since 1932; and burgess rolls*. Birmingham; Federation of Family History Societies; 1989. Pp 51.

49. Gilbert, Victor F. (comp.). 'Theses and dissertations on British labour history, 1989' [with additions to previous entries], *Labour History R.* 55/2 (1990), 6–14.

50. Goodall, Francis. 'Bibliography' [of business history, 1989], *Business Archives* 60 (1990), 65–72.

51. Graham, T.W. (ed.). 'A list of articles on Scottish history published during the year 1988', *Scottish Historical R.* 68 (1989), 185–95.

52. Grant, A. (comp.). 'A list of essays on Scottish history in books published during the year 1988', *Scottish Historical R.* 68 (1989), 196–202.

53. Gregory, M. 'The seventeenth- and eighteenth-century archives of the Bar Convent, York', *Catholic Archives* 10 (1990), 3–7.

54. Hale, Matthew; Hawkins, Richard; Partridge, Michael S. (comp.). 'List of publications on the economic and social history of Great Britain and Ireland published in 1989', *Economic History R.* 2nd ser. 43 (1990), 697–734.

55. Hall, Lesley A. 'The Eugenics Society archives in the Contemporary Medical Archives Centre [Wellcome Inst. Library]', *Medical History* 34 (1990), 327–33.

56. Hallam, Elizabeth M. 'Nine centuries of keeping the public records', Bc132, 23–42.

57. Harris, Eileen; Savage, Nicholas (ed.). *British architectural books and writers, 1556–1785*. Cambridge; Cambridge UP; 1990. Pp 528.

58. Hassall, M.W.C.; Tomlin, R.S.O. 'Roman Britain in 1989, ii: inscriptions', *Britannia* 21 (1990), 365–78.

59. Heath, Peter. 'Between reform and Reformation: the English church in the fourteenth and fifteenth centuries' [a bibliographical survey], *J. of Ecclesiastical History* 41 (1990), 647–78.

60. Higgs, Edward. 'The Public Record Office, the historian, and information technology', Bc132, 101–10.

61. Holmes, Malcolm J.; Knight, Richard G. *Camden past and present: a guide to Camden's archives and local studies collections.* London; London Borough of Camden Library & Arts Department; 1989. Pp 74.

62. Howell, David. 'The Ramsay MacDonald papers in the John Rylands University Library of Manchester: an initial discussion', *B. of the John Rylands University Library of Manchester* 72/2 (1990), 101–20.

63. Hume, John Robert. *Scotland's industrial past: an introduction to Scotland's industrial history with a catalogue of preserved material.* Edinburgh; National Museum of Scotland; 1990. Pp 80.

64. Jackson, Anthony R. 'Archives of an educational drama pioneer: a survey of the Peter Slade Collection in the John Rylands University Library of Manchester', *B. of the John Rylands University Library of Manchester* 72/2 (1990), 153–66.

65. Jones, Philip Henry. *A bibliography of the history of Wales.* Cardiff; Wales UP; 3rd edn. 1989. Pp 72 + 21 microfiche.

66. Kenyon, John R. 'Post-medieval Britain in periodic literature in 1988', *Post-Medieval Archaeology* 23 (1989), 69–75.

67. Kenyon, John R. *Castles, town defences and artillery fortifications in Britain and Ireland: a bibliography,* vol. 3. London; CBA (Research report no. 72); 1990. Pp iv, 88.

68. Korsten, Frans. *A catalogue of the library of Thomas Baker.* Cambridge; Cambridge UP; 1990. Pp 480.

69. Kushner, Tony. 'Jewish Communists in twentieth-century Britain: the Zaidman collection' [in Sheffield University Library], *Labour History R.* 55/2 (1990), 66–75.

70. Latham, David; Latham, Sheila. *An annotated critical bibliography of William Morris.* London; Harvester Wheatsheaf; 1990. Pp 256.

71. Lorimer, R.J.R. 'Government record keeping: a tale from the Department of Employment', Bc132, 61–66.

72. Marsh, Christopher. 'In the name of God? Will-making and faith in early modern England', Bc132, 215–50.

73. Martin, G.H. 'The future of the public records', Bc132, 43–48.

74. Martin, G.H. 'The public records in 1988', Bc132, 17–22.

75. McNaughtan, Adam. 'A century of saltmarket literature, 1790–1890', Bc139, 165–80.

76. McNiven, Peter. 'Handlist of the papers of Edward Augustus Freeman in the John Rylands University Library of Manchester', *B. of the John Rylands University Library of Manchester* 72/2 (1990), 27–71.

77. Messick, Frederic M. 'With Churchill: a bibliography of his associates', *B. of Bibliography* 46 (1989), 195–203.

78. Meynell, Geoffrey Guy. *A bibliography of Dr Thomas Sydenham, 1624–1689.* Folkestone; Winterdown; 1990. Pp 225.

79. Mitchell, Karen Jane. 'ICI—a brief history and guide to the archives', *Business Archives* 60 (1990), 1–13.

80. Moon, Marjorie. *Benjamin Tabart's juvenile library: a bibliography of books for children published, written, edited and sold by Mr. Tabart, 1801–1820.* Winchester; St Paul's Bibliographies; 1990. Pp 192.

81. Morgan, Raine (comp.). 'Annual list and brief review of articles on agrarian history, 1988', *Agricultural History R.* 38 (1990), 83–94.

82. Myers, Robin. *The archive of the Stationers' Company, 1554–1984: an account of the records.* Winchester; St Paul's Bibliographies; 1990. Pp 500.

83. Nicol, Alexandra. 'Liaison: public records held in other record offices', Bc132, 139–50.

84. Nixon, Malcolm I. 'Business records deposited in 1988', *Business Archives* 60 (1990), 73–86.

85. Ollerenshaw, Philip. 'British business history: a review of recent periodical literature', *Business History* 32/1 (1990), 76–99.

86. Orde, Anne; Rollason, David. 'Bibliography of the writings of W.R. Ward', Bc115, 347–67.

87. Padfield, Timothy R. 'Preservation and conservation: will our public records survive another 150 years?', Bc132, 67–74.

88. Partridge, Michael S. *The duke of Wellington, 1769–1852: a bibliography.* London; Meckler; 1990. Pp 150.

89. Peacock, Alison. 'The papers of Joseph Barlow Brooks (1874–1952) in the Methodist Archives and Research Centre', *B. of the John Rylands University Library of Manchester* 72/2 (1990), 121–34.

90. Pelteret, David A.E. *Catalogue of English post-conquest vernacular documents.* Woodbridge; Boydell; 1990. Pp x, 137.

91. Perkins, J. 'A list of publications of J.B. Trapp', Bc129, 295–303.

92. Post, J.B. 'Public Record Office publication: past performance and future prospects', Bc132, 89–100.

93. Price, Helen. 'Some theses accepted in the United Kingdom, 1986–1987', *J. of Imperial & Commonwealth History* 18 (1990), 397–402.

94. Pryce, Huw; Griffith, W.P. (comp.). 'Articles relating to the history of Wales published mainly in 1988', *Welsh History R.* 15 (1990–1), 317–30.

95. Ratcliffe, F.W. 'The contribution of book-trade studies to scholarship', Bc139, 1–11.

96. Refausse, Raymond. 'The Representative Church Body Library, Dublin', *Catholic Archives* 10 (1990), 21–25; 39.

97. Rexroth, Frank (ed.). *Research on British history in the Federal Republic of Germany, 1983–1988: an annotated bibliography.* London; German Historical Inst.; 1990. Pp 139.

98. Richmond, Lesley M.; Turton, Alison (ed.). *The brewing industry: a guide to historical records.* Manchester; Manchester UP; 1990. Pp 304.

99. Rimmer, David. 'Coventry City Record Office', *Archives* 19 (1990), 199–212.

100. Robbins, Keith G. (ed.). *The Blackwell biographical dictionary of*

*British political life in the twentieth century.* Oxford; Blackwell; 1990. Pp 460.

101. Roberts, Julian; Watson, Andrew G. *John Dee's library catalogue.* London; Bibliographical Soc.; 1990. Pp 250.

102. Rolph, Avril; Kerr, Linda; Allen, Jane. 'An introduction to books for lesbian history studies', Bc1, 188–227.

103. Roper, Michael. 'The international role of the Public Record Office', Bc132, 9–16.

104. Russell, Colin A.; Russell, Shirley P. 'The archives of Sir Edward Falkland: resources, problems and methods', *British J. for the History of Science* 23 (1990), 175–85.

105. Scott, John. *A matter of record: documentary sources in social research.* Cambridge; Polity; 1990. Pp 200.

106. Shorrocks, Derek M.S. 'The role of the [Somerset Archaeological and Natural History] Society in the preservation of the county's archive heritage', *Somerset Archaeology & Natural History* 133 (1990 for 1989), 260–68.

107. Short, D. Mary. *A bibliography of printed items related to the city of Lincoln.* Lincoln; Lincoln Record Soc. Publications no. 79; 1990. Pp 408.

108. Simpson, Murray C.T. (comp.). *A catalogue of the library of Revd. James Nairn (1629–1678), bequeathed by him to Edinburgh University Library.* Edinburgh; Edinburgh UP; 1990. Pp 260.

109. Slingerland, Jean Harris (ed.). *The Wellesley index to Victorian periodicals, 1824–1900, vol. 5: epitome and index, etc.* London; Routledge; 1989. Pp xiv, 923.

110. Smith, Brian S. 'The National Register of Archives and other nationwide finding aids', Bc132, 111–18.

111. Smith, Christopher. 'The archives of the Plymouth diocese', *Catholic Archives* 10 (1990), 17–20; 39.

112. Smith, K.J. 'Sampling and selection: current policies', Bc132, 49–60.

113. Smyth, Susan J.(ed.). *The Koestler archive in Edinburgh University Library: a checklist.* Edinburgh; Edinburgh University Library; 1987. Pp 95.

114. Spufford, Peter. 'A printed catalogue of the names of testators', Bc132, 167–86.

115. Spufford, Peter. 'The Index Library: a centenary history, 1988', Bc132, 119–38.

116. Stevenson, Sara; Morrison-Low, A.D. (ed.). *Scottish photography: a bibliography, 1839–1989.* Edinburgh; Salvia; 1990. Pp 48.

117. Takahashi, Motoyasu. 'The number of wills proved in the sixteenth and seventeenth centuries: graphs, with tables and commentary', Bc132, 187–214.

118. Thick, Anne. 'The Hampshire Archives Trust and the archives of the Hampshire General Friendly Society', *Business Archives* 60 (1990), 56–60.

119. Tough, Alistair. 'Trade unions and their records', *Archives* 19 (1990), 121–44.

120. Tranter, Margery. 'Joan Thirsk: a bibliography', Bc77, 369–82.
121. Wallace, Janet. 'The central archives of the British Museum', *Archives* 19 (1990), 213–23.
122. Weatherill, Lorna. 'Probate inventories and consumer behaviour in England, 1660–1740', Bc132, 251–72.
123. Webster, E. 'Some Dean Clough archives' [in Calderdale Archives Department], *Halifax Antiq. Soc. T.* (1989 for 1988), 41–56.
124. White, Bruce (ed.). 'Victorian periodicals, 1988: an annotated bibliography', *Victorian Periodicals R.* 22 (1989), 167–83.
125. Wiener, Joel H. 'Sources for the study of newspapers', Bc87, 155–65.
126. Wood, Jennifer. 'Bibliographic guide to research on hospitals', *Local Population Studies* 45 (1990), 62–65.

## (b) *Works of Reference*

1. Ashton, T.S. 'Business history', Bc24, 8–9.
2. Atkins, Peter J. *The directories of London, 1677–1977.* London; Mansell; 1990. Pp 752.
3. Banks, Olive. *The biographical dictionary of British feminists, vol. 2: 1930–1945.* Hemel Hempstead; Harvester Wheatsheaf; 1990. Pp 224.
4. Barker, Felix; Jackson, Peter. *The history of London in maps.* London; Barrie & Jenkins; 1990. Pp 192.
5. Bell, Gary M. *A handlist of British diplomatic representatives, 1509–1688.* London; Royal Historical Soc. (Guides and handbooks no. 16); 1990. Pp viii, 306.
6. Bell, Maureen; Parfitt, George; Shepherd, Simon. *A biographical dictionary of women writers, 1580–1720.* Hemel Hempstead; Harvester Wheatsheaf; 1990. Pp 240.
7. Bennett, Bryan; Hamilton, Anthony. *Edward Arnold: 100 years of publishing.* London; Arnold; 1990. Pp 128.
8. Besley, Edward M. *Coins and medals of the English Civil War.* London; Seaby; 1990. Pp 128.
9. Billcliffe, Roger (comp.). *The Royal Glasgow Institute of the Fine Arts, 1861–1989: a dictionary of exhibitors at the annual exhibitions, vol. 1: A-D.* Glasgow; Woodend; 1990. Pp 400.
10. Coates, Richard. *The place-names of St Kilda: nomina hirtensia.* Lampeter; Mellen; 1990. Pp 240.
11. Coates, Richard. *Toponymic topics: essays on the early toponymy of the British Isles.* Brighton; Younsmere; 1988. Pp 256.
12. Connor, Jennifer J. 'Medieval library history: a survey of the literature in Great Britain and north America', *Libraries & Culture* 24 (1989), 459–74.
13. Crossley, David Waytt. *Guide to post-medieval archaeology in Britain.* Leicester; Leicester UP; 1990. Pp 224.
14. Darton, Mike. *The dictionary of Scottish place-names.* Moffat; Lochar; 1990. Pp 288.
15. Foster, Janet. 'An introductory guide to hospital records', *Local Population Studies* 45 (1990), 57–61.

16. Gard, Robin. 'Catholic lay societies in England and Wales, 1870–1970: a preliminary list', *Catholic Archives* 10 (1990), 48–57.
17. Graham, E. Dorothy (comp.). *Chosen by God: a list of the female travelling preachers of early Primitive Methodism*. Nantwich; Wesley Historical Soc.; 1989. Pp iv, 31.
18. Hill, John (ed.). *Hertfordshire militia lists: Harpenden*. Ware; Hertfordshire Family & Population History Soc. (Militia series, no. 12); 1989. Pp 63.
19. Hodson, Yolande. *Ordnance surveyors' drawings, 1789–1840: a guide to the original manuscript maps of the first Ordnance Survey of England and Wales*. Reading; Research Publications; 1989; Pp 154.
20. Hudson, Ann. 'Index for volumes 139–143, 1986–1990', *J. of the British Arch. Association* 143 (1990), 153–75.
21. Jones, Barri; Mattingly, David. *An atlas of Roman Britain*. Oxford; Blackwell; 1990. Pp 320.
22. Mallalieu, Huon Lancelot (ed.). *The dictionary of British watercolour artists up to 1920*, vol. 3. Woodbridge; Antique Collectors' Club; 1990. Pp 200.
23. Manley, K.A. (comp.). 'Sources for library history: Norfolk and Suffolk', *Library History* 8 (1990), 145–49.
24. Maxted, Ian. *Books with Devon imprints: a handlist to 1800*. Exeter; Maxted; 1989. Pp ix, 219.
25. McIntyre, Colin. *Monuments of war: how to read a war memorial*. London; Hale; 1990. Pp 192.
26. McKinley, Richard A. *The surnames of Sussex*. Oxford; Leopard's Head (English surnames series 5); 1988. Pp xii, 498.
27. Medlycott, Mervyn. 'Local census listings', *Genealogists' Magazine* 23 (1990), 281–84.
28. Mills, Anthony David (ed.). *The place-names of Dorset*, part 3. Nottingham; English Place-Name Soc. Publications vol. 59/60; 1989. Pp 400.
29. Morris, Janet. *A Latin glossary for family and local historians*. Birmingham; Federation of Family History Societies; 1989. Pp 39.
30. Mullen, A.L.T. (ed.). *The Military General Service Medal roll, 1793–1814*. London; London Stamp Exchange; 1990. Pp 700.
31. Palmer, Marilyn. 'Industrial archaeology: a thematic or a period discipline?', *Antiquity* 64/243 (1990), 275–85.
32. Porter, Stephen. *Exploring urban history: sources for the local historian*. London; Batsford; 1990. Pp 160.
33. Royle, Edward. 'Newspapers and periodicals in historical research', Bc87, 48–59.
34. Schneider, Jurgen; Sotscheck, Ralf. *Irland: eine Bibliographie selbständiger deutschsprachiger Publikationen: 16. Jahrhundert bis 1989* [Ireland: a bibliography of separate publications in German, from the sixteenth century to 1989]. [Place]; Buchner; 1990. Pp 379.
35. Slaven, Anthony; Checkland, Sydney George (ed.). *Dictionary of Scottish business biography, vol. 2: processing, distributing, services*. Aberdeen; Aberdeen UP; 1990. Pp 447.

36. Spalding, Frances; Collins, Judith. *The dictionary of British twentieth-century painters, sculptors and other artists.* Woodbridge; Antique Collectors' Club; 1990. Pp 700.

37. Spiers, Sheila M. (comp.). *The kirkyard of Drumblade.* Aberdeen; Aberdeen & North-East Scotland Family History Soc.; 1989. Pp 44.

38. Spiers, Sheila M. (comp.). *The kirkyard of Newhills.* Aberdeen; Aberdeen & North-East Scotland Family History Soc.; 1990. Pp 49.

39. Spiers, Sheila M. (comp.). *The kirkyard of Rathen.* Aberdeen; Aberdeen & North-East Scotland Family History Soc.; 1989. Pp 37.

40. Williams, David H. 'A catalogue of Welsh ecclesiastical seals as known down to AD 1600. Part V: other monastic seals', *Archaeologia Cambrensis* 137 (1989 for 1988), 119–34.

41. Williams, David H. 'A catalogue of Welsh ecclesiastical seals as known down to AD 1600. Part VI: personal seals with religious devices', *Archaeologia Cambrensis* 138 (1990 for 1989), 67–77.

## (c) *Historiography*

1. Adamson, J.S.A. 'Eminent Victorians: S.R. Gardiner and the liberal as hero', *Historical J.* 33 (1990), 641–57.

2. Ankersmit, F.R. 'Historiography and post modernism', *History & Theory* 28 (1989), 137–53.

3. Anon. 'Introduction: defining the field' [journalism], Bc87, xi-xiv.

4. Anon. *Approaches towards a machine-readable structure for biographical databases.* Kenilworth; Eighteenth-Century British Biography; 1990. Pp 96.

5. Bennett, J.M. 'Feminism and history', *Gender & History* 1 (1989), 251–72.

6. Boucher, David. 'Philosophy, history and practical life: the emergence of the history of political thought in England', *Australian J. of Politics & History* 35 (1989), 220–37.

7. Bradshaw, Brendan. 'Nationalism and historical scholarship in modern Ireland', *Irish Historical Studies* 26 (1989), 329–51.

8. Brett, Caroline. 'John Leland and the Anglo-Norman historian', Bc137, 59–76.

9. Brock, Jeanette M.; Tagg, Stephen K. 'Using SPSS-X to create a suitable database for estimating Scottish population movement, 1861–1911', *History & Computing* 2 (1990), 17–23.

10. Brotherstone, Terry. 'Cultural history and revolutionary theory: the examples of Jacques Barzun and Leon Trotsky', Bc4, 142–58.

11. Burgess, Glenn. 'On revisionism: an analysis of early Stuart historiography in the 1970s and 1980s', *Historical J.* 33 (1990), 609–27.

12. Burke, Peter. 'The comparative approach to European witchcraft', Bc105, 435–41.

13. Cairncross, Alec K. 'In praise of economic history', *Economic History R.* 2nd ser. 42 (1989), 173–85.

14. Cartledge, Paul. 'The "Tacitism" of Edward Gibbon (two hundred years on)', *Mediterranean Historical R.* 4 (1989), 251–70.

15. Chapman, William. 'The organizational context in the history of archaeology: Pitt Rivers and other British archaeologists in the 1860s', *Antiquaries J.* 69 (1989), 23–42.
16. Chartres, John; Hey, David. 'Introduction' [Joan Thirsk], Bc77, 1–16.
17. Coats, A.W. 'Disciplinary self-examination, departments, and research traditions in economic history: the Anglo-American story', *Scandinavian Economic History R.* 38 (1990), 3–18.
18. Cogswell, Thomas. 'Coping with revisionism in early Stuart history' [review article], *J. of Modern History* 62 (1990), 538–51.
19. Corfield, Penelope J. 'Defining urban work', Bc27, 207–30.
20. Counihan, Joan. 'Ella Armitage, castle studies pioneer', *Fortress* 6 (1990), 51–59.
21. Cowan, Ian B. 'Thomas Ian Rae, 1926–1989: an appreciation', *Scottish Historical R.* 69 (1990), 114–15.
22. Crafts, N.F.R. 'The new economic history and the industrial revolution', Bc25, 25–43.
23. d'Avray, David. 'The comparative study of memorial preaching', *T. of the Royal Historical Soc.* 5th ser. 40 (1990), 25–42.
24. Denley, Peter. 'Computing and postgraduate training in Britain: a discussion paper', *History & Computing* 2 (1990), 135–38.
25. Devereux, E.J. 'Empty tuns and unfruitful grafts: Richard Grafton's historical publications', *Sixteenth Century J.* 21 (1990), 33–56.
26. Donche, Pieter, 'HISTCAL, a program for historical chronology', *History & Computing* 2 (1990), 97–106.
27. Donoghue, Daniel. 'Layamon's ambivalence', *Speculum* 65 (1990), 537–63.
28. Dukes, Paul. 'Introduction' [culture and revolution], Bc4, 1–7.
29. Dumville, David. *Histories and pseudo-histories of the insular middle ages*. Aldershot; Variorum; 1990. Pp 350.
30. Eatwell, Roger. 'Conceptualizing the Right: Marxism's central errors', Bc6, 18–31.
31. Eatwell, Roger. 'The nature of the Right, 1: is there an "essentialist" philosophical core?', Bc6, 47–61.
32. Eatwell, Roger. 'The nature of the Right, 2: the Right as a variety of "styles of thought" ', Bc6, 62–78.
33. Eatwell, Roger. 'The rise of "Left-Right" terminology: the confusions of social science', Bc6, 32–46.
34. Fernandez-Armesto, F. 'Armada myths: the formative phase', Bc130, 19–40.
35. Fernley-Sander, Mary. 'Philosophical history and the Scottish Reformation: William Robertson and the Knoxian tradition', *Historical J.* 33 (1990), 323–38.
36. Fraser, Derek. 'Introduction' [Asa Briggs], Bc104, 1–9.
37. Freeman, June. 'The crafts as poor relations', *Oral History* 18 (1990), 24–32.
38. Goldstein, Erik. 'Historians outside the Academy: G.W. Prothero and the experience of the Foreign Office Historical Section, 1917–1920', *Historical Research* 63 (1990), 195–211.

39. Goode, John. 'E.P. Thompson and "the significance of literature"', Bc3, 183–203.
40. Gordon, Eleanor; Breitenbach, Esther. 'Introduction' [women's work in Scotland], Bc90, 1–6.
41. Gray, Robert. 'History, Marxism and theory', Bc3, 153–82.
42. Greenhalgh, Michael. 'Graphical data in art history and the humanities: their storage and display', *History & Computing* 1 (1989), 121–34.
43. Harvey, Charles; Jones, Geoffrey. 'Business history in Britain into the 1990s', *Business History* 32/1 (1990), 5–16.
44. Harvey, Charles; Press, Jon. 'Issues in the history of mining and metallurgy', *Business History* 32/3 (1990), 1–14.
45. Henningsen, Gustav; Ankarloo, Bengt. 'Introduction' [early modern witchcraft: historiography], Bc105, 1–15.
46. Higgs, Edward. 'Household and work in the nineteenth-century censuses of England and Wales', *J. of the Soc. of Archivists* 11 (1990), 73–77.
47. Hobart, M.E. 'The paradox of historical constructionism', *History & Theory* 28 (1989), 43–58.
48. Holdsworth, Christopher J. 'R. Allen Brown', Bc72, 1–5.
49. Keene, Derek J. 'Continuity and development in urban trades: problems of concepts and the evidence', Bc27, 1–16.
50. Kiralfy, Albert. 'Independent legal systems under a common dynastic rule: the examples of England and Hungary', *J. of Legal History* 11 (1990), 118–28.
51. Knoespel, Kenneth J. 'Newton in the school of time: the *Chronology of the ancient kingdoms amended* and the crisis of seventeenth-century historiography', *Eighteenth-Century Theory & Interpretation* 30 (1989), 19–41.
52. Lee, C.H. 'Corporate behaviour in theory and history, i: the evolution of theory', *Business History* 32/1 (1990), 17–31.
53. Lee, C.H. 'Corporate behaviour in theory and history, ii: the historian's perspective', *Business History* 32/2 (1990), 163–79.
54. Low, David A. 'William Keith Hancock, 1898–1988', *J. of Imperial & Commonwealth History* 18 (1990), 5–8.
55. Low, Raimund (ed.). *Historiographie der Arbeiterbewegung in Frankreich and Grossbritannien: Archive und Institutionen, Stand und Trends der Forschung* [Historiography of the working-class movement in France and Britain: archives and institutions, present status and research trends]. Vienna; Europa; 1989. Pp 103.
56. Maidment, B.E. 'Victorian periodicals and academic discourse', Bc87, 143–54.
57. Martel, Gordon. 'Toynbee, McNeill, and the myth of history', *International History R.* 12 (1990), 330–48.
58. Mathias, Peter. 'The industrial revolution: concept and reality', Bc25, 1–24.
59. McClelland, Keith. 'Introduction' [E.P. Thompson], Bc3, 1–11.
60. McNeill, William Hardy. *Arnold J. Toynbee: a life*. Oxford; Oxford UP; 1989. Pp viii, 346.

61. Morris, R.J. 'Externalities, the market, power structures and the urban agenda', *Urban History Yearbook* 17 (1990), 99–109.
62. Newton, J. '*Family fortunes*: "new history" and "new historicism"', *Radical History* 43 (1989), 5–22.
63. Parker, Christopher. *The English historical tradition*. Edinburgh; Donald; 1989. Pp 260.
64. Parker, David. 'French absolutism, the English state and the utility of the base-superstructure model', *Social History* 15 (1990), 287–301.
65. Patterson, T.C. 'Post-structuralism, post-modernism: implications for historians', *Social History* 14 (1989), 83–88.
66. Phillips, Paul T. *Britain's past in Canada: the teaching and writing of British history*. Vancouver; British Columbia UP; 1989. Pp xi, 187.
67. Phillips, William H. 'The economic performance of late Victorian Britain: traditional historians and growth', *J. of European Economic History* 18 (1989), 393–414.
68. Piggott, Stuart. *Ancient Britons and the antiquarian imagination*. London; Thames & Hudson; 1989. Pp 176.
69. Pomata, G. 'Versions of narrative: overt and covert narrators in nineteenth-century historiography', *History Workshop J.* 27 (1989), 1–17.
70. Powell, W. Raymond. 'Antiquaries in conflict: Philip Morant versus Richard Gough', *Essex Archaeology & History* 3rd ser. 20 (1989), 143–46.
71. Prior, Mary. 'Conjugal love and the flight from marriage: poetry as a source for the history of women and the family', Bc44, 179–203.
72. Pullan, Brian. 'John Kenneth Hyde, 1930–1986', *B. of the John Rylands University Library of Manchester* 72/3 (1990), 3–11.
73. Reed, Mick; Wells, Roger A.E. 'An agenda for modern English rural history?', Bc78, 215–23.
74. Richmond, Lesley M. 'A national documentation strategy for business?', *Business Archives* 59 (1990), 37–46.
75. Richter, Melvin. 'Reconstructing the history of political languages: Pocock, Skinner and the "Geschichtliche Grundbegriffe"', *History & Theory* 29 (1990), 38–70.
76. Robbins, Keith G. 'National identity and history: past, present and future', *History* 75 (1990), 369–87.
77. Robertson, J.C. 'Moving on from holes and corners: recent currents in urban archaeology', *Urban History Yearbook* 17 (1990), 1–13.
78. Rosaldo, Renato. 'Celebrating Thompson's heroes: social analysis in history and anthropology', Bc3, 103–24.
79. Royle, Edward. 'Historians and *The making of the English working class*, 1963–1988', *Halifax Antiq. Soc. T.* (1989 for 1988), 73–82.
80. Schöttler, P. 'Historians and discourse analysis', *History Workshop J.* 27 (1989), 37–65.
81. Schurer, Kevin; Oeppen, J. 'Calculating days of the week and some related problems with using calendars of the past', *History & Computing* 2 (1990), 107–18.

82. Schurer, Kevin; Oeppen, J. 'Saturday's child: coping with the calendars of the past', *Local Population Studies* 45 (1990), 43–56.

83. Sewell, William H., Jr. 'How classes are made: critical reflections on E.P. Thompson's theory of working-class formation', Bc3, 50–77.

84. Sharpe, Pamela. 'The total reconstitution method: a tool for class-specific study?', *Local Population Studies* 44 (1990), 41–51.

85. Shaw, Martin. 'From total war to democratic peace: exterminism and historical pacifism', Bc3, 233–51.

86. Shinn, Ridgway F. *Arthur Berriedale Keith, 1879–1944: the chief ornament of Scottish learning.* Aberdeen; Aberdeen UP; 1990.

87. Slavin, Arthur J. 'G.R. Elton and the Tudor age: telling the story', Bc147, 249–63.

88. Slavin, Arthur J. 'Telling the story: G.R. Elton and the Tudor age', *Sixteenth Century J.* 21 (1990), 151–60.

89. Smith, Godfrey. 'Asa Briggs: a personal profile', Bc104, 10–21.

90. Smith, J.E. 'Gender and class in working-class history', *Radical History* 44 (1989), 152–58.

91. Soper, Kate. 'Socialist humanism', Bc3, 204–32.

92. Southall, Humphrey; Oliver, Ed. 'Drawing maps with a computer or without', *History & Computing* 2 (1990), 146–54.

93. Stevenson, David R. 'David Hume, historicist', *The Historian* [USA] 52 (1990), 209–18.

94. Tilly, L.A. 'Gender, women's history, and social history', *Social Science History* 13 (1989), 439–80.

95. Trainor, Richard H. 'Using computers in historical teaching and research: the British experience', *Tijdschrift voor Geschiedenis* 103 (1990), 373–80.

96. Turner, J.M. 'After Thompson—Methodism and the English working class: an essay in historiography', *Halifax Antiq. Soc. T.* (1989 for 1988), 57–72.

97. Twigg, John. 'Evolution, obstacles, and aims: the writing of Oxford and Cambridge college histories', *History of Universities* 8 (1989), 179–99.

98. Tyson, Diana B. 'Problem people in the *Petit Bruit* by Rauf de Boun', *J. of Medieval History* 16 (1990), 351–61.

99. Underdown, David. 'Puritanism, revolution, and Christopher Hill', *History Teacher* 22 (1988), 67–76.

100. Wallace, Jeff. 'Taking possession of the ordinary man's mind' [literary studies and history of science], *Literature & History* ns 1 (1990), 58–74.

101. Wilkes, J.J. 'A prospect of Roman Britain', Bc30, 245–50.

102. Wilson, Adrian. 'The ceremony of childbirth and its interpretation', Bc44, 68–107.

103. Winstone, Harry V.F. *Woolley of Ur: the life of Sir Leonard Woolley.* London; Secker & Warburg; 1990. Pp 256.

104. Wood, Ellen Meiksins. 'Falling through the cracks: E.P. Thompson and the debate on base and superstructure', Bc3, 125–52.

105. Wrightson, Keith. 'The enclosure of English social history', *Rural History* 1 (1990), 73–81.

# B. GENERAL

(a) *Long Periods—National*

1. Aldrich, Megan (ed.). *The Craces: royal decorators, 1768–1899.* London; Murray; 1990. Pp 224.
2. Alexander, Ziggy. ' "Let it lie upon the table": the status of black women's biography in the UK', *Gender & History* 2 (1990), 22–33.
3. Andrews, D.T. 'Marriage history as social history', *Canadian J. of History* 24 (1989), 381–85.
4. Aston, Margaret. 'Segregation in church', Bc128, 237–94.
5. Aylmer, G.E. 'The peculiarities of the English state', *J. of Historical Sociology* 3 (1989), 91–108.
6. Babington, Anthony. *Military intervention in Britain: from the Gordon riots to the Gibraltar killings.* London; Routledge; 1990. Pp 304.
7. Baldwin, David. *The Chapel Royal: ancient and modern.* London; Duckworth; 1990. Pp ii, 480.
8. Barley, Maurice W. *Houses and history.* London; Faber & Faber; 1986. Pp 290.
9. Barratt Brown, M. 'Commercial and industrial capital in England: a reply to Geoffrey Ingham', *New Left R.* 178 (1989), 124–28.
10. Barrett, T.H. *Singular listlessness: a short history of Chinese books and British scholars.* London; Wellsweep; 1989. Pp 125.
11. Bartrip, Peter W.J. *Mirror of medicine: the history of the 'British Medical Journal', 1840–1990.* Oxford; Oxford UP; 1990. Pp 320.
12. Bateman, D.I. ' "Heroes for present purposes?" A look at the changing idea of communal land ownership in Britain', *J. of Agricultural Economics* 40 (1989), 269–89.
13. Beacham, M.J.A. 'Dovecotes in England: an introduction and gazetteer', *T. of the Ancient Monuments Soc.* 34 (1990), 85–131.
14. Bebbington, D.W. *Evangelicalism in modern Britain: a history from the 1730s to the 1980s.* London; Unwin Hyman; 1989. Pp xi, 364.
15. Belchem, John. *Industrialization and the working class: the English experience, 1750–1900.* Aldershot; Gower; 1989. Pp 310.
16. Benson, John. *The working class in Britain, 1850–1939.* Harlow; Longman, 1989. Pp xvii, 219.
17. Berridge, Virginia. 'The Society for the Study of Addiction, 1884–1988', *British J. of Addiction* 85 (1990), 983–1087.
18. Birkett, Dea; Wheelwright, Julie. ' "How could she?" Unpalatable facts and feminists' heroines', *Gender & History* 2 (1990), 49–58.
19. Black, I. 'Geography, political economy and the circulation of capital in early industrial England', *J. of Historical Geography* 15 (1989), 366–84.
20. Bolin-Hort, Per. *Work, family, and the State: child labour and the organization of production in the British cotton industry, 1780–1920.* Lund; Lund UP (Bibliotheca Historica Lundensis 66); 1989. Pp 328.
21. Bosley, Peter. *Light railways in England and Wales.* Manchester; Manchester UP; 1990. Pp 240.

22. Boyer, George R. *An economic history of the English Poor Law, 1750–1850*. Cambridge; Cambridge UP; 1990. Pp 297.

23. Bramah, Edward; Bramah, Joan. *Coffee makers: 300 years of art and design*. London; Quiller; 1989. Pp 192.

24. Brereton, John Maurice. *A history of the Royal Regiment of Wales (24th/41st Foot) and its predecessors, 1689–1989*. Cardiff; The Royal Regiment of Wales; 1989. Pp xxxi, 512.

25. Brown, Jane. *The art and architecture of English gardens: designs for the garden from the collection of the Royal Institute of British Architects, 1609 to the present day*. London; Weidenfeld & Nicolson; 1989. Pp 320.

26. Buckland, P.C. 'Ballast and building stone: a discussion', Bc135, 114–25.

27. Burk, Kathleen. *Morgan Grenfell, 1838–1988: the biography of a merchant bank*. Oxford; Oxford UP; 1989. Pp xv, 348.

28. Byng-Hall, John; Thompson, Paul. 'The power of family myths', Bc131, 216–24.

29. Campbell, James. *Stubbs and the English state*. Reading; Department of History, the University; 1988. (Stenton Lecture no. 21). Pp 19.

30. Canny, Nicholas J. 'The British Atlantic world: working towards a definition', *Historical J*. 33 (1990), 479–97.

31. Carlton, Charles. *Royal mistresses*. London; Routledge; 1989. Pp 208.

32. Chadwick, Whitney. *Women, art, and society*. London; Thames & Hudson; 1990. Pp 384.

33. Chapman, Stanley. 'The decline and rise of textile merchanting, 1880–1990', *Business History* 32/4 (1990), 171–90.

34. Charlton, Clive. 'Urological circles', Bc126, 59–65.

35. Chartres, John. 'No English Calvados? English distillers and the cider industry in the seventeenth and eighteenth centuries', Bc77, 313–42.

36. Chase, Malcolm. 'From millennium to anniversary: the concept of jubilee in late eighteenth- and nineteenth-century England', *Past & Present* 129 (1990), 132–47.

37. Clark, Gregory. 'Enclosure, land improvement, and the price of capital: a reply to Jones', *Explorations in Economic History* 27 (1990), 356–62.

38. Coley, Noel G. 'Physicians, chemists, and the analysis of mineral waters: "The most difficult part of chemistry"', *Medical History*, Supplement 10 (1990), 56–66.

39. Collins, Michael. *Banks and industrial finance in Britain, 1800–1939*. Basingstoke; Macmillan; 1990. Pp 112.

40. Crimmins, James Edward. *Religion, secularization and political thought: from Locke to Mill*. London; Routledge; 1990. Pp 256.

41. Cunningham, Hugh. 'The employment and unemployment of children in England, c.1680–1851', *Past & Present* 126 (1990), 115–50.

42. Currie, C.R.J. 'Time and chance: a reply to comments', *Vernacular Architecture* 21 (1990), 5–9.

43. Davenport-Hines, Richard P.T. *Sex, death and punishment: attitudes to sex and sexuality in Britain since the Renaissance*. London; Collins; 1990. Pp 439.

44. Davies, John. *Hanes Cymru* [History of Wales in English]. London; Allen Lane; 1990. Pp 728.

45. Davies, Peter. *Fyffes and the banana: musa sapientum—a centenary history, 1888–1988.* London; Athlone; 1990. Pp xviii, 401.

46. Dent, J.G. 'The pound weight and the pound sterling: the relationship between weight and coinage and its consequences', *Folk Life* 27 (1989), 80–84.

47. Dunleavy, Patrick; *et al.* 'Prime ministers and the Commons: patterns of behaviour, 1868–1987', *Public Administration* 68 (1990), 123–40.

48. Dymond, David. 'A lost social institution: the camping close', *Rural History* 1 (1990), 165–92.

49. Eccleshall, Robert. *English Conservatism since the Restoration: an introduction and anthology.* London; Unwin Hyman; 1990. Pp 254.

50. Farnie, D.A. 'The textile machine-making industry and the world market, 1870–1960', *Business History* 32/4 (1990), 150–70.

51. Farnie, D.A.; Henderson, W.O. (ed.). *Industry and innovation: selected essays of W.H. Chaloner.* London; Cass; 1990. Pp 331.

52. Fine, Ben. *The coal question: political economy and industrial change from the nineteenth century to the present day.* London; Routledge; 1990. Pp 256.

53. Fine, Ben; Leopold, Ellen. 'Consumerism and the industrial revolution', *Social History* 15 (1990), 151–79.

54. Fisher, Stephen. *Lisbon as a port town: the British seaman and other maritime themes.* Exeter; Exeter UP; 1989. Pp 146.

55. Fiske, Jane (ed.). *The Oakes diaries: business, politics and the family in Bury St Edmunds, 1778–1827, I. Introduction and James Oakes's diaries, 1778–1800.* Woodbridge; Boydell for Suffolk Record Soc.; 1990. Pp 418.

56. Foreman, Susan. *Loaves and fishes: an illustrated history of the Ministry of Agriculture, Fisheries and Food, 1889–1989.* London; HMSO; 1989. Pp ix, 150.

57. Fox, Harold S.A. 'Social relations and ecological relationships in agrarian change: an example from medieval and early modern England', *Geografiska Annaler* 70 (1988), 105–15.

58. Fox, Maurice Rayner. *Dyemakers of Great Britain, 1856–1976: a history of chemists, companies, products and changes.* Manchester; Imperial Chemical Industries; 1987. Pp 296.

59. Frow, Ruth; Frow, Edmund (ed.). *Political women, 1800–1850* [a collection of documents with commentary]. Pluto Press; London; 1989. Pp 220.

60. Fry, Plantagenet Somerset. *The Tower of London: cauldron of England's past.* London; Quiller; 1990. Pp 188.

61. Gascoigne, John. 'From Bentley to the Victorians: the rise and fall of British Newtonian natural theology', *Science in Context* 2 (1988), 219–56.

62. Gillespie, Raymond; Canny, Nicholas J. 'Migration and opportunity: a comment', *Irish Economic & Social History* 16 (1989), 90–100.

63. Girouard, Mark. *The English town.* London; Yale UP; 1990. Pp 336.

64. Godsell, Andrew. *A history of the Conservative Party*. Fleet; Godsell; 1989. Pp 87.
65. Golland, J. ' "Compell'd to weep . . . ": the apprenticeship system', *Genealogists' Magazine* 23 (1989), 121–27.
66. Gore, Ann; Gore, Alan. *The history of English interiors*. Oxford; Phaidon; 1990. Pp 192.
67. Grove, Eric J. 'The armed forces and society in Britain', Bc83, 105–112.
68. Halmesvirta, Anssi. *The British conception of the Finnish "race", nation and culture, 1760–1918*. Helsinki; Suomen Historiallinen Seura (Studia Historica 34); 1990. Pp 324.
69. Hardyment, Christina. *From mangle to microwave: mechanization of the household*. Oxford; Polity; 1988. Pp 250.
70. Harley, David. 'A sword in a madman's hand: professional opposition to popular consumption in the waters' literature of southern England and the midlands, 1570–1870', *Medical History*, Supplement 10 (1990), 48–55.
71. Harvie, Christopher. 'Political thrillers and the condition of England from the 1840s to the 1980s', Bc61, 217–48.
72. Henham, Brian; Sharp, Brian. *Badges of extinction: the eighteenth- and nineteenth-century badges of insurance office firemen*. London; Quiller; 1989. Pp 96.
73. Henry, L. 'Men's and women's mortality in the past', *Population* 44 (1989), 177–201.
74. Heywood, Audrey. '*Colica pictonum*: taking the cure in Bath', Bc126, 101–110.
75. Hillam, Christine (ed.). *The roots of dentistry: for the Lindsay Society and for the 'History of Dentistry'*. London; British Dental Association; 1990. Pp 64.
76. Hinton, David Alban. *Archaeology, economy and society: England from the fifth to the fifteenth century*. London; Seaby; 1990. Pp 256.
77. Hitchens, Christopher. *Blood, class and nostalgia: Anglo-American ironies*. London; Chatto & Windus; 1990. Pp 398.
78. Howard, Peter. *The artists' vision*. London; Routledge; 1990. Pp 272.
79. Hoyles, Martin. *A new history of English gardening*. London; Journeyman; 1990. Pp 415.
80. Hughes, R. Elwyn. 'The rise and fall of the "antiscorbutics": some notes on the traditional cures for "land scurvy" ', *Medical History* 34 (1990), 52–64.
81. Hurst, Norman (comp.). '*Naval Chronicle', 1799–1818: index to births, marriages and deaths*. Coulsdon; Hurst; 1989. Pp 158.
82. Inikori, Joseph E. 'The credit needs of the African trade and the development of the credit economy in England', *Explorations in Economic History* 27 (1990), 197–231.
83. Jeffreys, Sheila. 'Does it matter if they did it?', Bc1, 19–28.
84. Johnston, John. *The Lord Chamberlain's blue pencil*. London; Hodder & Stoughton; 1990. Pp 256.
85. Jones, E.L. 'Enclosure, land improvement, and the price of capital: a comment', *Explorations in Economic History* 27 (1990), 350–55.

86. Jones, Pamela Fletcher. *The Jews of Britain: a thousand years of history.* Adlestrop; Windrush; 1990. Pp 208.

87. Karsten, Peter. ' "Bottomed on justice": a reappraisal of critical legal studies scholarship concerning breachers of labor contracts by quitting or firing in Britain and the US, 1630–1880', *American J. of Legal History* 34 (1990), 213–61.

88. Katz, David S. 'The conundrum of the Bodleian Bowl: an Anglo-Jewish mystery story', *Bodleian Library Record* 13 (1990), 290–99.

89. Knafla, Louis A. (ed.). *Essays from 'Criminal Justice History', vol. 1: crime, police and the courts in British history.* Westport (Ct); Meckler; 1990. Pp 310.

90. Krystanek, Karol; Guldon, Zenon. 'Jews and Scotsmen in Sandomierz in the sixteenth to eighteenth centuries' [in Polish; English summary], *Studies in History* 31 (1988), 527–42.

91. Kussmaul, Ann. *A general view of the rural economy of England, 1538–1840.* Cambridge; Cambridge UP; 1990. Pp 216.

92. Lawrence, Margaret. *The encircling hop: a history of hops and brewing.* Sittingbourne; Sawd; 1990. Pp 144.

93. Lewis, Geoffrey. *For instruction and recreation: a centenary history of the Museums Association.* London; Quiller; 1990. Pp 96.

94. Lipman, Vivian D. *A history of the Jews in Britain since 1858.* Leicester; Leicester UP; 1990. Pp 274.

95. Litten, Julian. 'Journeys to paradise: funerary transport, 1600–1850', *Genealogists' Magazine* 23 (1990), 169–76.

96. Lloyd-Jones, Roger. 'The first Krondatieff: the long wave and the British industrial revolution', *J. of Interdisciplinary History* 20 (1989–90), 581–605.

97. Lummis, Trevor; Marsh, Jan. *The woman's domain: women and the English country house.* London; Viking; 1990. Pp 256.

98. Lund, Alfred. *The red duster: living and working conditions in the Merchant Navy, 1850–1950.* Whitby; Lund; 1989. Pp 156.

99. Manchester, Keith; Roberts, C. 'The palaeopathology of leprosy in Britain—a review', *World Archaeology* 21 (1989), 265–72.

100. Marks, Gary. 'Variations in Union political activity in the United States, Britain, and Germany from the nineteenth century', *Comparative Politics* 22 (1989), 83–104.

101. Marwick, Arthur. 'Introduction' and 'conclusion' [arts, literature and society], Bc61, 1–22; 303–19.

102. Mass, William; Lazonick, William. 'The British cotton industry and international competitive advantage: the state of the debates', *Business History* 32/4 (1990), 9–65.

103. McCloskey, Donald N. 'The open fields of England: rent, risk, and the rate of interest, 1300–1815', Bc21, 5–51.

104. McKibbin, Ross. *The ideologies of class: social relations in Britain, 1880–1950.* Oxford; Oxford UP; 1990. Pp 328.

105. Melman, Billie. 'Desexualizing the Orient: the harem in English travel writing by women, 1763–1914', *Mediterranean Historical R.* 4 (1989), 301–39.

106. Menefee, Samuel Pyeatt. 'Dead reckoning: the church porch watch in British society', Bc103, 80–99.

107. Mercer, Eric. 'Time and chance: a timely rejoinder', *Vernacular Architecture* 21 (1990), 1–3.

108. Mingay, Gordon E. *A social history of the English countryside*. London; Routledge; 1990. Pp 272.

109. Mokyr, Joel. 'The great conundrum' [demography], *J. of Modern History* 62 (1990), 78–88.

110. Morris, Polly. 'Sodomy and male honor: the case of Somerset, 1740–1850', *J. of Homosexuality* 16 (1988), 383–406.

111. Murray, M. 'Property and "patriarchy" in English history', *J. of Historical Sociology* 2 (1989), 303–27.

112. Naggar, Betty. 'Old-clothes men: eighteenth and nineteenth centuries', *Jewish Historical Studies* 31 (1988–90), 171–91.

113. Norris, Pippa. *British by-elections: the volatile electorate*. Oxford; Oxford UP; 1990. Pp 280.

114. Nuttgens, Patrick. *The home front: housing the people, 1840–1990*. London; BBC; 1989. Pp 192.

115. Olby, Robert C. (ed.). *Companion to the history of modern science*. London; Routledge; 1989. Pp 992.

116. Parker, Stephen. *Informal marriage, cohabitation and the law, 1750–1989*. Basingstoke; Macmillan; 1990. Pp 184.

117. Parkes, Oscar. *British battleships*. London; Cooper; 1990. Pp 696.

118. Parsons, David. 'Review and prospect: the stone industry in Roman, Anglo-Saxon and medieval England', Bc135, 1–15.

119. Popplewell, Lawrence. *Coastguard and preventive upon the shipwreck coast*. Southbourne; Melledgen; 1990. Pp 48.

120. Porter, Roy (ed.). *The medical history of waters and spas*. London; *Medical History*, Supplement no. 10; 1990. Pp xii, 150.

121. Quinn, David Beers. 'Atlantic Islands' [and St Brendan], Bc74, 77–93.

122. Ranieri, F. 'From status to profession: the professionalisation of lawyers as a research field in modern European legal history', *J. of Legal History* 10 (1989), 180–90.

123. Reed, Michael. *The landscape of Britain: from the beginnings to 1914*. London; Routledge; 1990. Pp xvi, 387.

124. Reed, Mick. 'Class and conflict in rural England: some reflections on a debate', Bc78, 1–28.

125. Resnick, D.P. 'Historical perspectives on literacy and schooling', *Daedalus* 119 (1989), 15–32.

126. Riley, James C. *Sickness, recovery and death*. Basingstoke; Macmillan; 1989. Pp 312.

127. Roaf, Susan; Beamon, Sylvia P. *The ice-houses of Britain*. London; Routledge; 1990. Pp 448.

128. Roberts, Brian K. 'Rural settlement and regional contrasts: questions of continuity and colonization', *Rural History* 1 (1990), 51–72.

129. Roberts, Ian. *Pontefract Castle*. Wakefield; West Yorkshire Archaeology Service; 1990. Pp 76.

130. Rose, Mary B. 'International competition and strategic response in the textile industries since 1870', *Business History* 32/4 (1990), 1–8.
131. Rosenberg, C.E. 'What is an epidemic? AIDS in historical perspective', *Daedalus* 118 (1989), 1–17.
132. Saint Marc, Michele. 'Monetary history in the long run: how are monetarization and monetarism implicated in France, in the UK and in the USA?', *J. of European Economic History* 18 (1989), 551–82.
133. Schwoerer, Lois G. 'Celebrating the Glorious revolution, 1689–1989', *Albion* 22 (1990), 1–20.
134. Shammas, Carole. *The pre-industrial consumer in England and America*. Oxford; Oxford UP; 1990. Pp 336.
135. Sharpe, James Anthony. *Judicial punishment in England*. London; Faber & Faber; 1990. Pp 160.
136. Sheldrake, John. *Industrial relations and politics in Britain, 1880–1989*. London; Pinter; 1990. Pp 192.
137. Shimada, Takau. '*Yefumi* and the rivalry between Britain and Holland in travel literature', Bc74, 223–26.
138. Short, Brian. 'The de-industrialisation process: a case study of the Weald, 1600–1850', Bc42, 156–74.
139. Silver, Harold. *Education, change and the policy process*. London; Falmer; 1990. Pp 236.
140. Slack, Paul; Clarkson, Leslie A. *The English Poor Law, 1531–1782*. Basingstoke; Macmillan; 1990. Pp 80.
141. Smith, Peter. 'Time and chance: a reply', *Vernacular Architecture* 21 (1990), 4–5.
142. Snell, K.D.M. 'Rural history and folklore studies: towards new forms of association', *Folklore* 100 (1989), 218–20.
143. Spring, Eileen. 'The heiress-at-law: English real property law from a new point of view', *Law & History R.* 8 (1990), 273–96.
144. Spufford, Margaret. 'The limitations of the probate inventory', Bc77, 139–74.
145. St John, John. *William Heinemann: a century of publishing, 1890–1990*. London; Heinemann; 1990. Pp xiv, 690.
146. Stanley, Liz. 'Moments of writing: is there a feminist autobiography?', *Gender & History* 2 (1990), 58–67.
147. Staves, Susan. *Married women's separate property in England, 1660–1833*. Cambridge (Ma); Harvard UP; 1990. Pp xiv, 290.
148. Stebbings, Chantal. 'The devolution of partnership property', *J. of Legal History* 11 (1990), 270–78.
149. Stoljar, Samuel. 'No obituary for Wennall *v.* Adney', *J. of Legal History* 11 (1990), 250–69.
150. Stone, Lawrence. *Road to divorce: England, 1530–1987*. Oxford; Oxford UP; 1990. Pp xx, 486.
151. Strong, Roy. *Lost treasures of Britain: five centuries of creation and destruction*. London; Viking; 1990. Pp 240.
152. Tait, Simon. *Palaces of discovery: the changing world of Britain's museums*. London; Quiller; 1989. Pp 184.

153. Tatton-Brown, T.W.T. *Great cathedrals of Britain.* London; BBC; 1989. Pp 224.
154. Teeven, Kevin M. *A history of the Anglo-American common law of contract.* London; Greenwood; 1990. Pp 295.
155. Thane, Pat M. 'Government and society in England and Wales, 1750–1914', Bc47, 1–62.
156. Thick, Malcolm. 'Garden seeds in England before the late eighteenth century, part 1: seed growing', *Agricultural History R.* 38 (1990), 58–71.
157. Thomas, Matthew T. *The Indian Army.* India; Lancer International; 1990. Pp 160.
158. Thompson, Francis M.L. 'Town and city', Bc45, 1–86.
159. Trench, Richard. *Travellers in Britain.* London; Aurum; 1990. Pp 208.
160. Trewin, Wendy. *The Royal General Theatrical Fund: a history, 1838–1988.* London; Soc. for Theatre Research; 1989. Pp 181.
161. Tricker, John. 'To mend a bone: a short history of the management of fractures', Bc126, 75–82.
162. Turner, Terence D. ' "Secret nostrums": aspects of the development of patent and proprietary medicines', Bc126, 159–68.
163. Tweedale, Geoffrey. *At the sign of the Plough: Allen and Hanburys and the British pharmaceutical industry, 1715–1990.* London; Murray; 1990. Pp 320.
164. van Helten, J.J.; Cassis, Y. (ed.). *Capitalism in a mature economy: financial institutions, capital exports and British industry, 1870–1939.* London; Elgar; 1990. Pp 248.
165. Vaughan, Mary. *Courtfield and the Vaughans.* London; Quiller; 1990. Pp 198.
166. Vitale, Ermanno. 'Hobbes e Bentham: contrattualismo e utilitarismo fra moderni e contemporanei' [Hobbes and Bentham: contractualism and utilitarianism from moderns and contemporaries], *Annali Fondazione Luigi Einaudi* 21 (1987), 89–114.
167. Wainwright, David. *Stone's ginger wine: fortunes of a family firm, 1740–1990.* London; Quiller; 1990. Pp 136.
168. Walton, John R. 'On estimating the extent of parliamentary enclosure', *Agricultural History R.* 38 (1990), 79–82.
169. Wellenreuter, Hermann. *Der Aufstieg des ersten Britischen Weltreiches: England und seine nordamerikanischen Kolonien, 1660–1763* [The rise of the first British Empire: England and its north American colonies, 1660–1763]. Dusseldorf (Germany); Schwann; 1987.
170. Wells, Roger. 'Social protest, class, conflict and consciousness, in the English countryside, 1700–1880', Bc78, 121–214.
171. Wendorf, Richard. *The elements of life: biography and portrait-painting in Stuart and Georgian England.* Oxford; Oxford UP; 1990. Pp 330.
172. West, Edwin G. *Adam Smith and modern economics: from market behaviour to public choice.* Aldershot; Elgar; 1990. Pp 256.
173. Whipp, Richard. *Patterns of labour: work and social change in the pottery industry.* London; Routledge; 1990. Pp 272.
174. Williams, David Innes. 'Specialists and special hospitals', Bc126, 11–28.

175. Williams, David M. 'Bulk passenger freight trades, 1750–1870', Bc76, 43–61.
176. Williams, Glynn; Ramsden, John. *Ruling Britannia: a political history of Britain, 1688–1988*. London; Longman; 1990. Pp 532.
177. Williamson, Jeffrey G. *Coping with city growth during the British industrial revolution*. Cambridge; Cambridge UP; 1990. Pp 368.
178. Woodward, Donald. ' "An essay on manures": changing attitudes to fertilization in England, 1500–1800', Bc77, 251–78.
179. Yeo, Richard. 'Genius, method, and morality: images of Newton in Britain, 1760–1860', *Science in Context* 2 (1988), 257–84.

## (b) *Long Periods—Local*

1. Addison, William. 'The making of the Essex landscape', Bc65, 47–56.
2. Aldsworth, F.G.; Bishop, John H. 'Recent observations on the tower of the church of St Mary the Virgin, Singleton, West Sussex', *Sussex Arch. Collections* 127 (1989), 61–71.
3. Allen, J.R.L. 'Reclamation and sea defence in Rumney parish, Monmouthshire', *Archaeologia Cambrensis* 137 (1989 for 1988), 135–40.
4. Andrews, David D.; Brooks, Howard. 'An Essex Dunwich: the lost church at Little Holland Hall', *Essex Archaeology & History* 3rd ser. 20 (1989), 74–83.
5. Andrews, David D.; *et al.* 'Harwich: its archaeological potential as revealed in excavations at George Street and Church Street', *Essex Archaeology & History* 3rd ser. 21 (1990), 57–91.
6. Anon. *Aspects of Nottinghamshire agricultural history*. Ely; Providence; 1989. Pp 78.
7. Anon. *Houses of the north York moors: a selective inventory*. London; Royal Commission on Historical Monuments; 1989. Pp v, 103.
8. Anon. *Territorial battalions of the regiments of Surrey and their successors*. Guildford; Queen's Royal Surrey Regiment Museum; 1988. Pp 134.
9. Anon. *The Scottish soldier, 1600–1914*. London; HMSO for National Museums of Scotland; 1987. Pp 35.
10. Atkins, Peter J. 'The spatial configuration of class solidarity in London's West End, 1792–1939', *Urban History Yearbook* 17 (1990), 36–65.
11. Auckland, Clifford. *The growth of a township: Maltby's story*. Rotherham; Rotherham Metropolitan Borough Council; 1989. Pp 163.
12. Aughton, Peter. *North Meols and Southport: a history*. Preston; Carnegie; 1988. Pp 220.
13. Baggs, A.P. 'Domestic buildings' [Lichfield], Bc99, 43–44.
14. Bailey, C.J. 'Thorner's Litton, a dissenting school in Dorset', *P. of the Dorset Natural History and Arch. Soc.* 111 (1989), 1–8.
15. Banks, Leslie; Stanley, Christopher. *The Thames: a history from the air*. Oxford; Oxford UP; 1990. Pp 192.
16. Barker, Katherine. 'The mizmaze at Leigh, near Sherborne, Dorset', *P. of the Dorset Natural History and Arch. Soc.* 111 (1989), 130–32.

17. Barker, Rosalin. *The book of Whitby*. Buckingham; Barracuda; 1990. Pp 132.

18. Barnsby, George J. *Birmingham working people: a history of the labour movement in Birmingham, 1650–1914*. Wolverhampton; Integrated Publishing Services; 1989. Pp v, 516.

19. Baylis, Audrey. *The story of Cleeve Prior*. Cleeve Prior; Baylis; 1988. Pp 83.

20. Beckett, John V. *The book of Nottingham*. Buckingham; Barracuda; 1990. Pp 148.

21. Beckwith, Ian. *The book of Lincoln*. Buckingham; Barracuda; 1990. Pp 148.

22. Bennett, John; Vernon, Robert W. *Mines of the Gwydyr Forest, part 1: Llanrwst mine and its neighbours*. Cuddington; Gwydyr Mines Publications; 1989. Pp 60.

23. Bentley, James. *Dare to be wise: a history of the Manchester Grammar School*. London; James & James; 1990. Pp 144.

24. Beresford, Maurice W.; Hurst, John G. *Wharram Percy: deserted medieval village*. London; Batsford for English Heritage; 1990. Pp 144.

25. Best, David. *A short history of Clitheroe*. Preston; Carnegie; 1988. Pp 64.

26. Bil, Albert. *The shieling, 1600–1840: the case of the central Scottish Highlands*. Edinburgh; Donald; 1990. Pp 300.

27. Bird, D.G.; Croker, Glenys; McCracken, J.S. 'Archaeology in Surrey, 1987', *Surrey Arch. Collections* 79 (1989), 179–89.

28. Blackmore, Lyn; Schwab, Irene. 'From the Templars to the tenement: a medieval and post-medieval site at 18 Shore Road, E9', *London & Middlesex Arch. Soc. T.* 37 (1986), 147–85.

29. Blair, J.S.G. *Ten Tayside doctors*. Edinburgh; Scottish Academic Press; 1990. Pp 120.

30. Blair, W. John; Townley, S.C. 'Cogges', Bc97, 54–75.

31. Blakeman, Pamela. *The book of Ely*. Buckingham; Barracuda; 1990. Pp 148.

32. Bolton, J.S. *From Royal Stewart to Shaw Stewart: their story*. London; Nenufra; 1989. Pp xiv, 82.

33. Booth, R.K. *York: the history and heritage of a city*. London; Barrie & Jenkins; 1990. Pp 168.

34. Born, Anne. *The Torbay towns*. Chichester; Phillimore; 1989. Pp xiii, 160.

35. Boston, Ray. *The essential Fleet Street: its history and influence*. London; Blandford; 1990. Pp 192.

36. Boyd, David H.A. *Leith Hospital, 1848–1988*. Edinburgh; Scottish Academic Press; 1990. Pp 180.

37. Boyer, George R. 'Malthus was right after all: poor relief and birth rates in south-eastern England', *J. of Political Economy* 97 (1989), 93–114.

38. Broad, John. 'The Verneys as enclosing landlords, 1600–1800', Bc77, 27–53.

39. Brown, Cynthia. *Northampton, 1835–1985: shoe town, new town*. Chichester; Phillimore; 1990. Pp xii, 240.

40. Brown, Joe; Lawson, Iain. *A history of Peebles, 1850–1990*. London; Mainstream; 1990. Pp 304.
41. Brown, Ronald S. *The book of Wealdstone: the history of a Victorian suburb*. Buckingham; Barracuda; 1989. Pp 124.
42. Burroughs, F.E. ' "Playing yerely at the orgayns and singynge in the Quyer . . . ": a history of music at Banbury parish church', *Cake & Cockhorse* 11/4 (1989), 90–100.
43. Butler, Lawrence. 'All Saints church, Crofton', *Yorkshire Arch. J.* 62 (1990), 125–32.
44. Byrne, Andrew. *Bedford Square: an architectural study*. London; Athlone; 1990. Pp 160.
45. Cadell, Patrick; Matheson, Ann (ed.). *For the encouragement of learning: Scotland's national library, 1689–1989*. London; HMSO; 1989. Pp xii, 316.
46. Cadman, Graham; Audouy, Michel. 'Recent excavations on Saxon and medieval quarries in Raunds, Northamptonshire', Bc135, 187–206.
47. Carter, G.A. *A history of Latchford from the Bronze Age to the twentieth century*. Warrington; Thomson; 1989. Pp 76.
48. Champ, Judith F. (ed.). *Oscott College, 1838–1988*. Birmingham; Archdiocese of Birmingham; 1987. Pp 36.
49. Chandler, C.J.; Digby, H.S.N. '*Off the map of history'? The development of north-east Wiltshire to 1600*. Swindon; Borough of Thamesdown; 1989. Pp 64.
50. Chesterton, George. *Malvern College, 125 years*. Upton-upon-Severn; Malvern Publishing Co.; 1990. Pp 160.
51. Clough, Monica. *Two houses: New Tarbat House, Easter Ross, Royston House, Edinburgh, and the family of Mackenzie, earls of Cromartie, 1656–1784*. Aberdeen; Aberdeen UP; 1990. Pp 176.
52. Cobb, William. *A history of Grays of York, 1695–1988; including an account of the under-sheriffs of Yorkshire from 1788*. York; Sessions; 1989. Pp 240.
53. Coldicott, Diana K. *Hampshire nunneries*. Chichester; Phillimore; 1989. Pp 200.
54. Cook, Robert. *The book of Winslow*. Buckingham; Barracuda; 1989. Pp 144.
55. Cooper, Janet. 'Bladon', Bc97, 14–36.
56. Cooper, Janet. 'Cassington', Bc97, 36–54.
57. Cooper, Janet. 'Hanborough', Bc97, 158–79.
58. Cooper, Janet. 'Kidlington', Bc97, 179–213.
59. Cooper, Janet. 'Shipton-on-Cherwell', Bc97, 254–67.
60. Copleston-Crow, Bruce. *Herefordshire place-names*. Oxford; BAR (British ser. 214); 1989. Pp xvi, 242.
61. Cox, D.C. *Shropshire County Council: a centenary history*. Shrewsbury; Shropshire County Council; 1989. Pp vi, 105.
62. Cremin, John. *St Agatha's, Kingston upon Thames: a parish history*. Sevenoaks; G.C. Press; 1989. Pp 196.
63. Crossley, Alan. 'Blenheim', Bc97, 430–70.
64. Crossley, Alan. 'Eynsham', Bc97, 98–158.

65. Crossley, Alan. 'Wootton Hundred (southern part)', Bc97, 1–2.
66. Crossley, Alan; Townley, S.C.; Colvin, Christina. 'Woodstock', Bc97, 325–423.
67. Davies, Roger. *Tarring: a walk through its history*. Tarring; Davies; 1990. Pp xx, 219.
68. Day, C.J. 'Begbroke', Bc97, 3–14.
69. Day, C.J. 'Combe', Bc97, 75–98.
70. Day, C.J. 'North Leigh', Bc97, 213–38.
71. Day, C.J. 'Old Woodstock', Bc97, 423–30.
72. Day, C.J. 'Wilcote', Bc97, 296–304.
73. Day, C.J. 'Yarnton', Bc97, 470–89.
74. Day, John C.; Watson, W.M. 'History of the book trade in the north—the first twenty-five years', Bc139, 187–93.
75. Deacon, Marjorie. *Great Chesterford: the people, 1600–1800*. Saffron Walden; Town Library; 1989. Pp 53.
76. Deakin, Derick (ed.). *Wythenshawe: the story of a garden city*. Chichester; Phillimore; 1990. Pp xiii, 179.
77. Dear, James; Taylor, Tom. *Aspects of Yellowbelly history: the settlement and development of the East, West and Wildmore fens: a history of the fens north of Boston*. Spalding; Chameleon International; 1988. Pp 176.
78. Delanoy, Michael. *The history of Windsor Castle*. London; Headline; 1990. Pp 224.
79. Delvin, S. *A history of Winchmore Hill*. London; Regency; 1989. Pp 120.
80. Dennison, E.; Russett, V. 'Duck decoys: their function and management with reference to Nyland decoy, Cheddar', *Somerset Archaeology & Natural History* 133 (1990 for 1989), 141–55.
81. Dibben, A.A. 'Blackchapel, Great Waltham', Bc65, 115–42.
82. Donaldson, Gordon. *The faith of the Scots*. London; Batsford; 1990. Pp 168.
83. Douglas, Audrey. 'Midsummer in Salisbury: the Tailors' Guild and confraternity, 1444–1642', *Renaissance & Reformation* 13 (1989), 35–51.
84. Drage, C. *Nottingham Castle: a place full royal*. Nottingham; T. of Thoroton Soc., 93; 1990 for 1989. Pp 151.
85. Earl, A.L. *Middlewich, 900–1900*. Chester; Ravenscroft; 1990. Pp vi, 180.
86. Eccles, Christine. *The Rose Theatre*. London; Hern; 1990. Pp 160.
87. Eddershaw, Margaret. *Grand fashionable nights: Kendal Theatre, 1575–1985*. Lancaster; Centre for North-west Regional Studies, Lancaster University (Occasional papers no. 17.); 1989. Pp vii, 57.
88. Edwards, Hywel Teifi. *The Eisteddfod*. Cardiff; Wales UP; new edn. 1990. Pp 96.
89. Emery, Norman; Warner, John; Pearson, Alan. 'Causeway House, Northumberland', *Archaeologia Aeliana* 5th ser. 18 (1990), 131–49.
90. English, Barbara. *The great landowners of East Yorkshire, 1530–1910*. London; Harvester Wheatsheaf; 1990. Pp x, 289.

91. Evans, Christopher. ' "Power on silt": towards an archaeology of the East India Company', *Antiquity* 64/244 (1990), 643–61.

92. Fairrie, Angus. *The northern meeting, 1788–1988: the story of the northern meeting—its games, its Highland Balls, its dances and dance music and its piping competitions.* Haddington; Pentland; 1988. Pp 305.

93. Farrar, Henry. *Windsor: town and castle.* Chichester; Phillimore; 1990. Pp 144.

94. Fenton, Alexander. *Scottish country life.* Edinburgh; Donald; 1989. Pp 160.

95. Ferguson, Anthony J.A.; Prescott, Donald. *A history of medicine in south west Durham.* Durham; South Durham Health Authority; 1989. Pp iv, 197.

96. Fildes, Valerie. 'Maternal feelings re-assessed: child abandonment and neglect in London and Westminster, 1550–1800', Bc44, 139–78.

97. Flinn, Derek (ed.). *Travellers in a bygone Shetland: an anthology.* Edinburgh; Scottish Academic Press; 1989. Pp xiv, 278.

98. Flynn, Philip. 'Scottish philosophers, Scotch reviewers, and the science of mind', *Dalhousie R.* 68 (1988), 259–83.

99. Forrest, Gordon; Hadley, Ted. *Policing Hereford and Leominster: an illustrated history of the city of Hereford police, 1835 to 1947, and Leominster borough police, 1836 to 1889.* Studley; Brewin; 1989. Pp 92.

100. Fowler, Marian. *Blenheim: biography of a palace.* London; Viking; 1989. Pp 320.

101. Fraser, Constance; Emsley, Kenneth. *Northumbria.* Chichester; Phillimore; 1990. Pp 208.

102. French, David. *The British way in warfare, 1688–2000.* London; Unwin Hyman; 1990. Pp xviii, 266.

103. Galinou, Mireille (ed.). *London's pride: the glorious history of the capital's gardens.* London; Anaya; 1990. Pp 224.

104. Gavine, David. 'Navigation and astronomy teachers in Scotland outside the universities', *Mariner's Mirror* 76 (1990), 5–12.

105. Gay, Ken. *Forest to suburb: the story of Hornsey retold.* London; Hornsey Historical Soc.; 1988. Pp 50.

106. Godwin, Jeremy. 'Early bowling-greens in Whitehaven', *T. of the Cumberland & Westmorland Antiq. & Arch. Soc.* 90 (1990), 267–78.

107. Gordon, Eric. *Eynsham Abbey, 1005–1228: a small window into a large room.* Chichester; Phillimore; 1990. Pp xi, 196.

108. Gray, V.W. 'The County Record Office: the unfolding of an idea', Bc65, 11–26.

109. Green, Angela. *Ashdown: a history of an Essex village.* Essex; Green; 1989. Pp xv, 233.

110. Green, H.M.; Thurley, Simon J. 'Excavations on the west side of Whitehall, 1960–1962. Part I: from the building of the Tudor palace to the construction of the modern offices of state', *London & Middlesex Arch. Soc. T.* 38 (1987), 59–130.

111. Greenslade, M.W. 'Communications' [Lichfield], Bc99, 44–47.

112. Greenslade, M.W. 'Introduction' [Lichfield], Bc99, 1–3.

113. Greenslade, M.W. 'Parish government and poor relief' [Lichfield], Bc99, 87–92.
114. Greenslade, M.W. 'Population' [Lichfield], Bc99, 39.
115. Greenslade, M.W. 'Public services' [Lichfield], Bc99, 95–109.
116. Greenslade, M.W. 'Roman Catholicism' [in Lichfield], Bc99, 155–56.
117. Greenslade, M.W.; Johnson, D.A. 'Burntwood', Bc99, 195–228.
118. Greenslade, M.W.; Johnson, D.A. 'Fisherwick with Tamhorn', Bc99, 237–52.
119. Greenslade, M.W.; Johnson, D.A. 'Hammerwich', Bc99, 258–73.
120. Greenslade, M.W.; Johnson, D.A.; Tringham, N.J. 'General history' [of Lichfield], Bc99, 4–36.
121. Greenslade, M.W.; Tringham, N.J. 'Guilds' [Lichfield], Bc99, 131–34.
122. Gwynne, Peter. *A history of Crawley*. Chichester; Phillimore; 1990. Pp viii, 176.
123. Handley, Stuart. 'Local legislative initiatives for economic and social developments in Lancashire, 1689–1731', *Parliamentary History* 9 (1990), 14–37.
124. Hands, Roger; Hands, Joan. *The book of Boxmoor*. Buckingham; Barracuda; 1989. Pp 148.
125. Harris, A.P. 'Building stone in Norfolk', Bc135, 207–16.
126. Harwood, Joy. *A portrait of Portsea, 1840–1940*. Southampton; Ensign; 1990. Pp 160.
127. Haskell, Patricia. 'Country and town' [Portsmouth], Bc136, 13–35.
128. Haskell, Patricia. 'Marsh and water' [Portsmouth], Bc136, 1–12.
129. Hassall, G.; Cooper, Janet. 'Wolvercote', Bc97, 304–25.
130. Hayfield, Colin. *Wharram remembered: a social view of 40 years of excavations at Wharram Percy, East Riding of Yorkshire*. Arley; Spring Hill Publications; 1990. Pp 48.
131. Healey, Hilary. 'Report on the pottery found during field-walking of the transect' [Lincolnshire], Bc67, part ii, 71–79.
132. Heaton, Paul M. *Welsh shipping, forgotten fleets*. Newport (Gwent); Heaton; 1989. Pp 91.
133. Heginbottom, J.A. 'Early Christian sites in Calderdale', *Halifax Antiq. Soc. T.* (1989 for 1988), 1–16.
134. Hendrie, William Fyfe. *Linlithgow: six hundred years a royal burgh*. Edinburgh; Donald; 1989. Pp 240.
135. Hill, Godfrey. 'History on the pavements', *Ceredigion* 11 (1988–9), 81–86.
136. Hillyard, Brian. 'Working towards a history of Scottish book collecting', Bc139, 181–86.
137. Hogg, Anthony. *The Hulton diaries, 1832–1928: a gradely Lancashire chronicle*. Chichester; Solo Mio; 1989. Pp 432.
138. Holland, Eric G. *Coniston copper*. Milnthorpe; Cicerone; 1988. Pp 307.
139. Holton-Krayenbuhl, Anne; *et al.* 'Ely Cathedral precincts: the north range', *Cambridge Antiq. Soc. P.* 78 (1990 for 1989), 47–69.
140. Honeybone, Michael. *The book of Bottesford: continuity and change in a Leicestershire village*. Buckingham; Barracuda; 1989. Pp 148.

141. Houston, R.A. 'Age at marriage of Scottish women, c.1660–1770', *Local Population Studies* 43 (1989), 63–66.

142. Howell, R.L. *The Pembroke Yeomanry.* Carmarthen; Dyfed County Council; 1987. Pp 24.

143. Hudson, Helen. *Cumberland Lodge: a house through history.* Chichester; Phillimore; 1989. Pp xv, 192.

144. Hull, Felix. 'Aspects of local cartography in Kent and Essex, 1585–1700', Bc65, 241–52.

145. Jacobs, Norman. *Colchester: the last hundred years.* Lowestoft; Tyndale & Panda; 1990. Pp 112.

146. Jerram-Burrows, Lily E. *Bygone Rochford.* Chichester; Phillimore; 1988. Pp 128.

147. Johnson, D.A. 'Charities for the poor' [in Lichfield], Bc99, 184–94.

148. Johnson, D.A. 'Education' [in Lichfield], Bc99, 170–84.

149. Johnson, D.A.; Greenslade, M.W. 'Churches' [Lichfield], Bc99, 134–55.

150. Johnson, Nicholas; Rose, Peter. 'Bodmin Moor, Cornwall—post survey observations', Bc142, 65–69.

151. Jones, B.C. 'St Alban's church and graveyard, Carlisle', *T. of the Cumberland & Westmorland Antiq. & Arch. Soc.* 90 (1990), 163–81.

152. Jones, Dilwyn. 'Aerial evidence from the survey area and its environs' [Lincolnshire], Bc67, part ii, 1–25.

153. Katz, David S. 'The Chinese Jews and the problem of biblical authority in eighteenth- and nineteenth-century England', *English Historical R.* 105 (1990), 893–919.

154. Kelly, J.N.D. *St Edmund Hall: almost seven hundred years.* Oxford; Oxford UP; 1989. Pp 176.

155. Knight, Roy Clement. *A history of the Swansea Arts Society (1886–1986): the first hundred years.* Swansea; Davies; 1987. Pp 106.

156. Lawrence, Ian. *Fontmell Magna in retrospect.* Fontmell Magna; Brambledown; 1988. Pp 64.

157. Lea, Roger (ed.). *Scenes from Sutton's past: a closer look at aspects of the history of Sutton Coldfield.* Sutton Coldfield; Westwood; 1989. Pp 160.

158. Leach, J.H. Colin. *A school at Shrewsbury: the four foundations.* London; James & James; 1990. Pp 160.

159. Lightfoot, Nigel; Skeggs, James. 'Searching for plague in Somerset', Bc126, 90–100.

160. Lockwood, David. *Dumfries story: a tribute to, William McDowall.* Dumfries; Farries; 1988. Pp 106.

161. Long, Jean (comp.). *Knuston Hall: a Northamptonshire saga.* Horsmonden; Hi Resolution; 1989. Pp 92.

162. Lowe, M.C. 'The turnpike trusts in Devon and their roads, 1753–1889', *Devon Association Report and T.* 122 (1990), 47–69.

163. MacArthur, E. Mairi. *Iona: the living memory of a crofting community, 1750–1914.* Edinburgh; Edinburgh UP; 1990. Pp 296.

164. Macdonald, Jessie. 'The place-names of Hawick and district', *Hawick Arch. Soc. T.* (1989), 10–19.

165. Maclean, Douglas. 'The origins and early development of the Celtic cross', *Markers* 7 (1990), 232–75.

166. Maclure, Stuart. *A history of education in London, 1870–1990.* London; Allen Lane; new edn. 1990. Pp 256.

167. Mair, Douglas (ed.). *The Scottish contribution to modern economic thought.* Aberdeen; Aberdeen UP; 1990.

168. Markham, John. *The book of Hull: the evolution of a great northern city.* Buckingham; Barracuda; 1989. Pp 132.

169. Marks, Lara. ' "Dear old Mother Levy's": the Jewish Maternity Home and Sick Room Helps Society, 1895–1939', *Social History of Medicine* 3 (1990), 61–88.

170. Marr, L. James; Cox, James S. *Guernsey bailiwick harbours and landing-places, c.2000 BC to 1987.* Guernsey; Toucan; 1987. Pp 80.

171. Marren, Peter. *Grampian battlefields: battles in north-east Scotland, AD 84–1745.* Aberdeen; Aberdeen UP; 1990. Pp 224.

172. Martin, G.H. 'Essex boroughs and their records', Bc65, 27–46.

173. Massie, Alan. 'Glasgow: a moving portrait', *History Today* 40/5 (1990), 4–9.

174. Matthews, Hugh. *Burgess Hill.* Chichester; Phillimore; 1989. Pp xiv, 185.

175. Maxted, Ian. 'Mobility and innovation in the book trades—some Devon examples', Bc139, 73–85.

176. McCarthy, M.R.; Summerson, H.R.T. *Carlisle Castle: a survey and documentary history.* London; English Heritage; 1990. Pp 292.

177. McDonnell, John. 'Upland Pennine hamlets', *Northern History* 26 (1990), 20–39.

178. McFadzean, Alen. *The iron moor: a history of the Lindal Moor and Whitriggs hematite mines.* Ulverston; Red Earth; 1989. Pp 148.

179. McIntosh, Marjorie K. 'New College, Oxford and its Hornchurch Estate, 1391–1675', Bc65, 171–84.

180. McKeague, P. 'Sutton packhorse bridge', *Bedfordshire Archaeology* 18 (1989), 64–80.

181. Mead, A.H. *A miraculous draught of fishes: a history of St Paul's school.* London; James & James; 1990. Pp 144.

182. Mead, Geoffrey. 'Aspects of Brighton's market garden industry', *Sussex Arch. Collections* 127 (1989), 262–63.

183. Mee, Frances. *A history of Selsey.* Chichester; Phillimore; 1990. Pp xviii, 160.

184. Meller, Hugh. *Exeter architecture.* Chichester; Phillimore; 1989. Pp 192.

185. Milburn, Geoffrey E.; Miller, Stuart Tindale. (ed.). *Sunderland: river, town and people. A history from the 1780s.* Sunderland; Reed; 1989. Pp 232.

186. Miles, A.E.W. *An early Christian chapel and burial ground on the Isle of Ensay, Outer Hebrides, Scotland, with a study of the skeletal remains.* London; BAR (British ser. 212); 1989. Pp iv, 203.

187. Miller, F.J.W. 'The Newcastle dispensary, 1777–1976', *Archaeologia Aeliana* 5th ser. 18 (1990), 177–95.

188. Miller, Stuart Tindale. *The book of Sunderland*. Buckingham; Barracuda; 1989. Pp 120.

189. Mitchell, D.J. *A history of Warwickshire County Council, 1889–1989: a century of county government*. Warwick; Warwickshire County Council; 1988. Pp xxiv, 249.

190. Moncreiff, Rhoderick; Moncreiff, Alison (ed.). *The annals of Kinross-shire, 490–1861: by Ebenezer Henderson*. Kinross; Fossoway Community Council; 1990. Pp 126.

191. Moore, Pam. *The industrial heritage of Hampshire and the Isle of Wight*. Chichester; Phillimore; 1990. Pp xi, 128.

192. Morgan, Nicholas J. *Pavement, Glasgow: Scott Rae Stevenson Ltd, 1838–1988*. Glasgow; Scott Rae Stevenson; 1988. Pp 36.

193. Morgan, Paul. 'The provincial book trade before the end of the Licensing Act', Bc139, 31–39.

194. Morris, R.J.B. 'Northampton's local legislation: 1430 to 1988', *Northamptonshire Past & Present* 8/1 (1989–90), 73–82.

195. Murray, Hugh; Riddick, Sarah; Green, Richard. *York through the eyes of the artist*. York; York City Art Gallery; 1990. Pp vi, 174.

196. Murray, Jane. 'Archaeological landscapes; recent RCAMS survey in S.W. Scotland', *Dumfriesshire & Galloway Natural History & Antiq. Soc. T.* 3rd ser. 62 (1988), 22–34.

197. Musgrove, Frank. *The north of England: a history from Roman times to the present*. Oxford; Blackwell; 1990. Pp 347.

198. Neale, Kenneth. 'Essex: an appreciation', Bc65, 253–60.

199. Neale, Kenneth. 'Frederick G. Emmison: archivist and scholar', Bc65, 1–10.

200. Nelson, E. Charles. 'Three centuries in Irish botanical gardens: an epitome and a bibliography', *Long Room* 34 (1989), 15–28.

201. Newman, Aubrey. 'Mapping the metropolis: London—a review essay', *Urban History Yearbook* 17 (1990), 122–25.

202. Newport, John James. *Records of Hooe, Battle, Sussex*. Battle; Newport; 1989. Pp 98.

203. Nichols, Harold. *Local maps of Nottingham to 1800: an inventory*. Nottingham; Nottingham County Council Leisure Services; 1987. Pp xii, 162.

204. Nolan, John. 'The castle of Newcastle-upon-Tyne after *c.*1600', *Archaeologia Aeliana* 5th ser. 18 (1990), 79–126.

205. O'Brien, C.; *et al.* 'Excavations at Newcastle quayside: the crown court site', *Archaeologia Aeliana* 5th ser. 17 (1989), 141–205.

206. Paley, Ruth. ' "An imperfect, inadequate and wretched system"? Policing London before Peel', *Criminal Justice History* 10 (1989), 95–130.

207. Pascoe, Stuart N. *The early history of Porthleven*. Redruth; Dyllansow Truran; 1989. Pp viii, 124.

208. Patrick, Miss; Bowie, Miss. *Fortiter vivamus: a centenary history of St Margaret's School, Edinburgh, 1890–1990*. Edinburgh; Mainstream; 1989. Pp 144.

209. Pearson, David. 'Cambridge bindings in Cosin's Library, Durham', Bc139, 41–60.

210. Perkin, Michael. 'Hampshire notices of printing presses, 1799–1867', Bc139, 151–64.

211. Phillips, Patricia. 'Lincolnshire wolds transect survey: objectives and results', Bc67, part ii, 27–69.

212. Phillips, Peter. 'A Catholic community: Shrewsbury. Part 1, 1750–1850', *Recusant History* 20 (1990), 239–61.

213. Phillips, Roger. *Tredegar: the history of the agricultural estate, 1300–1956*. Upton-upon-Severn; Self Publishing Association; 1990. Pp 360.

214. Pitts, Michael. 'What future for Avebury?', *Antiquity* 64/243 (1990), 259–74.

215. Pocock, Douglas C.D.; Norris, Roger C. *A history of County Durham*. Chichester; Phillimore; 1990. Pp 128.

216. Pounds, N.J.G. 'Buildings, building stones and building accounts in south-west England', Bc135, 228–37.

217. Powell, R.F. Peter. 'The place-names of Devynock hundred, III: Cantref & Glyn', *Brycheiniog* 23 (1988–9), 85–108.

218. Price, David Trevor William. *A history of Saint David's University College, Lampeter, vol. 2: 1898–1971*. Cardiff; Wales UP; 1990. Pp xvi, 270.

219. Proctor, Molly Geraldine. *Honnors: a century full circle—a Maidstone corn and seed merchants' story*. Rochester; Honnors; 1989. Pp 96.

220. Quail, Sarah. 'Stone towers' [Portsmouth], Bc136, 53–67.

221. Quail, Sarah. 'The voice of the people' [Portsmouth], Bc136, 121–40.

222. Quail, Sarah. 'The way people worshipped' [Portsmouth], Bc136, 100–20.

223. Railton, Margaret; Barr, Marshall. *History of the Royal Berkshire Hospital, 1839–1989*. Reading; Royal Berkshire Hospital; 1989. Pp ix, 355.

224. Rees, Eiluned. 'The Welsh printing house from 1718 to 1818', Bc139, 101–24.

225. Richards, Paul. *King's Lynn*. Chichester; Phillimore; 1990. Pp 256.

226. Richardson, Rosamond. *Swanbrooke Down: a century of change in an English village*. London; Macdonald; 1990. Pp 320.

227. Riley, Raymond. 'Wooden walls and ironclads' [Portsmouth], Bc136, 36–52.

228. Robinson, David. *Pastors, parishes and people in Surrey*. Chichester; Phillimore; 1989. Pp 38.

229. Robinson, P.W. 'Stone Trough Brewery', *Halifax Antiq. Soc. T.* (1990 for 1989), 7–22.

230. Robinson, Vaughan; McCarroll, Danny (ed.). *The Isle of Man: celebrating a sense of place*. Liverpool; Liverpool UP; 1990. Pp 311.

231. Robson, Brian. 'Premature obituaries: change and adaptation in the great cities', Bc28, 45–54.

232. Rogers, C. Paul. 'Scots law in post-revolutionary and nineteenth-century America: the neglected jurisprudence', *Law & History R.* 8 (1990), 205–35.

233. Rolls, Roger. 'From balneology to physiotherapy: the development of physical treatment in Bath', Bc126, 111–18.

234. Ronnquist, Ralf. *Historia och nationalitet: Skotsk etno-territorialitet i ett historiskt perspektiv* [History and nationality: Scottish ethno-territoriality from an historical perspective]. Lund; Lund UP; 1990. Pp 273.

235. Roper, Elinor M.C. *Seedtime: the history of Essex seeds.* Chichester; Phillimore; 1989. Pp xvi, 294.

236. Ryan, P.M.; *et al.* 'Ashmans, Woodham Walter: a post-medieval house and its setting', *Essex Archaeology & History* 3rd ser. 20 (1989), 120–32.

237. Schueller, Robert. *A history of Chobham.* Chichester; Phillimore; 1989. Pp 192.

238. Scowcroft, Philip L. *Singing together: the centenary history of Doncaster Choral Society, 1888–1988.* Doncaster; Doncaster Library Service; 1988. Pp 63.

239. Senior, J.R. 'Hildenley limestone: a fine quality dimensional and artifact stone from Yorkshire', Bc135, 147–68.

240. Senior, Michael. *Disputed border: the history of the north Wales marches from Chester to Shrewsbury.* Llanrwst; Gwasg Carreg Gwalch; 1989. Pp 48.

241. Smith, Christopher. 'The excavation of the Exchequer Gate, Denbigh, 1982–1983', *Archaeologia Cambrensis* 137 (1989 for 1988), 108–12.

242. Smith, Graham. *Smuggling in the Bristol Channel, 1700–1850.* Newbury; Countryside Books; 1989. Pp 176.

243. Smith, Peter. 'The RCAHM Wales in my time, 1949–1989', *T. of the Ancient Monuments Soc.* 34 (1990), 29–83.

244. Smith, Robert. *The granite city: a history of Aberdeen.* Edinburgh; Donald; 1989. Pp 200.

245. Smith, Robert. *The royal glens.* Edinburgh; Donald; 1990. Pp 250.

246. Snetzler, M.F.; Hall, R. *Devon extracts, 1665–1850, vol. 2: Plymouth, 1665–1765.* Bideford; Devon Family History Soc.; 1989. Pp 178.

247. Snowden, Keith. *Thornton Dale through the ages.* Pickering; Castleden Publications; 1989. Pp 48.

248. Spick, Bill. *The book of Arnold.* Buckingham; Barracuda; 1990. Pp 128.

249. Stagg, D.J. 'Silvicultural enclosure in the New Forest to 1780', *P. of the Hampshire Field Club & Arch. Soc.* 45 (1989), 135–45.

250. Stanley, M.F. 'Carved in bright stone: sources of building stone in Derbyshire', Bc135, 169–86.

251. Stapleton, Guy (ed.). *Memories of Moreton: contributions to the history of Moreton in Marsh, Gloucestershire.* Shipston-on-Stour; Drinkwater; 1989. Pp ii, 94.

252. Stevenson, Stephanie. *Anstruther: a history.* Edinburgh; Donald; 1989. Pp 256.

253. Stocker, David; Everson, Paul. 'Rubbish recycled: a study of the re-use of stone in Lincolnshire', Bc135, 83–101.

254. Storey, Edward. *Fen, fire and flood: scenes from Fenland history.* Peterborough; Cambridgeshire Libraries; 1989. Pp 56.

255. Strawhorn, John. *The history of Ayr: royal burgh and county town.* Edinburgh; Donald; 1989. Pp 336.

256. Summerell, Max. *The book of Wendover*. Buckingham; Barracuda; 1989. Pp 160.

257. Summers, Norman. *A prospect of Southwell: an architectural history of the church and domestic buildings of the Collegiate Foundation.* Southwell; Kelham House Publications; rev. edn. 1988. Pp xviii, 152.

258. Swan, Vivien G.; *et al.* 'East Lilling, north Yorkshire: the deserted medieval village reconsidered', *Yorkshire Arch. J.* 62 (1990), 91–109.

259. Tatton-Brown, T.W.T. 'The history of St Gregory's priory', *Archaeologia Cantiana* 107 (1990 for 1989), 314–27.

260. Thomas, Charles. 'The names of the batteries on the garrison, St Mary's, Isles of Scilly', Bc142, 251–59.

261. Thomas, Harry. *The history of the Gloucestershire Constabulary, 1839–1985.* Gloucester; Gloucestershire Constabulary; 1987. Pp 352.

262. Thomas, John; Farrington, John. *The Callander & Oban railway.* Newton Abbot; Thomas (The history of the railways of the Scottish Highlands 4); 1990. Pp 220.

263. Thompson, Arthur. *A short history of the Settlement, 1892–1989.* Middlesbrough; Newport Settlement; 1989. Pp 24.

264. Thomson, John A. *The smuggling coast: the customs port of Dumfries, forty miles of the Solway Firth.* Dumfries; Farries; 1989. Pp 101.

265. Thorpe, Josephine (ed.). *North Devon watermills.* Barnstable; North Devon Arch. Soc.; 1989. Pp 68.

266. Todd, Barbara. 'Freebench and free enterprise: widows and their property in two Berkshire villages', Bc77, 175–200.

267. Torrens, Hugh S. 'The four Bath philosophical societies, 1779–1959', Bc126, 180–88.

268. Townley, S.C. 'South Leigh', Bc97, 238–53.

269. Townley, S.C. 'Stanton Harcourt', Bc97, 267–96.

270. Travers, Ben. 'Trading patterns in the east midlands, 1660–1800', *Midland History* 15 (1990), 65–82.

271. Tringham, N.J. 'Boundaries and gates' [Lichfield], Bc99, 39–40.

272. Tringham, N.J. 'Parliamentary representation' [Lichfield], Bc99, 92–95.

273. Tringham, N.J. 'Protestant nonconformity' [in Lichfield], Bc99, 156–59.

274. Tringham, N.J. 'Social and cultural activities' [in Lichfield], Bc99, 159–70.

275. Tringham, N.J. 'Street names' [Lichfield], Bc99, 40–42.

276. Tringham, N.J. 'The cathedral and the close' [Lichfield], Bc99, 47–67.

277. Tringham, N.J. 'Town government' [Lichfield], Bc99, 73–87.

278. Tringham, N.J.; Greenslade, M.W. 'Economic history' [Lichfield], Bc99, 109–31.

279. Tringham, N.J.; Greenslade, M.W. 'Manor and other estates' [Lichfield], Bc99, 67–72.

280. Tringham, N.J.; Johnson, D.A. 'Curborough and Elmhurst', Bc99, 229–37.

281. Tringham, N.J.; Johnson, D.A. 'Freeford', Bc99, 253–58.

282. Tringham, N.J.; Johnson, D.A. 'Streethay', Bc99, 273–82.

283. Tringham, N.J.; Johnson, D.A. 'Wall with Pipehill', Bc99, 283–94.

284. Tyson, Blake. 'Newlaithes Hall, Carlisle: the evolution and extinction of

a Cumbrian courtyard farm', *T. of the Cumberland & Westmorland Antiq. & Arch. Soc.* 90 (1990), 235–52.

285. Urdank, Albion M. 'The consumption of rental property: Gloucestershire plebeians and the market economy, 1750–1860', *J. of Interdisciplinary History* 21 (1990–1), 261–81.

286. Varley, Edwina (ed.). *History of Leatherhead: a town at the crossroads.* Leatherhead; Leatherhead & District Local History Soc.; 1988. Pp 384.

287. Veriod, Bryan S. *A history of the Norwich City Fire Brigade.* Norwich; Veriod; 1986. Pp xv, 144.

288. Walker, David Maxwell. *A legal history of Scotland*, vol. 2. London; Green; 1990. Pp 700.

289. Wallace, Joyce Moyra. *Further traditions of Trinity and Leith.* Edinburgh; Donald; 1990. Pp 150.

290. Wallis, P.J. 'Cross-regional connexions' [in the book trade], Bc139, 87–100.

291. Walter, Don. *The book of Harrow.* Buckingham; Barracuda; 1990. Pp 148.

292. Warren, Kenneth. *Consett iron, 1840 to 1980: a study in industrial location.* Oxford; Oxford UP; 1990. Pp 193.

293. Waterson, Edward; Meadows, Peter. *Lost houses of York and the North Riding.* Thornton-le-Clay; Raines; 1990. Pp 72.

294. Watkin, Bruce W. *A history of Wiltshire.* Chichester; Phillimore; 1989. Pp 128.

295. Watson, R.C. 'According to the custom of the province of York', *Lancashire Local History* 5 (1989), 5–14.

296. Webb, John. 'Leisure and pleasure' [Portsmouth], Bc136, 141–53.

297. Webb, John. 'Port and garrison town' [Portsmouth], Bc136, 68–82.

298. Webb, John. 'Portsmouth and its past', Bc136, 154–68.

299. Webb, John. 'The way people lived' [Portsmouth], Bc136, 83–99.

300. Wellard, Gordon. *The story of Camberley, 1798–1987: the Victorian village that became a modern town.* Camberley; Wellard; 1989. Pp 134.

301. Whetter, James. *The history of Gorran Haven*, part 1. St Austell; Lyfrow Trelyspen; 1990. Pp 120.

302. Whitney, Charles E. *Bygone Hythe: with Saltwood, Seabrook and Lympe.* Chichester; Phillimore; 1989. Pp 128.

303. Whyte, Ian D. *Edinburgh and the Borders: landscape heritage.* Newton Abbot; David & Charles; 1990. Pp 208.

304. Wildsmith, Osmond. *A history of Wolverhampton transport, vol. 1: 1833 to 1930.* Birmingham; Birmingham Transport History Group; 1989. Pp 128.

305. Willetts, Arthur. *The Black Country nail trade.* Dudley; Dudley Leisure Services; 1989. Pp 34.

306. Williams, Ken. *The story of Typhoo.* London; Quiller; 1990. Pp 132.

307. Wirdnam, Audrey. *Pidela: an account of the village of Tolpuddle, Dorset, from early times.* Tolpuddle; Beechcote; 1989. Pp 88.

308. Withers, C.W.J. 'Highland migration to Aberdeen, *c.*1649–1891', *Northern Scotland* 9 (1989), 21–44.

309. Wong, Maria Lin. *Chinese-Liverpudlians: history of the Chinese community in Liverpool*. Birkenhead; Liver; 1989. Pp 100.
310. Woodall, Joy. *The book of Solihull*. Buckingham; Barracuda; 1990. Pp 124.
311. Wratten, Don. *The book of Radlett and Aldenham*. Buckingham; Barracuda; 1990. Pp 132.

## (c) *Collective Volumes*

1. Anon (ed.). *Not a passing phase: reclaiming lesbians in history, 1840–1985*. London; Women's Press; 1989. Pp 264.
2. Angerman, Arina (ed.). *Current issues in women's history*. London; Routledge; 1989. Pp 350.
3. Kaye, Harvey J.; McClelland, Keith (ed.). *E.P. Thompson: critical perspectives*. Cambridge; Polity; 1990. Pp 300.
4. Dukes, Paul; Dunkley, John (ed.). *Culture and revolution*. London; Pinter; 1990. Pp 165.
5. Salter, Stephen; Stevenson, John (ed.). *The working class and politics in Europe and America, 1929–1945*. Harlow; Longman; 1990. Pp 272.
6. Eatwell, Roger; O'Sullivan, Noel (ed.). *The nature of the Right: European and American politics and political thought since 1789*. London; Pinter; 1989. Pp 203.
7. Troen, Selwyn Ilan; Shemesh, Moshe (ed.). *The Suez-Sinai crisis, 1956: retrospective and reappraisal*. Cass; 1989. Pp ix, 400.
8. Pravda, Alex; Duncan, Peter J.S. (ed.). *Soviet-British relations since the 1970s*. Cambridge; Cambridge UP; 1990. Pp x, 220.
9. Foot, Michael R.D. (ed.). *Holland at war against Hitler: Anglo-Dutch relations, 1940–1945*. London; Cass; 1990.
10. Zametica, John (ed.). *British officials and British foreign policy, 1945–1950*. Leicester; Leicester UP; 1990. Pp 224.
11. Deighton, Anne (ed.). *Britain and the first Cold War*. London; Macmillan; 1990. Pp 320.
12. Hawkes, Sonia Chadwick (ed.). *Weapons and warfare in Anglo-Saxon England*. Oxford; Oxford University Committee for Archaeology; 1990. Pp 218.
13. Gash, Norman (ed.). *Wellington: studies in the military and political career of the first duke of Wellington*. Manchester; Manchester UP; 1990. Pp v, 336.
14. Tracey, James D. (ed.). *The rise of merchant empires: long-distance trade in the early modern world, 1350–1750*. Cambridge; Cambridge UP; 1990. Pp 430.
15. Tinkler, Keith J. (ed.). *The history of geomorphology*. Unwin Hyman; 1989. Pp xviii, 384.
16. Moore, James R. (ed.). *History, humanity and evolution: essays for John C. Greene*. Cambridge; Cambridge UP; 1989. Pp 464.
17. Feingold, Mordechai (ed.). *Before Newton: the life and times of Isaac Barrow*. Cambridge; Cambridge UP; 1990. Pp 368.
18. Taton, Rene; Wilson, Curtis (ed.). *The general history of astronomy,*

*vol. 2: planetary astronomy from the Renaissance to the rise of astrophysics, part A: Tycho Brahe to Newton.* Cambridge; Cambridge UP; 1989. Pp 250.

19. Kroh, J. (ed.). *The early developments in radiation chemistry.* London; Royal Society of Chemists; 1989. Pp 514.

20. Nutton, Vivian (ed.). *Medicine at the courts of Europe, 1500–1837.* London; Routledge (Wellcome Institute ser. in the History of Medicine); 1989. Pp 336.

21. Galenson, David W. (ed.). *Markets in history: economic studies of the past.* Cambridge; Cambridge UP; 1989. Pp 355.

22. Davenport-Hines, Richard P.T. (ed.). *Business in the age of depression and war* [reprints from *Business History*]. London; Cass; 1990. Pp 332.

23. Graham, Andrew; Seldon, Anthony (ed.). *Government and economies in the postwar world: economic policies and comparative performance, 1945–1985.* London; Routledge; 1990. Pp 336.

24. Davenport-Hines, Richard P.T. (ed.). *Capital, entrepreneurs and profits* [Reprints from *Business History*]. London; Cass; 1990. Pp 367.

25. Mathias, Peter; Davis, John A. (ed.). *The first industrial revolutions.* Oxford; Blackwell; 1990. Pp x, 224.

26. Slater, Terry R. (ed.). *The built form of western cities: essays for M.R.G. Conzen on the occasion of his 80th birthday.* Leicester; Leicester UP; 1990. Pp 350.

27. Corfield, Penelope J.; Keene, Derek J. (ed.). *Work in towns, 850–1850.* Leicester; Leicester UP; 1990. Pp 250.

28. Lawton, Richard (ed.). *The rise and fall of great cities.* London; Pinter; 1989. Pp 224.

29. Goodman, Anthony; Mackay, Angus (ed.). *The impact of humanism on western Europe.* Harlow; Longman; 1990. Pp 272.

30. Todd, Malcolm (ed.). *Research on Roman Britain, 1960–1989.* [Place]; Soc. for the Promotion of Roman Studies (Britannia monograph ser. vol. 11); 1989. Pp 267.

31. Stanley, Eric G. (ed.). *British Academy papers on Anglo-Saxon England* [Reprints from *Proceedings*]. Oxford; Oxford UP for British Academy; 1990. Pp 364.

32. Williams, Daniel (ed.). *England in the twelfth century: proceedings of the 1988 Harlaxton Symposium.* Woodbridge; Boydell & Brewer; 1990. Pp xii, 308.

33. Morrill, John (ed.). *Oliver Cromwell and the English revolution.* Harlow; Longman; 1990. Pp 352.

34. MacGregor, Arthur (ed.). *The late king's goods: collections, possessions, and patronage of Charles I in the light of the Commonwealth sale inventories.* Oxford; Oxford UP; 1989. Pp 600.

35. Gorst, Tony; Johnman, Lewis; Lucas, W. Scott (ed.). *Postwar Britain, 1945–1965: themes and perspectives.* London; Pinter/Inst. of British Contemporary Studies; 1989. Pp 254.

36. Dean, David M.; Jones, Norman L. (ed.). *The parliaments of Elizabethan England.* Oxford; Blackwell; 1990. Pp 224.

37. Hellmuth, Eckhart (ed.). *The transformation of political culture:*

*England and Germany in the late-eighteenth century.* Oxford; Oxford UP; 1990. Pp 560.

38. Cesarani, David (ed.). *The making of modern Anglo-Jewry.* Oxford; Blackwell; 1990. Pp 256.

39. Green, Francis (ed.). *The restructuring of the UK economy.* Hemel Hempstead; Harvester Wheatsheaf; 1989. Pp 320.

40. Harper-Bill, Christopher; Harvey, Ruth (ed.). *The ideals and practice of medieval knighthood, III: papers from the fourth Strawberry Hill Conference, 1988.* Woodbridge; Boydell; 1990. Pp 192.

41. Griffiths, Jeremy; Pearsall, Derek (ed.). *Book-production and publishing in Britain, 1375–1475.* Cambridge; Cambridge UP; 1989. Pp x, 438.

42. Hudson, Pat (ed.). *Regions and industries: a perspective on the industrial revolution in Britain.* Cambridge; Cambridge UP; 1989. Pp xiii, 277.

43. Harvey, Charles; Turner, John (ed.). *Labour and business in modern Britain* [Reprints from *Business History*]. London; Cass; 1989. Pp 117.

44. Fildes, Valerie (ed.). *Women as mothers in pre-industrial England: essays in memory of Dorothy McLaren.* London; Routledge; 1990. Pp 225.

45. Thompson, Francis M.L. (ed.). *The Cambridge social history of Britain, 1750–1950, vol. 1: regions and communities.* Cambridge; Cambridge UP; 1990. Pp xv, 588.

46. Thompson, Francis M.L. (ed.). *The Cambridge social history of Britain, 1750–1950, vol. 2: people and their environment.* Cambridge; Cambridge UP; 1990. Pp xv, 373.

47. Thompson, Francis M.L. (ed.). *The Cambridge social history of Britain, 1750–1950, vol. 3: social agencies and institutions.* Cambridge; Cambridge UP; 1990. Pp xiii, 492.

48. Gaskell, S. Martin (ed.). *Slums.* Leicester; Leicester UP; 1990. Pp 240.

49. Swift, Roger; Gilley, Sheridan (ed.). *The Irish in Britain, 1815–1939.* London; Pinter; 1989. Pp 256.

50. Myers, Robin; Harris, Michael (ed.). *Fakes and frauds: varieties of deception in print and manuscript.* Winchester; St Paul's Bibliographies; 1989. Pp 136.

51. Mason, Tony (ed.). *Sport in Britain: a social history.* Cambridge; Cambridge UP; 1989. Pp 384.

52. Holt, Richard (ed.). *Sport and the working class in modern Britain.* Manchester; Manchester UP; 1990. Pp 221.

53. Higham, Robert (ed.). *Landscape and townscape in the south-west.* Exeter; Exeter UP; 1989. Pp 144.

54. Simpson, Grant G. (ed.). *Scotland and Scandinavia.* Edinburgh; Donald; 1990. Pp 250.

55. Devine, Tom M. (ed.). *Conflict and stability in Scottish society, 1700–1850.* Edinburgh; Donald; 1990. Pp ix, 139.

56. Jones, Peter (ed.). *Philosophy and science in the Scottish Enlightenment.* Edinburgh; Donald; 1989. Pp 240.

57. Devine, Tom M. (ed.). *Improvement and Enlightenment: proceedings of*

*the Scottish Historical Studies Seminar, University of Strathclyde, 1987–1988*. Edinburgh; Donald; 1989. Pp 156.

58. Fraser, W. Hamish; Morris, R.J. (ed.). *People and society in Scotland: vol. 2, 1830–1914*. Edinburgh; Donald; 1990. Pp xvi, 363.

59. Rodger, Richard (ed.). *Scottish housing: policy and politics, 1885–1985*. Leicester; Leicester UP; 1989. Pp 250.

60. Vaughan, W.E. (ed.). *A new history of Ireland, vol. 5. Ireland under the Union, i: 1801–1870*. Oxford; Oxford UP; 1989.

61. Marwick, Arthur (ed.). *The arts, literature, and society*. London; Routledge; 1990. Pp 332.

62. Bradshaw, Brendan; Duffy, Eamon (ed.). *Humanism, reform and the Reformation: the career of St John Fisher*. Cambridge; Cambridge UP; 1989. Pp 260.

63. Gough, Hugh; Dickson, David J. (ed.). *Ireland and the French revolution*. Dublin; Irish Academic Press; 1990. Pp xii, 255.

64. Ó Corráin, Donnchadh; Breatnach, Liam; McCone, Kim (ed.). *Sages, saints and storytellers: Celtic studies in honour of Professor James Carney*. Maynooth; An Sagart; 1989. Pp xvi, 472.

65. Neale, Kenneth (ed.). *An Essex tribute: essays presented to Frederick G. Emmison as a tribute to his life and work for Essex history and archives*. London; Leopard's Head; 1987. Pp xv, 268.

66. Blair, W. John (ed.). *St Frideswide's monastery, at Oxford: archaeological and architectural studies* [Reprints from articles in *Oxoniensis* vol. 53 (1988)]. Gloucester; Sutton; 1990. Pp 296.

67. Phillips, Patricia (ed.). *Archaeology and landscape studies in north Lincolnshire*. Oxford; BAR (British ser. 208); 1989. 2 parts. Pp 201, 181.

68. Bayly, Christopher A. (ed.). *The Raj: India and the British, 1600–1947*. London; National Portrait Gallery; 1990. Pp 432.

69. Hicks, Michael A. (ed.). *Profit, piety and the professions in later medieval England*. Gloucester; Sutton; 1990. Pp xxii, 170.

70. Marsden, Gordon (ed.). *Victorian values: personalities and perspectives in nineteenth-century society*. London; Longman; 1990. Pp viii, 232.

71. Fernie, Eric; Crossley, Paul (ed.). *Medieval architecture and its intellectual context: studies in honour of Peter Kidson*. London; Hambledon; 1990. Pp 304.

72. Chibnall, Marjorie (ed.). *Anglo-Norman studies, 12*. Woodbridge; Boydell (Proceedings of the Battle conference, 1989); 1990. Pp 252.

73. Deegan, Marilyn; Scragg, Donald G. (ed.). *Medicine in early medieval England*. Manchester; Manchester Centre for Anglo-Saxon Studies; 1989. Pp 40.

74. Ireland, John de Courcy; Sheehy, David C. (ed.). *Atlantic visions: international conference proceedings of the Society of St Brendan the navigator*. Dublin; Boole; 1989. Pp ix, 229.

75. Williams, Glanmor; Jones, Robert Owen (ed.). *The Celts and the renaissance: tradition and innovation—proceedings of the Eighth International Congress of Celtic Studies 1987*. Cardiff; Wales UP; 1990. Pp xi, 187.

76. Fischer, Lewis R.; Nordvik, Helge W. (ed.). *Shipping and trade, 1750–1950: essays in international maritime economic history.* Pontefract; Lofthouse; 1990. Pp xii, 325.

77. Chartres, John; Hey, David (ed.). *English rural society, 1500–1800: essays in honour of Joan Thirsk.* Cambridge; Cambridge UP; 1990. Pp 384.

78. Reed, Mick; Wells, Roger A.E. (ed.). *Class, conflict and protest in the English countryside, 1700–1880* [Mainly reprints from *J. of Peasant Studies*]. London; Cass; 1990. Pp 236.

79. Constantine, Stephen (ed.). *Emigrants and empire: British settlement in the dominions between the wars.* Manchester; Manchester UP; 1990. Pp x, 208.

80. Clark, Jonathan Charles Douglas (ed.). *Ideas and politics in modern Britain.* Basingstoke; Macmillan; 1990. Pp 288.

81. Charlot, Monica; Marx, Roland (ed.). *Londres, 1851–1901.* Paris; Autrement; 1990. Pp 240.

82. Harris, Tim; Seaward, Paul; Goldie, Mark (ed.). *The politics of religion in Restoration England.* Oxford; Blackwell; 1990. Pp xii, 259.

83. Raven, G.J.A.; Rodger, N.A.M. (ed.). *Navies and armies: the Anglo-Dutch relationship in war and peace, 1688–1988.* Edinburgh; Donald; 1990. Pp x, 118.

84. Power, Thomas P.; Whelan, Kevin (ed.). *Endurance and emergence: Catholics in Ireland in the eighteenth century.* Dublin; Irish Academic Press; 1990. Pp 204.

85. Comerford, R.V.; Cullen, Mary; Hill, Jacqueline R.; Lennon, Colm (ed.). *Religion, conflict and coexistence in Ireland: essays presented to Monsignor Patrick Corish.* Dublin; Gill and Macmillan; 1990. Pp 360.

86. Sher, Richard B.; Smitten, Jeffrey R. (ed.). *Scotland and America in the age of the Enlightenment.* Edinburgh; Edinburgh UP; 1990. Pp xii, 307.

87. Brake, Laurel; Jones, Alex; Madden, Lionel (ed.). *Investigating Victorian journalism.* London; Macmillan; 1990. Pp 224.

88. Coughlan, Patricia (ed.). *Spenser and Ireland: an interdisciplinary perspective.* Cork; Cork UP; 1989. Pp 130.

89. Medwin, Alisoun Gardner; Williams, Janet Hadley (ed.). *A Day Estivall: essays on the music, poetry and history of Scotland and England & poems previously unpublished: in honour of Helena Mennie Shire.* Aberdeen; Aberdeen UP; 1990. Pp 192.

90. Gordon, Eleanor; Breitenbach, Esther (ed.). *The world is ill-divided: women's work in Scotland in the nineteenth and early twentieth centuries.* Edinburgh; Edinburgh UP; 1990. Pp 194.

91. Ford, Boris (ed.). *Cambridge guide to the Arts in Britain, vol. 4: the seventeenth century.* Cambridge; Cambridge UP; 1989. Pp xii, 356.

92. Ford, Boris (ed.). *Cambridge guide to the Arts in Britain, vol. 7: the later Victorian age.* Cambridge; Cambridge UP; 1989. Pp xiii, 363.

93. Ford, Boris (ed.). *Cambridge guide to the Arts in Britain, vol. 8: the Edwardian age and the inter-war years.* Cambridge; Cambridge UP; 1989. Pp xi, 367.

94. McVeagh, John (ed.). *All before them. English literature and the wider world, vol. 1: 1660–1780.* London; Ashfield; 1990. Pp xi, 305.
95. Black, Jeremy (ed.). *British politics and society from Walpole to Pitt, 1742–1789.* London; Macmillan; 1990. Pp 274.
96. Friedland, Klaus (ed.). *Maritime aspects of migration.* Cologne; Bohlau (Quellen und Darstellungen zur Hansischen Geschichte, neue folge 34); 1989. Pp 465.
97. Crossley, Alan (ed.). *A history of the county of Oxford, vol. 12: Wootton hundred (south), including Woodstock.* London; Oxford UP (Victoria history of the counties of England); 1990. Pp 528.
98. Clarkson, Leslie A. (ed.). *The industrial revolution: a compendium* [Reprints of four pamphlets of the Economic History Soc., 1984–1988]. Basingstoke; Macmillan; 1990. Pp ix, 308.
99. Greenslade, M.W. (ed.). *A history of the county of Stafford, vol. 14: Lichfield.* London; Oxford UP (Victoria history of the counties of England); 1990. Pp 319.
100. Taylor, John; Childs, Wendy R. (ed.). *Politics and crisis in fourteenth-century England.* Gloucester; Sutton; 1990. Pp xvi, 157.
101. Anglo, Sydney (ed.). *Chivalry in the Renaissance.* Woodbridge; Boydell; 1990. Pp xvi, 284.
102. Brown, David (ed.). *Newman, a man for our time: centenary essays.* London; SPCK; 1990. Pp 176.
103. Davidson, Hilda Ellis (ed.). *The seer in Celtic and other traditions.* Edinburgh; Donald; 1989. Pp x, 146.
104. Fraser, Derek (ed.). *Cities, class and communication: essays in honour of Asa Briggs.* London; Harvester Wheatsheaf; 1990. Pp 264.
105. Ankarloo, Bengt; Henningsen, Gustav (ed.). *Early modern European witchcraft.* Oxford; Oxford UP; 1990. Pp xii, 476.
106. Gordon, Peter; Szreter, Richard (ed.). *History of education: the making of a discipline* [Reprints from various sources, 1914–1983]. London; Woburn; 1989. Pp vii, 240.
107. Brown, Tony (ed.). *Edward Carpenter and his circle: late Victorian radicalism.* London; Cass; 1990. Pp [200].
108. Anon. *Camden miscellany, XXX.* London; Royal Historical Soc. (Camden fourth ser. vol. 39); 1990. Pp 256.
109. Williams, Ann; Erskine, R.W.H. (ed.). *The Oxfordshire Domesday.* London; Alecto; 2 vols. 1990. Pp i–viii, 1–45; 29; fos. 154–61.
110. Williams, Ann; Erskine, R.W.H. (ed.). *The Shropshire Domesday.* London; Alecto; 2 vols. 1990. Pp i–viii, 1–61; 40; fos. 252–61.
111. Williams, Ann; Erskine, R.W.H. (ed.). *The Sussex Domesday.* London; Alecto; 2 vols. 1990. Pp i–viii, 1–64; 42; fos. 16–29v.
112. Niles, John D.; Amodio, Mark (ed.). *Anglo-Scandinavian England: Norse-English relations in the period before the Conquest.* Lanham (Md); UP of America; 1989. Pp xi, 81.
113. McEldowney, J.F.; O'Higgins, Paul (ed.). *The common law tradition: essays in Irish legal history.* Dublin; Irish Academic Press; 1990. Pp 249.
114. Wilson, P.R. (ed.). *The Crambeck Roman pottery industry.* Leeds; Yorkshire Arch. Soc.; 1989. Pp viii, 107.

115. Robbins, Keith G. (ed.). *Protestant Evangelicalism: Britain, Ireland, Germany and America, c.1750-c.1950: essays in honour of W.R. Ward.* Oxford; Blackwell for Ecclesiastical Soc.; 1990. xii, 369.

116. Tranter, Stephen N.; Tristram, Hildegard (ed.). *Early Irish history: media and communication.* Tubingen; Gunter Nair Verlag; 1989. Pp 306.

117. Williams, Ann; Erskine, R.W.H. (ed.). *The Cambridgeshire Domesday.* London; Alecto; 2 vols. 1990. Pp 44; 26; fos. 189–202.

118. Williams, Ann; Erskine, R.W.H. (ed.). *The Derbyshire Domesday.* London; Alecto; 2 vols. 1990. Pp i-viii, 1–58; 38; fos. 272–80v.

119. Williams, Ann; Erskine, R.W.H. (ed.). *The Leicestershire Domesday.* London; Alecto; 2 vols. 1990. Pp i-viii, 1–50; 30; fos. 230–37v.

120. Williams, Ann; Erskine, R.W.H. (ed.). *The Nottinghamshire Domesday.* London; Alecto; 2 vols. 1990. Pp i-viii, 1–63; 42; fos. 280–94.

121. McKitterick, Rosamond (ed.). *The uses of literacy in early medieval Europe.* Cambridge; Cambridge UP; 1990.

122. Bachrach, B.S.; Nicholas, David (ed.). *Law, custom and the social fabric in medieval Europe.* Kalamazoo (MI); Western Michigan UP; 1990. Pp xxvi, 304.

123. Loades, Judith (ed.). *Monastic studies: the continuity of tradition.* Bangor; Headstart; 1990. Pp 325.

124. McGrail, Sean (ed.). *Maritime Celts, Frisians and Saxons: papers presented to a conference at Oxford in November 1988.* London; CBA (Research report 71); 1990. Pp 150.

125. Maguire, William A. (ed.). *Kings in conflict: the revolutionary war in Ireland and its aftermath, 1689–1750.* Belfast; Blackstaff; 1990. Pp 203.

126. Rolls, Roger; Guy, Jean (ed.). *A pox on the provinces: proceedings of the 12th congress of the British Society for the History of Medicine.* Bath; Bath UP; 1990. Pp 250.

127. Ker, Ian Turnbull; Hill, Alan G. (ed.). *Newman after a hundred years.* Oxford; Oxford UP; 1990. Pp 496.

128. Sheils, W.J.; Wood, Diana (ed.). *Women in the Church.* Oxford; Blackwell (Studies in Church history, vol. 27); 1990. Pp xxi, 515.

129. Chaney, Edward; Mack, Peter (ed.). *England and the continental renaissance.* Woodbridge; Boydell 1990. Pp 288.

130. Gallagher, P.; Cruickshank, D.W. (ed.). *God's obvious design: papers for the Spanish Armada Symposium, Sligo 1988.* Woodbridge; Boydell for Tamesis; 1990. Pp vii, 256.

131. Samuel, Raphael; Thompson, Paul (ed.). *The myths we live by.* London; Routledge; 1990. Pp 272.

132. Martin, G.H.; Spufford, Peter (ed.). *The records of the nation: the Public Record Office, 1838–1988; the British Record Society, 1880–1988.* Woodbridge; Boydell; 1990. Pp 320.

133. Gibson, Margaret T.; Nelson, Janet L. (ed.). *Charles the Bald: court and kingdom.* Exeter; Exeter UP; 1990. Pp xvi, 176.

134. Smith, Joseph (ed.). *The origins of NATO.* Aldershot; Variorum; 2nd edn. 1990. Pp xvi, 364.

135. Parsons, David (ed.). *Stone: quarrying and building in England, AD 43–1525.* Chichester; Phillimore; 1990. Pp xi, 240.
136. Webb, John; Quail, Sarah; Haskell, Patricia; Riley, Raymond. *The spirit of Portsmouth: a history.* Chichester; Phillimore; 1990.
137. Brown, R.A. (ed.). *Anglo-Norman studies, 11.* Woodbridge; Boydell (Proceedings of the Battle conference, 1988); 1989. Pp x, 295.
138. Smith, Christopher; Dubois, Elfrieda (ed.). *France et Grande Bretagne de la chute de Charles Ier à celle de Jacques II, 1649–1688.* Norwich; Soc. for Seventeenth Century French Studies; 1990. Pp 273.
139. Isaac, Peter. *Six centuries of the provincial book trade in Britain.* Winchester; St Paul's Bibliographies; 1990. Pp xii, 212.
140. Murray, C. van Driel- (ed.). *Roman military equipment: the sources of evidence. Proceedings of the Fifth Roman Military Equipment Conference.* Oxford; BAR (International ser. 476); 1989. Pp viii, 377.
141. Barrett, John C.; Fitzpatrick, Andrew P.; Macinnes, Lesley (ed.). *Barbarians and Romans in north-west Europe from the later Republic to late Antiquity.* Oxford; BAR (International ser. 471); 1989. Pp 241.
142. Bowden, Mark; Mackay, Donnie A.; Topping, Peter (ed.). *From Cornwall to Caithness: some aspects of British Field Archaeology. Papers presented to Norman V. Quinnell.* Oxford; BAR (British ser. 209); 1989. Pp x, 269.
143. Hogan, Daire; Osborough, W.N. (ed.). *Brehons, serjeants and attorneys: studies in the history of the Irish legal profession.* Dublin; Irish Academic Press; 1990. pp xii, 265.
144. Collins, Bruce. *British culture and economic decline.* London; Weidenfeld & Nicolson; 1990. Pp ix, 200.
145. Helmstadter, Richard J.; Lightman, Bernard (ed.). *Victorian faith in crisis: essays on continuity and change in nineteenth-century religious belief.* London; Macmillan; 1990. Pp xi, 391.
146. Cruickshanks, Eveline (ed.). *By force or by default? The revolution of 1688–1689.* Edinburgh; Donald; 1989. Pp xi, 200.
147. Schochet, Gordon J. (ed.). *Reformation, Humanism, and 'revolution': proceedings of the Folger Institute for British political thought.*, vol. 1. Washington (DC); Folger Shakespeare Library; 1990. Pp xiv, 327.
148. Contamine, Philippe (ed.). *L'état et les aristocraties, xiiè-xviiè siècle: France, Angleterre, Écosse.* Paris; Presses le l'École normale superieure; 1989. Pp396.
149. Schochet, Gordon J.; Tatspaugh, Patricia E.; Brobeck, Carol (ed.). *Law, literature and the settlement of regimes.* Washington (DC); Folger Shakespeare Library; 1990. Pp xvii, 236.
150. Dubrow, Helen; Strier, Richard (ed.). *The historical Renaissance: new essays on Tudor and Stuart literature and culture.* Chicago; Chicago UP; 1988. Pp ix, 377.

(d) *Genealogy and Heraldry*

1. Anon. *Registers of the church of St Bartholomew's, Edgbaston, Warwickshire: marriages, 1813–1831.* Birmingham; Birmingham & Midland Soc. for Genealogy & Heraldry; 1990. Pp 141.

2. Anon. *Registers of the Church of St Peter's, Norbury, Staffordshire: baptisms and burials, 1538–1812, and marriages 1538–1837.* Birmingham; Birmingham & Midland Soc. for Genealogy & Heraldry; 1990. Pp 147.

3. Anon. *The surrendered nonconformist registers of the parish of Sedgley including Coseley, Staffordshire.* Birmingham; Birmingham & Midland Soc. for Genealogy & Heraldry; 1989. Pp 83.

4. Bangs, Jeremy Dupertuis. 'The Pilgrims and other English in Leiden records: some new Pilgrim documents', *New England Historical & Genealogical Register* 143 (1989), 195–212.

5. Beattie, Alastair G.; Beattie, Margaret H. (ed.). *Pre–1855 gravestone inscriptions in Upper Donside.* Edinburgh; Scottish Genealogy Soc.; 1989. Pp 123.

6. Bloore, John. *Computer programs for the family historian, vol. 1: commercial programs.* Birmingham; Birmingham & Midland Soc. for Genealogy & Heraldry; 1989. Pp 36.

7. Chadd, Margaret. *The Collett saga: an account of the Collett family.* Norwich; Elvery Dowers; 1988. Pp 208.

8. Charnock, Denys. *Oldacre: a Gloucestershire family and business, 1881–1986.* Lewes; Book Guild; 1990. Pp 272.

9. Cowper, A.S.; Ross, I. (ed.) *Pre–1855 tombstone inscriptions in Sutherland burial grounds.* Edinburgh; Scottish Genealogy Soc.; 1989. Pp 331.

10. Dalby, Mark. *The Cocker connection: Yorkshire, van Dieman's Land, Melbourne, British Columbia, Mexico, Tonga and Michigan.* London; Regency; 1989. Pp 160.

11. Farris, Noel. *The Wymondleys.* Hertford; Hertfordshire Publications; 1989. Pp vi, 322.

12. Gibson, William. 'Clerical dynasticism: the Compton family of Minstead and Sopley', *Hatcher Review* 3/30 (1990), 488–99.

13. Goulstone, John. 'Genealogical links with our pagan past: dioscuric elements in the Anglo-Saxon pedigrees', *Genealogists' Magazine* 23 (1990), 161–68.

14. Hyde, Myrtle Stevens. 'The English ancestry of Elizabeth Aldous, wife of Henry Brock of Dedham, Massachusetts', *New England Historical & Genealogical Register* 144 (1990), 124–37.

15. Jones, J. Gwynfor. *The history of the Gwydir family, and memoirs.* Llandysul; Gomer; 1990. Pp xxxviii, 233.

16. McKinley, Richard A. *A history of British surnames.* London; Longman; 1990. Pp 230.

17. Mitchell, Alison. *Pre–1855 gravestone inscriptions: index for Carrick, Ayrshire.* Edinburgh; Scottish Genealogy Soc.; 1988. Pp 200.

18. Notcutt, Michael Edward; Sartin, Marian Phyllis. *The Notcutt family history, 1515–1989.* Chatham; Bachman & Turner; 1989. Pp 192.

19. Offley, Edward Murray; *et al. The Offley family in England: historical references and extracts from Norman to Stuart times.* Hitchen; Offley Family Soc.; 1989. Pp 64.

20. Owen, Hugh. *The Lowther family.* Chichester; Phillimore; 1990. Pp 432.

21. Paine, Sidney L. 'The English ancestry of Stephen Paine of Rehoboth, Plymouth colony', *New England Historical & Genealogical Register* 143 (1989), 291–302.
22. Pedler, Sir Frederick. *A wider Pedler family history.* Chichester; Phillimore; 1989. Pp 128.
23. Pepys, Nadine (ed.). *Lineage of the Camoys family.* Reading; Pepys; 1989. Pp vi, 526.
24. Plummer, John. 'Two John Jacksons from Dartmouth, Devon', *New England Historical & Genealogical Register* 144 (1990), 29–38.
25. Prideaux, R.M. *Prideaux: a west country clan.* Chichester; Phillimore; 1989. Pp 352.
26. Richardson, Douglas. 'The Riddlesdale alias Loker family of Bures Saint Mary, Suffolk, England, and Sudbury, Massachusetts', *New England Historical & Genealogical Register* 143 (1989), 325–31.
27. Rogers, Colin D. 'Unknown civilians: some problems of identification', *Genealogists' Magazine* 23 (1990), 177–80.
28. Rowse, A.L. *The controversial Colensos.* Redruth; Dyllansow Truran; 1989. Pp 160.
29. Smith, Chris John (comp.). *The heraldry of Warwickshire parish churches and associated buildings, vol. 2: archdeaconry of Coventry (central).* Birmingham; Birmingham & Midland Soc. for Genealogy & Heraldry; 1989. Pp 63.
30. Spiers, Sheila M. (comp.). *The kirkyard of Fyvie.* Aberdeen; Aberdeen & North-East Scotland Family History Soc.; 1989. Pp 79.
31. Titford, John. *The Titford family, 1547–1947: come wind come weather.* Chichester; Phillimore; 1988. Pp 192.
32. Wilton, Robert. *The Wiltons of Cornwall.* Chichester; Phillimore; 1989. Pp xiv, 170.
33. Yurdan, Marilyn. *Irish family history.* London; Batsford; 1990. Pp 160.

# C. ROMAN BRITAIN

*See also* Aa44,58,b21,c101; Bc30,114,140–141; De15.

(a) *Archaeology*

1. Allason-Jones, Lindsay. *Ear-rings in Roman Britain.* Oxford; BAR (British ser. 201); 1989. Pp xxvi, 205.
2. Anon. *Hadrian's Wall: historical map and guide.* Southampton; Ordnance Survey; 1989. Map.
3. Barber, Bruno; Bowsher, David; Whittaker, Ken. 'Recent excavations of a cemetery of *Londinium*', *Britannia* 21 (1990), 1–12.
4. Bellhouse, R.L. *Roman sites on the Cumberland coast: a new schedule of coastal sites.* Kendal; Cumberland & Westmorland Antiq. & Arch. Soc. (Research ser. vol. 3). Pp viii, 72.
5. Bewley, R.H. *Prehistoric and Romano-British settlement in the Solway*

*plain, Cumbria.* Oxford; Oxford Academic Publications; 1989. Pp 150.

6. Bishop, M.C.; Dore, J.N. *Corbridge: excavations of the Roman fort and town, 1947–1980.* London; English Heritage; 1989. Pp x, 323, fiche 4.
7. Blagg, T.F.C. 'Art and architecture', Bc30, 203–17.
8. Blagg, T.F.C. 'Building stone in Roman Britain', Bc135, 33–50.
9. Blood, K.; Bowden, M.C.B. 'The Roman fort at Haltonchesters: an analytic field survey', *Archaeologia Aeliana* 5th ser. 18 (1990), 55–62.
10. Brigham, T. 'A reassessment of the second basilica in London, AD 100–400: excavations at Leadenhall Court, 1984–1986', *Britannia* 21 (1990), 53–97.
11. Brigham, T. 'The late Roman waterfront in London', *Britannia* 21 (1990), 99–183.
12. Britnell, Jenny. *Caersws Vicus, Powys: excavations at the old primary school, 1985–1986.* Oxford; BAR (British ser. 205); 1989. Pp iv, 136.
13. Corder, P. 'A pair of fourth-century Romano-British pottery kilns near Crambeck with a note on the distribution of Crambeck ware by Margaret Birley', Bc114, 25–35.
14. Corder, P. 'The Roman pottery at Crambeck, Castle Howard', Bc114, 3–24.
15. Cracknell, Philip M. 'A group of marked brooches from Gloucester', *Britannia* 21 (1990), 197–206.
16. Daniels, Charles. *The eleventh pilgrimage of Hadrian's Wall.* Newcastle-upon-Tyne; Soc. of Antiquaries of Newcastle-upon-Tyne & Cumberland & Westmorland Antiq. & Arch. Soc.; 1989. Pp 95.
17. Davison, David P. *The barracks of the Roman army from the 1st to 3rd centuries AD: a comparative study of the barracks from fortresses, forts and fortlets with an analysis of building types and construction, stabling and garrisons.* Oxford; BAR (International ser. 472); 1989. Pp xiv, 914.
18. Evans, Jeremy. 'Crambeck; the development of a major northern pottery industry', Bc114, 43–90.
19. Evans, Jeremy; Scull, Christopher. 'Fieldwork on the Roman fort site at Blennerhasset, Cumbria', *T. of the Cumberland & Westmorland Antiq. & Arch. Soc.* 90 (1990), 127–37.
20. Gaffney, Vincent; Tingle, Martin. *The Maddle Farm project: an integrated survey of prehistoric and Roman landscapes on the Berkshire Downs.* Oxford; BAR (British ser. 200); 1989. Pp ix, 262.
21. Griffith, F.M. 'Aerial reconnaissance in mainland Britain in the summer of 1989', *Antiquity* 64/242 (1990), 14–33.
22. Hinchliffe, J.; Bartlett, A. 'A survey of the Roman pottery production site at Jamie's Craggs, Crambeck', Bc114, 91–95.
23. Jackson, Ralph; Leahy, Kevin. 'A Roman surgical forceps from Littleborough and a note on the type', *Britannia* 21 (1990), 271–74.
24. Jermy, Kenneth E. 'The "North Cheshire Ridge" Roman road', *Britannia* 21 (1990), 283–83.
25. Johnson, Stephen. *Hadrian's Wall.* London; Batsford for English Heritage; 1990. Pp 143.

26. Keevil, A.J. 'The Fosseway at Bath', *Somerset Archaeology & Natural History* 133 (1990 for 1989), 75–101.
27. Keppie, Lawrence J.F. 'Excavation of a Roman temporary camp at Annan Hill, Dumfriesshire, 1985–1986', *Dumfriesshire & Galloway Natural History & Antiq. Soc. T.* 3rd ser. 62 (1988), 13–21.
28. King, E.M.; Moore, M. 'The Romano-British settlement at Crambe, North Yorkshire', Bc114, 105–07.
29. Macinnes, Lesley. 'Baubles, bangles and beads: trade and exchange in Roman Scotland', Bc141, 108–16.
30. Mackay, Donnie A. 'The Great Chesters aqueduct: a new survey', *Britannia* 21 (1990), 285–89.
31. Maloney, Catherine. *The archaeology of Roman London, vol. 1: the upper Walbrook valley in the Roman period.* York; CBA (Research report 69); 1990. Pp 160.
32. Manning, W.H. *Report on the excavations at Usk, vol. iv: the fortress excavations, 1972–1974.* Cardiff; Wales UP; 1989. Pp 216.
33. Marsden, P. 'A reassessment of Blackfriars ship 1', Bc124, 66–74.
34. Mason, D.J.P. 'The use of earthenware tubes in Roman vault construction: an example from Chester', *Britannia* 21 (1990), 214–22.
35. McLinden, J.A. 'Roman coins from Hayton, East Yorkshire', *Yorkshire Arch. J.* 62 (1990), 13–28.
36. Moore, W.F.; Ross, M.S. 'The Romano-British settlement, Common Mead Lane, Gillingham, Dorset', *P. of the Dorset Natural History and Arch. Soc.* 111 (1989) 57–70.
37. Neal, David Stanley, et al. *Excavation of the Iron Age, Roman, and medieval settlement at Gorhambury.* London; English Heritage (Historic Buildings and Monuments Commission for England: Arch. report no. 14); 1990. Pp 258.
38. O'Leary, T.J.; Blockley, Kevin; Musson, Chris. *Pentre Farm, Flint 1976–1981: an official building in the Roman lead mining district.* Oxford; BAR (British ser. 207); 1989. Pp iv, 136.
39. Peddie, John. 'In search of a Roman road', *Hatcher Review* 3/30 (1990), 480–87.
40. Perrin, J.R.; Williams, D.F. *The archaeology of York, vol. 16: Roman pottery from the Colonia—General Accident and Rougier Street.* London; CBA; 1990. Pp 140.
41. Philp, Brian J. *The Roman house with Bacchic murals at Dover.* Dover; Kent Arch. Rescue Unit; 1989. Pp 290.
42. Richardson, A.; Allan, T.M. 'The Roman road over the Kirkstone Pass: Ambleside to Old Penrith', *T. of the Cumberland & Westmorland Antiq. & Arch. Soc.* 90 (1990), 105–25.
43. Rule, M. 'The Romano-Celtic ship excavated at St Peter Port, Guernsey', Bc124, 49–56.
44. Thomas, Charles. 'The context of Tintagel: a new model for the diffusion of post-Roman Mediterranean imports', *Cornish Archaeology* 27 (1988), 7–27.
45. Thomas, Gordon D. 'Excavations at the Roman civil settlement at Inveresk', *Soc. of Antiquaries of Scotland P.* 118 (1988), 139–76.

46. Thomas, Gordon D. 'The re-excavation of the Inveresk hypocaust', *Soc. of Antiquaries of Scotland P.* 118 (1988), 177–79.
47. Timby, Jane. 'Severn valley wares: a reassessment', *Britannia* 21 (1990), 243–51.
48. Tomalin, David. 'A Roman symmetrical flanged bronze strainer found in Surrey and its counterparts in Highland Britain', *Surrey Arch. Collections* 79 (1989), 53–65.
49. Turner, Rick C. 'A Romano-British cemetery at Lanchester, Durham', *Archaeologia Aeliana* 5th ser. 18 (1990), 63–77.
50. van Driel-Murray, C. 'The Vindolanda chamfrons and miscellaneous items of leather horse gear', Bc140, 281–318.
51. Waddelove, A.C.; Waddelove, E. 'Archaeology and research into sea-level during the Roman era: towards a methodology based upon the highest astronomical tide', *Britannia* 21 (1990), 253–66.
52. Waddelove, A.C.; Waddelove, E.; Jones, G.D.B. 'The Roman fort at Ruthin, Clwyd', *Britannia* 21 (1990), 299–302.
53. Webster, Graham. 'A late Celtic sword-belt with a ring and button found at Coleford, Gloucestershire', *Britannia* 21 (1990), 294–95.
54. Webster, Graham. 'Part of a Celtic linch-pin', *Britannia* 21 (1990), 293–94.
55. Webster, Janet. 'An unusual brooch from Caerleon', *Britannia* 21 (1990), 297–99.
56. Wenham, L.P. 'Cliff House Farm, near Crambe, North Riding, 1960–1965', Bc114, 99–103.
57. Williams, Tim. 'The foundation and early development of Roman London: a social context', *Antiquity* 64/244 (1990), 599–607.
58. Winterbottom, S. 'Saddle covers, chamfrons and possible horse armour from Carlisle', Bc140, 319–36.
59. Yule, Brian. 'The "dark earth" of late Roman London', *Antiquity* 64/244 (1990), 620–28.

## (b) *History*

1. Adams, J.N. 'The *forfex* and the *veterinarius* Virilis (Vindolanda Inv. No. 86/470) and ancient methods of castrating horses', *Britannia* 21 (1990), 267–71.
2. Allason-Jones, Lindsay. 'Introductory remarks on the nature of Roman trade in the north of Britain', Bc140, 13–24.
3. Black, Ernest W. 'Caesar's second invasion of Britain, Cassivellaunus, and the Trinobantes', *Essex Archaeology & History* 3rd ser. 21 (1990), 6–10.
4. Blagg, T.F.C. 'Architectural munificence in Britain: the evidence of inscriptions', *Britannia* 21 (1990), 13–31.
5. Blockley, Kevin. *Prestatyn, 1984–1985: an Iron Age farmstead and Romano-British industrial settlement in North Wales.* Oxford; BAR (British ser. 210); 1989. Pp xi, 231.
6. Bowman, A.K.; Thomas, J.D.; Adams, J.N. 'Two letters from Vindolanda', *Britannia* 21 (1990), 33–52.

7. Breeze, David J. 'The impact of the Roman army on North Britain', Bc141, 227–34.

8. Breeze, David J. 'The northern frontiers', Bc30, 37–60.

9. Breeze, David J. 'Why did the Romans fail to invade Scotland?', *Soc. of Antiquaries of Scotland P*. 118 (1988), 3–22.

10. Burgess, R.W. 'The Dark Ages return to fifth-century Britain: the "restored" Gallic chronicle exploded', *Britannia* 21 (1990), 185–95.

11. Burnham, Barry C; Wacher, John S. *The small towns of Roman Britain*. London; Batsford; 1990. Pp 384.

12. Cepas, Adela. *The north of Britannia and the north-west of Hispania: an epigraphic comparison*. Oxford; BAR (International ser. 470); 1989. Pp v, 182.

13. Cleary, Simon Esmonde. 'Constantine I to Constantine III', Bc30, 235–44.

14. Crossan, Carl; Smoothy, Martyn; Wallace, Colin. 'Salvage recording of Iron Age and Roman remains at Ickleton Road, Great Chesterford, Essex', *Essex Archaeology & History* 3rd ser. 21 (1990), 11–18.

15. Cule, John. 'The province of Britain: Wales, druidic magic and Roman medicine', Bc126, 1–10.

16. Daniels, Charles. 'The Flavian and Trajanic northern frontier', Bc30, 31–35.

17. Donaldson, G.H. 'A reinterpretation of RIB 1912 from Birdoswald', *Britannia* 21 (1990), 207–14.

18. Down, Alec. *Roman Chichester*. Chichester; Phillimore; 1988. Pp 160.

19. Fulford, Michael G. 'The economy of Roman Britain', Bc30, 175–201.

20. Giot, Pierre Roland. 'The attraction of coasts and islands, from later pre-history to the Dark Ages', Bc74, 125–31.

21. Grant, Annie. 'Animals in Roman Britain', Bc30, 135–46.

22. Haselgrove, Colin. 'The later Iron Age in southern Britain and beyond', Bc30, 1–18.

23. Heard, Kieron; Sheldon, Harvey; Thompson, Peter. 'Mapping Roman Southwark', *Antiquity* 64/244 (1990), 608–19.

24. Henig, Martin. 'Religion in Roman Britain', Bc30, 219–34.

25. Higham, N.J. 'Roman and native in England north of the Tees: acculturation and its limitations', Bc141, 153–74.

26. Jackson, Ralph. 'A new *collyrium* stamp from Cambridge and a corrected reading of the stamp from Caistor-by-Norwich', *Britannia* 21 (1990), 275–83.

27. Jones, Martin. 'Agriculture in Roman Britain: the dynamics of change', Bc30, 127–34.

28. Keppie, Lawrence J.F. 'Beyond the northern frontier: Roman and native in Scotland', Bc30, 61–73.

29. Mann, J.C. 'Hadrian's Wall west of the Irthing: the role of VI Victrix', *Britannia* 21 (1990), 289–92.

30. Mann, J.C. 'The function of Hadrian's Wall', *Archaeologia Aeliana* 5th ser. 18 (1990), 51–54.

31. Mann, J.C. 'The history of the Antonine Wall: a reappraisal', *Soc. of Antiquaries of Scotland P*. 118 (1988), 131–37.

32. Maxfield, Valerie A. 'Conquest and aftermath', Bc30, 19–29.
33. Maxfield, Valerie A. 'Hadrian's Wall in its imperial setting', *Archaeologia Aeliana* 5th ser. 18 (1990), 1–27.
34. Maxwell, Gordon S. *A battle lost: Romans and Caledonians at Mons Graupius.* Edinburgh; Edinburgh UP; 1989. Pp 112.
35. Maxwell, Gordon S. *The Romans in Scotland.* Edinburgh; Mercat; 1989. Pp xii, 200.
36. Miles, David. 'The Romano-British countryside', Bc30, 115–26.
37. Millett, Martin. *The Romanization of Britain: an essay in archaeological interpretation.* Cambridge; Cambridge UP; 1990. Pp 220.
38. Milne, Gustav. 'Maritime traffic between the Rhine and Roman Britain: a preliminary note', Bc124, 82–84.
39. Potter, T.W. 'The Roman fenland: a review of recent work', Bc30, 147–73.
40. Rudling, David R. 'Late Iron Age and Roman Billericay: excavations, 1987', *Essex Archaeology & History* 3rd ser. 21 (1990), 19–47.
41. Saddington, D.B. 'The origin and nature of the German and British fleets', *Britannia* 21 (1990), 223–32.
42. Sainsbury, Iain; Welfare, Humphrey. 'The Roman fort at Bewcastle: an analytical field survey', *T. of the Cumberland & Westmorland Antiq. & Arch. Soc.* 90 (1990), 139–46.
43. Southern, P. 'Signals versus illumination on Roman frontiers', *Britannia* 21 (1990), 233–42.
44. Stephens, G.R. 'Roman inscribed building-stones from Wales', *Archaeologia Cambrensis* 137 (1989 for 1988), 99–107.
45. Todd, Malcolm. 'The early cities', Bc30, 75–89.
46. Wacher, John S. 'Cities from the second to fourth centuries', Bc30, 91–114.

# D.  ENGLAND 450–1066

*See also* Bc12,31,66,112,124,133,d13; Ca44; Da4; Ea30,h19.

(a) *General*

1. Beech, George. 'England and Aquitaine in the century before the Norman Conquest', *Anglo-Saxon England* 19 (1990), 81–101.
2. Brown, A.E.; Taylor, Christopher C. 'The origins of dispersed settlement; some results from fieldwork in Bedfordshire', *Landscape History* 11 (1989), 61–81.
3. Head, Anthony. ' "The gift of elves": Queen Emma', *Hatcher Review* 3/30 (1990), 471–79.
4. Hills, Catherine. 'Roman Britain to Anglo-Saxon England', *History Today* 40/10 (1990), 46–52.
5. Howe, Nicholas. *Migration and myth-making in Anglo-Saxon England.* London; Yale UP; 1989. Pp xiii, 198.

6. Keynes, Simon. 'Changing faces: Offa, king of Mercia', *History Today* 40/11 (1990), 14–19.
7. Lebecq, S. 'On the use of the word "Frisian" in the 6th–10th centuries written sources: some interpretations', Bc124, 85–90.
8. Lifshitz, Felice. 'The *Encomium Emmae Reginae*: a "political pamphlet" of the eleventh century?', *The Haskins Soc. J.* 1 (1989), 39–50.
9. Lindow, John. 'Norse mythology and Northumbria: methodological notes', Bc112, 25–40.
10. Lowe, Kathryn A. 'A new edition of the will of Wulfgyth', *Notes and Queries* ns 36 (1989), 295–98.
11. McKinnell, John. 'Norse mythology and Northumbria: a response', Bc112, 41–52.
12. Niles, John D.; Amodio, Mark. 'Introduction: the Vikings and England', Bc112, vii-xi.
13. Stanley, Eric G. 'Introduction' [Anglo-Saxon England], Bc31, ix-xiii.
14. Ward, Benedicta. *The Venerable Bede*. London; Chapman; 1990. Pp 160.

## (b) *Politics and Institutions*

1. Andersson, Theodore M. 'The Viking policy of Æthelred the Unready', Bc112, 1–11.
2. Bascombe, Kenneth. 'Two charters of King Suebred of Essex', Bc65, 85–96.
3. Brown, Phyllis R. 'The Viking policy of Æthelred: a response', Bc112, 13–15.
4. Davis, R.H.C. 'Did the Anglo-Saxons have warhorses?', Bc12, 141–44.
5. Gardiner, Mark. 'Some lost Anglo-Saxon charters and the endowment of Hastings College', *Sussex Arch. Collections* 127 (1989), 39–48.
6. Gillingham, John. 'Chronicles and coins as evidence for levels of tribute and taxation in late tenth- and early eleventh-century England', *English Historical R.* 105 (1990), 939–50.
7. Halsall, Guy. 'Anthropology and the study of pre-Conquest warfare and society: the ritual war in Anglo-Saxon England', Bc12, 155–77.
8. Harmer, Florence E. *Anglo-Saxon writs*. Stamford; Watkins; 2nd edn. 1989. Pp xliv, 604.
9. Hart, Cyril. 'The ealdordom of Essex', Bc65, 57–84.
10. Hooper, Nicholas. 'The Anglo-Saxons at war', Bc12, 191–202.
11. Keynes, Simon. 'Royal government and the written word in late Anglo-Saxon England', Bc121, 226–57.
12. Lawson, M.K. 'Danegeld and heregeld once more', *English Historical R.* 105 (1990), 951–61.
13. Potts, Cassandra. 'Normandy or Brittany? A conflict of interest at Mont Saint Michel (966–1035)', Bc72, 135–51.
14. Roffe, David R. 'From thegnage to barony: sake and soke, title and tenants-in-chief', Bc72, 157–76.
15. Stafford, Pauline. 'Charles the Bald, Judith and England', Bc133, 139–53.

16. Williams, Ann. 'A vice-comital family in pre-Conquest Warwickshire', Bc137, 279–95.
17. Yorke, Barbara. *Kings and kingdoms of early Anglo-Saxon England.* London; Seaby; 1990. Pp vi, 218.

## (c) *Religion*

1. Blair, W. John. 'St Frideswide's monastery: problems and possibilities', Bc66, 221–58.
2. Clayton, Mary. *The cult of the Virgin Mary in Anglo-Saxon England.* Cambridge; Cambridge UP; 1990. Pp 300.
3. Foot, Sarah. 'What was an early Anglo-Saxon monastery?', Bc123, 48–57.
4. Nelson, Janet L. 'Women and the word in the earlier middle ages', Bc128, 53–78.
5. Olson, Lynette. *Early monasteries in Cornwall.* Woodbridge; Boydell; 1989. Pp xxiv, 135.
6. Ortenberg, Veronica. 'Archbishop Sigeric's journey to Rome in 990', *Anglo-Saxon England* 19 (1990), 197–246.
7. Sawyer, Peter. 'Æthelred II, Olaf Tryggvason, and the conversion of Norway', Bc112, 17–24.
8. Sutherland, Diana S. 'Burnt stone in a Saxon church and its implications', Bc135, 102–13.
9. Thomas, Charles. 'Christians, chapels, churches and charters—or, "proto-parochial provisions for the pious in a peninsular" (Land's End)', *Landscape History* 11 (1989), 19–26.
10. Wood, Ian N. 'Ripon, Francia and the Franks Casket in the early middle ages', *Northern History* 26 (1990), 1–19.

## (d) *Economic Affairs and Numismatics*

1. Biddle, Martin. 'The study of Winchester: archaeology and history in a British town, 1961–1983', Bc31, 299–342.
2. Carver, M.O.H. 'Pre-Viking traffic in the North Sea', Bc124, 117–25.
3. Fulford, Michael G. 'Byzantium and Britain: a Mediterranean perspective on post-Roman Mediterranean imports in western Britain and Ireland', *Medieval Archaeology* 33 (1989), 1–6.
4. Gildas, Bernier. 'Ships, harbours and navigation between the Continent and the Celtic Islands during the early middle ages', Bc74, 155–57.
5. Hodges, Richard. 'Trade and market origins in the ninth century: relations between England and the Continent', Bc133, 203–23.
6. Metcalf, D.M. 'Large danegelds in relation to war and kingship: their implications for monetary history, and some numismatic evidence', Bc12, 179–89.
7. Metcalf, D.M.; Northover, J.P. 'Coinage alloys from the time of Offa and Charlemagne to *c*.864', *Numismatic Chronicle* 149 (1989), 101–20.
8. Milne, Gustav; Goodburn, Damian. 'The early medieval port of London, AD 700–1200', *Antiquity* 64/244 (1990), 629–36.

9. Wood, Ian N. 'The Channel from the 4th to the 7th centuries AD', Bc124, 93–97.

(e) *Intellectual and Cultural*

1. Bately, J.M. 'The compilation of the Anglo-Saxon chronicle, 60 BC to AD 890: vocabulary as evidence', Bc31, 261–98.
2. Blair, W. John (ed.). *Saint Frideswide, patron of Oxford: the earliest texts*. Oxford; Perpetua; 1988. Pp 44.
3. Cameron, M.L. 'Bald's *Leechbook* and cultural interactions in Anglo-Saxon England', *Anglo-Saxon England* 19 (1990), 5–12.
4. Chambers, R.W. 'Bede', Bc31, 29–56.
5. Davidson, Hilda Ellis. 'Introduction' [the Seer], Bc103, 1–8.
6. Dickins, B. 'John Mitchell Kemble and Old English scholarship', Bc31, 57–91.
7. Gameson, Richard. 'The Anglo-Saxon artists of the Harley 603 psalter', *J. of the British Arch. Association* 143 (1990), 29–48.
8. Gilbert, J.E.P. 'The Lindisfarne Gospels—how many artists?', *Durham University J.* 82 (1990), 153–60.
9. Gneuss, Helmut. 'The study of language in Anglo-Saxon England', *B. of the John Rylands University Library of Manchester* 72/1 (1990), 3–32.
10. Godden, M.R. 'Money, power and morality in late Anglo-Saxon England', *Anglo-Saxon England* 19 (1990), 41–65.
11. Grant, Lindy. 'The choir of St-Etienne at Caen', Bc71, 113–25.
12. Heslop, T.A. 'The production of *de luxe* manuscripts and the patronage of king Cnut and queen Emma', *Anglo-Saxon England* 19 (1990), 151–94.
13. Irvine, Susan E. 'Bones of contention: the context of Ælfric's homily on St Vincent', *Anglo-Saxon England* 19 (1990), 117–32.
14. Kelly, Susan. 'Anglo-Saxon lay society and the written word', Bc121, 36–62.
15. Kornbluth, Genevra A. 'The Alfred Jewel: reuse of Roman "spolia"', *Medieval Archaeology* 33 (1989), 32–37.
16. Lang, James T. *Corpus of Anglo-Saxon stone sculpture, vol. 3: York and eastern Yorkshire*. Oxford; Oxford UP for British Academy; 1989. Pp 480.
17. Lendinara, Patrizia. 'The Abbo glossary in London British Library Cotton Domitian i', *Anglo-Saxon England* 19 (1990), 133–49.
18. Mavor, James W. Jr; Dix, Byron E. 'An Icelandic horizon calendar, key to Vinland', Bc74, 143–54.
19. McIntosh, A. 'Wulfstan's prose', Bc31, 111–44.
20. McKitterick, Rosamond. 'Anglo-Saxon missionaries in Germany: reflections on the manuscript evidence', *T. of the Cambridge Bibliographical Soc.* 9 (1989), 291–329.
21. Ó Carrágain, Éamonn. 'The Ruthwell crucifixion poem and its iconographic and liturgical contexts', *Peritia* 6–7 (1990 for 1987–8), 1–71.
22. O'Reilly, Jennifer. 'Early medieval text and image: the wounded and exalted Christ', *Peritia* 6–7 (1990 for 1987–8), 72–118.

23. Raw, Barbara Catherine. *Anglo-Saxon crucifixion iconography and the art of the monastic revival*. Cambridge; Cambridge UP; 1990. Pp 288.
24. Sherlock, David. 'Anglo-Saxon monastic sign language at Christ Church, Canterbury', *Archaeologia Cantiana* 107 (1990 for 1989), 1–27.
25. Sims-Williams, Patrick. *Religion and literature in the west of England, 600–800*. Cambridge; Cambridge UP; 1990. Pp 460.
26. Sisam, K. 'Anglo-Saxon royal genealogies', Bc31, 145–204.
27. Tudor-Craig, Pamela. 'Controversial sculptures: the Southwell Tympanum, the Glastonbury Respond, the Leigh Christ', Bc72, 211–31.
28. van Houts, Elisabeth M.C. 'Historiography and hagiography at Saint-Wandrille: the *Inventio et Miracula Sancti Vulfranni*', Bc72, 233–51.
29. Whitelock, Dorothy M. 'The Old English Bede', Bc31, 227–60.
30. Worssam, B.C.; Tatton-Brown, T.W.T. 'The stone of the Reculver columns and the Reculver cross', Bc135, 51–69.
31. Yapp, W. Brunsdon. 'The animals of the Ormside Cup', *T. of the Cumberland & Westmorland Antiq. & Arch. Soc.* 90 (1990), 147–61.
32. Yapp, W. Brunsdon. 'The font at Melbury Bubb: an interpretation', *P. of the Dorset Natural History and Arch. Soc.* 111 (1989), 128–29.

## (f) *Society and Archaeology*

1. Adams, Kenneth A. 'Monastery and village at Crayke, north Yorkshire', *Yorkshire Arch. J.* 62 (1990), 29–50.
2. Blair, W. John. 'Thornbury, Binsey: a probable defensive enclosure associated with Saint Frideswide', Bc66, 3–20.
3. Bone, Peter. 'The development of Anglo-Saxon swords from the fifth to the eleventh century', Bc12, 63–70.
4. Brown, A.E.; Gelling, Margaret; Orr, Cristine. 'The details of the Anglo-Saxon landscape: Badby revisited', *Northamptonshire Past & Present* 8/2 (1990–91), 95–103.
5. Campbell, James. 'The sale of land and the economics of power in early England: problems and possibilities', *The Haskins Soc. J.* 1 (1989), 23–37.
6. Crumlin-Pedersen, O. 'Boats and ships of the Angles and Jutes', Bc124, 98–116.
7. Deegan, Marilyn. 'Pregnancy and childbirth in the Anglo-Saxon medical texts: a preliminary survey', Bc73, 17–26.
8. Fellows-Jensen, Gillian. 'Place-names as a reflection of cultural interaction', *Anglo-Saxon England* 19 (1990), 13–21.
9. Filmer-Sankey, W. 'A new boat burial from the Snape Anglo-Saxon cemetery, Suffolk', Bc124, 126–34.
10. Gale, David. 'The Seax', Bc12, 71–83.
11. Gelling, Margaret. 'The place-names Burton and variants', Bc12, 145–53.
12. Haldenby, David. 'An Anglian site on the Yorkshire wolds', *Yorkshire Arch. J.* 62 (1990), 51–63 [with further report by Peter Didsbury, pp. 63–67].

13. Hall, Richard. *Viking Age archaeology in Britain and Ireland*. Princes Risborough; Shire; 1990. Pp 64.
14. Härke, Heinrich. 'Early Saxon weapon burials: frequencies, distributions and weapon combinations', Bc12, 49–61.
15. Härke, Heinrich. 'Knives in early Saxon burials: blade-length and age at death', *Medieval Archaeology* 33 (1989), 144–47.
16. Härke, Heinrich. ' "Warrior graves"? The background of the Anglo-Saxon weapon burial rite', *Past & Present* 126 (1990), 22–43.
17. Hawkes, Sonia Chadwick. 'Weapons and warfare in Anglo-Saxon England: an introduction', Bc12, 1–9.
18. Holmes, John. 'A Saxon church at Findon', *Sussex Arch. Collections* 127 (1989), 252–54.
19. Hooke, Della. 'Studies on Devon charter boundaries', *Devon Association Report and T.* 122 (1990), 193–211.
20. Hooke, Della. *Worcestershire Anglo-Saxon charter bounds*. Woodbridge; Boydell (Studies in Anglo-Saxon history no. 11); 1990. Pp 456.
21. Johnson, D.A. 'The place-name' [Lichfield], Bc99, 37–39.
22. Lang, James T. *Anglo-Saxon sculpture*. Princes Risborough; Shire; 1988. Pp 60.
23. Lang, Janet; Ager, Barry. 'Swords of the Anglo-Saxon and Viking periods in the British Museum: a radiographic study', Bc12, 85–122.
24. Mainman, A.J (ed.). *The archaeology of York, vol. 16: Anglo-Scandinavian pottery from 16–22 Coppergate*. London; CBA for the York Arch. Trust; 1990. Pp 165.
25. Moffat, Brian. 'Investigations into medieval medical practice: the remnants of some herbal treatments on archaeological sites and in archives', Bc73, 33–40.
26. Poulton, Rob. 'Rescue excavations on an early Saxon cemetery site and a later (probably late Saxon) execution site at the former Goblin Works, Ashtead, near Leatherhead', *Surrey Arch. Collections* 79 (1989), 69–97, + fiche.
27. Rubin, Stanley. 'The Anglo-Saxon physician', Bc73, 7–15.
28. Rutter, Jan. 'The search for a small Anglo-Saxon bound at Shaftesbury', *P. of the Dorset Natural History and Arch. Soc.* 111 (1989), 125–27.
29. Scull, Christopher *et al.* 'Excavations in the cloister of St Frideswide's Priory, 1985', Bc66, 21–73.
30. Smith, A.H. 'Place-names and the Anglo-Saxon settlement', Bc31, 205–26.
31. Tweddle, Dominic. 'Craft and industry in Anglo-Scandinavian York', Bc27, 17–41.
32. Wenham, S.J. 'Anatomical interpretations of Anglo-Saxon weapon injuries', Bc12, 123–39.

# E. ENGLAND 1066–1500

See also Aa59,90,c27,29,98; Bc32,40–41,66,69,71–73,100,109–111,117–123,135,137; Dd8,f1; Fe85.

(a) *General*

1. Ayton, Andrew. 'Domesday Book re-bound, *c.*1346', *Notes and Queries* ns 36 (1989), 298–99.
2. Bates, David. 'Two Ramsey Abbey writs and the Domesday survey', *Historical Research* 63 (1990), 337–39.
3. Biddick, Kathleen A. 'People and things: power in early English development', *Comparative Studies in Soc. & History* 32 (1990), 3–23.
4. Blair, W. John. 'An introduction to the Oxfordshire Domesday', Bc109, 1–19.
5. Bridbury, A.R. 'Domesday Book: a re-interpretation', *English Historical R.* 105 (1990), 284–309.
6. Cain, T.D. 'An introduction to the Leicestershire Domesday', Bc119, 1–21.
7. Carpenter, David. 'The minority of Henry III', *History Today* 40/7 (1990), 9–14.
8. Carpenter, David. *The minority of Henry III*. London; Methuen; 1990. Pp xviii, 472.
9. Childs, Wendy R.; Taylor, John. 'Introduction' [14th-century politics], Bc100, ix-xvi.
10. Christelow, Stephanie Evans. 'All the king's men: prosopography [of eleventh- and twelfth-century England and Normandy] and the Santa Barbara School', *Medieval Prosopography* 11 (1990), 1–15.
11. Crouch, David. *William Marshal: court, career and chivalry in the Angevin Empire, 1147–1219*. London; Longman; 1990. Pp xii, 233.
12. Davies, Robert Rees. *Domination and conquest: the experience of Ireland, Scotland and Wales, 1100–1300*. Cambridge; Cambridge UP (Wiles lectures, Queen's University Belfast); 1990. Pp xvii, 134.
13. Dockray, Keith. 'Patriotism, pride and paranoia: England and the English in the fifteenth century', *The Ricardian* 8/110 (1990), 430–42.
14. Dyer, Christopher C. *Standards of living in the middle ages: social change in England, c.1200–1520*. Cambridge; Cambridge UP; 1989. Pp xvi, 297.
15. Eales, Richard. 'Royal power and castles in Norman England', Bc40, 49–78.
16. Frame, Robin. *The political development of the British Isles, 1100–1400*. Oxford; Oxford UP; 1990. Pp x, 256.
17. Glasscock, R.E. 'An introduction to the Cambridgeshire Domesday', Bc117, 1–17.
18. Gransden, Antonia. 'The chronicles of medieval England and Scotland: part 1', *J. of Medieval History* 16 (1990), 129–50.

19. Hicks, Michael A. 'Introduction' [poverty, piety and the professions], Bc69, x-xxii.
20. Holt, Richard; Rosser, Gervase (ed.). *The English medieval town: a reader in English urban history, 1200–1540* [reprints with introduction]. Harlow; Longman; 1990. Pp viii, 291.
21. Huneycutt, Lois L. 'Images of queenship in the high middle ages', *The Haskins Soc. J.* 1 (1989), 61–71.
22. James, S.A.L.; Seal D. 'An introduction to the Sussex Domesday', Bc111, 1–27.
23. Keefe, Thomas K. 'Counting those who count: a computer-assisted analysis of charter witness-lists and the itinerant court in the first year of the reign of King Richard I', *The Haskins Soc. J.* 1 (1989), 135–45.
24. Keen, Maurice. *English society in the later middle ages, 1348–1500.* London; Allen Lane (The Penguin social history of Britain); 1990. Pp 332.
25. Kellett, Arnold. 'King John in Knaresborough: the first known royal maundy', *Yorkshire Arch. J.* 62 (1990), 69–90.
26. Kellett, Arnold. 'King John's maundy', *History Today* 40/4 (1990), 34–39.
27. Kelly, H.A. 'Croyland observations', *The Ricardian* 8/108 (1990), 334–41.
28. Lewis, Christopher P. 'An introduction to the Shropshire Domesday', Bc110, 1–27.
29. Lewis, Christopher P. 'The earldom of Surrey and the date of Domesday Book', *Historical Research* 63 (1990), 329–36.
30. Loyn, Henry. '1066: should we have celebrated?', *Historical Research* 63 (1990), 119–27.
31. Mason, Emma. 'The hero's invincible weapon: an aspect of Angevin propaganda', Bc40, 121–37.
32. Mortimer, Richard. 'The charters of Henry II: what are the criteria for authenticity?', Bc72, 119–34.
33. Palliser, D.M. *Domesday York.* York; the University (Borthwick Paper no. 78); 1990. Pp iv, 31.
34. Pollard, Anthony James. *North-eastern England during the Wars of the Roses: lay society, war and politics, 1450–1500.* Oxford; Oxford UP; 1990. Pp xvii, 445.
35. Prestwich, J.O.; Davis, R.H.C. 'Last words on Geoffrey de Mandeville', *English Historical R.* 105 (1990), 670–72.
36. Prestwich, Michael. *English politics in the thirteenth century.* Basingstoke; Macmillan; 1990. Pp vi, 177.
37. Richmond, Colin. *The Paston family in the fifteenth century: the first phase.* Cambridge; Cambridge UP; 1990. Pp 269.
38. Roffe, David R. 'An introduction to the Derbyshire Domesday', Bc118, 1–27.
39. Roffe, David R. 'An introduction to the Nottinghamshire Domesday', Bc120, 1–31.
40. Roffe, David R. 'Domesday Book and northern society: a reassessment', *English Historical R.* 105 (1990), 310–36.

41. Tatton-Brown, T.W.T. *Canterbury in Domesday Book.* Canterbury; Canterbury Arch. Trust (Canterbury Heritage Series no. 1); 1987. Pp 41.
42. Thomson, J.A.F. 'The death of Edward V: Dr Richmond's dating reconsidered', *Northern History* 26 (1990), 207–11.
43. Warren, W.L. 'Painter's *King John*—forty years on', *The Haskins Soc. J.* 1 (1989), 1–9.
44. White, Graeme J. 'The end of Stephen's reign', *History* 75 (1990), 3–22.

## (b) *Politics*

1. Arthurson, Ian; Kingwell, Nicholas. 'The proclamation of Henry Tudor as king of England, 3 November 1483', *Historical Research* 63 (1990), 100–06.
2. Barron, Caroline. 'The deposition of Richard II', Bc100, 132–49.
3. Bates, David. *William the Conqueror.* London; Philip; 1989. Pp viii, 198.
4. Bennett, Michael J. 'Henry VII and the northern rising of 1489', *English Historical R.* 105 (1990), 34–59.
5. Bevan, B. *King Richard II.* London; Rubicon; 1990. Pp 182.
6. Bradbury, Jim. 'The early years of the reign of Stephen, 1135–1139', Bc32, 17–30.
7. Brown, Shirley Ann. 'The Bayeux Tapestry: why Eustace, Odo and William?', Bc72, 7–28.
8. Davis, Virginia. 'William Waynflete and the Wars of the Roses', *Southern History* 11 (1989), 1–22.
9. Dyer, Christopher C. 'The rising of 1381 in Suffolk: its origins and participants', *P. of the Suffolk Inst. of Arch. & History* 36 (1988), 274–87.
10. Facinelli, Diane A. 'Treasonous criticisms of Henry IV: the loyal poet of *Richard the Redeless* and *Mum and the Sothsegger*', *J. of the Rocky Mountain Medieval & Renaissance Assoc.* 10 (1989), 51–62.
11. Friedrichs, Rhoda L. 'The two last wills of Ralph, lord Cromwell', *Nottingham Medieval Studies* 34 (1990), 93–112.
12. Hicks, Michael A. 'Did Edward V outlive his reign or did he outreign his life?', *The Ricardian* 8/108 (1990), 342–45.
13. Hollister, C. Warren. 'The viceregal court of Henry I', Bc122, 131–44.
14. Horrox, Rosemary E. *Richard III: a study of service.* Cambridge; Cambridge UP; 1989. Pp x, 358.
15. Hunt, Edwin S. 'A new look at the dealings of the Bardi and Peruzzi with Edward III', *J. of Economic History* 50 (1990), 149–62.
16. Jewell, Helen M. '*Piers Plowman*—a poem of crisis: an analysis of political instability in Langland's England', Bc100, 59–80.
17. Leland, John L. 'A further note on the [Sir Edward] Dalyngrygge case', *Medieval Prosopography* 11 (1990), 85–87.
18. Marius, Richard. 'Community, consent, and coercion', Bc147, 17–38.
19. Maund, K.L. 'The Welsh alliances of Earl Ælfgar of Mercia and his family in the mid-eleventh century', Bc137, 181–90.

20. Maurer, Helen. 'Bones in the Tower: a discussion of time, place and circumstance. Part 1', *The Ricardian* 8/111 (1990), 474–93.

21. Ormrod, W.M. *The reign of Edward III: crown and political society in England, 1327–1377*. London; Yale UP; 1990. Pp xiii, 280.

22. Osberg, Richard H. 'The Lambeth Palace Library manuscript account of Henry VI's 1432 London entry', *Medieval Studies* 52 (1990), 255–67.

23. Prestwich, Michael. 'The Ordinances of 1311 and the politics of the early fourteenth century', Bc100, 1–18.

24. Saul, Nigel. 'The Commons and the abolition of badges', *Parliamentary History* 9 (1990), 302–15.

25. Taylor, John. 'The Good parliament and its sources', Bc100, 81–96.

26. Teunis, H.B. 'Benoît of St Maure and William the Conqueror's *amor*', Bc72, 199–209.

27. Virgoe, Roger. 'Aspects of the county community in the fifteenth century', Bc69, 1–13.

28. Ward, Jennifer C. 'Royal service and reward: the Clare family and the Crown, 1066–1154', Bc137, 261–78.

29. Watts, John. '*De consulatu Stiliconis*: texts and politics in the reign of Henry VI', *J. of Medieval History* 16 (1990), 251–67.

30. Wigram, Isolde; Thone, Marlow. 'A local dispute and the politics of 1483: two reactions', *The Ricardian* 8/109 (1990), 414–16.

31. Williams, Barrie. 'Richard III and the house of Dudley', *The Ricardian* 8/108 (1990), 346–50.

32. Williams, Joanna M. 'The political career of Francis, viscount Lovell (1456–?)', *The Ricardian* 8/109 (1990), 382–402.

33. Young, Charles R. 'Divided loyalties: the Neville family and the Barons' War against King Henry III, 1264–1265', Bc122, 145–61.


## (c) *Constitution, Administration and Law*

1. Barron, Caroline. 'London and parliament in the Lancastrian period', *Parliamentary History* 9 (1990), 343–67.

2. Beilby, Mark. 'The profits of expertise: the rise of the civil lawyers and chancery equity', Bc69, 72–90.

3. Bonfield, Lloyd; Poos, L.R. 'The development of the deathbed transfer in medieval English manor courts', *Cambridge Law J.* 47 (1988), 403–27.

4. Brand, Paul. 'The drafting of legislation in mid-thirteenth century England', *Parliamentary History* 9 (1990), 243–85.

5. Brown, A.L. *The governance of late medieval England, 1272–1461*. London; Arnold; 1989. Pp viii, 248.

6. Butt, Ronald. *A history of parliament: the middle ages*. London; Constable; 1989. Pp xvi, 475.

7. Cherry, John. 'Symbolism and survival: medieval horns of tenure', *Antiquaries J.* 69 (1989), 111–18.

8. Clark, Elaine. 'City orphans and custody laws in medieval England', *American J. of Legal History* 34 (1990), 168–87.

9. Clark, Linda. 'The benefits and burdens of office: Henry Bourgchier

(1408–1483), viscount Bourgchier and earl of Essex, and the treasurer-ship of the Exchequer', Bc69, 119–36.

10. Clayton, Dorothy J. *The administration of the county palatine of Chester, 1442–1485*. Manchester; Manchester UP (Chetham Soc. 3rd ser. vol. 35); 1990. Pp xii, 313.

11. Doe, Norman. 'Legal reasoning and Sir Roger Townshend, JCP (d. 1493)', *J. of Legal History* 11 (1990), 191–99.

12. Green, Judith A. *English sheriffs to 1154*. London; HMSO; 1990. Pp 105.

13. Gross, Anthony. 'Langland's rats: a moralist's view of parliament', *Parliamentary History* 9 (1990), 286–301.

14. Harper-Bill, Christopher (ed.). *English episcopal acta, vol. 6: Norwich, 1070–1214*. Oxford; Oxford UP; 1990. Pp lxxxviii, 439.

15. Melikan, Rose. 'Shippers, salvors, and sovereigns: competing interests in the medieval law of shipwreck', *J. of Legal History* 11 (1990), 163–82.

16. Moreton, Charles E. 'A "best betrustyd frende": a late medieval lawyer [Roger Townshend] and his clients', *J. of Legal History* 11 (1990), 183–90.

17. Murray, Jacqueline. 'On the origins and role of "wise women" in causes for annulment on the grounds of male impotence', *J. of Medieval History* 16 (1990), 235–49.

18. Ormrod, W. M. 'Agenda for legislation, 1322–c.1340', *English Historical R.* 105 (1990), 1–33.

19. Ormrod, W.M. 'The Peasants' Revolt and the government of England', *J. of British Studies* 29 (1990), 1–30.

20. Ramsay, Nigel. 'What was the legal profession?', Bc69, 62–71.

21. Rawcliffe, Carole. 'Parliament and the settlement of disputes by arbitration in the later middle ages', *Parliamentary History* 9 (1990), 316–42.

22. Rawcliffe, Carole; Clark, Linda. 'Parliament and communities in the middle ages: introduction', *Parliamentary History* 9 (1990), 233–42.

23. Thorn, F.R. 'Hundreds and wapentakes' [in Cambridgeshire], Bc117, 18–26.

24. Thorn, F.R. 'Hundreds and wapentakes' [in Derbyshire], Bc118, 28–38.

25. Thorn, F.R. 'Hundreds and wapentakes' [in Leicestershire], Bc119, 22–30.

26. Thorn, F.R. 'Hundreds and wapentakes' [in Nottinghamshire], Bc120, 32–42.

27. Thorn, F.R. 'Hundreds and wapentakes' [in Oxfordshire], Bc109, 20–29.

28. Thorn, F.R. 'Hundreds and wapentakes' [in Shropshire], Bc110, 28–40.

29. Thorn, F.R. 'Hundreds and wapentakes' [in Sussex], Bc111, 28–42.

30. Turner, Ralph V. 'The Mandeville inheritance, 1189–1236: its legal, political, and social context', *The Haskins Soc. J.* 1 (1989), 147–72.

31. Turner, Ralph V. 'Who was the author of *Glanvill*? Reflections on the education of Henry II's common lawyers', *Law & History R.* 8 (1990), 97–127.

32. Vale, Brigette. 'The profits of the law and the "rise" of the Scropes:

Henry Scrope (d. 1336) and Geoffrey Scrope (d. 1340), Chief Justices to Edward II and Edward III', Bc69, 91–102.

33. Waugh, Scott L. 'Women's inheritance and the growth of bureaucratic monarchy in twelfth- and thirteenth-century England', *Nottingham Medieval Studies* 34 (1990), 71–92.

## (d) *External Affairs*

1. Bradbury, Jim. 'Geoffrey V of Anjou, count and knight', Bc40, 21–38.
2. Giry-Deloison, Charles. 'France, Burgundy and England', *History Today* 40/8 (1990), 47–52.
3. Haegeman, Marc. *De anglofilie in het graafschap Vlaanderen tussen 1379 en 1435: politieke en economische aspecten* [Anglophilia in the county of Flanders from 1379 to 1435: political and economic aspects]. Kortrijk; U.G.A. (Standen en Landen, 90); 1988. Pp 279.
4. Horn, Michael. 'Der Kardinalbischof Imar von Tusculum als Legat in England, 1144/1145' [The Cardinal-Bishop Imar von Tusculum as legate in England, 1144/1145], *Historisches Jahrbuch* 110 (1990), 492–505.
5. Huffman, Joseph P. 'Prosopography and the Anglo-imperial connection: a Cologne *ministerialis* family and its English relations', *Medieval Prosopography* 11 (1990), 53–134.
6. Jenks, Stuart. 'Die *Carta mercatoria*: ein Hansisches Privileg' [The *Carta mercatoria*: a Hanseatic privilege], *Hansische Geschichtsblätter* 108 (1990), 45–86.
7. Phillpotts, Christopher John. 'John of Gaunt and English policy towards France, 1389–1395', *J. of Medieval History* 16 (1990), 363–86.
8. Tuck, Anthony. 'Richard II and the Hundred Years War', Bc100, 117–31.

## (e) *Religion*

1. Anderson, Freda. 'Three Westminster abbots: a problem of identity', *Church Monuments* 4 (1989), 3–15.
2. Anderson, J.J. 'Gawain and the hornbook', *Notes and Queries* ns 37 (1990), 160–63.
3. Andrews, David D.; Nurse, Bernard. 'The hospital of St Leonard's at Newport', *Essex Archaeology & History* 3rd ser. 20 (1989), 84–91.
4. Barrow, Julia. 'Vicars choral and chaplains in northern European cathedrals, 1100–1250', *Studies in Church History* 26 (1989), 87–97.
5. Beech, George. 'Aquitanians and Flemings in the refoundation of Bardney Abbey (Lincolnshire) in the later eleventh century', *The Haskins Soc. J.* 1 (1989), 73–90.
6. Bell, D.N. 'A Cistercian at Oxford: Richard Dove of Buckfast and London, BL Sloane 513', *Studia Monastica* 31 (1989), 69–87.
7. Bestul, Thomas H. 'The meditations of Alexander of Ashby: an edition', *Medieval Studies* 52 (1990), 24–81.

8. Burger, Michael. '*Officiales* and the *familiae* of the bishops of Lincoln, 1258–1299', *J. of Medieval History* 16 (1990), 39–53.

9. Burgess, Clive. 'Late medieval wills and pious convention: testamentary evidence reconsidered', Bc69, 14–33.

10. Butterill, C.A. 'The cartulary of Flamstead', *Revue Bénédictine* 99 (1989), 293–312.

11. Catto, J.I. 'Sir William Beauchamp between chivalry and Lollardy', Bc40, 39–48.

12. Cigman, Gloria. '*Luceat lux vestra*: the Lollard preacher as truth and light', *R. of English Studies* 40 (1989), 479–96.

13. Coldstream, Nicola. '*Cui bono?* The saint, the clergy and the new work at St Albans', Bc71, 143–49.

14. Cooke, Kathleen. 'Donors and daughters: Shaftesbury Abbey's benefactors, endowments and nuns c.1086–1130', Bc72, 29–45.

15. Coppack, Glyn. *Abbeys and priories*. London; Batsford for English Heritage; 1990. Pp 159.

16. Cowdrey, H.E.J. 'William I's relations with Cluny further considered', Bc123, 75–85.

17. Davis, Virginia. 'Medieval English clergy database', *History & Computing* 2 (1990), 75–87.

18. Dawtry, Anne Frances. 'Monasticism in Cheshire, 1092–1300: a tale of mediocrity', Bc123, 64–74.

19. de Vine, S.W. 'The Franciscan friars, the feoffment to uses, and canonical theories of property enjoyment before 1535', *J. of Legal History* 10 (1989), 1–22.

20. Dinn, Robert. 'Baptism, spiritual kinship, and popular religion in late medieval Bury St Edmunds', *B. of the John Rylands University Library of Manchester* 72/3 (1990), 93–106.

21. Doyle, A.I. 'The English provincial book trade before printing', Bc139, 13–29.

22. Duffy, Eamon. '*Holy maydens, holy wyfes*: the cult of women saints in fifteenth- and sixteenth-century England', Bc128, 175–96.

23. Duggan, Anne J. (ed.). 'A new Becket letter: *Sepe quidem cogimur*', *Historical Research* 63 (1990), 86–99.

24. Dutton, Marsha L. 'The conversion and vocation of Ælred of Rievaulx: a historical hypothesis', Bc32, 31–49.

25. Elkins, Sharon K. *Holy women of twelfth-century England*. Chapel Hill; North Carolina UP; 1988. Pp xx, 244.

26. Franklin, Michael. 'The bishops of Winchester and the monastic revolution', Bc72, 47–65.

27. Gillespie, Vincent. 'Vernacular books of religion', Bc41, 317–44.

28. Given-Wilson, Chris. 'The bishop of Chichester and the second Statute of Praemunire, 1365', *Historical Research* 63 (1990), 128–42.

29. Golding, Brian. 'Hermits, monks and women in twelfth-century France and England: the experience of Obazine and Sempringham', Bc123, 127–45.

30. Greatrex, Joan. 'In commendation of a monastic Emden: prosopographic source material for English medieval Benedictine history', Bc123, 322–25.

31. Haines, Roy Martin. *Ecclesia anglicana: studies in the English church of the later middle ages.* Toronto; Toronto UP; 1989. Pp xv, 411.

32. Halsey, Richard. 'The twelfth-century church of St Frideswide's Priory', Bc66, 115–67.

33. Hanna, Katharine A. (ed.). *The cartularies of Southwick priory,* part 1. Winchester; Hampshire County Council (Hampshire record ser. vol. 9); 1988. Pp 305.

34. Harper-Bill, Christopher. 'The struggle for benefices in twelfth-century East Anglia', Bc137, 113–32.

35. Head, Thomas. 'The marriages of Christina of Markyate', *Viator* 21 (1990), 75–101.

36. Henderson, George. '*Sortes biblicae* in twelfth-century England: the list of episcopal prognostics in Cambridge, Trinity College MS R.7.5', Bc32, 113–35.

37. Hicks, Michael A. 'The English Minoresses and their early benefactors, (1990 for 1989), 13–31.

38. Hidden, Norman. 'The hospital or priory or free chapel of St John the Baptist in Hungerford', *Wiltshire Arch. & Natural History Magazine* 83 1990 for 1989, 13–31.

39. Holdsworth, Christopher J. 'Baldwin of Forde, Cistercian and archbishop of Canterbury', *Friends of Lambeth Library: Annual Report* (1989 for 1990), 13–31.

40. Horner, Patrick J. ' "The king taught us the lesson": Benedictine support for Henry V's suppression of the Lollards', *Medieval Studies* 52 (1990), 190–220.

41. Hudson, Anne. 'Lollard book production', Bc41, 125–42.

42. Hudson, Anne (ed.). *English Wycliffite sermons,* vol. 3. Oxford; Oxford UP; 1990. Pp clv, 323.

43. Johnson, Charles (ed.). *Hugh the Chanter: the history of the Church of York, 1066–1127.* Oxford; Oxford UP; 2nd edn. 1990. Pp 304.

44. Luttrell, Anthony (ed.). 'The Hospitallers' western accounts, 1373–1374 and 1374–1375', Bc108, 1–22.

45. Martin, Judy; Walker, Lorna E.M. 'At the feet of St Stephen Muret: Henry II and the order of Grandmont *redivivus*', *J. of Medieval History* 16 (1990), 1–12.

46. Mason, Emma. 'Westminster Abbey and the monarchy between the reigns of William I and John (1066–1216)', *J. of Ecclesiastical History* 41 (1990), 199–216.

47. Oliva, Marilyn. 'Aristocracy or meritocracy? Office-holding patterns in late medieval English nunneries', Bc128, 197–208.

48. Petersohn, Jurgen. 'Jubilaumsfrommigkeit vor dem Jubelablass: Jubeljahr, Reliquientranslation und *remissio* in Bamberg (1189) und Canterbury (1220)' [Jubilee piety before the Jubilee indulgence: jubilee year, translation of relics and *remissio* in Bamberg and Canterbury], *Deutsches Archiv für Erforschung des Mittelalters* 45 (1989), 31–53.

49. Rosenthal, Joel T. 'Lancastrian episcopal wills: directing and distributing', *Medieval Prosopography* 11 (1990), 35–84.

50. Rubin, Miri. 'Corpus Christi: inventing a feast', *History Today* 40/7 (1990), 15–21.

51. Ruud, Marylou. 'Monks in the world: the case of Gundulf of Rochester', Bc137, 245–60.

52. Sayers, Jane. 'Violence in the medieval cloister', *J. of Ecclesiastical History* 41 (1990), 533–42.

53. Smith, Julie A. 'An image of a preaching bishop in late medieval England: the 1498 woodcut portrait of Bishop John Alcock', *Viator* 21 (1990), 301–22.

54. Swanson, R.N. 'Problems of the priesthood in pre-Reformation England', *English Historical R.* 105 (1990), 845–69.

55. Swanson, R.N. '*Sede vacante* administration in the medieval diocese of Carlisle: the accounts of the vacancy of December 1395 to March 1396', *T. of the Cumberland & Westmorland Antiq. & Arch. Soc.* 90 (1990), 183–94.

56. Swanson, R.N. 'The rolls of Roger de Meuland, bishop of Coventry and Lichfield (1285–1295)', *J. of the Soc. of Archivists* 11 (1990), 37–40.

57. Swanson, R.N. *The register of John Catterick, bishop of Coventry and Lichfield, 1415–1419.* Woodbridge; Boydell for Canterbury & York Soc.; 1990. Pp 112.

58. Tatton-Brown, T.W.T. 'Church building on Romney marsh in the later middle ages', *Archaeologia Cantiana* 107 (1990 for 1989), 253–65.

59. Taylor, Pamela. 'Clerkenwell and the religious foundations of Jordan de Bricett: a re-examination', *Historical Research* 63 (1990), 17–28.

60. Theilmann, John M. 'English peasants and medieval miracle lists', *The Historian* [USA] 52 (1990), 286–303.

61. Theilmann, John M. 'Political canonization and political symbolism in medieval England', *J. of British Studies* 29 (1990), 241–66.

62. Thompson, Benjamin. 'The Statute of Carlisle, 1307, and the alien priories', *J. of Ecclesiastical History* 41 (1990), 543–83.

63. Walker, John. 'The motives of patrons of the order of St Lazarus in England in the twelfth and thirteenth centuries', Bc123, 171–81.

64. Webb, Diana M. 'Women and home: the domestic setting of late medieval spirituality', Bc128, 159–73.

65. Wilson, Christopher. 'The tomb of Henry IV and the holy oil of St Thomas of Canterbury', Bc71, 181–90.

66. Winkless, Doreen. *Hailes, Gloucestershire: the story of a medieval abbey.* Stocksfield; Spredden; 1990. Pp 80.

67. Young, Abigail Ann. '*Accessus ad Alexandrum*: the *Praefatio* to the *Postilla in Iohannis Evangelium* of Alexander of Hales (1186?–1245)', *Medieval Studies* 52 (1990), 1–23.

## (f) *Economic Affairs*

1. Alcock, N.W. 'The Catesbys in Coventry: a medieval estate and its archives', *Midland History* 15 (1990), 1–36.

2. Alexander, Ann; *et al.* 'Patrington: a fifteenth-century manorial account', *Yorkshire Arch. J.* 62 (1990), 141–52.

3. Allmand, Christopher. 'Taxation in medieval England: the example of murage', *Villes, bonnes villes, cités et capitales. Études d'histoire urbaine (XII-XVII siècle) offertes à Bernard Chevalier*, ed. Monique Bourin (Tours; University of Tours; 1989), pp 223–30.

4. Andrews, David D. 'A late medieval cutlery manufacturing site at Weaverhead Lane, Thaxted', *Essex Archaeology & History* 3rd ser. 20 (1989), 110–19.

5. Bailey, Mark. 'Sand into gold: the evolution of the foldcourse system in west Suffolk, 1200–1600', *Agricultural History R.* 38 (1990), 40–57.

6. Biddick, Kathleen A. 'Malthus in a straightjacket? Analyzing agrarian change in medieval England' [review article], *J. of Interdisciplinary History* 20 (1989–90), 623–35.

7. Britnell, R.H. 'Bailiffs and burgesses in Colchester, 1400–1525', *Essex Archaeology & History* 3rd ser. 21 (1990), 103–09.

8. Britnell, R.H. 'Feudal reaction after the Black Death in the palatinate of Durham', *Past & Present* 128 (1990), 28–47.

9. Childs, Wendy R. 'Finance and trade under Edward II', Bc100, 19–37.

10. Childs, Wendy R. *The trade and shipping of Hull, 1300–1500.* Beverley; East Yorkshire Local History Soc.; 1990. Pp 41.

11. Condon, Margaret. 'From caitiff and villain to *pater patriae*: Reynold Bray and the profits of office', Bc69, 137–68.

12. Cook, B.J. 'The royal household and the mint (1279–1399)', *Numismatic Chronicle* 149 (1989), 121–33.

13. Despretz, Claude. 'Le système manorial d'agriculture au 14è siècle en Angleterre', *Revue du Nord* 72 (1990), 483–93.

14. Dyer, Christopher C. 'The past, the present and the future in medieval rural history', *Rural History* 1 (1990), 37–49.

15. Farmer, D.L. 'Two Wiltshire manors and their markets', *Agricultural History R.* 37 (1989), 1–11.

16. Gerrard, S. 'The medieval and early modern Cornish stamping mill', *Industrial Archaeology R.* 12 (1989), 9–19.

17. Gervers, Michael. 'The textile industry in Essex in the late twelfth and thirteenth centuries: a study based on occupational names in charter sources', *Essex Archaeology & History* 3rd ser. 20 (1989), 34–73.

18. Gervers, Michael; Long, Gillian; McCulloch, Michael. 'The DEEDS database of mediaeval charters: design and coding for the RDBMS Oracle 5', *History & Computing* 2 (1990), 1–11.

19. Harvey, P.D.A. 'Non-agrarian activities in twelfth-century English estate surveys', Bc32, 101–11.

20. Higham, Mary C. 'Some evidence for twelfth- and thirteenth-century linen and woollen textile processing', *Medieval Archaeology* 33 (1989), 38–52.

21. Hybel, Nils. *Crisis or change: the concept of crisis in the light of agrarian structural reorganization in late medieval England.* Lund (Sweden); Almqvist & Wiksell; 1989. Pp xxiv, 334.

22. Jewell, Helen M. 'Women at the courts of the manor of Wakefield, 1348–1350', *Northern History* 26 (1990), 59–81.

23. Keen, Laurence. 'Coastal salt production in Norman England', Bc137, 133–80.

24. Ketteringham, L.L. 'Two medieval pottery kilns at Limpsfield Chart', *Surrey Arch. Collections* 79 (1989), 125–45.

25. Kowaleski, Maryanne. 'Town and country in late medieval England: the hide and leather trade', Bc27, 57–73.

26. Martin, G.H. 'The early history of the London Saddlers' Guild', *B. of the John Rylands University Library of Manchester* 72/3 (1990), 145–54.

27. Matzat, W. 'Long strip field lay-outs and their later subdivisions', *Geografiska Annaler* 70 (1988), 133–47.

28. Monnas, L. 'Silk cloths purchased for the great wardrobe of the kings of England, 1325–1462', *Textile History* 20 (1989), 283–307.

29. Moorhouse, Stephen. 'The quarrying of stone roofing slates and rubble in West Yorkshire during the middle ages', Bc135, 126–46.

30. Mundill, R.R. 'Anglo-Jewry under Edward I: credit agents and their clients', *Jewish Historical Studies* 31 (1988–90), 1–21.

31. Nightingale, Pamela. 'Monetary contraction and mercantile credit in later medieval England', *Economic History R.* 2nd ser. 43 (1990), 560–75.

32. Patterson, Robert B. 'Robert fitz Harding of Bristol: profile of an early Angevin burgess-baron patrician and his family's urban involvement', *The Haskins Soc. J.* 1 (1989), 109–22.

33. Penn, Simon A.C.; Dyer, Christopher C. 'Wages and earnings in late medieval England: evidence from the enforcement of the labour laws', *Economic History R.* 2nd ser. 43 (1990), 356–76.

34. Piper, Alan; Foster, Meryl. 'Evidence of the Oxford booktrade, about 1300', *Viator* 20 (1989), 155–59.

35. Postles, David. 'Securing the gift in Oxfordshire charters in the twelfth and early thirteenth centuries', *Archives* 19 (1990), 183–91.

36. Pretty, Jules N. 'Sustainable agriculture in the middle ages: the English manor', *Agricultural History R.* 38 (1990), 1–19.

37. Roberts, Brian K. 'Norman village plantations and long strip fields in northern England', *Geografiska Annaler* 70 (1988), 169–77.

38. Rokeah, Zefira Entin. 'Money and the hangman in late thirteenth-century England: Jews, Christians and coinage offences alleged and real (Part 1)', *Jewish Historical Studies* 31 (1988–90), 83–109.

39. Scrase, A.J. 'A French merchant in fourteenth-century Wells', *Somerset Archaeology & Natural History* 133 (1990 for 1989), 131–40.

40. Scrase, A.J. 'Development and change in burgage plots; the example of Wells', *J. of Historical Geography* 15 (1989), 349–65.

41. Staniland, K. 'The great wardrobe accounts as a source for historians of fourteenth-century clothing and textiles', *Textile History* 20 (1989), 275–81.

42. Swanson, Heather. 'Artisans in the urban economy: the documentary evidence from York', Bc27, 42–56.

43. Ward, Jennifer C. ' "Richer in land than in inhabitants": south Essex in the middle ages, *c.*1066–*c.*1340', Bc65, 97–108.

44. Witney, K.P. 'Development of the Kentish marshes in the aftermath of the Norman conquest', *Archaeologia Cantiana* 107 (1990 for 1989), 29–50.
45. Witney, K.P. 'The woodland economy of Kent, 1066–1348', *Agricultural History R.* 38 (1990), 20–39.

## (g) *Social Structure and Population*

1. Carr, David R. 'The problem of urban patriciates: office holders in fifteenth-century Salisbury', *Wiltshire Arch. & Natural History Magazine* 83 (1990), 118–35.
2. Contamine, Philippe. 'L'état et les aristocraties', Bc148, 11–26.
3. DeWindt, Edwin Brezette (ed.). *The court rolls of Ramsey, Hepmangrove and Bury, 1268–1600.* Canada; Pontifical Inst. of Mediaeval Studies; 1990. Pp xii, 297 + 1310 on fiche.
4. Eckhardt, Caroline D. 'Chaucer's franklin and others of the Vavasour family', *Modern Philology* 87 (1990), 239–48.
5. Evans, Dafydd. 'The nobility of knight and falcon', Bc40, 79–99.
6. Finch, A.J. 'Parental authority and the problem of clandestine marriage in the later middle ages', *Law & History R.* 8 (1990), 189–204.
7. Fleming, Donald F. '*Milites* as attestors to charters in England, 1101–1300', *Albion* 22 (1990), 185–98.
8. Franklin, Peter. 'Heriots and deaths in medieval England: a note', *Local Population Studies* 45 (1990), 71–73.
9. Genet, Jean-Philippe. 'Le lien personnel dans la litterature politique anglaise aux xivè et xvè siècles', Bc148, 161–87.
10. Goldberg, P.J.P. 'Urban identity and the poll taxes of 1377, 1379, and 1381', *Economic History R.* 2nd ser. 43 (1990), 194–216.
11. Goldberg, P.J.P. 'Women's work, women's role, in the late medieval north', Bc69, 34–50.
12. Green, Judith A. 'Aristocratic loyalties on the northern frontier of England, c.1100–1174', Bc32, 83–100.
13. Harf-Lancner, Laurence. 'L'enfer de la cour: la cour d'Henri II Plantagenêt et la mesnie Hellequin (dans l'oeuvre de Jean de Salisbury, de Gautier Map, de Pierre de Blois et de Giraud de Barri)', Bc148, 27–50.
14. Harris, Barbara J. 'Property, power, and personal relations: elite mothers and sons in Yorkist and early Tudor England', *Signs* 15 (1990), 606–32.
15. Hart, John. 'Leprosy in Cornwall and Devon: problems and perspectives', Bc142, 261–69.
16. Hawkins, Duncan. 'The Black Death and the new London cemeteries of 1348', *Antiquity* 64/244 (1990), 637–42.
17. Hillaby, Joe. 'A magnate among the marchers: Hamo of Hereford, his family and clients, 1218–1253', *Jewish Historical Studies* 31 (1988–90), 23–82.
18. Hindle, Brian Paul. *Medieval town plans.* Princes Risborough; Shire; 1990. Pp 64.

19. Howes, Audrey M. 'The career of Robert Michelson, merchant, ship master and burgess of Kingston upon Hull, 1464–1490', *The Ricardian* 8/110 (1990), 443–48.

20. Hudson, John. 'Life-grants and the development of inheritance in Anglo-Norman England', Bc72, 67–80.

21. Manchester, Keith. 'Medieval leprosy: the disease and its management', Bc73, 27–32.

22. Moore, John S. 'Domesday slavery', Bc137, 191–220.

23. Oggins, Robin S. 'Falconry and medieval social status', *Mediaevalia* 12 (1989 for 1986), 43–55.

24. Powell, W. Raymond. 'Domesday Book and feudal topography', *Essex Archaeology & History* 3rd ser. 21 (1990), 48–56.

25. Rigby, Stephen. 'Urban society in early fourteenth-century England: the evidence of the lay subsidies', *B. of the John Rylands University Library of Manchester* 72/3 (1990), 169–84.

26. Saul, Nigel. 'Conflict and consensus in English local society', Bc100, 38–58.

27. Saul, Nigel. 'Some Etchingham ephemera or more scenes from provincial life', *Sussex Arch. Collections* 127 (1989), 254–56.

28. Shahar, Shulamith. *Childhood in the middle ages*. London; Routledge; 1990. Pp 352.

29. Sil, Narasngha P. 'Sir Thomas Heneage of Hainton: a Henrician gentleman', *J. of the Rocky Mountain Medieval & Renaissance Assoc.* 10 (1989), 63–74.

30. Turner, Ralph V. 'Changing perceptions of the new administrative class in Anglo-Norman and Angevin England: the *curiales* and their conservative critics', *J. of British Studies* 29 (1990), 93–117.

31. Turner, Ralph V. 'The children of Anglo-Norman royalty and their upbringing', *Medieval Prosopography* 11 (1990), 17–52.

32. Walker, Simon K. 'Autorité des magnats et pouvoir de la *gentry* en Angleterre à la fin du moyen âge', Bc148, 189–211.

33. Walker, Simon K. 'Sir Richard Abberbury (*c.*1330–1399) and his kinsmen: the rise and fall of a gentry family', *Nottingham Medieval Studies* 34 (1990), 113–40.

34. Walker, Simon K. *The Lancastrian affinity, 1361–1399*. Oxford; Oxford UP; 1990. Pp 280.

35. Williams, Daniel. 'The Peverils and the Essebies, 1066–1166: a study in early feudal relationships', Bc32, 241–59.

36. Wormald, Jenny. 'L'état et aristocratie et l'idée de contrat en Écosse, xvè-xviiè siècle', Bc148, 213–30.

## (h) *Naval and Military*

1. Baker, Derek. 'Ailred of Rievaulx and Walter Espec', *The Haskins Soc. J.* 1 (1989), 91–98.

2. Ballard, Mark. 'An expedition of English archers to Liège in 1467, and the Anglo-Burgundian marriage alliance', *Nottingham Medieval Studies* 34 (1990), 152–74.

3. Bennett, Matthew. 'The means and limitations of military power in the middle ages', *Sandhurst J. of Military Studies* 2 (1990), 1–14.
4. Bennett, Matthew. 'Wace and warfare', Bc137, 37–58.
5. Bliese, John. 'The battle rhetoric of Ælred of Rievaulx', *The Haskins Soc. J.* 1 (1989), 99–107.
6. Cazel, Fred A., Jr. 'Intertwined careers: Hubert de Burgh and Peter des Roches', *The Haskins Soc. J.* 1 (1989), 173–81.
7. Counihan, Joan. 'The growth of castle studies in England and on the Continent since 1850', Bc137, 77–86.
8. Davies, S.M.; Graham, A.H. 'Trowbridge castle excavations, 1988: an interim report', *Wiltshire Arch. & Natural History Magazine* 83 (1990), 50–56.
9. Griffiths, Rhidian. 'Prince Henry and Wales, 1400–1408', Bc69, 51–61.
10. Hammond, Peter William. *The battles of Barnet and Tewkesbury*. Gloucester; Sutton; 1990. Pp 192.
11. Hodges, Geoffrey. *Ludford Bridge and Mortimer's Cross: the Wars of the Roses in Herefordshire and the Welsh Marches and the accession of Edward IV*. Almeley; Logaston; 1989. Pp 80.
12. Kerr, Brian. 'Windsor castle round tower: results of rescue excavation and recording, 1989–1990', *Castle Studies Group Newsletter* 4 (1990), 6–10.
13. Lester, G.A. 'Chaucer's unkempt knight', *English Language Notes* 27 (1989), 25–29.
14. Lewis, Carenza. 'Paired mottes in East Chelborough, Dorset', Bc142, 159–71.
15. Lindenbaum, Sheila. 'The Smithfield tournament of 1390', *J. of Medieval and Renaissance Studies* 20 (1990), 1–20.
16. Mahoney, Dhira B. 'Malory's great guns', *Viator* 20 (1989), 291–310.
17. Neillands, Robin. *The Hundred Years War, 1337–1453*. London; Routledge; 1990. Pp 272.
18. Neumann, J. 'Hydrographic and ship-hydrodynamic aspects of the Norman invasion, AD 1066', Bc137, 221–44.
19. Peirce, Ian. 'The development of the medieval sword, *c*.850–1300', Bc40, 139–58.
20. Pounds, N.J.G. *The medieval castle in England and Wales: a social and political history*. Cambridge; Cambridge UP; 1990. Pp xvii, 357.
21. Pugh, T.B. 'Richard, duke of York, and the rebellion of Henry Holand, duke of Exeter, in May 1454', *Historical Research* 63 (1990), 248–62.
22. Sherborne, James. 'The defence of the realm and the impeachment of Michael de la Pole in 1386', Bc100, 97–116.
23. Stansfield, Michael. 'John Holland, duke of Exeter and earl of Huntingdon (d. 1447) and the costs of the Hundred Years War', Bc69, 103–18.
24. Strickland, Matthew. 'Securing the north: invasion and the strategy of defence in twelfth-century Anglo-Scottish warfare', Bc72, 177–98.
25. Sumption, Jonathan. *The Hundred Years War: trial by battle*. London; Faber & Faber; 1990. Pp xi, 659.

26. Suppe, Robert B. 'Castle guard and the castlery of Clun', *The Haskins Soc. J.* 1 (1989), 123–34.
27. Vale, Malcolm G.A. *The Angevin legacy and the Hundred Years War, 1250–1340.* Oxford; Blackwell; 1990. Pp xiv, 317.
28. Williams, C.L. Sinclair. 'A valiant constable of Colchester Castle, AD 1155', *Essex Archaeology & History* 3rd ser. 20 (1989), 30–33.


## (i) *Intellectual and Cultural*

1. Aers, David. 'Reading *Piers Plowman*: literature, history and criticism', *Literature & History* ns 1 (1990), 4–23.
2. Anderson, Freda. 'St Pancras Priory, Lewes: its architectural development to 1200', Bc137, 1–36.
3. Barker, Lynn K. 'MS Bodl. Canon. Pat. Lat. 131 and a lost Lactantius of John of Salisbury: evidence in search of a French critic of Thomas Becket', *Albion* 22 (1990), 21–37.
4. Barr, Helen. 'The dates of *Richard the Redeless* and *Mum and the Sothsegger*', *Notes and Queries* ns 37 (1990), 270–75.
5. Barrow, Julia. 'Education and recruitment of cathedral canons in England and Germany, 1100–1225', *Viator* 20 (1989), 117–38.
6. Binski, Paul. 'Reflections on *La estoire de Seint Aedward le rei*: hagiography and kingship in thirteenth-century England', *J. of Medieval History* 16 (1990), 333–50.
7. Blake, N.F. 'Manuscript to print', Bc41, 403–32.
8. Boffey, Julia; Thompson, John J. 'Anthologies and miscellanies: production and choice of texts', Bc41, 279–315.
9. Brooke, Christopher N.L. 'Chancellors of the university of Cambridge, *c.*1415–1535', Bc62, 233–34.
10. Christianson, C. Paul. 'A community of book artisans in Chaucer's London', *Viator* 20 (1989), 207–18.
11. Christianson, C. Paul. 'Evidence for the study of London's late medieval manuscript-book trade', Bc41, 87–108.
12. Coates, Alan E. 'The library of Durham College, Oxford', *Library History* 8 (1990), 125–31.
13. Cox, James S. (ed.). *The English fifteenth-century commonplace book.* St Sampson (Guernsey); Toucon; 1989. Pp 56.
14. Crick, Julia C. (comp.). *'History of the Kings of Britain'*, vol. 3: a summary catalogue of the manuscripts. Woodbridge; Boydell; 1989. Pp xxiv, 376.
15. Doyle, A.I. 'Publication by members of the religious orders', Bc41, 109–23.
16. Dronke, Peter. 'On the continuity of the medieval English love-lyric', Bc129, 7–22.
17. Edwards, A.S.G.; Pearsall, Derek. 'The manuscripts of the major English poetic texts', Bc41, 257–78.
18. Evans, G.R. *Anselm.* London; Cassell; 1989. Pp 108.
19. Getz, Faye Marie. 'Charity, translation, and the language of medical

learning in medieval England', *B. of the History of Medicine* 64 (1990), 1–17.

20. Gibson, Gail McMurray. *The theatre of devotion: East Anglian drama and society in the late middle ages.* London; Chicago UP; 1989. Pp xvi, 252.

21. Glenn, John. 'Adelard of Bath and the applications of geometry: a note', Bc32, 51–53.

22. Gransden, Antonia. 'Prologues in the historiography of twelfth-century England', Bc32, 55–81.

23. Gullick, Michael. 'A twelfth-century manuscript of the letters of Thomas Becket', *English Manuscript Studies 1100–1700* 2 (1990), 1–31.

24. Harris, Kate. 'Patrons, buyers and owners: the evidence for ownership, and the role of book owners in book production and the book trade', Bc41, 163–99.

25. Hunt, Tony. *Popular medicine in thirteenth-century England: introduction and texts.* Woodbridge; Boydell; 1990. Pp xii, 466.

26. Jansen, Sharon L. 'Toward a history of the vernacular book trade in England, 1300–1500', *B. of Bibliography* 46 (1989), 92–117.

27. Knorr, Wilbur R. 'John of Tynemouth alias John of London: emerging portrait of a singular medieval mathematician', *British J. for the History of Science* 23 (1990), 293–330.

28. Knorr, Wilbur R. 'Paraphrase editions of Latin mathematical texts: *De Figuris ysoperimetris*', *Medieval Studies* 52 (1990), 132–89.

29. Kretzmann, Norman; Kretzmann, Barbara Ensign (ed.). *The 'Sophismata' of Richard Kilvington* [English text and commentary]. Cambridge; Cambridge UP; 1990. Pp 392.

30. Kretzmann, Norman; Kretzmann, Barbara Ensign (ed.). *The 'Sophismata' of Richard Kilvington* [Latin text]. Oxford; Oxford UP (Auctores Britannici medii aevi 12); 1990. Pp xx, 156.

31. Loyn, Henry. 'Epic and Romance', Bc32, 153–63.

32. Lyall, R.J. 'Materials: the paper revolution', Bc41, 11–29.

33. McKendrick, Scot. '*La Grande Historie Cesar* and the manuscripts of Edward IV', *English Manuscript Studies 1100–1700* 2 (1990), 109–38.

34. McLoughlin, John. '*Amicitia* in practice: John of Salisbury (*c.*1120–1180) and his circle', Bc32, 165–81.

35. Meale, Carol. 'Patrons, buyers and owners: book production and social status', Bc41, 201–38.

36. Michael, M.A. 'Destruction, reconstruction and invention: the Hungerford Hours and English manuscript illumination of the early fourteenth century', *English Manuscript Studies 1100–1700* 2 (1990), 33–108.

37. Mooney, Linne R. 'Lydgate's *Kings of England* and another verse chronicle of the kings', *Viator* 20 (1989), 255–89.

38. Pearsall, Derek. 'Introduction' [book-production], Bc41, 1–10.

39. Richardson, Malcolm. 'The earliest known owners of *Canterbury Tales* MSS and Chaucer's secondary audience', *The Chaucer R.* 25 (1990), 17–32.

40. Sheppard, Jennifer M. 'The twelfth-century library and scriptorium at Buildwas: assessing the evidence', Bc32, 193–204.

41. Smith, William. 'Two medieval Salisbury wills', *J. of the Soc. of Archivists* 10 (1989), 118–22.
42. Sutton, Anne F.; Visser-Fuchs, Livia. 'Richard III's books: ix', *The Ricardian* 8/111 (1990), 494–514.
43. Sutton, Anne F.; Visser-Fuchs, Livia. 'Richard III's books: vii and viii: the interest of these books to Richard III and later owners', *The Ricardian* 8/109 (1990), 403–13.
44. Sutton, Anne F.; Visser-Fuchs, Livia. 'Richard III's books: viii(2), cont.', *The Ricardian* 8/108 (1990), 351–62.
45. Sutton, Anne F.; Visser-Fuchs, Livia. 'The prophecy of G', *The Ricardian* 8/110 (1990), 449–50.
46. Tierney, Brian. 'Medieval foundations of Elizabethan political thought', Bc149, 1–3.
47. van Gijsen, Annelies. 'Pygmalion, or the image of women in medieval literature', Bc2, 221–30.
48. Vickerstaff, J.J. 'Thomas Langley and the nature of public education in Durham City, 1400–1550', *Durham University J.* 82 (1990), 1–7.
49. Voigts, Linda Ehrsam. 'Scientific and medical books', Bc41, 345–402.
50. Waldron, Ronald. 'Trevisa's "Celtic complex" re-visited', *Notes and Queries* ns 36 (1989), 303–307.
51. Walsh, Martin W. '*Babio*: toward a performance reconstruction of secular farce in twelfth-century England', Bc32, 219–40.
52. Wathey, Andrew. 'The production of books of liturgical polyphony', Bc41, 143–61.

## (j) *Visual Arts*

1. Ailes, Adrian. 'Heraldry in twelfth-century England: the evidence', Bc32, 1–16.
2. Anderson, Freda. 'Two Romanesque capitals from Lewes Priory', *Sussex Arch. Collections* 127 (1989), 49–60.
3. Ashdown, John; Fisher, Ian; Munby, Julian. 'The roof carpentry of Oxford Cathedral', Bc66, 195–204.
4. Bettey, J.H. 'The medieval churches of Bristol: anniversary address, 1989', *T. of the Ancient Monuments Soc.* 34 (1990), 1–27.
5. Bony, Jean. 'The stonework planning of the first Durham Master', Bc71, 19–34.
6. Brodie, Allan M. 'The sculpture of Burmington manor, Warwickshire', Bc71, 91–101.
7. Courtenay, Lynn T. 'The Westminster Hall roof: a new archaeological source', *J. of the British Arch. Association* 143 (1990), 95–111.
8. Crossley, Paul. 'Lincoln and the Baltic: the fortunes of a theory', Bc71, 169–80.
9. Cunningham, Jane. 'Auckland Castle: some recent discoveries', Bc71, 81–90.
10. Currie, C.R.J. 'Gazetteer of archaic roofs in Herefordshire and Worcestershire churches', *Vernacular Architecture* 21 (1990), 18–32.

11. Draper, Peter. ' "Seeing that it was done in all the noble churches in England' ", Bc71, 137–42.
12. Edwards, John. 'New light on Christ of the Trades, and other medieval wall-paintings at St Mary's, Purton', *Wiltshire Arch. & Natural History Magazine* 83 (1990), 105–17.
13. Fergusson, Peter. '*Porta patens esto*: notes on early Cistercian gatehouses in the north of England', Bc71, 47–59.
14. Foot, Mirjam M. 'English decorated bookbindings', Bc41, 65–86.
15. Gem, Richard. 'The first Romanesque cathedral of Old Salisbury', Bc71, 9–18.
16. Green, Julia; *et al.* 'Medieval floor-tiles from St Frideswide's Priory', Bc66, 103–14.
17. Heslop, T.A. 'Romanesque painting and social distinction: the Magi and the Shepherds', Bc32, 137–52.
18. Heslop, T.A. 'The iconography of the Angel Choir at Lincoln Cathedral', Bc71, 151–58.
19. Holden, E.W. 'Slate roofing in medieval Sussex—a reappraisal', *Sussex Arch. Collections* 127 (1989), 73–88.
20. Jansen, Virginia. 'Medieval "service" architecture: undercrofts', Bc71, 73–79.
21. King, James F. 'The Old Sarum master: a twelfth-century sculptor in south-west England', *Wiltshire Arch. & Natural History Magazine* 83 (1990), 70–95.
22. Leedy, Walter. 'King's College, Cambridge: observations on its context and foundations', Bc71, 209–17.
23. Marcombe, David; Manchester, Keith. 'The Melton Mowbray "leper head": an historical and medical investigation', *Medical History* 34 (1990), 86–91.
24. McAleer, Philip J. 'Southwell, Worksop, and stylistic tendencies in English twelfth-century facade design', Bc71, 61–72.
25. Milner, Lesley. 'Warkworth Keep, Northumberland: a reassessment of its plan and date', Bc71, 219–28.
26. Mitchell, D.M. ' "By your leave my masters": British taste in table linen in the fifteenth and sixteenth centuries', *Textile History* 20 (1989), 49–77.
27. Morris, Richard K. 'Mouldings and the analysis of medieval style', Bc71, 239–47.
28. Morris, Richard K. 'The Gothic mouldings of the Latin and Lady Chapels' [Christ Church, Oxford], Bc66, 169–83.
29. Oosterwijk, Sophie; Norton, Christopher. 'Figure sculpture from the twelfth century Minster', *Friends of York Minster Annual Report* (1990), 11–30.
30. Platt, Colin. *The architecture of medieval Britain.* London/Newhaven; Yale UP; 1990. Pp x, 325.
31. Rodley, Lyn. 'The writing on the wall (or not): an aspect of Byzantine influence on western art', Bc32, 183–92.
32. Routh, Pauline Sheppard; Knowles, Richard. 'The Markenfield collar', *Yorkshire Arch. J.* 62 (1990), 133–40.

33. Scott, Kathleen L. 'Design, decoration and illustration', Bc41, 31–64.
34. Taylor, Christopher C. 'Somersham Palace, Cambridgeshire: a medieval landscape for pleasure?', Bc142, 211–24.
35. Tracy, Charles. 'The St David's cathedral bishop's throne and its relationship to contemporary fourteenth-century ecclesiastical furniture in England', *Archaeologia Cambrensis* 137 (1989 for 1988), 113–18.
36. Tracy, Charles. *English Gothic choir-stalls, 1400–1550.* Woodbridge; Boydell; 1990. Pp x, 210.
37. Tudor-Craig, Pamela. 'St Bernard and the Canterbury capitals', Bc32, 205–17.
38. Vale, Malcolm G.A. 'Cardinal Henry Beaufort and the "Albergati" portrait', *English Historical R.* 105 (1990), 337–54.
39. White, Adam. 'Westminster Abbey in the early seventeenth century: a powerhouse of ideas', *Church Monuments* 4 (1989), 15–53.
40. Wormald, Francis. 'The survival of Anglo-Saxon illumination after the Norman Conquest', Bc31, 92–110.
41. Wormald, Francis. *Collected writings, II: studies in English and continental art of the later middle ages* ed. J.J.G. Alexander, T.J. Brown and Joan Gibbs. London; Miller; 1988. Pp 242.

## (k) *Topography*

1. Andrews, David D.; Stenning, David F. 'Wealden houses and urban topography at the lower end of Maldon High St', *Essex Archaeology & History* 3rd ser. 20 (1989), 103–09.
2. Aston, Michael. 'The development of medieval rural settlement in Somerset', Bc53, 19–40.
3. Ayers, B.S. 'Building a fine city: the provision of flint, mortar and freestone in medieval Norwich', Bc135, 217–27.
4. Bond, C.J. 'Central place and medieval new town: the origins of Thame, Oxfordshire', Bc26, 83–108.
5. Bonney, D.J.; Dunn, C.J. 'Earthwork castles and settlement at Hamstead Marshall, Berkshire', Bc142, 173–82.
6. Butler, Lawrence; Wade-Martins, Peter. *The deserted medieval village of Thuxton, Norfolk.* Dereham; Norfolk Arch. Unit (East Anglian archaeology reports no. 46); 1989. Pp 69.
7. Campbell, B.M.S.; Power, J.P. 'Mapping the agricultural geography of medieval England', *J. of Historical Geography* 15 (1989), 24–39.
8. Courtney, Paul. 'Excavations in the outer precinct of Tintern Abbey', *Medieval Archaeology* 33 (1989), 99–143.
9. Davey, Norman. 'Medieval timber buildings in Potterne', *Wiltshire Arch. & Natural History Magazine* 83 (1990), 57–69.
10. Everson, Paul. 'Lost and found in Lincolnshire: two problems in archaeological inventorizing', Bc142, 55–64.
11. Farley, Michael; Manchester, Keith. 'The cemetery of the leper hospital of St Margaret, High Wycombe, Buckinghamshire', *Medieval Archaeology* 33 (1989), 82–89.

12. Fox, Harold S.A. 'Peasant farmers, patterns of settlement and *pays*: transformations in the landscapes of Devon and Cornwall during the later middle ages', Bc53, 41–73.

13. Franklin, Peter. 'Thornbury woodlands and deer parks, part 1: the earls of Gloucester's deer parks', *T. of the Bristol & Gloucestershire Arch. Soc.* 107 (1989), 149–69.

14. Hall, Catherine; Lovatt, Roger. 'The site and foundation of Peterhouse', *Cambridge Antiq. Soc. P.* 78 (1990 for 1989), 5–46.

15. Hart, Cyril. 'Oundle: its province and eight hundreds', *Northampton-shire Past & Present* 8/1 (1989–90), 3–23.

16. Holgate, Robin. 'The excavation of a late medieval hall-house at Brook Lane, near Horsham, West Sussex', *Sussex Arch. Collections* 127 (1989), 123–31.

17. Houghton, John. 'Lewes during the fifteenth century', *Sussex Arch. Collections* 127 (1989), 256–57.

18. Hughes, M. 'Hampshire castles and the landscape, 1066–1216', *Landscape History* 11 (1989), 27–60.

19. James, Thomas B. *The palaces of medieval England, c.1050–1550: royalty, nobility, the episcopate and their residences from Edward the Confessor to Henry VIII.* London; Seaby; 1989. Pp 192.

20. Jones, M.J. 'Thirteenth-century gardens in Carisbrooke Castle', *P. of the Isle of Wight Natural History and Arch. Soc.* 9 (1989), 135–36.

21. Laxton, R.R.; Litton, C.D. 'Construction of a Kent master dendrochronological sequence for oak, AD 1158 to 1540', *Medieval Archaeology* 33 (1989), 90–98.

22. Leech, Roger H. 'Aspects of the medieval defences of Bristol: the town wall, the castle barbican and the jewry', Bc142, 235–50.

23. Liddell, William. 'The bounds of the forest of Essex', Bc65, 109–14.

24. Martin, David. 'Three moated sites in north-east Sussex, part 1: Glottenham', *Sussex Arch. Collections* 127 (1989), 89–122.

25. Martin, Janet D. 'St Michael's church and parish, Leicester', *Leicester-shire Arch. and Historical Soc. T.* 64 (1990), 21–25.

26. Munby, Julian. 'Christ Church, Priory House: discoveries in St Frideswide's dormitory', Bc66, 185–93.

27. Royle, Edward (ed.). *1190–1990, Clifford's Tower Commemoration: a programme and handbook . . . in solemn commemoration of the 800th anniversary of the massacre in York Castle.* York; the 1190 Clifford's Tower 1990 Commemoration Committee; 1990. Pp 132.

28. Samuel, Mark. 'The fifteenth-century garner at Leadenhall, London', *Antiquaries J.* 69 (1989), 119–53.

29. Slater, Terry R. 'English medieval new towns with composite plans: evidence from the midlands', Bc26, 60–82.

30. Sturdy, David. 'Excavations in the Latin Chapel and outside the east end of Oxford Cathedral, winter 1962/3', Bc66, 75–102.

31. Swan, Vivien G.; Mackay, Donnie A. 'Roxby Hill, Thornton Dale: the lost village of Roxby?', Bc142, 183–95.

32. Tatton-Brown, T.W.T. 'Building stone in Canterbury, c.1070–1525', Bc135, 70–82.

33. Taylor, Christopher C. 'Spaldwick, Cambridgeshire', *Cambridge Antiq. Soc. P.* 78 (1990 for 1989), 71–75.
34. Ward, Simon. *Excavations at Chester: the lesser mediaeval religious houses—sites investigated, 1964–1983*. Chester; Chester City Council (Grosvenor Museum archaeological reports no. 6); 1990. Pp xiv, 294.
35. Woodward, Donald. 'The accounts of the building of Trinity House, Hull, 1465–1476', *Yorkshire Arch. J.* 62 (1990), 153–70.
36. Wooldridge, Kevin. '49–52 St John's Square, Clerkenwell, London EC1. Excavation and recording of the standing building' [within the precincts of St John's priory], *London & Middlesex Arch. Soc. T.* 38 (1987), 131–50.

# F. ENGLAND AND WALES 1500–1714

*See also* Aa11,78,117,122,b5–6,8,c11,18,34,51,70,87–88; Bc17–18,33–34, 36,62,82,91,101,130,138,146–147,150,d4;    Eg3,i48,j26,39,k19;    Ga3,13, e22,i81; Kh2.

(a) *General*

1. Archer, Ian; *et al.* (ed.). *Hugh Alley's caveat. The markets of London in 1598: Folger MS V. a. 318.* London; London Topographical Soc. vol. 137; 1988. Pp 105.
2. Bershadsky, Edith. 'Controlling the terms of debate: John Selden and the tithes controversy', Bc149, 187–220.
3. Carswell, John. *The porcupine: the life of Algernon Sidney.* London; Murray; 1989. Pp xiii, 274.
4. Chambers, D.S. 'A Mantuan in London in 1557: further research on Annibale Litolfi', Bc129, 73–108.
5. Childs, John (ed.). 'Lord Cutts's letters, 1695', Bc108, 371–414.
6. Daultrey, S. 'The weather of north-west Europe during the summer and autumn of 1588', Bc130, 113–42.
7. Gray, Charles. 'Category confusion as a confused category', Bc149, 221–36.
8. Kelley, Donald R. '*Jurisconsultus perfectus*: the lawyer as Renaissance man', Bc149, 143–70.
9. Kipling, Gordon Lee (ed.). *The receyt of the Ladie Kateryne.* Oxford; Early English Text Soc. (Original ser. 296); 1990. Pp 200.
10. Lightbown, Ronald W. 'The Protestant confessor, or the tragic history of Mr Molle', Bc129, 239–56.
11. Mendle, Michael; 'The Thomason collection: a reply to Stephen J. Greenberg' [followed by 'Rebuttal to Michael Mendle' by S.J. Greenberg], *Albion* 22 (1990), 85–98.
12. Morrill, John. 'Introduction' [Oliver Cromwell], Bc33, 1–18.
13. Morrill, John. 'Textualizing and contextualizing Cromwell' [review article], *Historical J.* 33 (1990), 629–39.

14. Mosler, D.F. 'The English revolution: an historiographical impasse?', *Australian J. of Politics & History* 35 (1989), 174–84.
15. Mueller, Janet. 'A Tudor queen finds voice: Katherine Parr's *Lamentation of a sinner*', Bc150, 15–47.
16. Owen, G. Dyfnallt (ed.). *The manuscripts of the marquess of Downshire, vol. 5: the papers of William Trumbull, September 1614–August 1616*. London; HMSO; 1989. Pp xix, 663.
17. Pettitt, Elizabeth L. (ed.). *Gresford parish registers, vol. 1: 1660–1714*. Wrexham; Clwyd Family History Soc.; 1988. Pp xxviii, 95.
18. Pound, John F. *Tudor and Stuart Norwich*. Chichester; Phillimore; 1988. Pp xii, 196.
19. Prior, Mary. 'Margerie Bonner: a waiting gentlewoman of seventeenth-century Wroxton', *Oxfordshire Local History* 2 (1989) 4–10.
20. Routh, Charles R.N. *Who's who in Tudor England*. London; Shepheard-Walwyn; 1989. Pp xiii, 476.
21. Stagl, J. 'The methodising of travel in the sixteenth century: a tale of three cities', *History & Anthropology* 4 (1989), 303–38.
22. Szechi, Daniel. 'Mythistory versus history: the fading of the revolution of 1688', *Historical J.* 33 (1990), 143–53.
23. White, Eileen. *Elizabethan York*. York; Yorkshire Architectural & Arch. Soc.; 1989. Pp 32.

## (b) *Politics*

1. Adams, Simon. 'England under the Tudors', *Historical J.* 33 (1990), 677–81.
2. Adamson, J.S.A. 'Oliver Cromwell and the Long Parliament', Bc33, 49–92.
3. Adamson, J.S.A. 'The baronial context of the English Civil War', *T. of the Royal Historical Soc.* 5th ser. 40 (1990), 93–120.
4. Allen, D.F. 'Attempts to revive the Order of Malta in Stuart England', *Historical J.* 33 (1990), 939–52.
5. Alsop, J.D. 'Reinterpreting the Elizabethan Commons: the parliamentary session of 1566', *J. of British Studies* 29 (1990), 216–40.
6. Anderson, Peter. 'The Armada and the Northern Isles', *Northern Studies* 25 (1988), 42–57.
7. Asch, Ronald G. 'Die englische Herrschaft in Irland und die Krise der Stuart-Monarchie im 17. Jahrhundert' [The English nobility in Ireland and the crisis of the Stuart monarchy in the seventeenth century], *Historisches Jahrbuch* 110 (1990), 370–408.
8. Aubrey, Philip. *Mr Secretary Thurloe: Cromwell's Secretary of State, 1652–1660*. London; Athlone; 1990. Pp xiii, 252.
9. Barber, Sarah. 'The engagement for the council of state and the establishment of the Commonwealth government', *Historical Research* 63 (1990), 44–57.
10. Black, Jeremy. 'England, France and the Glorious revolution', *France et Grand Bretagne de la chute de Charles Ier à celle de Jacques II* ed. C. Smith and E. Dubois (Norwich, 1990), 47–54.

11. Bordes, Helene. 'Les personnages de la famille royale Britannique d'apres *l'année sainte*', Bc138, 77–89.
12. Brigden, Susan (ed.). 'The letters of Richard Scudamore to Sir Philip Hoby, September 1549-March 1555', Bc108, 67–148.
13. Carruthers, Bruce G. 'Politics, popery, and property: a comment on North and Weingast', *J. of Economic History* 50 (1990), 693–98.
14. Cogswell, Thomas. 'A low road to extinction? Supply and redress of grievances in the parliaments of the 1620s', *Historical J.* 33 (1990), 283–303.
15. Cogswell, Thomas. 'The politics of propaganda: Charles I and the people in the 1620s', *J. of British Studies* 29 (1990), 187–215.
16. Cope, Esther S. 'The bishops and parliamentary politics in early Stuart England', *Parliamentary History* 9 (1990), 1–13.
17. Cromartie, Ian D.T. 'The printing of parliamentary speeches, November 1640–July 1642', *Historical J.* 33 (1990), 23–44.
18. Cust, Richard. 'Charles I and a draft declaration for the 1628 parliament', *Historical Research* 63 (1990), 143–61.
19. Davis, J.C. 'Puritanism and revolution: themes, categories, methods and conclusions', *Historical J.* 33 (1990), 693–703.
20. De Krey, Gary S. 'London radicals and revolutionary politics, 1675–1683', Bc82, 133–62.
21. Dean, David M. 'Parliament and locality', Bc36, 139–62.
22. Dean, David M. 'Parliament, Privy Council, and local politics in Elizabethan England: the Yarmouth-Lowestoft fishing dispute', *Albion* 22 (1990), 39–64.
23. Dean, David M.; Jones, Norman L. 'Introduction: representation, ideology and action in the Elizabethan parliaments', Bc36, 1–13.
24. Dowling, Maria (ed.). 'William Latymer's *Chronickille of Anne Bulleyne*', Bc108, 23–66.
25. Dunlop, Colin; Smyth, Charles. *Thomas Cranmer: two studies.* Doncaster; Brynmill; 1989. Pp 24.
26. Eales, Jacqueline. *Puritans and Roundheads: the Harleys of Brampton Bryan and the outbreak of the English Civil War.* Cambridge; Cambridge UP; 1989. Pp xviii, 225.
27. Edie, Carolyn A. 'The public face of royal ritual: sermons, medals, and civic ceremony in later Stuart coronations', *Huntington Library Q.* 53 (1990), 311–36.
28. Graves, M.A.R. 'Managing Elizabethan parliaments', Bc36, 37–63.
29. Greaves, Richard L. *Enemies under his feet: radicals and nonconformists in Britain, 1664–1677.* Stanford; Stanford UP; 1990. Pp xiv, 324.
30. Groenhuis, G. 'De Glorious revolution van 1688 herdacht' [The Glorious revolution of 1688 reconsidered], *Bijdragen en mededelingen betreffende de Geschiedenis der Nederlanden* 105 (1990), 394–403.
31. Gwyn, Peter. *The king's cardinal: the rise and fall of Cardinal Wolsey.* London; Barrie & Jenkins; 1990. Pp xxii, 666.
32. Harris, Barbara J. 'Women and politics in early Tudor England', *Historical J.* 33 (1990), 259–81.
33. Harris, Tim. 'Introduction: revising the Restoration', Bc82, 1–28.

34. Hartley, T.E. 'The sheriff and county elections', Bc36, 163–89.
35. Haynes, Alan. *Robert Cecil, first earl of Salisbury, 1563–1612: servant of two sovereigns.* London; Owen; 1989. Pp 240.
36. Hayton, David. 'Moral reform and country politics in the late seventeenth-century House of Commons', *Past & Present* 128 (1990), 48–91.
37. Hayton, David. 'The propaganda war', Bc125, 106–21.
38. Hibbert, Christopher. *The virgin queen: a personal history of Elizabeth I.* London; Viking; 1990. Pp 288.
39. Hill, Christopher. *A nation of change and novelty: radical politics, religion and literature in seventeenth-century England.* London; Routledge; 1990. Pp xii, 272.
40. Hirst, Derek. 'The Lord Protector, 1653–1658', Bc33, 119–48.
41. Hirst, Derek; Bowler, Shaun. 'Voting in Hertford, 1679–1721', *History & Computing* 1 (1989), 14–18.
42. Hopkins, Lisa. *Elizabeth I and her court.* London; Vision; 1990. Pp 188.
43. Hutton, Ronald. *The British republic, 1649–1660.* Basingstoke; Macmillan; 1990. Pp 160.
44. Jones, Clyve. 'The politics and the financial costs of an episcopal appointment in the early eighteenth century: the promotion of William Wake to the bishopric of Lincoln in 1705', *Huntington Library Q.* 53 (1990), 119–29.
45. Kishlansky, Mark A. 'Saye what', *Historical J.* 33 (1990), 917–37.
46. Lambert, Sheila. 'Committees, religion, and parliamentary encroachment on royal authority in early Stuart England', *English Historical R.* 105 (1990), 60–95.
47. Lee, Patricia-Ann. ' "A bodye politique to governe": Aylmer, Knox, and the debate on queenship', *The Historian* [USA] 52 (1990), 242–61.
48. Loades, David M. 'The reign of Mary Tudor: historiography and research', *Albion* 21 (1989), 547–58.
49. Lock, Geoffrey. 'The 1689 Bill of Rights', *Political Studies* 37 (1989), 540–61.
50. Lockyer, Roger. *The early Stuarts: a political history of England, 1603–1642.* London; Longman; 1989. Pp x, 411.
51. MacGregor, Arthur. 'The king's goods and the Commonwealth sale: materials and context', Bc34, 13–52.
52. May, Steven. 'Sir Philip Sidney and Queen Elizabeth', *English Manuscript Studies 1100–1700* 2 (1990), 257–67.
53. McDonald, F.M.S. 'The timing of General George Monck's march into England, 1 January, 1660', *English Historical R.* 105 (1990), 363–76.
54. McGuire, James. 'James II and Ireland, 1685–1690', Bc125, 45–57.
55. Miller, John. 'The Glorious revolution', Bc125, 29–44.
56. Moreton, Charles E. 'The Walsingham conspiracy of 1537', *Historical Research* 63 (1990), 29–43.
57. Morrill, John. 'Cromwell and his contemporaries', Bc33, 259–81.
58. Morrill, John. 'The making of Oliver Cromwell', Bc33, 19–48.
59. Nutkiewicz, Michael. 'A rapporteur of the English Civil War: the

courtly politics of James Howell (1594?–1666)', *Canadian J. of History* 25 (1990), 21–40.

60. Pearman, Robert. *The first earl Cadogan, 1672–1726.* London; Haggerston; 1988. Pp 144.

61. Perry, Maria. *The word of a prince: the life of Elizabeth I from contemporary documents.* Woodbridge; Boydell; 1990. Pp xvi, 304.

62. Popofsky, Linda S. 'The crisis over tonnage and poundage in parliament in 1629', *Past & Present* 126 (1990), 44–75.

63. Quilligan, Maureen. 'Sidney and his queen', Bc150, 171–96.

64. Rowlands, E. 'The Harleys and the battle for power in post-revolution Radnorshire', *Welsh History R.* 15 (1990–1), 21–33.

65. Russell, Conrad. 'English parliaments, 1593–1606: one epoch or two?', Bc36, 191–213.

66. Russell, Conrad. *The causes of the English Civil War: the Ford lectures delivered in the university of Oxford, 1987–1988.* Oxford; Oxford UP; 1990. Pp xvi, 236.

67. Russell, Conrad. *Unrevolutionary England, 1603–1642.* London; Hambledon; 1990. Pp xxxii, 313.

68. Russell, Elizabeth. 'Mary Tudor and Mr Jorkins', *Historical Research* 63 (1990), 263–76.

69. Schwoerer, Lois G. 'Images of Queen Mary II, 1689–1695', *Renaissance Q.* 42 (1989), 717–48.

70. Scott, Jonathan. 'England's troubles: exhuming the Popish plot', Bc82, 107–31.

71. Slavin, Arthur J. 'Thomas Cromwell and the printers: the Boston pardons', Bc147, 235–47.

72. Smith, Alan Gordon Rae (ed.). *The 'Anonymous life' of William Cecil, lord Burghley.* Lampeter; Mellen; 1990. Pp 152.

73. Spalding, Ruth (ed.). *Contemporaries of Bulstrode Whitelocke, 1605–1675: biographies, illustrated by letters and other documents.* Oxford; Oxford UP (British Academy Records of Social & Economic History ns); 1989. Pp xxvi, 526.

74. Spalding, Ruth (ed.). *The diary of Bulstrode Whitelocke, 1605–1675.* Oxford; Oxford UP (British Academy Records of Social & Economic History ns); 1990. Pp xvi, 893.

75. Starkey, David J. 'Castiglione at the court of Henry VIII? Was there a Renaissance court after all?', Bc147, 163–90.

76. Statt, Daniel. 'The City of London and the controversy over immigration, 1660–1722', *Historical J.* 33 (1990), 45–61.

77. Stevens, Douglas J. *War and peace in west Somerset, 1620–1670.* London; Stevens; 1988. Pp 122.

78. Stevenson, David. 'Cromwell, Scotland and Ireland', Bc33, 149–80.

79. Tennant, P.E. 'Parish and people: South Warwickshire and the Banbury area in the Civil War', *Cake & Cockhorse* 13/6 (1990), 121–52.

80. Thomas, W.S.K. *Stuart Wales: 1603–1714.* Llandysul; Gomer; 1988. Pp xxiv, 216.

81. Wootton, David. 'From rebellion to revolution: the crisis of the winter

of 1642/3 and the origins of civil war radicalism', *English Historical R.* 105 (1990), 654–69.
82. Young, Michael B. 'Charles I and the erosion of trust, 1625–1628', *Albion* 22 (1990), 217–35.

(c) *Constitution, Administration and Law*

1. Ashley, Roger. 'Getting and spending: corruption in the Elizabethan ordnance', *History Today* 40/11 (1990), 47–53.
2. Aylmer, G.E. 'Buckingham as an administrative reformer?', *English Historical R.* 105 (1990), 355–62.
3. Ball, R.M. 'Tobias Eden, change and conflict in the Exchequer Office, 1672–1698', *J. of Legal History* 11 (1990), 70–89.
4. Buck, A.R. 'The politics of land law in Tudor England, 1529–1540', *J. of Legal History* 11 (1990), 200–17.
5. Chapman, Murray L. (ed.). 'A sixteenth-century trial for felony in the court of Great Sessions for Montgomeryshire', *Montgomeryshire Collections* 78 (1990), 167–70.
6. Cockburn, James Swanston. *Calendar of assize records: Kent indictments, 1649–1659.* London; HMSO; 1989. Pp vii, 436.
7. Cornwall, Julian. 'The letter of the law: Hatfield Peverel in the lay subsidy of 1524–1525', Bc65, 143–52.
8. Elton, Sir Geoffrey R. '*Lex terrae victrix*: the triumph of parliamentary law in the sixteenth century', Bc36, 15–36.
9. Emmison, Frederick George (ed.). *Essex wills, vol. 5: the archdeaconry courts, 1583–1592.* Chelmsford; Essex Record Office (publications no. 101); 1989. Pp xviii, 401.
10. Erickson, Amy Louise. 'Common law versus common practice: the use of marriage settlements in early modern England', *Economic History R.* 2nd ser. 43 (1990), 21–39.
11. Foster, Elizabeth Read. 'Henry Elsyng, "Judicature in parliament"', *Parliamentary History* 9 (1990), 158–62.
12. Gibson, Jeremy S.W. 'The background to the surrender of Banbury's charter in 1683; and the parliamentary representation of the borough, 1660–1698', *Cake & Cockhorse* 11/7 (1990), 175–80.
13. Gray, Vera. 'A leat on Roborough Down and an early seventeenth-century tinners' dispute', *Devon Association Report and T.* 122 (1990), 71–82.
14. Helmholz, Richard H. *Roman canon law in Reformation England.* Cambridge; Cambridge UP; 1990. Pp xxiv, 209.
15. Holmes, P.J. 'The last Tudor Great Councils', *Historical J.* 33 (1990), 1–22.
16. Horden, John. 'The fate of monastic churches in Cumbria: a consideration of the position at law', Bc123, 255–66.
17. Hoyle, Richard W. ' "Vain projects": the Crown and its copyholders in the reign of James I', Bc77, 73–104.
18. Johnston, Alexandra F. 'English guilds and municipal authority', *Renaissance & Reformation* 13 (1989), 69–88.

19. Lammers, Guido. *Council und County: Untersuchungen zum elisabethanischen Privy Council und seinen Beziehungen zur Grafschaft Norfolk, 1558–1603* [Council and county: investigations into the Elizabethan Privy Council and its connections in the county of Norfolk, 1558–1603]. Frankfurt; Lang; 1988. Pp 368.
20. Lemmings, David. *Gentlemen and barristers: the Inns of Court and the English Bar, 1680–1730.* Oxford; Oxford UP; 1990. Pp xiv, 213.
21. Lockwood, H.H. 'Those greedy hunters after concealed lands', Bc65, 153–70.
22. Loncar, Kathleen. 'John Selden's *History of tithes*: a charter for the landlord', *J. of Legal History* 11 (1990), 218–38.
23. Maguire, William A. 'The land settlement' [in Ireland], Bc125, 139–56.
24. Manning, Roger B. 'Antiquarianism and the seigneurial reaction: Sir Robert and Sir Thomas Cotton and their tenants', *Historical Research* 63 (1990), 277–88.
25. Milne-Tyte, Robert. *Bloody Jeffreys: the hanging judge.* London; Deutsch; 1989. Pp 221.
26. Roberts, Peter R. 'The Welsh language, English law and Tudor legislation', *Honourable Soc. of Cymmrodorion T.* (1989), 19–75.
27. Sanderson, John. 'Charles Dallison and the rule of law', *J. of Legal History* 11 (1990), 239–49.
28. Von Friedeburg, Robert. 'Reformation of manners and the social composition of offenders in an East Anglian cloth village: Earls Colne, Essex, 1531–1642', *J. of British Studies* 29 (1990), 347–85.
29. Wunderli, Richard M. 'Evasion of the office of alderman in London, 1532–1672', *London J.* 15 (1990), 3–18.

## (d) *External Affairs*

1. Black, Jeremy. 'England, France and the Glorious revolution', Bc138, 47–54.
2. Bremer, Francis J. *Puritan crisis: New England and the English civil wars, 1630–1670.* New York; Garland; 1989. Pp xx, 398.
3. Cruickshank, D.W.; Gallagher, P. 'A note on Cuellar and his letter', Bc130, 195–200.
4. Cruickshank, D.W.; Gallagher, P. (ed.). 'Francisco de Cuellar: *Carta de uno que fue en la Armada de Ingalaterra y cuenta la jornada* [Letter of one who was in the Armada of England and an account of the journey], Bc130, 201–22.
5. Dubois, Elfrieda. 'Exilés et pays d'accueil, la France et l'Angleterre au dix-septième siècle', Bc138, 103–14.
6. Duchhardt, Heinz. 'Die Glorious revolution und das internationale System' [The Glorious revolution and the international system], *Francia* 16/2 (1989), 29–37.
7. Erpenbeck, Dirk. 'Die Englander in Narva zu schwedischen Zeit' [The English in Narva during the Swedish period], *Zeitschrift für Ostforschung* 38 (1989), 481–97.
8. Fausz, J. Frederick. 'An "abundance of blood shed on both sides":

England's first Indian war, 1609–1614', *Virginia Magazine of History & Biography* 98 (1990), 3–56.

9. Frey, Linda; Frey, Marsha. 'The bounds of immunity: the Sá case [concerning Dom Pataleone de Sá e Meneses]: politics, law, and diplomacy in Commonwealth England', *Canadian J. of History* 25 (1990), 41–60.

10. Gallagher, P.; Cruickshank, D.W. 'The Armada of 1588 reflected in serious and popular literature of the period', Bc130, 167–86.

11. Gallagher, P.; Cruickshank, D.W. (ed.). 'Francisco de Cuellar: *Letter from one who sailed . . .* ', Bc130, 223–48.

12. Gibbs, G.C. 'The European origins of the Glorious revolution', Bc125, 9–28.

13. Goyet, Therese. 'Politique et religion en Angleterre vues par Bossuet', Bc138, 55–61.

14. Israel, Jonathan I. 'The Amsterdam stock exchange and the English revolution of 1688', *Tijdschrift voor Geschiedenis* 103 (1990), 412–40.

15. Lorimer, Joyce (ed.). *English and Irish settlement on the river Amazon, 1550–1646.* London; Hakluyt Soc. 2nd ser. 171; 1989. Pp xxvi, 499.

16. Lovejoy, David. 'The first American revolution, 1689', Bc4, 22–32.

17. MacCaffrey, Wallace. 'Parliament and foreign policy', Bc36, 65–90.

18. Massarella, Derek. *A world elsewhere: Europe's encounter with Japan in the sixteenth and seventeenth centuries.* London; Yale UP; 1990. Pp xiii, 442.

19. McBride, Robert. 'Introduction' [France et Grande-Bretagne], Bc138, 9–17.

20. Rodger, N.A.M. 'The British view of the functioning of the Anglo-Dutch alliance, 1688–1795', Bc83, 12–32.

21. Scott, Hamish M. *British foreign policy in the age of the American revolution.* Oxford; Oxford UP; 1990. Pp xiv, 378.

22. Shaw, L.M.E. *Trade, Inquisition, and the English nation in Portugal, 1650–1690.* Manchester; Carcanet; 1989. Pp x, 230.

23. Sher, Richard B. '1688 and 1788: William Robertson on revolution in Britain and France', Bc4, 98–109.

24. Sturdy, David J. 'Le ménage à trois: les relations entre l'Irlande, l'Angleterre et la France (1660–1690)', Bc138, 35–45.

25. Thistlethwaite, Frank. *Dorset pilgrims: the story of west country pilgrims who went to New England in the early seventeenth century.* London; Barrie & Jenkins; 1989. Pp ix, 294.

26. van der Cruysse, Dirk. 'Entre les Stuarts, les Orange et les Hanovre: Madame Palatine et l'Angleterre', Bc138, 23–33.

27. Wernham, Richard Bruce (ed.). *List and analysis of state papers preserved in the Public Record Office. Foreign ser. Elizabeth I, vol. 5: July 1593–December 1594.* London; HMSO; 1989. Pp viii, 635.

(e) *Religion*

1. Abbott, William M. 'James Ussher and "Ussherian" episcopacy, 1640–1656: the primate and his "Reduction" manuscript', *Albion* 22 (1990), 237–59.

2. Acheson, Robert J. *Radical Puritans in England, 1550–1660.* London; Longman; 1990. Pp viii, 112.

3. Adams, Michael. 'Peter Chamberlen's *Case of conscience*', *Huntington Library Q.* 53 (1990), 281–309.

4. Adams, Simon. 'A Godly peer? Leicester and the Puritans', *History Today* 40/1 (1990), 14–19.

5. Allison, Antony F. 'Richard Smith's Gallican backers and Jesuit opponents, part III: the continuation of the controversy, 1631–*c*.1643', *Recusant History* 20 (1990), 164–206.

6. Alsop, J.D. 'Revolutionary Puritanism in the parishes? The case of St Olave, Old Jewry', *London J.* 15 (1990), 29–37.

7. Anderson, P.J. 'A fifth monarchist appeal and the response of an independent church at Canterbury, 1653', *Baptist Q.* 33 (1989), 72–80.

8. Ashton, R. 'Displaced Protestants', *Seventeenth-Century French Studies* 11 (1989), 163–68.

9. Aston, Margaret. 'Iconoclasm at Rickmansworth, 1522: troubles of churchwardens', *J. of Ecclesiastical History* 40 (1989), 524–52.

10. Atkinson, David W. ' "Who cares how Noah got them all in": the religious views of Sir Thomas Browne', *Anglican & Episcopal History* 59 (1990), 31–48.

11. Barry, Jonathan. 'The politics of religion in Restoration Bristol', Bc82, 163–89.

12. Bernard, G.W. 'The Church of England, *c*.1529–*c*.1642', *History* 75 (1990). 181–206.

13. Blom, J.M. 'The adventures of an angel-guardian in seventeenth-century England' [Jeremias Druxelius's *The Angel-guardian's clock*], *Recusant History* 20 (1990), 48–57.

14. Bossy, John. 'The Society of Jesus in the wars of religion', Bc123, 229–44.

15. Bradshaw, Brendan. 'Bishop John Fisher, 1469–1535: the man and his work', Bc62, 1–24.

16. Brooke, Christopher N.L. 'Fisher's career and itinerary, *c*.1469–1535', Bc62, 235–49.

17. Brooke, Christopher N.L. 'The university chancellor' [John Fisher], Bc62, 47–66.

18. Brooks, Peter Newman. *Cranmer in context.* Cambridge; Lutterworth; 1989. Pp x, 134.

19. Brownlow, F.W. 'John Shakespeare's recusancy: new light on an old document', *Shakespeare Q.* 40 (1989), 186–91.

20. Chadwick, Henry. 'Royal ecclesiastical supremacy', Bc62, 169–203.

21. Clark, Stuart. 'Protestant demonology: sin, superstition, and society, *c*.1520–*c*.1630', Bc105, 45–81.

22. Collett, Barry. 'The civil servant and monastic reform: Richard Fox's translation of the Benedictine Rule for women, 1517', Bc123, 211–28.

23. Connolly, S.J. 'The penal laws', Bc125, 157–72.

24. Cornwall, Robert D. 'The search for the primitive Church: the use of early Church Fathers in the High Church Anglican tradition', *Anglican & Episcopal History* 59 (1990), 303–29.

25. Coster, William. 'Purity, profanity, and Puritanism: the churching of women, 1500–1700', Bc128, 377–87.
26. Cross, Claire. 'A metamorphosis of ministry: former Yorkshire monks and friars in the sixteenth-century English Protestant church', *J. of the United Reformed Church Historical Soc.* 4 (1989), 289–304.
27. Cross, Claire. 'Community solidarity among Yorkshire religious after the Dissolution', Bc123, 245–54.
28. Cross, Claire. 'The religious life of women in sixteenth-century Yorkshire', Bc128, 307–24.
29. Crouzet, F.M. 'Walloons, Huguenots and the Bank of England', *Huguenot Soc. P.* 25 (1990), 167–78.
30. Daniell, David. 'The authorised version of the Bible', Bc91, 40–51.
31. Davies, Ceri. 'The 1588 translation of the Bible and the world of Renaissance learning', *Ceredigion* 11 (1988–9), 1–18.
32. Davis, J.C. 'Cromwell's religion', Bc33, 181–208.
33. Disbrey, Claire. 'George Fox and some theories of innovation in religion', *Religious Studies* 25 (1989), 61–74.
34. Dottie, R.G. 'John Crosse of Liverpool and recusancy in early seventeenth-century Lancashire', *Recusant History* 20 (1990), 31–47.
35. Dzelzainis, Martin. ' "Undouted realities": Clarendon on sacrilege', *Historical J.* 33 (1990), 515–40.
36. Evans, J. Wyn. 'The Reformation and St David's cathedral', *J. of Welsh Ecclesiastical History* 7 (1990), 1–16.
37. Evans, N. 'The Holy Ghost Guild and the Beccles town land feoffees in the sixteenth and seventeenth century', *P. of the Suffolk Inst. of Arch. & History* 37 (1989), 31–44.
38. Fincham, Kenneth. *Prelate as pastor: the episcopate of James I.* Oxford; Oxford UP; 1990. Pp xvii, 360.
39. Fletcher, Anthony. 'Oliver Cromwell and the godly nation', Bc33, 209–33.
40. Goldie, Mark. 'Danby, the bishops and the Whigs', Bc82, 75–105.
41. Greatex, Joan. 'On ministering to "certayne devoute and religiouse women": Bishop Fox and the Benedictine nuns of Winchester diocese on the eve of the Dissolution', Bc128, 223–35.
42. Greaves, Richard L. 'Coventicles, sedition, and the Toleration Act of 1689', *Eighteenth-Century Life* 13 (1988), 1–13.
43. Gruffydd, R. Geraint. 'Michael Roberts o Fon a'r Beibl bach' [Michael Roberts of Anglesey and the little Bible], *Anglesey Antiquarian Soc. & Field Club T.* (1989), 25–41.
44. Guy, John A. 'Perceptions of heresy, 1200–1550', Bc147, 39–61.
45. Guy, John A. 'Thomas More and Christopher St German: the battle of the books', Bc147, 307–27.
46. Haigh, Christopher. 'The English Reformation: a premature birth, a difficult labour and a sickly child', *Historical J.* 33 (1990), 449–59.
47. Hall, David S. *Richard Robinson, 1628–1693 and the Quakers of Wensleydale.* York; Sessions; 1989. Pp 90.
48. Haydon, Colin M. 'Samuel Peploe and Catholicism in Preston, 1714', *Recusant History* 20 (1990), 76–80.

49. Holroyde, H. 'Protestantism and dissent in the parish of Halifax, 1509–1640', *Halifax Antiq. Soc. T.* (1989 for 1988), 17–40.

50. Ingle, H. Larry. 'George Fox as enthusiast: an unpublished epistle', *J. of the Friends' Historical Soc.* 55 (1989), 265–70.

51. Jansen, Paule. 'Jansenisme et Grande-Bretagne de la chute de Charles Ier à celle de Jacques II (1649–1688)', Bc138, 91–101.

52. Jones, J. Gwynfor. 'Reformation bishops of Llandaff, 1558–1601', *Morgannwg* 32 (1989), 38–69.

53. Jones, J. Gwynfor. 'The Reformation bishops of St Asaph', *J. of Welsh Ecclesiastical History* 7 (1990), 17–40.

54. Jones, J. Gwynfor. 'William Morgan, translator of the Bible and bishop of Llandaff', *Gwent Local History* 66 (1989), 37–48.

55. Jones, J. Gwynfor. *The translation of the scriptures into Welsh, 1588.* Cardiff; Collegiate Faculty of Theology; 1988. Pp 32.

56. Jones, Norman L. 'Religion in parliament', Bc36, 117–38.

57. Key, Newton E. 'Comprehension and the breakdown of consensus in Restoration Herefordshire', Bc82, 191–215.

58. Knafla, Louis A. 'Common law and custom in Tudor England', Bc149, 171–86.

59. Lake, Peter. 'Puritanism, Arminianism and a Shropshire axe-murder', *Midland History* 15 (1990), 37–64.

60. Laurence, Anne. 'A priesthood of she-believers: women and congregations in mid-seventeenth century England', Bc128, 345–63.

61. Laurence, Anne. *Parliamentary army chaplains, 1642–1651.* Woodbridge; Boydell for the Royal Historical Soc.; 1990. Pp xxii, 199.

62. MacCulloch, Diarmaid. *The later Reformation in England, 1547–1603.* Basingstoke; Macmillan; 1990. Pp 216.

63. Marc'Hadour, Germain. 'Fisher and More: a note', Bc62, 103–08.

64. Marshall, John. 'John Locke's religious, educational and moral thought' [review article], *Historical J.* 33 (1990), 993–1001.

65. Matar, N.I. 'Some notes on George Fox and Islam', *J. of the Friends' Historical Soc.* 55 (1989), 271–76.

66. Montagu, Jennifer. 'Edward Altham as a hermit', Bc129, 271–82.

67. Mueller, Janet. 'Devotion as difference: intertextuality in Queen Katherine Parr's *Prayers or Meditations* (1545)', *Huntington Library Q.* 53 (1990), 171–97.

68. Nuttall, Geoffrey F. ' "The sun-shine of liberty": the Toleration Act and the ministry', *J. of the United Reformed Church Historical Soc.* 4 (1989), 239–55.

69. Penny, D. Andrew. *Freewill or predestination: the battle over saving grace in mid-Tudor England.* Woodbridge; Boydell for the Royal Historical Soc.; 1990. Pp x, 246.

70. Redworth, Glyn. *In defence of the Church Catholic: the life of Stephen Gardiner.* Oxford; Blackwell; 1990. Pp 320.

71. Roberts, Enid Pierce. 'Gabriel Goodman [dean of Westminster] and his native homeland', *Honourable Soc. of Cymmrodorion T.* (1989), 77–104.

72. Robison, William B. 'The Reformation and local government in

England: the case of Surrey, 1529–1570', *Lamar J. of Humanities* 14 (1988), 61–84.

73. Rosenmeier, Jesper. 'John Cotton on usury', *William & Mary Q.* 3rd ser. 47 (1990), 548–65.

74. Salazar, Philippe-Joseph. 'L' *Apologie pour les Catholiques d'Angleterre* d'Antoine Arnauld: éloquence, controverse, tradition', Bc138, 115–28.

75. Scarisbrick, J.J. 'Fisher, Henry VIII and the Reformation crisis', Bc62, 155–68.

76. Scott, Geoffrey. 'A Benedictine conspirator: Henry Joseph Johnston, (*c.*1656–1723)', *Recusant History* 20 (1990), 58–75.

77. Seaward, Paul. 'Gilbert Sheldon, the London Vestries, and the defence of the Church', Bc82, 49–73.

78. Simon, Irene. 'The preacher' [Isaac Barrow], Bc17, 303–32.

79. Somerville, C.J. 'Anglican, Puritan, and sectarian in empirical perspective', *Social Science History* 13 (1989), 109–35.

80. Spinks, Brian D. 'A seventeenth-century reformed liturgy of penance and reconciliation', *Scottish J. of Theology* 42 (1989), 183–97.

81. Spurr, John. 'Schism and the Restoration church', *J. of Ecclesiastical History* 41 (1990), 408–24.

82. Thompson, Stephen. 'Parochial patronage and the episcopate, *c.*1520', Bc62, 251–52.

83. Thompson, Stephen. 'Statistics of episcopal residence, *c.*1486–1535', Bc62, 250.

84. Thompson, Stephen. 'The bishop in his diocese', Bc62, 67–80.

85. Thompson, Stephen. 'The episcopate and ordinations, *c.*1487–1546', Bc62, 253–54.

86. Tudor, Philippa. ' "All youthe to learne the Creade and tenne commaundementes": unpublished draft injunctions of Henry VIII's reign', *Historical Research* 63 (1990), 212–17.

87. Tudor, Philippa. 'Protestant books in London in Mary Tudor's reign', *London J.* 15 (1990), 19–28.

88. Wabuda, Susan. 'Shunamites and nurses of the English Reformation: the activities of Mary Glover, niece of Hugh Latimer', Bc128, 335–44.

89. Wilson, Janet. 'A catalogue of the "unlawful" books found in John Stow's study on 21 February, 1568/9', *Recusant History* 20 (1990), 1–30.

90. Wykes, David L. 'Bardon Park meeting-house: the registration of nonconformist places of worship under the Act of Toleration (1689)', *Leicestershire Arch. and Historical Soc. T.* 64 (1990), 31–34.

91. Wykes, David L. 'Religious dissent and the penal laws: an explanation of business success?', *History* 75 (1990), 39–62.

## (f) *Economic Affairs*

1. Alsop, J.D. 'Parliament and taxation', Bc36, 91–116.
2. Alsop, J.D. 'Sea surgeons, health and England's maritime expansion: the West African trade, 1553–1660', *Mariner's Mirror* 76 (1990), 215–21.
3. Benson, Joel D. *Cooperation to competition: English perspective and*

*policy on Anglo-Dutch economic relations during the reign of James I.* New York; Lang (American University Studies 9th ser. vol. 81); 1990. Pp xiv, 272.

4. Brown, Henry Phelps. 'Gregory King's notebook and the Phelps Brown-Hopkins price index', *Economic History R.* 2nd ser. 43 (1990), 99–103.

5. Coleman-Smith, Richard; Pearson, Terry. *Excavations in the Donyatt potteries.* Chichester; Phillimore; 1988. Pp 448.

6. Corfield, Penelope J.; Harte, N.B. (ed.). *London and the English economy, 1500–1700* [collected essays of F.J. Fisher]. London; Hambledon; 1989. Pp ix, 208.

7. Edwards, Peter. 'The horse trade of Shropshire in the early modern period', Bc77, 227–49.

8. Fairclough, Keith. 'A successful Elizabethan project: the River Lea improvement scheme', *J. of Transport History* 3rd ser. 11 (1990), 54–65.

9. Haselgrove, Dennis. 'The seventeenth-century "Cock Ale-House" at Temple Bar and some Fulham stoneware bottles', *London & Middlesex Arch. Soc. T.* 37 (1986), 187–219.

10. Heslip, Robert. 'Brass money', Bc125, 122–35.

11. Hey, David. 'The origins and early growth of the Hallamshire cutlery and allied trades', Bc77, 343–67.

12. Hoyle, Richard W. 'Tenure and the land market in early modern England: or a late contribution to the Brenner debate', *Economic History R.* 2nd ser. 43 (1990), 1–20.

13. Hutchings, Naomi. 'The plan of Whatborough: a study of the sixteenth-century map of enclosure', *Landscape History* 11 (1989), 83–92.

14. Jenkins, H.J.K. 'A mid-seventeenth century scheme for navigation on the river Nene', *Northamptonshire Past & Present* 8/1 (1989–90), 25–30.

15. Keirn, Tim; Melton, Frank T. 'Thomas Manley and the rate-of-interest debate, 1668–1673', *J. of British Studies* 29 (1990), 147–73.

16. Kiernan, David T. *The Derbyshire lead industry in the sixteenth century.* Chesterfield; Derbyshire Record Soc. vol. 14; 1989. Pp 288.

17. Murison, Barbara. 'Getting and spending: William Blathwayt and Dyrham Park', *History Today* 40/12 (1990), 22–28.

18. Pearsall, A.W.H. 'The Royal Navy and trade protection, 1688–1714', *Renaissance & Modern Studies* 30 (1989), 109–23.

19. Phillips, Richard. 'Grassroots change in an early modern economy: the emergence of a rural consumer society in Berkshire', *Southern History* 11 (1989), 23–39.

20. Power, Michael J. 'The East London working community in the seventeenth century', Bc27, 103–20.

21. Robertson, Mary L. 'Profit and purpose in the development of Thomas Cromwell's landed estates', *J. of British Studies* 29 (1990), 317–46.

22. Rothstein, N.K. 'Canterbury and London: the silk industry in the late seventeenth century', *Textile History* 20 (1989), 33–47.

23. Samuel, Edgar. 'The readmission of the Jews to England in 1656, in the context of English economic policy', *Jewish Historical Studies* 31 (1988–90), 153–69.

24. Simpson, Murray C.T. 'Some aspects of book purchasing in Restoration Scotland: two letters from James Fall to the earl of Tweeddale, May 1678', *Edinburgh Bibliographical Soc. T.* 6/1 (1990), 2–9.
25. Steensgaard, Niels. 'The growth and composition of the long-distance trade of England and the Dutch Republic before 1750', Bc14, 102–52.
26. Thompson, R.H.; Gyford, Janet. 'The Witham hoard of seventeenth-century tokens and George Robinson the issuer', *Essex Archaeology & History* 3rd ser. 20 (1989), 133–42.

## (g) Social History (General)

1. Atkinson, Colin B.; Stoneman, William P. ' "These griping greefes and pinching pangs": attitudes to childbirth in Thomas Bentley's *The monument of matrones* (1582)', *Sixteenth Century J.* 21 (1990), 193–203.
2. Barry, Jonathan (ed.). *The Tudor and Stuart town: a reader in English urban history, 1530–1688* [reprints with introduction]. Harlow; Longman; 1990. Pp ix, 340.
3. Bedells, John. 'The gentry of Huntingdonshire', *Local Population Studies* 44 (1990), 30–40.
4. Beier, A.L. ' "Utter strangers to industry, morality and religion": John Locke on the poor', *Eighteenth-Century Life* 13 (1988), 28–41.
5. Boulton, Jeremy. 'London widowhood revisited: the decline of female remarriage in the seventeenth and early eighteenth centuries', *Continuity & Change* 5 (1990), 323–55.
6. Bray, Alan. 'Homosexuality and the signs of male friendship in Elizabethan England', *History Workshop J.* 29 (1990), 1–19.
7. Broce, Gerald; Wunderli, Richard M. 'The funeral of Henry Percy, sixth earl of Northumberland', *Albion* 22 (1990), 199–215.
8. Brown, Keith M. 'Gentlemen and thugs in seventeenth-century Britain', *History Today* 40/10 (1990), 27–32.
9. Burnett, Mark Thornton. 'Masters and servants in moral and religious treatises, *c.*1580–*c.*1642', Bc61, 48–75.
10. Carlson, Eric Josef. 'Marriage reform and the Elizabethan High Commission', *Sixteenth Century J.* 21 (1990), 437–51.
11. Colman, Sylvia. 'Base-cruck usages in Suffolk', *Vernacular Architecture* 21 (1990), 10–15.
12. Cook, Harold J. 'Policing the health of London: the College of Physicians and the early Stuart monarchy', *Social History of Medicine* 2 (1989), 1–33.
13. Corkery, John Martin. 'Attitudes to naming practices by the Church in England during the sixteenth and seventeenth centuries', *Genealogists' Magazine* 23 (1990), 292–97.
14. Crawford, Patricia. 'The construction and experience of maternity in seventeenth-century England', Bc44, 3–38.
15. Cressy, David. 'Death and the social order: the funerary preferences of Elizabethan gentlemen', *Continuity & Change* 5 (1990), 99–119.
16. Cressy, David. 'The Protestant calendar and the vocabulary of celebration in early modern England', *J. of British Studies* 29 (1990), 31–52.

17. Cumming, Valerie. ' "Great vanity and excesse in Apparell". Some clothing and furs of Tudor and Stuart royalty', Bc34, 322–50.

18. Day, J.F.R. 'Primers of honour: heraldry, heraldry books, and English renaissance literature', *Sixteenth Century J.* 21 (1990), 93–103.

19. Dils, Joan A. 'Epidemics, mortality and the Civil War in Berkshire, 1642–1646', *Southern History* 11 (1989), 40–52.

20. Dobson, M.J. 'Mortality gradients and disease exchanges: comparisons between old England and colonial America', *Social History of Medicine* 2 (1989), 259–97.

21. Down, T.; Carter, Roger W. 'Tatworth Middle Field', *Somerset Archaeology & Natural History* 133 (1990 for 1989), 103–24.

22. Eales, Jacqueline. 'Samuel Clarke and the "lives" of godly women in seventeenth-century England', Bc128, 365–76.

23. Faraday, M.A. 'The Radnorshire hearth tax return of 1670, part 1', *T. of the Radnorshire Soc.* 59 (1989), 29–58.

24. Fitzmaurice, James. 'Fancy and the family: self-characterizations of Margaret Cavendish', *Huntington Library Q.* 53 (1990), 198–209.

25. Glanville, Philippa. 'The City of London' [seventeenth century], Bc91, 164–77.

26. Gomme, Andor. 'Architecture' [seventeenth century], Bc91, 52–103.

27. Gomme, Andor. 'Belton House, Grantham', Bc91, 222–33.

28. Grell, Ole Peter. 'Plague in Elizabethan and Stuart London: the Dutch response', *Medical History* 34 (1990), 424–39.

29. Guy, John R. 'The shadow of the fever van', Bc126, 39–49.

30. Heal, Felicity. *Hospitality in early modern England.* Oxford; Oxford UP; 1990. Pp x, 452.

31. Hembry, Phyllis M. *The English spa, 1560–1815: a social history.* London; Athlone; 1990. Pp xiv, 401.

32. Howard, Maurice. *The early Tudor country house.* London; Philip; 1987. Pp 256.

33. James, Susan E. 'A Tudor divorce: the marital history of William Parr, marquess of Northampton', *T. of the Cumberland & Westmorland Antiq. & Arch. Soc.* 90 (1990), 199–204.

34. Kunze, Bonnelyn Young. ' "Poore and in necessity": Margaret Fell and Quaker female philanthropy in northwest England in the late seventeenth century', *Albion* 21 (1989), 559–80.

35. Lane, Joan. 'Provincial medical apprentices and masters in early modern England', *Eighteenth-Century Life* 13 (1988), 14–27.

36. Large, Peter. 'Rural society and agricultural change: Ombersley, 1580–1700', Bc77, 105–37.

37. Laurence, Anne. 'Women's psychological disorders in seventeenth-century Britain', Bc2, 203–20.

38. Llewellyn, Nigel. 'Claims to status through visual codes: heraldry on post-Reformation funeral monuments', Bc101, 145–60.

39. MacDonald, Michael. *Witchcraft and hysteria in Elizabethan London: Edward Jorden and the Mary Glover case.* London; Routledge; 1990. Pp 368.

40. MacDonald, Michael; Murphy, Terence R. *Sleepless souls: suicide in early modern England.* Oxford; Oxford UP; 1990. Pp xvi, 384.

41. MacGregor, Arthur. 'The household below stairs: officers and equipment of the Stuart court', Bc34, 367–86.
42. MacGregor, Arthur. ' "The king's disport": sport, games and pastimes of the early Stuarts', Bc34, 403–21.
43. Mayhew, Graham. 'Order, disorder and popular protest in early modern Rye', *Sussex Arch. Collections* 127 (1989), 167–87.
44. Morgan, Roger. 'Timber tennis courts of the sixteenth century', *International J. of the History of Sport* 6 (1989), 378–88.
45. Muchembled, Robert. 'Satanic myths and cultural reality', Bc105, 139–60.
46. Mulligan, Lotte; Richards, Judith. 'A "radical" problem: the poor and the English reformers in the mid-seventeenth century', *J. of British Studies* 29 (1990), 118–46.
47. Murphy, Kenneth; *et al.* 'Analyses of a cesspit fill from the Tudor merchant's house, Tenby, Dyfed', *B. of the Board of Celtic Studies* 36 (1989), 246–62.
48. Newall, Fiona. 'Wet nursing and child care in Aldenham, Hertfordshire, 1595–1726: some evidence on the circumstances and effects of seventeenth-century child rearing practices', Bc44, 122–38.
49. Newman, Christine M. 'The Reformation and Elizabeth Bowes: a study of a sixteenth-century northern gentlewoman', Bc128, 325–33.
50. Pollock, Linda A. 'Embarking on a rough passage: the experience of pregnancy in early modern society', Bc44, 39–67.
51. Prior, Mary. 'Wives and wills, 1558–1700', Bc77, 201–25.
52. Prior, Roger. 'A second Jewish community in Tudor London', *Jewish Historical Studies* 31 (1988–90), 137–52.
53. Raftis, J. Ambrose. *Early Tudor Godmanchester: survivals and new arrivals*. London; Pontifical Inst. of Medieval Studies; 1990. Pp xiv, 466.
54. Riley, James C. 'The sickness experience of the Josselins' children', *J. of Family History* 14 (1989), 347–63.
55. Roberts, Michael. 'Women and work in sixteenth-century English towns', Bc27, 86–102.
56. Robertson, J.C. 'Counting London's horn cores: sampling what?', *Post-Medieval Archaeology* 23 (1989), 1–11.
57. Robson, Ralph. *The rise and fall of English Highland clans: Tudor responses to a medieval problem*. Edinburgh; Donald; 1989. Pp viii, 245.
58. Rose, Craig. 'London's charity schools, 1690–1730', *History Today* 40/3 (1990), 17–23.
59. Rowland, Robert. ' "Fantasticall and devilishe persons": European witch-beliefs in comparative perspective', Bc105, 161–90.
60. Runbini, Dennis. 'Sexuality and Augustan England: sodomy, politics, élite circles and society', *J. of Homosexuality* 16 (1988), 349–81.
61. Schnucker, Robert V. 'Puritan attitudes towards childhood discipline, 1560–1634', Bc44, 108–21.
62. Southgate, B.C. ' "Removing epidemick ignorance": an attempt to promote popular learning in late seventeenth-century England?', *History of European Ideas* 11 (1989), 645–51.

63. Taylor, David C. 'Old Mistral, Cobham: a sixteenth-century warrener's house identified', *Surrey Arch. Collections* 79 (1989), 117–24.

64. Thick, Malcolm. 'Root crops and the feeding of London's poor in the late sixteenth and early seventeenth centuries', Bc77, 279–96.

65. Thirsk, Joan. 'The fashioning of the Tudor-Stuart gentry', *B. of the John Rylands University Library of Manchester* 72/1 (1990), 69–85.

66. Thurley, Simon J. 'The sixteenth-century kitchens at Hampton Court', *J. of the British Arch. Association* 143 (1990), 1–28.

67. Tittler, Robert. ' "The Tudor revolution in government" and the English country town', *Locus* 2 (1990), 145–52.

68. Underwood, Malcolm. 'John Fisher and the promotion of learning', Bc62, 25–46.

69. Veevers, Erica. *Images of love and religion: Queen Henrietta Maria and court entertainments.* Cambridge; Cambridge UP; 1989. Pp xii, 244.

70. Wall, Alison. 'Elizabethan precept and feminine practice: the Thynne family of Longleat', *History* 75 (1990), 23–38.

71. Warne, Heather. 'Stanmer: a restructured settlement', *Sussex Arch. Collections* 127 (1989), 189–210.

72. Webster, W.F. (ed.). *Nottinghamshire hearth tax, 1664, 1674.* Nottingham; Thoroton Soc. (Record ser. 37); 1988. Pp lxii, 183.

73. Whittet, T. Douglas. 'Welsh apothecaries' and barber-surgeons' tokens and their issuers', *Archaeologia Cambrensis* 138 (1990 for 1989), 99–109.

## (h) *Social Structure and Population*

1. Anon. *Registers of the church of Holy Trinity, Coventry (War): baptisms, 1561–1653.* Birmingham; Birmingham & Midland Soc. for Genealogy & Heraldry; 1989. Pp 177.

2. Clark, G. 'London nurse children: a source of female employment in the rural domestic economy between 1540 and 1750', *Genealogists' Magazine* 23 (1989), 91–101.

3. Clark, G. 'London's first evacuees: a population study of nurse children', *Local Historian* 19 (1989), 100–06.

4. Hollinshead, J.E. 'The gentry of south-west Lancashire in the later sixteenth century', *Northern History* 26 (1990), 82–102.

5. Hulton, Mary. *Ten Tudor families: Coventrian wills and inventories.* Coventry; Coventry Branch of the Historical Association (Coventry and Warwickshire pamphlet no. 13.); 1987. Pp 106.

6. Jenkins, David. 'The demography of late Stuart Montgomeryshire, c.1660–1720', *Montgomeryshire Collections* 78 (1990), 73–113.

7. Lee, Ross. *Law and local society in the time of Charles I: Bedfordshire and the Civil War.* Bedford; Bedfordshire Historical Record Soc. vol. 65; 1986. Pp 164.

8. Pettegree, Andrew. ' "Thirty years on": progress towards integration amongst the immigrant population of Elizabethan London', Bc77, 297–312.

9. Ward, Jennifer C. 'Wealth and family in early sixteenth-century Colchester', *Essex Archaeology & History* 3rd ser. 21 (1990), 110–17.

(i) *Naval and Military*

1. Adams, Simon. 'New light on the "reformation" of John Hawkins: the Ellesmere naval survey of January, 1584', *English Historical R.* 105 (1990), 96–111.
2. Anon. *The siege of Bradford: an account of Bradford in the Civil War, together with the text of 'The rider of the white horse', a rare pamphlet of 1643.* Bradford; Bradford Libraries & Information Service; 1989. Pp 43.
3. Awty, Brian G. 'Parson Levett and English cannon founding', *Sussex Arch. Collections* 127 (1989), 133–45.
4. Awty, Brian G. 'The Arcana family of Cesena as gunfounders and military engineeers', *Newcomen Soc. T.* 59 (1990 for 1987/8), 61–80.
5. Blatcher, Margaret. 'Chatham dockyard and a little-known shipwright, Matthew Baker (1530–1613)', *Archaeologia Cantiana* 107 (1990 for 1989), 155–72.
6. Calvar, J. 'The *Nueva coleccion documental de las hostilidades entre Espana e Inglaterra (1568–1604)*' [The new documentary collection on the hostilities between Spain and England, 1568–1604], Bc130, 187–94.
7. Childs, John (ed.). 'Captain Henry Herbert's narrative of his journey through France with his regiment, 1671–1673. And: ane account of our regements marches from the winter quarters to ther entrance in France', Bc108, 271–370.
8. Cook, Harold J. 'Practical medicine and the British armed forces after the "Glorious revolution" ', *Medical History* 34 (1990), 1–26.
9. Furgol, Edward M. *A regimental history of the covenanting armies, 1639–1651.* Edinburgh; Donald; 1990. Pp xvii, 471.
10. Gilchrist, John H. 'Latitude errors and the New England voyages of [Martin] Pring and [George] Waymouth', *American Neptune* 50 (1990), 5–17.
11. Gonzalez-Arnao Conde-Luque, Mariano. 'La aventura de la Armada' [The adventure of the Armada], *Historia* 16/148 (1988), 75–88.
12. Heslinga, E.S. van Eryk. 'A competitive ally: the delicate balance of naval alliance and maritime competition between Great Britain and the Dutch Republic, 1674–1795', Bc83, 1–11.
13. Higueras, D.; San Pio, M.P. 'Irish wrecks of the great Armada: the testimony of the survivors', Bc130, 143–66.
14. Johnston, David. 'Hobbes's mortalism', *History of Political Thought* 10 (1989), 647–63.
15. Le Fevre, Peter. 'Jasper Churchill: another naval Churchill', *Mariner's Mirror* 76 (1990), 67–69.
16. Le Fevre, Peter. 'The earl of Torrington's court-martial, 10 December 1690', *Mariner's Mirror* 76 (1990), 243–49.
17. Lynch, James B. 'Edmund Custis and his "wreck-fishing" invention', *American Neptune* 50 (1990), 18–25.
18. Martin, C. 'The ships of the Spanish Armada', Bc130, 41–68.
19. Martin, Graham. 'Prince Rupert and the surgeons', *History Today* 40/12 (1990), 38–43.

20. McGurk, J.J.N. 'Casualties and welfare measures for the sick and wounded of the nine year war in Ireland, 1593–1602', *J. of the Soc. for Army Historical Research* 68 (1990), 22–35; 188–204.

21. Milford, Elizabeth. 'The navy at peace: the activities of the early Jacobean navy, 1603–1618', *Mariner's Mirror* 76 (1990), 23–36.

22. Moisan, Thomas. 'Robert Herrick's *Rex Tragicus*, and the *Troublesome Times*', *Viator* 21 (1990), 349–84.

23. Moulakis, Athanasios. 'Pride and the meaning of *Utopia*', *History of Political Thought* 11 (1990), 241–56.

24. Mulder, David. *The alchemy of revolution: Gerrard Winstanley's occultism and seventeenth-century English communism*. New York; Lang; 1990. Pp xi, 364.

25. Murtagh, Harman. 'The war in Ireland, 1689–1691', Bc125, 61–91.

26. Norman, A.V.B. 'Arms, armour and militaria', Bc34, 351–66.

27. O'Donnell, H. 'The requirements of the duke of Parma for the conquest of England', Bc130, 85–100.

28. Peachey, Stuart (ed.). *The Edgehill campaign and the letters of Nehemiah Wharton*. Leigh-on-Sea; Partizan; 1989. Pp 60.

29. Pearsall, A.W.H. 'The war at sea', Bc125, 92–105.

30. Phelan, Ivan P. 'Marlborough as logistician', *J. of the Soc. for Army Historical Research* 68 (1990), 36–48; 103–19.

31. Rodriguez-Salgado, M.J. 'The Spanish story of the 1588 Armada reassessed', *Historical J.* 33 (1990), 461–78.

32. Ryan, A.N. ' "God of his mercy keep us from sickness": disease and defeat in the age of Francis Drake', *B. of Liverpool Medical History Soc.* no. 3 (July 1990), 26–32.

33. Schokkenbroek, J.C.A. 'The role of the Dutch fleet in the conflict of 1588', Bc130, 101–12.

34. Simpson, Clive. *Town and castle: Stafford during the Civil War*. Leigh-on-Sea; Partizan; 1989. Pp 36.

35. Thompson, I.A.A. 'Spanish Armada gun policy and procurement', Bc130, 69–84.

36. Williams, J. Gwynn. 'The castles of Wales during the Civil War, 1642–1647', *Archaeologia Cambrensis* 137 (1989 for 1988), 1–26.

37. Woolrych, Austin. 'Cromwell as a soldier', Bc33, 93–118.

38. Woolrych, Austin. 'The Cromwellian Protectorate: a military dictatorship?', *History* 75 (1990), 207–31.

39. Zahedieh, Nuala. ' "A frugal, prudential and hopeful trade": privateering in Jamaica, 1655–1689', *J. of Imperial & Commonwealth History* 18 (1990), 145–68.

40. Zwitzer, H.L. 'The British and Netherlands armies in relation to the Anglo-Dutch alliance, 1688–1795', Bc83, 33–48.

## (j) *Political Thought and History of Ideas*

1. Andreadis, H. 'The Sapphic-Platonics of Katherine Philips, 1632–1664', *Signs* 15 (1989), 34–60.

2. Anglo, Sydney. 'A Machiavellian solution to the Irish problem: Richard Beacon's *Solon his follie* (1594)', Bc129, 153–64.
3. Beer, Barrett L. 'John Ponet's *Shorte Treatise of Politike Power* reassessed', *Sixteenth Century J.* 21 (1990), 373–83.
4. Behrens, Rudolf. 'John Locke et l'évolution de la rhétorique "cartésienne" à la fin du xviiè siècle', Bc138, 63–76.
5. Berkowitz, David Sandler. *John Selden's formative years: politics and society in early seventeenth-century England*. London; Golden Cockerel; 1989. Pp 376.
6. Box, Ian. *The social thought of Francis Bacon*. Lewiston (NY)/ Lampeter; Mellen; 1989. Pp 206.
7. Collins, Stephen L. *From divine cosmos to sovereign state: an intellectual history of consciousness and the idea of order in Renaissance England*. New York/Oxford; Oxford UP; 1989. Pp x, 235.
8. Condren, Conal. *George Lawson's 'Politica' and the English revolution*. Cambridge; Cambridge UP; 1990. Pp 211.
9. Conrad, F.W. 'A preservative against tyranny: Sir Thomas Elyot and the rhetoric of counsel', Bc147, 191–206.
10. Davis, J.C. 'Fear, myth and furore: reappraising the "Ranters" ', *Past & Present* 129 (1990), 79–103.
11. Dawson, Jane. 'Revolutionary conclusions: the case of the Marian exiles', *History of Political Thought* 11 (1990), 257–72.
12. Elton, Sir Geoffrey R. 'Thomas More and Thomas Cromwell', Bc147, 95–110.
13. Gallagher, P. (ed.). 'Antonio Gonzalez-Guerrero: *Carta irlandesa*' [Irish letter], Bc130, 249–75.
14. Glausser, Wayne. 'Three approaches to Locke and the slave trade', *J. of the History of Ideas* 51 (1990), 199–216.
15. Gombrich, E.H. ' "My library was dukedom large enough": Shakespeare's Prospero and Prospero Visconti of Milan', Bc129, 185–90.
16. Gray, Douglas. 'Some pre-Elizabethan examples of an Elizabethan art', Bc129, 23–36.
17. Hamowy, Ronald. 'Cato's letters, John Locke, and the republican paradigm', *History of Political Thought* 11 (1990), 273–94.
18. Harris, Tim. ' "Lives, liberties and estates": rhetorics of liberty in the reign of Charles II', Bc82, 217–41.
19. Holtgen, Karl Josef. 'An unknown manuscript translation by John Thorpe of du Cerceau's *Perspective*', Bc129, 215–28.
20. Kelley, Donald R. 'Ideas of resistance before Elizabeth' [duplicated in Bc149], Bc150, 48–76.
21. Kelley, Donald R. 'Ideas of resistance before Elizabeth' [duplicated in Bc150], Bc149, 5–28.
22. Klein, Jurgen. *Francis Bacon oder die Modernisierung Englands* [Francis Bacon or the modernization of England]. Hildesheim; Olms (Anglistische und Amerikanistische Texte und Studien, 4); 1987. Pp viii, 206.
23. Kraye, Jill; Davies, M.C. 'Erasmus and the canonization of Aristotle: the letter to John More', Bc129, 37–52.

24. Levack, Brian P. 'Law and ideology: the civil law and theories of absolutism in Elizabethan and Jacobean England', Bc150, 240–91.
25. Levack, Brian P. 'The civil law, theories of absolutism, and political conflict in late sixteenth- and early seventeenth-century England', Bc149, 29–48.
26. Lindsay, William D. 'Gerrard Winstanley's theology of creation: an approval', *Toronto J. of Theology* 4 (1988), 178–90.
27. Lowe, Ben. 'War and the commonwealth in mid-Tudor England', *Sixteenth Century J.* 21 (1990), 171–91.
28. Lurie, Raymond. 'Some ideas of the commonwealth in early Tudor England', Bc147, 293–306.
29. McCoy, Richard C. ' "The wonderful spectacle" and obscure ordo: progress of Elizabeth I's coronation', Bc149, 99–111.
30. McGrath, Elizabeth. 'Local heroes: the Scottish Humanist Parnassus for Charles I', Bc129, 257–70.
31. Michael, Emily; Michael, Fred S. 'Corporeal ideas in the seventeenth century', *J. of the History of Ideas* 50 (1989), 31–48.
32. Nelson, Richard. 'Liberalism, republicanism and the politics of therapy: John Locke's legacy of medicine and reform', *R. of Politics* 51 (1989), 29–54.
33. Porter, H.C. 'Fisher and Erasmus', Bc62, 81–101.
34. Rhodes, Dennis E. '*Il Moro*: an Italian view of Sir Thomas More', Bc129, 67–72.
35. Sacks, David Harris. 'Private profit and public good: the problem of the state in Elizabethan theory and practice', Bc149, 121–42.
36. Simmons, A. John. 'Locke's state of nature', *Political Theory* 17 (1989), 449–70.
37. Skinner, Quentin. 'Thomas Hobbes on the proper signification of liberty', *T. of the Royal Historical Soc.* 5th ser. 40 (1990), 121–51.
38. Slavin, Arthur J. 'Platonism and the problem of counsel in *Utopia*', Bc147, 207–34.
39. Sommerville, Johann. 'Oliver Cromwell and English political thought', Bc33, 234–58.
40. Spurr, John. ' "Virtue, religion and the government": the Anglican uses of providence', Bc82, 29–47.
41. Zagorin, Perez. 'Hobbes on our mind', *J. of the History of Ideas* 51 (1990), 317–35.

## (k) *Cultural and History of Science*

1. Adler, Doris. '*Pericles*: Jacobean whistling in the dark', Bc149, 49–57.
2. Ainsworth, Stewart. 'Howley Hall, West Yorkshire: field survey', Bc142, 197–209.
3. Anglo, Sydney. 'Introduction' [Chivalry], Bc101, xi–xvi.
4. Ardolino, Frank. ' "In Paris? Mass, and well remembered!": Kyd's *The Spanish Tragedy* and the English reaction to the St Bartholomew's Day massacre', *Sixteenth Century J.* 21 (1990), 401–09.
5. Baker-Smith, Dominic. ' "Inglorious glory": 1513 and the Humanist attack on chivalry', Bc101, 129–44.

6. Barker, Nicolas. 'The books of Henry Howard, [1st] earl of Northampton', *Bodleian Library Record* 13 (1990), 375–81.
7. Barker, Nicolas. 'The perils of publishing in the sixteenth century: Pietro Bizari and William Parry, two Elizabethan misfits', Bc129, 125–42.
8. Barroll, Leeds. 'Prince Ulric and the Red Bull playhouse', Bc149, 59–72.
9. Batey, Mavis; Cole, Catherine. 'The great staircase tower at Christ Church', Bc66, 211–20.
10. Baxandall, Michael. 'English *Disegno*', Bc129, 203–214.
11. Beard, Geoffrey. 'Decorative and applied arts', Bc91, 276–307.
12. Bennett, J.A. 'Magnetical philosophy and astronomy from Wilkins to Hooke', Bc18, 222–30.
13. Berry, Herbert. 'The first public playhouses, especially the Red Lion', *Shakespeare Q.* 40 (1989), 133–48.
14. Biddle, Martin. 'Wolsey's Bell-Tower', Bc66, 205–10.
15. Binns, J.W. *Intellectual culture in Elizabethan and Jacobean England: the Latin writings of the age.* Leeds; Cairns; 1990. Pp xxv, 761.
16. Binns, J.W.; Davies, H. Neville. 'Christian IV and *The Dutch Courtesan*', *Theatre Notebook* 44 (1990), 118–23.
17. Box, Ian. 'Medicine and medical imagery in Bacon's "Great Instauration"', *Historical Reflections/Reflections historiques* 16 (1989), 351–65.
18. Brackenridge, J.B. 'Newton's unpublished dynamical principles: a story in simplicity', *Annals of Science* 47 (1990), 3–31.
19. Breight, Curtis Charles. 'Caressing the great: viscount Montague's entertainment of Elizabeth at Cowdray, 1591', *Sussex Arch. Collections* 127 (1989), 147–66.
20. Bristol, Michael D. *Carnival and theatre: plebeian culture and the structure of authority in Renaissance Britain.* London; Routledge; 1990. Pp 256.
21. Burchfield, Robert. 'A profile of the grammar of three sixteenth-century lives of Sir Thomas More and of an unrelated "drab" prose work by Anthony Gilby', Bc129, 109–24.
22. Bushnell, Rebecca. 'Time and history in early English classical drama', Bc149, 73–86.
23. Canova-Green, Marie-Claude. 'Le relais français dans l'implantation de l'opéra en Angleterre (1660–1685)', Bc138, 239–48.
24. Capp, Bernard. 'John Taylor "the Water-Poet": a cultural amphibian in seventeenth-century England', *History of European Ideas* 11 (1989), 537–44.
25. Carley, James P. 'John Leland and the contents of English pre-Dissolution libraries: Lincolnshire', *T. of the Cambridge Bibliographical Soc.* 9 (1989), 330–57.
26. Carter, Jennifer. 'British universities and revolution, 1688–1718', Bc4, 8–21.
27. Clare, Janet. *'Art made tongue-tied by authority': Elizabethan and Jacobean dramatic censorship.* Manchester; Manchester UP; 1990. Pp xiii, 224.
28. Combe, Kirk. 'Clandestine protest against William III in Dryden's

translations of Juvenal and Persius', *Modern Philology* 87 (1989), 36–50.

29. Corbett, Margery. 'John Ogilby's *Africa* (London, 1670): some notes on the illustrations', *Quaerendo* 19 (1989), 299–307.

30. Corthell, Ronald J. ' "The secrecy of man". Recusant discourse and the Elizabethan subject', *English Literary Renaissance* 19 (1989), 272–90.

31. Duncan-Jones, Katherine. ' "Thy deayth my undoinge": John Langford's copy of the 1605 edition of Sidney's *Arcadia*', *Bodleian Library Record* 13 (1990), 360–64.

32. Eade, J.C. 'Looking for directions: Elias Ashmole's astrology in action', *Eighteenth-Century Life* 13 (1988), 42–52.

33. Edmond, Mary. 'Bury St Edmunds: a seventeenth-century art centre', *Walpole Soc.* 53 (1989 for 1987), 106–18.

34. Elton, Sir Geoffrey R. 'Humanism in England', Bc29, 259–78.

35. Evett, David. 'Some Elizabethan allegorical paintings: a preliminary enquiry', *J. of the Warburg & Courtauld Institutes* 52 (1989), 140–66.

36. Ewbank, Inga-Stina. 'Masques and pageants', Bc91, 104–17.

37. Feingold, Mordechai. 'Isaac Barrow: divine, scholar, mathematician', Bc17, 1–104.

38. Feingold, Mordechai. 'Isaac Barrow's library', Bc17, 333–72.

39. Fletcher, John M.; Upton, Christopher A. 'The Merton College Library roof, 1502–1503', *Library History* 8 (1989), 104–09.

40. Flower, R. 'Laurence Nowell and the discovery of England in Tudor times', Bc31, 1–28.

41. Flynn, Dennis. 'Donne and the ancient Catholic nobility', *English Literary Renaissance* 19 (1989), 305–23.

42. Gardiner, Anne Barbeau. 'John Dryden's *Love triumphant* and English hostility to foreigners, 1688–1693', *Clio* 18 (1989), 153–70.

43. Gascoigne, John. 'Isaac Barrow's academic milieu: interregnum and Restoration Cambridge', Bc17, 250–90.

44. Gascoigne, John. *Cambridge in the age of the Enlightenment: science, religion and politics from the Restoration to the French revolution.* Cambridge; Cambridge UP; 1989. Pp xii, 358.

45. Glanville, Philippa. *Silver in Tudor and early Stuart England: a social history and catalogue of the national collection, 1480–1660.* London; Victoria & Albert Museum; 1990. Pp 528.

46. Gouk, Penelope. 'Horological, mathematical and musical instruments: science and music at the court of Charles I', Bc34, 387–402.

47. Grafton, Anthony. 'Barrow as a scholar', Bc17, 291–302.

48. Gruffydd, R. Geraint. 'The Renaissance and Welsh literature', Bc75, 17–39.

49. Gunn, Steven. 'Chivalry and the politics of the early Tudor court', Bc101, 107–28.

50. Hagedorn, Suzanne C. 'Matthew Parker and Asser's *Ælfredi regis res gestae*', *Princeton University Library Chronicle* 51 (1989), 75–90.

51. Hammersmith, James P. 'The proof-reading of the Beaumont and Fletcher Folio of 1647, sections 7 and 8A-C', *Papers of the Bibliographical Soc. of America* 82 (1989), 187–99.

52. Haskell, Francis. 'Charles I's collection of pictures', Bc34, 203–31.
53. Hicks, Michael A. 'John Nettleton, Henry Savile of Banke, and the post-medieval vicissitudes of Byland Abbey library', *Northern History* 26 (1990), 212–17.
54. Hope, Charles. 'Titian, Philip II and Mary Tudor', Bc129, 53–66.
55. Hopton, Andrew (ed.). *Roger Crab: 'The English hermite' and 'Dagons-downfall'*. London; Aporia; 1989. Pp 44.
56. Howard-Hill, T.H. 'The evolution of the form of plays in English during the Renaissance', *Renaissance Q.* 43 (1990), 112–45.
57. Howarth, David. 'Charles I, sculpture and sculptors', Bc34, 73–113.
58. Hunter, Michael. 'Alchemy, magic and moralism in the thought of Robert Boyle', *British J. for the History of Science* 23 (1990), 387–410.
59. Hunter, Michael. *Establishing the new science: the experience of the early Royal Society*. Woodbridge; Boydell; 1989. Pp xiv, 382.
60. Jacques, D. ' "The chief ornament" of Gray's Inn: the walks from Bacon to Brown', *Garden History* 17 (1989), 41–67.
61. Jardine, Lisa; Grafton, Anthony. ' "Studied for action": how Gabriel Harvey read his Livy', *Past & Present* 129 (1990), 30–78.
62. Jervis, Simon. ' "Shadows, not substantial things": furniture in the Commonwealth inventories', Bc34, 277–306.
63. Jordan, Constance. '*King Lear* and the "effectual truth" ', Bc149, 87–97.
64. Kennerley, E. 'Lancaster inns and alehouses, 1600–1730', *Lancashire Local History* 5 (1989), 40–51.
65. King, Donald. 'Textile furnishings', Bc34, 307–21.
66. King, John N. 'Queen Elizabeth I: representations of the Virgin Queen', *Renaissance Q.* 43 (1990), 30–74.
67. King, John N. *Tudor royal iconography: literature and art in an age of religious crisis*. Princeton (NJ); Princeton UP; 1989. Pp xx, 286.
68. Kinnamon, Noel. 'The Sidney Psalms: the Penshurst and Tixall manuscripts', *English Manuscript Studies 1100–1700* 2 (1990), 139–61.
69. Kinney, Arthur F. 'Sir Philip Sidney and the uses of history', Bc150, 293–314.
70. Larminie, Vivienne (ed.). 'The undergraduate account book of John and Richard Newdigate, 1618–1621', Bc108, 149–270.
71. Le Fanu, William Richard. *Nehemiah Grew: a study and bibliography of his writings*. Winchester; St Paul's Bibliographies; 1990. Pp xvii, 182.
72. Levin, R. 'Women in the Renaissance theatre audience', *Shakespearian Q.* 40 (1989), 165–74.
73. Lightbown, Ronald W. 'Charles I and the art of the goldsmith', Bc34, 233–55.
74. Lightbown, Ronald W. 'Charles I and the tradition of European princely collecting', Bc34, 53–72.
75. Lightbown, Ronald W. 'The king's *regalia, insignia* and jewellery', Bc34, 257–75.
76. Lindley, Phillip. ' "Una grande opera al mio Re": gilt-bronze effigies in England from the middle ages to the Renaissance' ["A great work of art for my king"], *J. of the British Arch. Association* 143 (1990), 112–30.

77. Llewellyn, Nigel. 'Accident or design? John Gildon's funeral monuments and Italianate taste in Elizabethan England', Bc129, 143–52.
78. Loomie, Albert J. 'New light on the Spanish ambassador's purchases from Charles I's collection, 1649–1653', *J. of the Warburg & Courtauld Institutes* 52 (1989), 256–67.
79. Mahoney, Michael S. 'Barrow's mathematics: between ancients and moderns', Bc17, 179–249.
80. Manley, Lawrence. 'From matron to monster: Tudor-Stuart London and the languages of urban description', Bc150, 347–74.
81. Massing, Jean Michel. 'Veleda, Susanna, Boadicea or Dorothy: anti-quarian discussions on some sixteenth-century ornamental bricks', Bc129, 283–94.
82. McClure, Peter; Wells, Robin Headlam. 'Elizabeth I as a second Virgin Mary', *Renaissance Studies* 4 (1990), 38–70.
83. Mellers, Wilfrid. 'Music: paradise and paradox in the seventeenth century', Bc91, 178–221.
84. Mendyk, Stan A.E. *'Speculum Britanniae': regional study, antiquarianism, and science in Britain to 1700*. London; Toronto UP; 1989. Pp xv, 358.
85. Michael, Fred S.; Michael, Emily. 'The theory of ideas in Gassendi and Locke', *J. of the History of Ideas* 51 (1990), 379–99.
86. Morgan, Paul. 'A king's printer at work: two documents of Robert Barker', *Bodleian Library Record* 13 (1990), 370–74.
87. Mullaney, Steven. *The place of the stage: license, play, and power in Renaissance England*. Chicago; Chicago UP; 1988. Pp xiii, 178.
88. Mullin, David. 'The archaeology of Camp Mill [Gloucestershire]: a reassessment', *Post-Medieval Archaeology* 23 (1989), 15–20.
89. Murdoch, John. 'Painting: from Astraea to Augustus', Bc91, 234–65.
90. Murray, Hugh. 'The heraldic window at Fountains Hall', *Yorkshire Arch. J.* 62 (1990), 171–86.
91. Nelson, Alan H. (ed.) *Records of early English drama: Cambridge.* London; Toronto UP; 1989. Pp xvi, 1503.
92. Orgel, Stephen. 'Counterfeit presentments: Shakespeare's *Ekphrasis*', Bc129, 177–84.
93. Parfitt, George. 'Literature and drama' [seventeenth century], Bc91, 118–63.
94. Phillips, Henry. 'La querelle de théâtre en France et en Angleterre', Bc138, 151–61.
95. Pollard, J.G. 'England and the Italian medal', Bc129, 191–202.
96. Potter, Lois. *Secret rites and secret writing: royalist literature, 1641–1660*. Cambridge; Cambridge UP; 1989. Pp xvi, 242.
97. Raines, Robert. 'Notes on Egbert van Heemskerck and the English taste for genre', *Walpole Soc.* 53 (1989 for 1987), 119–42.
98. Rebhorn, Wayne A. 'The crisis of the aristocracy in *Julius Caesar*', *Renaissance Q.* 43 (1990), 75–111.
99. Roberts, Jane. 'The limnings, drawings and prints in Charles I's collection', Bc34, 115–29.
100. Roberts, R.J. 'New light on the career of Giacomo Castelvetro' [as bookseller in England], *Bodleian Library Record* 13 (1990), 365–69.

101. Robertson, J.C. 'Caroline culture: bridging court and country', *History* 75 (1990), 388–416.
102. Robertson, J.C. 'Furnishings seized in London, 1575', *Furniture History* 25 (1989), 36–41.
103. Rykwert, Joseph. 'The seventeenth century', Bc91, 2–38.
104. Saumarez-Smith, Charles. *The building of Castle Howard*. London; Faber & Faber; 1990. Pp 240.
105. Sessions, William Kaye. *The spread of British printing, 1557 to 1695: 'do not think that you can blind the crows'*. York; Ebor; 1988. Pp 211.
106. Shapin, Steven. 'Robert Boyle and mathematics: reality, representation, and experimental practice', *Science in Context* 2 (1988), 23–58.
107. Shapiro, Alan E. 'The *Optical Lectures* and the foundations of the theory of optical imagery', Bc17, 105–78.
108. Shilling, H. 'Politik und Gesellschaft—die Renaissance des historischen Interesses am Politischen' [Politics and society—the Renaissance of the historical interest in politics], *Bijdragen en mededelingen betreffende de Geschiedenis der Nederlanden* 104 (1989), 56–65.
109. Slights, William W.E. 'The edifying margins of renaissance English books', *Renaissance Q.* 42 (1989), 682–716.
110. Smith, H.S.A. 'A Manchester science library: Chetham's Library in 1684', *Library History* 8 (1989), 110–15.
111. Smith, Peter. 'Architecture in Wales during the Renaissance', Bc75, 101–46.
112. Stocker, Margarita; Raylor, Timothy. 'A new Marvell manuscript: Cromwellian patronage and politics', *English Literary Renaissance* 20 (1990), 106–62.
113. Strong, Roy. 'Sir Francis Carew's garden at Beddington', Bc129, 229–38.
114. Swift, Katherine. 'The French-booksellers in the Strand: Huguenots in the London book trade, 1685–1730', *Huguenot Soc. P.* 25 (1990), 123–39.
115. Thomas, James H. 'Richard Churcher (1659–1723): educational philanthrope', *Hatcher Review* 3/29 (1990), 424–36.
116. Treadwell, Michael. 'On false and misleading imprints in the London book trade, 1660–1750', Bc50, 29–46.
117. Trousdale, Marion. 'The grace of government in *The Winter's Tale*', Bc149, 113–20.
118. Walber, Karl Josef. *Charles Blount (1654–1693), Fruhaufklärer: leben und werk* [Charles Blount (1654–1693), precursor of the Enlightenment: life and work]. Bern; Lang; 1988. Pp 389.
119. Warntz, William. 'Newton, the Newtonians, and the *Geographia generalis Varenii*', *Association of American Geographers' Annual* 79 (1989), 165–91.
120. Webber, Teresa. 'Patrick Young, Salisbury Cathedral manuscripts and the Royal Collection', *English Manuscript Studies 1100–1700* 2 (1990), 283–90.
121. Welfare, Humphrey. 'John Aubrey—the first archaeological surveyor?', Bc142, 17–28.

122. White, Adam. 'Nicholas Stone and early Stuart sculpture', Bc91, 266–75.
123. White, Paul Whitfield. 'Calvinist and Puritan attitudes towards the stage in Renaissance England', *Explorations in Renaissance Culture* 14 (1988), 41–55.
124. Wilson, Curtis. 'The Newtonian achievement in astronomy', Bc18, 233–74.
125. Wilson-North, W.R. 'Formal garden earthworks at Moreton Corbet castle, Shropshire', Bc142, 225–28.
126. Woudhuysen, H.R. 'A "lost" Sidney document', *Bodleian Library Record* 13 (1990), 353–59.

# G. BRITAIN 1714–1815

*See also* Aa12,88,b30,c93; Bc13,37,95; Fb41,60,76,c20,f25,g31,58,h2,i40, k115–116; Hl25; Kh2.

## (a) *General*

1. Bidgood, Ruth. 'Thomas Price of Gwarafog and Strand House and his family', *Brycheiniog* 23 (1988–9), 49–63.
2. Black, Jeremy. 'Introduction' [British politics and society from Walpole to Pitt], Bc95, 1–28; 235–37.
3. Black, Jeremy. *Eighteenth-century Europe, 1700–1789*. Basingstoke; Macmillan; 1990. Pp 481.
4. Bradbury, David John (comp.). *Mansfield in the news, 1771–1780*. Mansfield; Wheel; 1990. Pp 48.
5. Corfield, Penelope J. 'Georgian Bath: the magical meeting place', *History Today* 40/11 (1990), 26–33.
6. Crimmins, James Edward. *Secular utilitarianism: social science and the critique of religion in the thought of Jeremy Bentham*. Oxford; Oxford UP; 1990. Pp xi, 348.
7. Drescher, Seymour. 'People and parliament: the rhetoric of the British slave trade', *J. of Interdisciplinary History* 20 (1989–90), 561–80.
8. Eley, Geoff. 'Edward Thompson, social history and political culture: the making of a working-class public, 1780–1850', Bc3, 12–49.
9. Gibson, Jeremy S.W. 'A few weeks in 1795', *Cake & Cockhorse* 11/4 (1989), 84–89.
10. Hargreaves, J.A. 'Methodism and Luddism in Yorkshire, 1812–1813', *Northern History* 26 (1990), 160–85.
11. Hellmuth, Eckhart. 'Towards a comparative study of political culture: the cases of late eighteenth-century England and Germany', Bc37, 1–38.
12. Huddart, William. *Unpathed waters: the life and times of Captain Joseph Huddart FRS, 1741–1816*. London; Quiller; 1990. Pp 250.

13. Kenyon, John P. 'Introduction' [Glorious revolution], Bc146, 1–7.
14. Lenman, Bruce P. 'Scotland and Ireland, 1742–1789', Bc95, 81–100; 254–58.
15. Lorch, Jennifer. *Mary Wollstonecraft: the making of a radical feminist.* Oxford; Berg; 1990. Pp 127.
16. MacDougall, Ian. *The prisoners at Penicuik.* Dalkeith; Midlothian District Council; 1989. Pp ii, 94.
17. Osbourne, John W.; Schweizer, Karl W. *Cobbett in his times.* London; Leicester UP; 1990. Pp 192.
18. Porter, Roy. 'English society in the eighteenth century revisited', Bc95, 29–52; 237–45.
19. Smout, T.C. 'Problems of nationalism, identity and improvement in later eighteenth-century Scotland', Bc57, 1–21.
20. Whatley, Christopher A. 'How tame were the Scottish lowlanders during the eighteenth century?', Bc55, 1–30.
21. Whyte, Ian D.; Whyte, Kathleen A. *On the trail of the Jacobites.* London; Routledge; 1990. Pp 264.
22. Wilson, Kathleen. 'Urban culture and political activism in Hanoverian England: the example of voluntary hospitals', Bc37, 165–84.

## (b) *Politics*

1. Barnes, June C.F. 'Freedom and liberty: Cumbria and the Borders during the period of the French revolution, 1789–1802', *T. of the Cumberland & Westmorland Antiq. & Arch. Soc.* 90 (1990), 253–65.
2. Baskerville, Stephen W. ' "Preferred linkage" and the analysis of voter behaviour in eighteenth-century England', *History & Computing* 1 (1989), 112–20.
3. Bass, Jeff D. 'An efficient humanitarianism: the British slave trade debates, 1791–1792', *Q. J. of Speech* 75 (1989), 152–65.
4. Black, Jeremy. 'Campaigning in Dorset in 1761', *Notes and Queries for Somerset & Dorset* 32 (1990), 850–51.
5. Black, Jeremy. 'Dr Johnson, eighteenth-century pamphleteering and the Tory view on foreign policy', *Factotum* 32 (Sept. 1990), 15–21.
6. Black, Jeremy. 'Eighteenth-century electioneering: Winchelsea in 1747', *Sussex Arch. Collections* 127 (1989), 259–60.
7. Black, Jeremy. 'Johnson's *Thoughts on the Falklands*: a Tory tract', *Literature & History* ns 1 (1990), 42–47.
8. Black, Jeremy. 'Lord Hervey's diet', *Scriblerian* 22 (1989), 86–87.
9. Black, Jeremy. 'New light on an Orkney MP of the early eighteenth century', *Historical Research* 63 (1990), 218.
10. Black, Jeremy. 'Party politics in eighteenth-century Britain', *Lamar J. of Humanities* 15 (1988), 27–38.
11. Black, Jeremy. 'Stopping the mouths of the public: the *Caledonian Mercury* and the Cromartyshire election of 1768', *Huntington library Q.* 53 (1990), 153–55.
12. Black, Jeremy. 'The British press and eighteenth-century revolution: the French case', Bc4, 110–20.

13. Black, Jeremy. 'The cost of an eighteenth-century election', *Notes and Queries for Somerset & Dorset* 32 (1990), 851–53.

14. Black, Jeremy. 'The Tucker papers', *Notes and Queries for Somerset & Dorset* 32 (1990), 817–23.

15. Black, Jeremy. *Robert Walpole and the nature of politics in early eighteenth-century Britain.* Basingstoke; Macmillan; 1990. Pp 160.

16. Butler, Mary; Todd, Janet, (ed.). *The works of Mary Wollstonecraft.* London; Pickering; 1989. 7 vols.

17. Christie, Ian R. 'The anatomy of the opposition in the parliament of 1784', *Parliamentary History* 9 (1990), 50–77.

18. Christie, Ian R. 'The changing nature of parliamentary politics, 1742–1789', Bc95, 101–122; 250–54.

19. Christie, Ian R. (ed.). 'John Robinson's "State" of the House of Commons, July 1780', Bc108, 441–98.

20. Claeys, Gregory. 'Whigs, liberals and radicals', *Historical J.* 33 (1990), 737–45.

21. Cruickshanks, Eveline. 'The revolution and the localities', Bc146, 28–43.

22. Daiches, David. '*Style periodique* and *style coupé*: Hugh Blair and the Scottish rhetoric of American Independence', Bc86, 209–26.

23. Dammers, Richard H. 'Bishop Fleetwood's *A sermon on the fast day* and the politics of *Spectator* 384', *Philological Studies* 68 (1989), 167–76.

24. Davis, Richard W. 'The politics of the confessional state, 1760–1832', *Parliamentary History* 9 (1990), 38–49.

25. Derry, John W. *Politics in the age of Fox, Pitt and Liverpool.* Basingstoke; Macmillan; 1990. Pp 216.

26. Devine, Tom M. 'The failure of radical reform in Scotland in the late eighteenth century: the social and economic context', Bc55, 51–64.

27. Dickinson, Harry T. 'Popular loyalism in Britain in the 1790s', Bc37, 503–33.

28. Dickinson, Harry T. 'Radicals and reformers in the age of Wilkes and Wyvill', Bc95, 123–146; 254–58.

29. Dinwiddy, John. 'Conceptions of revolution in the English radicalism of the 1790s', Bc37, 535–60.

30. Faller, Lincoln. 'King William, "K.J.", and James Whitney: the several lives and affiliations of a Jacobite robber', *Eighteenth-Century Life* 12 (1988), 88–104.

31. Hackmann, W. Kent. 'George Grenville and English politics in 1763', *Yale University Library Gazette* 64 (1990), 158–66.

32. Hackmann, W. Kent. 'William Beckford's profit from three Jamaican offices', *Historical Research* 63 (1990), 107–09.

33. Harris, Tim. 'London crowds and the revolution of 1688', Bc146, 44–64.

34. Hatley, Victor A. 'The headless trunk: a study in Northampton politics, 1795–1796', *Northamptonshire Past & Present* 8/2 (1990–91), 105–20.

35. Hay, Carla H. 'John Sawbridge and "popular politics" in late eighteenth-century Britain', *The Historian* [USA] 52 (1990), 551–65.

36. Haydon, Colin M. 'The Gordon riots in the English provinces', *Historical Research* 63 (1990), 354–59.
37. Hellmuth, Eckhart. ' "The palladium of all other English liberties": reflections on the liberty of the press in England during the 1760s and 1770s', Bc37, 467–501.
38. Ide, Isabel. 'Wiltshire members of parliament and their involvement with the South Sea Company', *Wiltshire Arch. & Natural History Magazine* 83 (1990), 136–46.
39. Innes, Joanna. 'Parliament and the shaping of eighteenth-century English social policy', *T. of the Royal Historical Soc.* 5th ser. 40 (1990), 63–92.
40. Jupp, Peter J. 'The landed elite and political authority in Britain, *c.*1760–1850', *J. of British Studies* 29 (1990), 53–79.
41. Lachman, David C. *The Marrow controversy, 1718–1723: an historical and theological controversy.* London; Rutherford House; 1988. Pp 508.
42. Lemmings, David. 'Lord Chancellor Cowper and the Whigs, 1714–1716', *Parliamentary History* 9 (1990), 163–74.
43. Lenman, Bruce P. 'Aristocratic "country" Whiggery in Scotland and the American revolution', Bc86, 180–92.
44. Middleton, Richard. 'The duke of Newcastle and the conduct of patronage during the Seven Years' War, 1757–1762', *British J. of Eighteenth-Century Studies* 12 (1989), 175–86.
45. Miller, John. 'James II and toleration', Bc146, 8–27.
46. Mitchell, Leslie George (ed.). *The writings and speeches of Edmund Burke, vol. 8: 1790–1794.* Oxford; Oxford UP; 1989. Pp 592.
47. Money, John. 'Freemasonry and the fabric of loyalism in Hanoverian England', Bc37, 235–71.
48. Monod, Paul. 'Theatre, Jacobitism and popular protest in London, 1689–1760', Bc146, 159–89.
49. Morrow, John. *Coleridge's political thought.* Basingstoke; Macmillan; 1990. Pp 232.
50. Perry, Keith. *British politics and the American revolution.* Basingstoke; Macmillan; 1990. Pp 192.
51. Schonhorn, Manuel. 'Defoe and James Shepheard's assassination plot of 1718: two new pamphlets', *Studies in English Literature, 1500–1900* 29 (1989), 447–62.
52. Scott-Moncrieff, Lesley (ed.). *The '45: to gather an image whole.* Edinburgh; Mercat; 1988. Pp 200.
53. Stevenson, John. 'Popular radicalism and popular protest, 1789–1815', *Britain and the French revolution, 1789–1815*, ed. Harry T. Dickinson (Basingstoke; Macmillan; 1989), pp 61–81.
54. Targett, Simon. 'A pro-government newspaper during the Whig ascendancy: Walpole's *London Journal*, 1722–1738', *Politics and the press in Hanoverian Britain*, ed. Jeremy Black (Lewiston, NY); Mellen; 1989), pp 1–32.

(c) *Constitution, Administration and Law*

1. Ball, R.M. 'The King's Remembrancer's Office in the eighteenth century', *J. of Legal History* 11 (1990), 90–113.
2. Castiglione, Dario. 'Hume's conventionalist analysis of justice', *Annali Fondazione Luigi Einaudi* 21 (1987), 139–73.
3. Christie, Ian R. (ed.). 'George III and the Southern Department: some unprinted royal correspondence', Bc108, 415–40.
4. Claeys, Gregory. 'The French revolution debate and British political thought', *History of Political Thought* 11 (1990), 59–80.
5. Jacobs, Struan. 'Bentham, science and the construction of jurisprudence', *History of European Ideas* 12 (1990), 583–94.
6. King, Peter. 'Gleaners, farmers and the failure of legal sanctions in England, 1750–1850', *Past & Present* 125 (1990), 116–50.
7. Mason, A. Stuart. *Essex on the map: the eighteenth-century land surveyors of Essex*. Chelmsford; Essex Record Office; 1990. Pp 138.
8. Schmidt, Albert J. 'The country attorney in late eighteenth-century England: Benjamin Smith of Horbling', *Law & History R.* 8 (1990), 237–71.
9. Sparrow, Elizabeth. 'The Alien Office, 1792–1806', *Historical J.* 33 (1990), 361–84.
10. Stimson, Shannon G. ' "A jury of the country": common sense philosophy and the jurisprudence of James Wilson', Bc86, 193–208.

(d) *External Affairs*

1. Bareham, Tony. ' "Paths to guide imagination's flight": some eighteenth-century poets abroad', Bc94, 247–62.
2. Bassett, David K. 'Anglo-Kedah relations, 1688–1765', *J. of the Malaysian Branch of the Royal Asiatic Soc.* 62/2 (1989), 1–17.
3. Bassett, David K. 'British "country" trade and local trade networks in the Thai and Malay states, *c.*1680–1770', *Modern Asian Studies* 23 (1989), 625–43.
4. Beasley, Jerry C. 'Smollett's novels and the wider world', Bc94, 171–84.
5. Bennett, Norman R. 'The golden age of the port wine system, 1781–1807', *International History R.* 12 (1990), 221–48.
6. Beretti, Francis. 'Regards britanniques sur la Corse et la Sardaigne (1796–1802)', *Études Corses* 16 (1988), 335–46.
7. Black, Jeremy. 'An analysis of Savoy-Piedmont in 1740', *Studi Piemontesi* 18 (1989), 229–32.
8. Black, Jeremy. 'Anglo-French relations in the age of the French revolution, 1787–1793', *Francia* 15 (1987), 407–34.
9. Black, Jeremy. 'Eighteenth-century intercepted despatches', *J. of the Soc. of Archivists* 11 (1990), 138–43.
10. Black, Jeremy. 'Florence in 1731', *Bollettino del centro interuniversitario di richerche sul viaggio in Italia* 7 (1986), 309–22.
11. Black, Jeremy. 'Foreign policy and the British state, 1742–1793', Bc95, 147–75; 258–60.

12. Black, Jeremy. 'Fragments from the Grand Tour' [letters from lord Dalrymple, 1715, and George, lord Lyttelton, 1763], *Huntington Library Q.* 53 (1990), 337–41.

13. Black, Jeremy. 'France in 1730', *Francia* 16 (1989), 39–59.

14. Black, Jeremy. 'On the "old system" and the "diplomatic revolution" of the eighteenth century', *International History R.* 12 (1990), 301–23.

15. Black, Jeremy. 'Portugal in 1760: the journal of a British tourist', *British Historical Soc. of Portugal: Annual Report and R.*, 15 (1988), 91–112.

16. Black, Jeremy. 'The British expeditionary force to Portugal in 1762', *British Historical Soc. of Portugal: Annual Report and R.* 16 (1989), 66–75.

17. Black, Jeremy. 'Tourism and cultural challenge: the changing scene of the eighteenth century', Bc94, 185–202.

18. Black, Jeremy. 'Turin in 1737', *Studi Piemontesi* 19 (1990), 487.

19. Black, Jeremy. *The rise of the European powers, 1679–1793.* London; Arnold; 1990. Pp 239.

20. Cannstein, Benno, Freiherr von. *Der Waldekkisch-Englische Subsidienvertrag von 1776: Zustandekommen, Ausgestaltung und Erfullung* [The Anglo-Waldeck subsidies treaty of 1776: its occurrence, arrangement and result]. Arlosen; Waldeckische Geschichtsverein; 1989. Pp 198.

21. Chapman, Pauline. *The French revolution: Madame Tussaud, witness extraordinary.* London; Quiller; 1989. Pp 176.

22. Childs, Virginia. *Lady Hester Stanhope: queen of the desert.* London; Weidenfeld & Nicolson; 1990. Pp 256.

23. Clark, Jennifer. 'John Bull's American connection: the allegorical interpretation of England and the Anglo-American relationship', *Huntington Library Q.* 53 (1990), 15–39.

24. Curley, Thomas M. 'Sterne's *A Sentimental Journey* and the tradition of travel literature', Bc94, 203–16.

25. Durant, Jack D. 'Sheridan and the wider world', Bc94, 263–76.

26. Fregosi, Paul. *Dreams of empire: Napoleon and the First World War, 1792–1815.* London; Hutchinson; 1989. Pp 373.

27. Gough, Hugh. 'The French revolution and Europe, 1789–1799', Bc63, 1–13.

28. Kaplan, Roger. 'The hidden war: British intelligence operations during the American revolution', *William & Mary Q.* 3rd ser. 47 (1990), 115–38.

29. Knight, Carol Lynn. *The American colonial press and the Townshend crisis, 1766–1770: a study in political imagery.* Lampeter; Mellen; 1990. Pp 296.

30. Korshin, Paul J. ' "Extensive view": Johnson and Boswell as travelers and observers', Bc94, 233–46.

31. Marshall, Peter J. 'The eighteenth-century Empire', Bc95, 177–200; 260–62.

32. Marshall, Peter J. 'The seventeenth and eighteenth centuries' [British in India], Bc68, 16–25.

33. McCaffrey, Donna T. 'Charles Townshend and plans for British East Florida', *Florida Historical Q.* 68 (1990), 324–40.

34. McVeagh, John. 'Goldsmith and nationality', Bc94, 217–32.
35. McVeagh, John (ed.). *English literature and the wider world: vol. 1, 1660–1780*. London [Entry duplicates BC 94]. Ashfield; 1990. Pp 305.
36. Renzing, Rudiger. *Pfalzer in Irland: Studien zur Geschichte deutscher Auswandererkolonien des frühen 18. Jahrhunderts* [Palatines in Ireland: studies of the history of German emigrants of the early eighteenth century]. Kaiserslautern; Institut für pfalzische Geschichte und Volkskunde; 1989. Pp. 456.
37. Sabor, Peter. ' "A safe bridge over the narrow seas": crossing the Channel with Samuel Richardson', Bc94, 159–70.
38. Sahlins, Marshall. 'Captain Cook at Hawaii', *J. of the Polynesian Society* 98 (1989), 371–423.
39. Sambrook, James. 'Thomson abroad: traversing realms unknown', Bc94, 141–58.
40. Severn, John K. 'The Wellesleys and Iberian diplomacy, 1808–1812', Bc13, 34–65.
41. Siry, Steven E. 'Anglo-American tensions and the decline of the Clintonian-Virginia alliance, 1803–1807', *Locus* 1 (1988), 11–26.
42. Thevenot-Totems, Marie-Helene. *La découverte de l'Écosse du xviiiè siècle: à travers les récits des voyageurs britanniques*. Paris; Didier; 1990. 2 vols.
43. Wood, Dennis. 'Constant in Britain, 1780–1787: a provisional chronology', *Annales Benjamin Constant* 7 (1987), 7–20.
44. Young, R.J. 'Slaves, coolies and bondsmen: a study of assisted migration in response to emerging English shipping networks in the Indian ocean, 1685–1765', Bc96, 391–402.

## (e) *Religion*

1. Barnard, Leslie W. 'Two eighteenth-century views of monasticism: Joseph Bingham and Edward Gibbon', Bc123, 283–91.
2. Barnard, Leslie W. *John Potter: an eighteenth-century archbishop*. London; Stockwell; 1989. Pp 128.
3. Black, Jeremy. 'A Worcester catastrophe in 1757', *Worcestershire Archaeology and Local History Newsletter* 40 (1988), 8–9.
4. Clifford, Alan C. *Atonement and justification: English evangelical theology, 1640–1790*. Oxford; Oxford UP; 1990. Pp 268.
5. Cray, Robert E. 'The boundaries of clerical modesty: the Reverend Alexander Campbell in the middle colonies, 1726–1734', *Anglican & Episcopal History* 59 (1990), 76–98.
6. Donovan, Robert Kent. 'The popular party of the church of Scotland and the American revolution', Bc86, 81–99.
7. Elliott, Bernard; Evans, Rupert. 'The French exiled clergy in Leicestershire from 1792', *Leicestershire Arch. and Historical Soc. T.* 64 (1990), 35–38.
8. Fitzpatrick, Martin. 'Heretical religion and radical political ideas in late eighteenth-century England', Bc37, 339–72.

9. Gilley, Sheridan. 'Catholic revival in the eighteenth century', Bc115, 99–108.

10. Gooch, Leo. 'Priests and patrons in the eighteenth century', *Recusant History* 20 (1990), 207–22.

11. Gurtler, Gernot O. 'Thomas J.F. Strickland of Sizergh (?1682–1740): the political cleric at his ecclesiastical zenith', *T. of the Cumberland & Westmorland Antiq. & Arch. Soc.* 90 (1990), 217–34.

12. Haikala, Sisko. 'Franskan vallankumous ja "brittilaiset jakobiinit" ' [The French revolution and the British Jacobins], *Historiallinen Aikakauskirja* 87 (1989), 296–310.

13. Harrison, Peter. *'Religion' and the religions in the English Enlightenment.* Cambridge; Cambridge UP; 1990. Pp 275.

14. Hempton, David. 'Religion in British society, 1740–1790', Bc95, 201–21; 262–64.

15. Jacobson, David L. 'The king's four churches: the established churches of America, England, Ireland, and Scotland in the early years of George III', *Anglican & Episcopal History* 59 (1990), 181–201.

16. Kinnear, Mary. 'The Correction Court in the diocese of Carlisle, 1704–1756', *Church History* 59 (1990), 191–206.

17. Landsman, Ned C. 'Witherspoon and the problem of provincial identity in Scottish evangelical culture', Bc86, 29–45.

18. Langford, Paul. 'The English clergy and the American revolution', Bc37, 275–307.

19. Markley, R. 'Isaac Newton's theological writings: problems and prospects', *Restoration Studies in English Literature & Culture* 13 (1989), 35–48.

20. Matar, N.I. 'The controversy over the restoration of the Jews: from 1754 until the London Society for Promoting Christianity among the Jews', *Durham University J.* 82 (1990), 29–44.

21. Maynard, W.B. 'Pluralism and non-residence in the archdeaconry of Durham, 1774–1856: the bishop and chapter as patrons', *Northern History* 26 (1990), 103–30.

22. McAllister, J. 'Colonial America, 1607–1776', *Economic History R.* 2nd ser. 42 (1989), 245–59.

23. Morgan, D. Densil. 'The theology of the Welsh Baptists, 1714–1760', *J. of Welsh Ecclesiastical History* 7 (1990), 41–54.

24. O'Brien, Susan. 'Women of the "English Catholic community": nuns and pupils at the Bar Convent, York, 1680–1790', Bc123, 267–82.

25. Podmore, C.J. 'The bishops and the brethren: Anglican attitudes to the Moravians in the mid-eighteenth century', *J. of Ecclesiastical History* 41 (1990), 622–46.

26. Rack, Henry D. 'Survival and revival: John Bennet, Methodism, and the Old Dissent', Bc115, 1–23.

27. Rack, Henry D. *Reasonable enthusiast: John Wesley and the rise of Methodism.* London; Epworth; 1989. Pp 672.

28. Richey, Russell E. 'Methodism and providence: a study in secularization', Bc115, 51–77.

29. Roberts, Alasdair. 'Mass in the kiln', *Innes R.* 41 (1990), 227–29.

30. Schmidt, Leigh Eric. 'Sacramental occasions and the Scottish context of presbyterian revivalism in America', Bc86, 65–80.
31. Sher, Richard B. 'Witherspoon's *Dominion of Providence* and the Scottish Jeremiad tradition', Bc86, 46–64.
32. Thomas, Graham C.G. 'George Whitefield and friends: the correspondence of some early Methodists', *National Library of Wales J.* 26 (1990), 251–80.
33. Valentine, S.R. 'The independent years of Wesley's John Bennet: 1752–1759', *J. of the United Reformed Church Historical Soc.* 4 (1989), 315–18.
34. Walsh, John. 'John Wesley and the community of goods', Bc115, 25–50.
35. Wright, Sheila. 'Quakerism and its implications for Quaker women: the women itinerant ministers of York Meeting, 1780–1840', Bc128, 403–14.

## (f) *Economic Affairs*

1. Anderson, B.L. 'Provincial aspects of the financial revolution of the eighteenth century', Bc24, 10–21.
2. Beckett, John V. 'Estate management in eighteenth-century England: the Lowther-Spedding relationship in Cumberland', Bc77, 55–72.
3. Beckett, John V. *The agricultural revolution.* Oxford; Blackwell (Historical Association Studies); 1990. Pp 96.
4. Beckett, John V.; Turner, Michael. 'Taxation and economic growth in eighteenth-century England', *Economic History R.* 2nd ser. 43 (1990), 377–403.
5. Black, Jeremy. 'Agricultural improvement in 1763: the role of foreign examples', *Agricultural History* 64 (1990), 90–92.
6. Black, Robert A.; Gilmore, Claire G. 'Crowding out during Britain's industrial revolution', *J. of Economic History* 50 (1990), 109–31.
7. Buchanan, B.J. 'The turnpike roads: a classic trap?', *J. of Transport History* 3rd ser. 11 (1990), 66–72.
8. Clarkson, Leslie A. 'The environment and dynamic of pre-factory industry in Northern Ireland', Bc42, 252–70.
9. Coutie, Heather (ed.). *The diary of Peter Pownall, a Bramhall farmer, 1765–1858: an introduction to local history.* Congleton; Old Vicarage Publications; 1989. Pp 144.
10. Crowley, John E. 'Neo-mercantilism and *The wealth of nations*: British commercial policy after the American revolution', *Historical J.* 33 (1990), 339–60.
11. Darity, W., Jr. 'Profitability of the British trade in slaves once again', *Explorations in Economic History* 26 (1989), 380–84.
12. Davis, John A. 'Industrialization in Britain and Europe before 1850: new perspectives and old problems', Bc25, 44–68.
13. Devine, Tom M. 'The tobacco lords of Glasgow', *History Today* 40/5 (1990), 17–21.
14. Evans, Neil. 'Two paths to economic development: Wales and the north-east of England', Bc42, 201–27.

15. Gemery, H.A.; Hogendorn, Jan; Johnson, Marion. 'Evidence on English/African terms of trade in the eighteenth century', *Explorations in Economic History* 27 (1990), 157–77.

16. Gibson, Alex. 'Proletarianization? The transition to full-time labour on a Scottish estate, 1723–1787', *Continuity & Change* 5 (1990), 357–89.

17. Green, Edmund M. 'The taxonomy of occupations in late eighteenth-century Westminster', Bc27, 164–81.

18. Hausman, William J. 'The British economy in transition, 1742–1789', Bc95, 53–79; 245–48.

19. Hoppit, Julian. 'Attitudes to credit in Britain, 1680–1790', *Historical J.* 33 (1990), 305–22.

20. Hoppit, Julian. 'Counting the industrial revolution', *Economic History R.* 2nd ser. 43 (1990), 173–93.

21. Hudson, Pat. 'Capital and credit in the West Riding wool textile industry, c.1750–1850', Bc42, 69–102.

22. Hudson, Pat. 'The regional perspective', Bc42, 5–40.

23. Inikori, Joseph E. 'Slavery and the revolution in cotton textile production in England', *Social Science History* 13 (1989), 343–79.

24. Jackson, R.V. 'Government expenditure and British economic growth in the eighteenth century: some problems of measurement', *Economic History R.* 2nd ser. 43 (1990), 217–35.

25. Lenman, Bruce P. 'The English and Dutch East India Companies and the birth of consumerism in the Augustan world', *Eighteenth-Century Life* 14 (1990), 47–65.

26. Marshall, John D. 'Stages of industrialisation in Cumbria', Bc42, 132–55.

27. Mathew, K.S. 'Maritime trade of Masulipatnam on the Coromandel coast of India during the second half of the eighteenth century', Bc76, 1–14.

28. Mingay, Gordon E. 'The diary of James Warne, 1758', *Agricultural History R.* 38 (1990), 72–78.

29. Neal, Larry. 'The Dutch and English East India companies compared: evidence from the stock and foreign exchange markets', Bc14, 195–223.

30. O'Brien, Padraig. *Warrington Academy, 1757–1786: its predecessors and successors.* Wigan; Owl Books; 1989. Pp 164.

31. O'Brien, Patrick Karl. 'The impact of the revolutionary and Napoleonic wars, 1793–1815, on the long-run growth of the British economy', *[F. Braudel Center] Review* 12 (1989), 335–95.

32. O'Donnell, Rory. *Adam Smith's theory of value.* Basingstoke; Macmillan; 1990. Pp 296.

33. Patterson, Margaret; Reiffen, David. 'The effect of the Bubble Act on the market for joint stock shares', *J. of Economic History* 50 (1990), 163–71.

34. Philipson, John; Isaac, Peter. 'A case of economic warfare in the late eighteenth century: 1. Three early paper-moulds in the collections of the Society; 2. Sir John Swinburne and the forged *assignats* from Haughton Mill', *Archaeologia Aeliana* 5th ser. 18 (1990), 151–63.

35. Phillips, John A. 'Municipal politics in later eighteenth-century

Maidstone: electoral polarization in the reign of George III', Bc37,185–203.

36. Probert, Simon. 'Beardown Warren, Princetown, Dartmoor', Bc142, 229–33.

37. Randall, Adrian J. 'New languages or old? Labour, capital and discourse in the industrial revolution', *Social History* 15 (1990), 195–216.

38. Randall, Adrian J. 'Peculiar perquisites and pernicious practices: embezzlement in the west of England woollen industry, *c.*1750–1840', *International R. of Social History* 35 (1990), 193–219.

39. Randall, Adrian J. 'Work, culture and resistance to machinery in the west of England woollen industry', Bc42, 175–200.

40. Rogers, Nicholas. 'Crowd and people in the Gordon Riots', Bc37, 39–55.

41. Rogers, Nicholas. 'The Gordon riots revisited', *Historical Papers* [Canada] (1988), 16–34.

42. Rowlands, Marie B. 'Continuity and change in an industrialising society: the case of the west midlands industries', Bc42, 103–31.

43. Schubert, B.S. 'Arbitrage in the foreign exchange markets of London and Amsterdam during the eighteenth century', *Explorations in Economic History* 26 (1989), 1–20.

44. Schwarz, L.D. 'Trends in real wage rates, 1750–1790: a reply to Hunt and Botham', *Economic History R.* 2nd ser. 43 (1990), 90–98.

45. Skinner, Andrew S. 'Adam Smith and America: the political economy of conflict', Bc86, 148–62.

46. Skinner, Andrew S. 'Sir James Steuart: economic theory and policy', Bc56, 117–44.

47. Sullivan, Richard J. 'The revolution of ideas: widespread patenting and invention during the English industrial revolution', *J. of Economic History* 50 (1990), 349–62.

48. Thomson, J.K.J. 'Scotland and Catalonia and the American market in the eighteenth century', *Scottish Economic & Social History* 9 (1989), 5–17.

49. Tranter, Neil L. 'The agricultural sector in the age of industrialization', *Historical J.* 33 (1990), 189–94.

50. Walton, John K. 'Proto-industrialisation and the first industrial revolution: the case of Lancashire', Bc42, 41–68.

51. Webster, Anthony. 'The political economy of trade liberalization: the East India Company Charter Act of 1813', *Economic History R.* 2nd ser. 43 (1990), 404–19.

52. Weiller, Kenneth J.; Mirowski, Philip. 'Rates of interest in eighteenth-century England', *Explorations in Economic History* 27 (1990), 1–28.

53. Whyte, Ian D. 'Proto-industrialisation in Scotland', Bc42, 228–51.

## (g) *Social Structure and Population*

1. Anon. *Gresford parish registers, vol. 2: 1714–1740*. Wrexham; Clwyd Family History Soc.; 1988. Pp xviii, 70.

2. Armstrong, W.A. 'The countryside', Bc45, 87–154.

3. Barrell, John. 'Visualizing the division of labour: William Pyne's *Microcosm*', Bc61, 95–132.

4. Borsay, Peter (ed.). *The eighteenth-century town: a reader in English urban history, 1688–1820* [reprints with introduction]. Harlow; Longman; 1990. Pp viii, 383.

5. Borsay, Peter; McInnes, Angus. 'The emergence of a leisure town: or an urban renaissance?', *Past & Present* 126 (1990), 189–202.

6. Bowles, Paul. 'Millar and Engels on the history of women and the family', *History of European Ideas* 12 (1990), 595–610.

7. Cruickshank, Dan; Burton, Neal. *Life in the Georgian city*. London; Viking; 1990. Pp 304.

8. Davis, Graham. 'Beyond the Georgian facade: the Avon street district of Bath', Bc48, 144–85.

9. Grubb, Farley. 'British immigration to Philadelphia: the reconstruction of ship passenger lists from May 1772 to October 1773', *Pennslyvania History* 55 (1988), 118–41.

10. Henstock, Adrian (ed.). *A Georgian country town, Ashbourne 1725–1825: vol. 1: fashionable society*. Ashbourne; Ashbourne Local History Group; 1989. Pp 96.

11. Humphries, Jane. 'Enclosures, common rights, and women: the proletarianization of families in the late eighteenth and early nineteenth centuries', *J. of Economic History* 50 (1990), 17–42.

12. Jones, Vivien (ed.). *Women in the eighteenth century: constructions of femininity*. London; Routledge; 1990. Pp 320.

13. Kent, David A. ' "Gone for a soldier": family breakdown and the demography of desertion in a London parish, 1750–1791', *Local Population Studies* 45 (1990), 27–42.

14. Koditschek, Theodore. *Class formation and urban-industrial society: Bradford, 1750–1850*. Cambridge; Cambridge UP; 1990. Pp 420.

15. Landau, Norma. 'The regulation of immigration, economic structures and definitions of the poor in eighteenth-century England', *Historical J.* 33 (1990), 541–71.

16. Landers, John. 'Age patterns of mortality in London during the "long eighteenth century": a test of the "high potential" model of metropolitan mortality', *Social History of Medicine* 3 (1990), 27–60.

17. Markus, Thomas A. 'Class and classification in the buildings of the late Scottish Enlightenment', Bc57, 78–107.

18. Mitchison, Rosalind. 'Scotland, 1750–1850', Bc45, 155–208.

19. Mitchison, Rosalind. 'Webster revisited: a re-examination of the 1755 "census" of Scotland', Bc57, 62–77.

20. Sharpe, Pamela. 'Marital separation in the eighteenth and early nineteenth centuries: a note', *Local Population Studies* 45 (1990), 66–70.

21. Trumbach, Randolph. 'Sodomitical assaults, gender role, and sexual development in eighteenth-century London', *J. of Homosexuality* 16 (1988), 407–19.

22. Turner, Michael. 'New towns for old? Urban reconstruction after fires in the south-west: the case of Blandford Forum, Dorset, 1731', Bc53, 75–89.

23. Weatherill, Lorna. *The account book of Richard Latham, 1724–1767.* Oxford; Oxford UP (British Academy Records of Social and Economic History ns); 1990. Pp 322.
24. Williams, James. 'Drumsleet barony; a list of feuars and their tenants in 1722', *Dumfriesshire & Galloway Natural History & Antiq. Soc. T.* 3rd ser. 62 (1988), 45–47.
25. Wright, S.J. 'Sojourners and lodgers in a provincial town: the evidence from eighteenth-century Ludlow', *Urban History Yearbook* 17 (1990), 14–35.

## (h) *Naval and Military*

1. Bauer, Frank. 'Die Schlacht von Waterloo (18. Juni 1815)' [The battle of Waterloo], *Militargeschichte* 29 (1990), 275–84.
2. Black, Jeremy. 'A new account of Culloden', *J. of the Soc. for Army Historical Research* 68 (1989), 119–20.
3. Breihan, John R. 'Army barracks in Devon during the French revolutionary and Napoleonic wars', *Devon Association Report and T.* 122 (1990), 133–58.
4. Breihan, John R. 'Army barracks in the north-east in the era of the French revolution', *Archaeologia Aeliana* 5th ser. 18 (1990), 165–76.
5. Breihan, John R. 'Barracks in Dorset during the French revolution and Napoleonic Wars', *P. of the Dorset Natural History and Arch. Soc.* 111 (1989), 9–14.
6. Conway, Stephen. ' "The great mischief Complain'd of": reflections on the misconduct of British soldiers in the revolutionary war', *William & Mary Q.* 3rd ser. 47 (1990), 370–90.
7. Davies, David. 'James II, William of Orange, and the admirals', Bc146, 82–108.
8. Esdaile, Charles J. 'The duke of Wellington and the command of the Spanish army, 1812–1814', Bc13, 66–86.
9. Esdaile, Charles J. *The duke of Wellington and the command of the Spanish army, 1812–1814.* Basingstoke; Macmillan; 1990. Pp 256.
10. Goodwin, Peter. *The bomb vessel Granado, 1742.* London; Conway Maritime; 1989. Pp 128.
11. Gruber, Ira D. 'The education of Sir Henry Clinton', *B. of the John Rylands University Library of Manchester* 72/1 (1990), 131–53.
12. Horward, Donald D. 'Wellington as a strategist, 1808–1814', Bc13, 87–116.
13. Houlding, J.A.; Yates, G. Kenneth. 'Corporal [George] Fox's memoir of service, 1766–1783: Quebec, Saratoga and the Convention Army', *J. of the Soc. for Army Historical Research* 68 (1990), 146–68.
14. Jenkins, H.J.K. 'The case of the "Courier", 1794–1798', *Mariner's Mirror* 76 (1990), 69–73.
15. Linney, C.A. 'The origins and formation of the first British lancer regiments, 1793–1823', *J. of the Soc. for Army Historical Research* 68 (1990), 82–102.

16. MacDougall, Philip. 'The formative years: Malta dockyards, 1800–1815', *Mariner's Mirror* 76 (1990), 205–13.
17. Mackay, Ruddock F. 'Lord St Vincent's early years (1735–1755)', *Mariner's Mirror* 76 (1990), 51–65.
18. Massey, Gregory de Van. 'The British expedition to Wilmington, January–November, 1781', *North Carolina Historical R.* 66 (1989), 387–411.
19. Patterson, William J. 'A forgotten hero in a forgotten war' [Colonel Joseph Wanton Morrison and the war of 1812], *J. of the Soc. for Army Historical Research* 68 (1990), 7–21.
20. Schom, Alan. *Trafalgar: countdown to battle, 1803–1805*. London; Joseph; 1990. Pp 418.
21. Starkey, Armstrong. 'War and culture, a case study: the Enlightenment and the conduct of the British army in America, 1755–1781', *War & Soc.* 8 (1990), 1–28.
22. Starkey, David J. 'War and the market for seafarers in Britain, 1736–1792', Bc76, 25–42.
23. Starkey, David J. *British privateering enterprise in the eighteenth century*. Exeter; Exeter UP (Maritime Studies no. 4); 1990. Pp 352.
24. Syrett, David. *The Royal Navy in American waters, 1775–1783*. Aldershot; Scolar; 1989. Pp 259.

## (i) *Intellectual and Cultural*

1. Allen, Brian. 'From Plassey to Seringapatam: India and British history painting, *c.*1760–*c.*1800', Bc68, 26–37.
2. Appleby, John H. 'Erasmus King: eighteenth-century experimental philosopher', *Annals of Science* 47 (1990), 375–92.
3. Barrell, Rex A. *Francis Atterbury (1662–1732), bishop of Rochester, and his French correspondents*. Lampeter; Mellen; 1990. Pp 104.
4. Bator, Paul G. 'The formation of the Regius chair of Rhetoric and Belles Lettres at the university of Edinburgh', *Q. J. of Speech* 75 (1989), 40–64.
5. Black, Jeremy. ' "Calculated upon a very extensive and useful plan"—the English provincial press in the eighteenth century', Bc139, 61–72.
6. Black, Jeremy. 'Going up to Oxford: Charles Weston's account in 1748', *Oxoniensia* 54 (1989), 414–15.
7. Black, Jeremy. 'Portraits for Scriblerians', *B. of the British Soc. for Eighteenth-Century Studies* 22 (1990), 12–14.
8. Born, Anne. 'This extraordinary man: John Wolcot/Peter Pindar (1738–1819)', *Devon Association Report and T.* 122 (1990), 83–102.
9. Brack, O.M. 'A pencil sketch of Samuel Johnson', *Factotum* 32 (Sept. 1990), 9–12.
10. Brewer, John; Tillyard, Stella. 'The moral vision of Thomas Bewick', Bc37, 375–408.
11. Burkett, Mary. 'Christopher Steele, 1733–1767', *Walpole Soc.* 53 (1989 for 1987), 193–225.
12. Campbell, Roy H. 'Scotland's neglected Enlightenment', *History Today* 40/5 (1990), 22–28.

13. Clark, Anna. 'Whores and gossips: sexual reputation in London, 1770–1825', Bc2, 231–48.

14. Cloudsley, Tim. 'Romanticism and the industrial revolution in Britain', *History of European Ideas* 12 (1990), 611–35.

15. Cooper, Albert. 'Benjamin Banks (1727–1795), the Salisbury violin-maker', *Hatcher Review* 3/29 (1990), 449–58.

16. Curley, Thomas M. 'Johnson's tour of Scotland and the idea of Great Britain', *British J. of Eighteenth-Century Studies* 12 (1989), 134–44.

17. Darling, John. 'The moral teaching of Francis Hutcheson', *British J. of Eighteenth-Century Studies* 12 (1989), 165–74.

18. Davis, Bertram H. *Thomas Percy: a scholar-cleric in the age of Johnson.* Philadelphia; Pennsylvania UP; 1989. Pp xi, 361.

19. Day, John C. 'Parochial libraries in Northumberland before 1830', *Library History* 8 (1989), 93–103.

20. Dean, Dennis R. 'James Hutton's role in the history of geomorphology', Bc15, 73–84.

21. Diamond, Peter J. 'Witherspoon, William Smith and the Scottish philosophy in revolutionary America', Bc86, 115–32.

22. Doerfel, Marianne. 'John Hartley, an eighteenth-century British head-master of a German public school', *British J. of Eighteenth-Century Studies* 12 (1989), 145–64.

23. Drummond, George. *Lord Provost George Drummond, 1687–1766.* Edinburgh; Scotland's Cultural Heritage; 1987. Pp 36.

24. Fenton, Alexander. 'The people below: Dougal Graham's chapbooks as a mirror of the lower classes in eighteenth-century Scotland', Bc89, 69–80.

25. Garner, Lawrence. *The Georgian legacy.* Shrewsbury; Swan Hill (Buildings of Shropshire vol. 2); 1990. Pp 112.

26. Gibson-Wood, Carol. 'Jonathan Richardson, lord Somers's collection of drawings, and early art-historical writing in England', *J. of the Warburg & Courtauld Institutes* 52 (1989), 167–87.

27. Glaister, Robert T.D. 'Education at Caerlanrig', *Hawick Arch. Soc. T.* (1989), 29–31.

28. Grady, Kevin. *The Georgian public buildings of Leeds and the West Riding.* Leeds; Thoresby Society (vol. 52); 1989. Pp xv, 192.

29. Griffin, Nicholas J. 'Possible theological perspectives in Thomas Reid's common sense philosophy', *J. of Ecclesiastical History* 41 (1990), 425–42.

30. Harris, Michael. 'Paper pirates: the alternative book trade in mid-eighteenth century London', Bc50, 47–69.

31. Hook, Andrew. 'Philadelphia, Edinburgh and the Scottish Enlightenment', Bc86, 227–41.

32. Hunter, David. 'The printing of opera and song books in England, 1703–1726', *Notes* 46 (1989), 328–51.

33. Innes, Joanna. 'Politics and morals: the reformation of manners movement in later eighteenth-century England', Bc37, 57–118.

34. Krauss, Anne McClenny. 'James Bremner, Alexander Reinagle and the influence of the Edinburgh musical society on Philadelphia', Bc86, 259–74.

35. Lawson-Peebles, Robert. 'William Smith in Aberdeen (1745) and Philadelphia (1778): fratricide and familialism', Bc4, 46–59.
36. Le Rougetel, Hazel. *The Chelsea gardener: Philip Miller and his circle, 1691–1771*. London; British Museum (Natural History); 1990. Pp 168.
37. Levine, Joseph M. ' "Et tu Brute?" history and forgery in eighteenth-century England', Bc50, 71–97.
38. Liscombe, Rhodri Windsor. 'The "diffusion of knowledge and taste": John Flaxman and the improvement of the study facilities at the Royal Academy', *Walpole Soc.* 53 (1989 for 1987), 226–38.
39. Livingston, Donald W. 'Hume, English barbarism and American independence', Bc86, 133–47.
40. Lobb, Douglas H.V. 'The Lobb brothers, woodcarvers to the aristocracy, part 2', *Genealogists' Magazine* 23 (1990), 285–89.
41. Maehle, Andreas-Holger. 'Literary responses to animal experimentation in seventeenth- and eighteenth-century Britain', *Medical History* 34 (1990), 27–51.
42. Markus, Thomas A. 'Buildings and the ordering of minds and bodies', Bc56, 169–224.
43. McKinney, David D. ' "The castle of my ancestors": Horace Walpole and Strawberry Hill', *British J. of Eighteenth-Century Studies* 13 (1990), 199–214.
44. McVeigh, Simon. 'The professional concert and rival subscription series in London, 1783–1793', *Royal Music Association Research Chronicle* 22 (1989), 1–35.
45. Michael, Emily; Michael, Fred S. 'Hutcheson's account of beauty as a response to Mandeville', *History of European Ideas* 12 (1990), 655–68.
46. Miles, Ellen G. 'A notebook of portrait compositions by Thomas Bardwell', *Walpole Soc.* 53 (1989 for 1987), 181–92.
47. Milhous, Judith; Hume, Robert D. 'Profits at Drury Lane, 1713–1716', *Theatre Research International* 14 (1989), 241–55.
48. Miller, Thomas P. 'Witherspoon, Blair and the rhetoric of civic humanism', Bc86, 100–14.
49. Morton, A.Q. 'Lectures on natural philosophy in London, 1750–1765: S.C.T. Demainbray (1710–1782) and the "inattention" of his countrymen', *British J. for the History of Science* 23 (1990), 411–34.
50. Mowl, Tim; Earnshaw, Brian. *John Wood: architect of obsession*. Bath; Millstream; 1988. Pp 224.
51. Myers, Sylvia Harcstark. *The bluestocking circle: women, friendship, and the life of the mind in eighteenth-century England*. Oxford; Oxford UP; 1990. Pp 360.
52. Mytum, Harold. 'An eighteenth-century summerhouse at Berry Hill, Nevern, Dyfed', *B. of the Board of Celtic Studies* 36 (1989), 263–67.
53. Noble, Andrew. 'James Boswell: Scotland's prodigal son', Bc57, 22–42.
54. Paulson, Ronald. *Breaking and remaking: aesthetic practice in England, 1700–1820*. New Brunswick (NJ); Rutgers UP; 1989. Pp 350.
55. Pearson, David. 'Unrecorded books from Samuel Johnson's library', *Factotum* 32 (Sept. 1990), 13–14.

56. Peterson, Charles E. 'Robert Smith, Philadelphia builder-architect: from Dalkeith to Princeton', Bc86, 275–99.
57. Physick, John. 'Westminster Abbey: designs for Poets' Corner and a new Roubiliac in the cloister', *Church Monuments* 4 (1989), 54–63.
58. Pitkin, Hanna Finichel. 'Slippery Bentham: some neglected cracks in the foundation of utilitarianism', *Political Theory* 18 (1990), 104–31.
59. Pittock, Murray. 'Jacobite literature: love, death and violence', Bc4, 33–45.
60. Porter, Roy. 'Erasmus Darwin: doctor of evolution?', Bc16, 39–69.
61. Pugsley, Steven. 'The Georgian landscape garden: Devon in the national context', Bc53, 91–104.
62. Ramsay, Nigel. 'Forgery and the rise of the London Scriveners' Company', Bc50, 99–108.
63. Raphael, D.D.; Sakamoto, Tatsuya. 'Anonymous writings of David Hume', *J. of the History of Politics* 28 (1990), 271–82.
64. Ribeiro, Alvaro (ed.). *The letters of Dr Charles Burney, vol. 1: 1751–1784.* Oxford; Oxford UP; 1990. Pp 520.
65. Rogers, David. 'In search of Mr Wilkinson' [18th-century book-collector], *Bodleian Library Record* 13 (1990), 406–14.
66. Russell, Francis. 'The Derby collection, 1721–1735', *Walpole Soc.* 53 (1989 for 1987), 143–80.
67. Russell, Gillian. 'Playing at revolution: the politics of the O.P. riots of 1809', *Theatre Notebook* 44/1 (1990), 17–26.
68. Schumann-Bacia, Eva. *Die Bank von England und ihr Architekt John Soane* [The Bank of England and its architect, John Soane]. Zurich; Artemis; 1989. Pp 202.
69. Searle, Arthur. *Haydn and England.* London; British Library; 1989. Pp 32.
70. Seidmann, Gertrud. 'Nathaniel Marchant, gem-engraver, 1739–1816', *Walpole Soc.* 53 (1989 for 1987), 1–105.
71. Simpson, John. 'Some eighteenth-century intellectual contacts between Scotland and Scandinavia', Bc54, 119–29.
72. Smitten, Jeffrey R. 'Moderatism and history: William Robertson's unfinished history of British America', Bc86, 163–79.
73. Spadafora, David. *The idea of progress in eighteenth-century Britain.* London; Yale UP; 1990. Pp 480.
74. Stoker, David. 'The genesis of *Collectanea Cantabrigiensia*', *T. of the Cambridge Bibliographical Soc.* 9 (1989), 372–80.
75. Tinkler, Keith J. 'Worlds apart: eighteenth-century writings on rivers, lakes and the terraqueous globe', Bc15, 37–71.
76. Ulman, H. Lewis (ed.). *The minutes of the Aberdeen Philosophical Society, 1758–1773.* Aberdeen; Aberdeen UP; 1990. Pp 264.
77. Wallis, Peter; Wallis, Ruth. 'Eighteenth-century medics—the PHIBB collective biography', Bc126, 129–39.
78. Wawn, Andrew. 'The Enlightenment traveller and the idea of Iceland: the Stanley expedition of 1789 reconsidered', *Scandinavica* 28 (May 1989), 5–16.
79. Withers, C.W.J. 'Improvement and Enlightenment: agriculture and

natural history in the work of the Rev. Dr John Walker (1731–1803)', Bc56, 102–16.

80. Wokler, Robert. 'Apes and races in the Scottish Enlightenment: Monboddo and Kames on the nature of man', Bc56, 145–68.

81. Zwicker, Steven N. 'Representing the revolution: politics and high culture in 1688', Bc146, 109–34.

## (j) *Science*

1. Ben-Chaim, Michael. 'Social mobility and scientific change: Stephen Gray's contribution to electrical research', *British J. for the History of Science* 23 (1990), 3–24.

2. Bloy, Marjorie. 'In spite of medical help: the puzzle of an eighteenth-century prime minister's illness', *Medical History* 34 (1990), 178–84.

3. Brunton, Deborah C. 'The transfer of medical education: teaching at the Edinburgh and Philadelphia medical schools', Bc86, 242–58.

4. Bynum, William F. 'Medicine at the English court, 1688–1837', Bc20, 262–89.

5. Delacy, Margaret. 'Puerperal fever in eighteenth-century Britain', *B. of the History of Medicine* 63 (1989), 521–56.

6. Doherty, Francis. 'The anodyne necklace: a quack remedy and its promotion', *Medical History* 34 (1990), 268–93.

7. Donovan, Arthur. 'The chemical revolution and the Enlightenment—and a proposal for the study of scientific change', Bc56, 87–101.

8. Fenby, David V. 'Chemical reactivity and heat in the eighteenth century', Bc56, 67–86.

9. Fissell, M.E. 'The "sick and dropping poor" in eighteenth-century Bristol and its region', *Social History of Medicine* 2 (1989), 35–58.

10. Hamlin, Christopher. 'Chemistry, medicine and the legitimization of English spas, 1740–1840', *Medical History*, Supplement 10 (1990), 67–81.

11. Heywood, Audrey. 'A trial of the Bath waters: the treatment of lead poisoning', *Medical History*, Supplement 10 (1990), 82–101.

12. James, J.G. 'Some steps in the evolution of early iron arched bridge designs', *Newcomen Soc. T.* 59 (1990 for 1987/8), 153–58.

13. James, J.G. 'Thomas Paine's iron bridge work, 1785–1803', *Newcomen Soc. T.* 59 (1990 for 1987/8), 189–221.

14. Kirkup, John. 'A pioneer accident service: Bath casualty hospital, 1788–1826', Bc126, 50–58.

15. Lane, Joan. 'Medical apprentices in eighteenth-century England', Bc126, 119–28.

16. MacDonald, Michael. 'Lunatics and the state in Georgian England', *Social History of Medicine* 2 (1989), 299–313.

17. Miller, D.P. ' "Into the valley of darkness": reflections on the Royal Society in the eighteenth century', *History of Science* 27 (1989), 155–66.

18. Porter, Roy (ed.). *The English malady (1733): George Cheyne*. London; Routledge; 1990. Pp 480.

19. Saul, G.M. 'John Rennie (1761–1821): one of his contributions to

waterworks technology', *Newcomen Soc. T.* 59 (1990 for 1987/8), 3–13.
20. Webb, Martha Ellen. 'The early medical studies and practice of Dr David Hartley', *B. of the History of Medicine* 63 (1989), 618–36.

# H. BRITAIN 1815–1914

*See also* Aa17–18,21,70,109,124,b17,c1,46,58,67; Bc70,87,92–93,102,107, 127,145,d1; Ga8,b40,c6,e21,f12,38,g14,18,i13,j4,10,14,19; Ib55,f21,54,68, 70,85,g6–7,10,13,28,h18,j27.

## (a) *General*

1. Armstrong, Margaret (ed.). *Thirlmere: across the bridges to chapel, 1849–1852—from the Reverend Basil R. Lawson, curate of Wythburn.* Keswick; Peel Wyke; 1989. Pp 88.
2. Auchmuty, Rosemary. 'By their friends we shall know them: the lives and networks of some women in north Lambeth, 1880–1940', Bc1, 77–98.
3. Briggs, Asa. 'The later Victorian age', Bc92, 3–38.
4. Bruff, Barry R. (ed.). *The village atlas: north & west Yorkshire, 1840–1910.* London; Village Press; 1990. Pp 204.
5. Bruff, Barry R. (ed.). *The village atlas: the growth of Derbyshire, Nottinghamshire and Leicestershire, 1834–1904.* London; Village Press; 1990. Pp 208.
6. Copelman, Dina M. 'Liberal ideology, sexual difference, and the lives of women: recent works in British history', *J. of Modern History* 62 (1990), 315–45.
7. Gale, Joanne; Sims, Jay. *Much Wenlock in Victorian times.* Shrewsbury; Shropshire Books; 1990. Pp 56.
8. Godfrey, Nanette; Snowden, Charmian. 'Wykham Park—from the early nineteenth century to the present day', *Cake & Cockhorse* 11/4 (1989), 78–83.
9. Gordon, Eleanor. 'Women's spheres', Bc58, 206–35.
10. Harrison-Barbet, Anthony. *Thomas Holloway, Victorian philanthropist: a biographical essay.* Gorran; Lyfrow Trelyspen; 1990. Pp 60.
11. Hey, Colin G. *Rowland Hill: Victorian genius and benefactor.* London; Quiller; 1989. Pp 192.
12. Howell, D.W.; Baber, C. 'Wales', Bc45, 281–354.
13. Jones, Douglas V. *Sidelights on a city: an evocation of Birmingham in the late nineteenth and early twentieth centuries.* Studley; Brewin; 1989. Pp 72.
14. Leak, Adrian. *The liberty of St Peter of York, 1800–1838.* York; the University (Borthwick paper no. 77); 1990. Pp iii, 39.
15. Lewer, David (ed.). *John Mowlem's Swanage diary, 1845–1851.* Wincanton; Dorset; 1990. Pp 128.

16. Mair, Craig. *David Angus: the life and adventures of a Victorian railway engineer.* Stevenage; Strong Oak; 1989. Pp xii, 218.
17. Mellers, Wilfrid; Hildyard, Rupert. 'The Edwardian age and the interwar years', Bc93, 2–44.
18. Mitchell, Tessa. *Strensall in the mid-nineteenth century.* York; Sessions; 1989. Pp 72.
19. Morgan, Nicholas J.; Trainor, Richard H. 'The dominant classes' [in Scotland], Bc58, 103–37.
20. Morris, R.J. 'Introduction: Scotland, 1830–1914. The making of a nation within a nation', Bc58, 1–7.
21. Plessis, Alain; Black, Jeremy; Le May, G.H.L. 'Le pouvoir: the City, Fleet Street, Westminster', Bc81, 188–216.
22. Price, Richard. 'Does the notion of Victorian England make sense?', Bc104, 152–71.
23. Ramm, Agatha (ed.). *'Beloved and darling child': last letters between Queen Victoria and her eldest daughter, 1886–1901.* Stroud; Sutton; 1990. Pp 256.
24. Reclus, Elisée; Baedecker, Karl. 'Gares, fiacres, bains et égouts . . . ', Bc81, 38–47.
25. Rowe, D.J. 'The north-east', Bc45, 415–70.
26. Runcie, Robert. 'Newman: an ecumenical perspective', Bc102, 159–66.
27. Shelston, Alan; Shelston, Dorothy. *The industrial city, 1820–1870.* London; Macmillan; 1990. Pp 172.
28. Steedman, Carolyn. *Childhood, culture and class in Britain: Margaret McMillan, 1860–1931.* London; Virago; 1990. Pp 343.
29. Walton, John K. 'The north-west', Bc45, 355–414.

## (b) *Politics*

1. Adburgham, Alison. *A radical aristocrat: the Rt. Hon. Sir William A. Molesworth, Bart., PC, MP, of Pencarrow, and his wife, Andalusia.* Padstow; Tabb House; 1990. Pp xv, 222.
2. Behagg, Clive. *Politics and production in the early nineteenth century.* London; Routledge; 1990. Pp x, 273.
3. Belchem, John. 'Beyond *Chartist Studies*: class, community and party in early Victorian populist politics', Bc104, 105–26.
4. Bendikat, Elfi. 'Politikstile, Konfliktlinien und Lagerstruktur im deutschen, britischen und franzosischen Parteisystem des späten 19. Jahrhunderts' [Political style, lines of conflict and group-structure in the German, British and French party systems in the late nineteenth century], *Politische Vierteljahresschrift* 30 (1989), 482–502.
5. Black, Shirley Burgoyne. 'Swing: the years 1827–1830 as reflected in a west Kent newspaper', *Archaeologia Cantiana* 107 (1990 for 1989), 89–106.
6. Brown, Lucy. 'The growth of a national press', Bc87, 133–40.
7. Brown, Tony. 'Introduction' [Edward Carpenter], Bc107, 1–16.
8. Cachin, Marie-Francoise. ' "Non-governmental society": Edward Carpenter's position in the British Socialist movement', Bc107, 58–73.

9. Challinor, Raymond. *A radical lawyer in Victorian England: W.P. Roberts and the struggle for workers' rights.* London; Tauris; 1990. Pp 302.

10. Clarke, Tony. 'Early Chartism in Scotland: a "moral force" movement?', Bc55, 106–21.

11. Craig, Frederick Walter Scott (ed.). *British parliamentary election results, 1832–1885.* Aldershot; Parliamentary Research Services; 2nd edn. 1989. Pp xvi, 746.

12. Dalton, Mary. 'The Pyt House riot and the Tisbury-Tasmania connection', *Hatcher Review* 3/30 (1990), 503–20.

13. Diamond, Michael. 'Political heroes of the Victorian music hall', *History Today* 40/1 (1990), 33–39.

14. Epstein, James A. 'The constitutional idiom: radical reasoning, rhetoric and action in early nineteenth-century England', *J. of Social History* 23 (1990), 553–74.

15. Fforde, Matthew. *Conservatism and collectivism, 1886–1914.* Edinburgh; Edinburgh UP; 1990. Pp 232.

16. Finlayson, Geoffrey. 'Wellington, the constitution, and the march of reform', Bc13, 196–213.

17. Foster, Ruscombe. 'Wellington and local government', Bc13, 214–37.

18. Freeden, Michael (ed.). *Minutes of the Rainbow circle, 1894–1924.* Woodbridge; Boydell for the Royal Historical Soc. (Camden 4th ser. vol. 38); 1989. Pp 370.

19. Gash, Norman. 'The duke of Wellington and the prime ministership, 1824–1830', Bc13, 117–38.

20. Gibson, William T. 'The Tories and church patronage: 1812–1830', *J. of Ecclesiastical History* 41 (1990), 266–74.

21. Gibson, William T. 'Wellington, the Whigs and the Exeter vacancy of 1830', *Devon Association Report and T.* 122 (1990), 41–46.

22. Gilley, Sheridan. 'Catholics and socialists in Scotland, 1900–1930', Bc49, 212–38.

23. Gutzke, David W. 'Rhetoric and reality: the political influence of British brewers, 1832–1914', *Parliamentary History* 9 (1990), 78–115.

24. Gutzke, David W. *Protecting the pub: brewers and publicans against temperance.* Woodbridge; Boydell (Royal Historical Soc. Studies in History 58); 1989. Pp xii, 266.

25. Hall, Catherine. 'The tale of Samuel and Jemima: gender and working-class culture in nineteenth-century England', Bc3, 78–102.

26. Hall, Robert G. 'Tyranny, work and politics: the 1818 strike wave in the English cotton district', *International R. of Social History* 34 (1989), 433–70.

27. Harris, Michael. 'London's local newspapers: patterns of change in the Victorian period', Bc87, 104–19.

28. Hirshfield, Claire. 'Fractured faith: Liberal party women and the suffrage issue in Britain, 1892–1914', *Gender & History* 2 (1990), 173–97.

29. Howe, A.C. 'Bimetallism, c.1880–1898: a controversy re-opened?', *English Historical R.* 105 (1990), 377–91.

30. Humphreys, Anne. 'Popular narrative and political discourse in *Reynold's Weekly Newspaper*', Bc87, 33–47.
31. Jenkins, T.A. 'The funding of the Liberal Unionist party and the honours system', *English Historical R.* 105 (1990), 920–38.
32. Jenkins, T.A. (ed.). *The parliamentary diaries of Sir John Trelawny, 1858–1865.* Woodbridge; Boydell for the Royal Historical Soc. (Camden 4th ser., vol. 40); 1990. Pp 256.
33. Jones, Aled. 'Local journalism in Victorian political culture', Bc87, 63–70.
34. Klarman, Michael. 'The trade union political levy, the Osborne judgment (1909), and the South Wales Miners' Federation', *Welsh History R.* 15 (1990–1), 34–57.
35. Knox, W. 'The political and workplace culture of the Scottish working class, 1832–1914', Bc58, 138–66.
36. Mandler, Peter. *Aristocratic government in the age of reform: Whigs and Liberals, 1830–1852.* Oxford; Oxford UP; 1990. Pp x, 307.
37. Marks, Gary. *Unions in politics: Britain, Germany and the United States in the nineteenth and early twentieth centuries.* Guildford; Princeton UP; 1989. Pp xvii, 277.
38. Mather, F.C. 'Achilles or Nestor? The duke of Wellington in British politics, 1832–1846', Bc13, 170–95.
39. Meacham, Standish. 'Lives in politics', *J. of Modern History* 62 (1990), 89–100.
40. Melling, Joseph. 'Clydeside rent struggles and the making of Labour politics in Scotland, 1900–1939', Bc59, 54–88.
41. Morris, J.N. 'A disappearing crowd? Collective action in late nineteenth-century Croydon', *Southern History* 12 (1990), 90–113.
42. Morris, R.J. 'Petitions, meetings and class formation amongst the urban middle classes in Britain in the 1830s', *Tijdschrift voor Geschiedenis* 103 (1990), 294–310.
43. Morrow, John (ed.). *Coleridge's writings, vol. 1: on politics and society.* Basingstoke; Macmillan; 1990. Pp xv, 253.
44. Moss, David J. *Thomas Attwood: the biography of a radical.* Montreal; McGill/Queen's UP; 1990. Pp 377.
45. Murray, Bruce K. 'Lloyd George, the navy estimates, and the inclusion of rating relief in the 1914 budget', *Welsh History R.* 15 (1990–1), 58–78.
46. Nenadic, Stana. 'Political reform and the "ordering" of middle-class protest', Bc55, 65–82.
47. Nield, Keith. 'Edward Carpenter: the uses of Utopia', Bc107, 17–32.
48. Norman, Edward. 'Stewart Headlam and the Christian socialists', Bc70, 159–69.
49. Noyce, Karen A. 'The duke of Wellington and the Catholic question', Bc13, 139–58.
50. O'Connell, Marvin R. 'Politics and prophecy: Newman and Lamennais', Bc127, 175–91.
51. O'Day, Alan. 'The political organization of the Irish in Britain, 1867–1890', Bc49, 183–211.

52. Palmer, Sarah. *Politics, shipping and the repeal of the Navigation Laws.* Manchester; Manchester UP; 1990. Pp x, 209.

53. Phillips, Andrew. 'Four Colchester elections: voting behaviour in a Victorian market town', Bc65, 199–227.

54. Prest, John. *Liberty and locality: parliament, permissive legislation and ratepayers' democracies in the mid-nineteenth century.* Oxford; Oxford UP; 1990. Pp 235.

55. Ramm, Agatha. *William Ewart Gladstone.* Cardiff; Wales UP (Political portraits); 1989. Pp 130.

56. Reay, Barry. *The last rising of the agricultural labourers: rural life and protest in nineteenth-century England.* Oxford; Oxford UP; 1990. Pp 245.

57. Robbins, Keith G. 'John Bright—Quaker politician: a centenary appreciation', *J. of the Friends' Historical Soc.* 55 (1989), 238–49.

58. Roberts, Stephen. 'The later radical career of Thomas Cooper, *c.*1845–1855', *Leicestershire Arch. and Historical Soc. T.* 64 (1990), 62–72.

59. Sack, James J. 'Wellington and the Tory press, 1828–1830', Bc13, 159–69.

60. Smith, E.A. *Lord Grey, 1764–1845.* Oxford; Oxford UP; 1990. Pp 338.

61. Stuurman, Siep. 'John Bright and Samuel van Houten: radical liberalism and the working classes in Britain and the Netherlands, 1860–1880', *History of European Ideas* 11 (1989), 593–604.

62. Tanner, Duncan. *Political change and the Labour Party, 1900–1918.* Cambridge; Cambridge UP; 1990. Pp 504.

63. Thompson, Dorothy. *Queen Victoria: gender and power.* London; Virago; 1990. Pp xix, 167.

64. Vincent, Andrew. 'Classical liberalism and its crisis of identity', *History of Political Thought* 11 (1990), 143–61.

65. Vincent, John. *Disraeli.* Oxford; Oxford UP (Past Masters ser.); 1990. Pp 127.

66. Walton, John K. *Disraeli.* London; Routledge; 1990. Pp 71.

67. Waters, Chris. *British socialists and the politics of popular culture, 1884–1914.* Manchester; Manchester UP; 1990. Pp 252.

68. Winstanley, Michael J. *Gladstone and the Liberal Party.* London; Routledge; 1990. Pp xi, 77.

69. Wright, Martin. 'Robert Blatchford, the Clarion movement and the crucial years of British socialism, 1891–1900', Bc107, 74–99.

## (c) *Constitution, Administration and Law*

1. Arnstein, Walter L. 'Queen Victoria opens parliament: the disinvention of tradition', *Historical Research* 63 (1990), 178–94.

2. Bee, Malcolm. 'A friendly society case study: the Compton Pilgrims Benefit Society', *Southern History* 12 (1990), 69–89.

3. Broomfield, Andrea. 'Towards a more tolerant society: *Macmillan's Magazine* and the women's suffrage question', *Victorian Periodicals R.* 23 (1990), 120–26.

4. Davies, Peter; Maile, Ben. *First post: from Penny Black to the present day.* London; Quiller; 1990. Pp 126.

5. Howell, Brian. *The police in late Victorian Bristol.* Bristol; Bristol Branch of the Historical Association (Local history pamphlets no. 71); 1989. Pp 29.

6. Jones, J. Graham. 'Alfred Thomas's National Institutions (Wales) Bills of 1891–1892', *Welsh History R.* 15 (1990–1), 218–39.

7. McGill, Barry. 'A Victorian office: the parliamentary counsel to the Treasury, 1869–1902', *Historical Research* 63 (1990), 110–16.

8. O'Toole, Barry J. *Private gain and public service: the Association of First Division Civil Servants.* London; Routledge; 1989. Pp xvi, 265.

9. Ranson, Susan. '*Caveat emptor*', *Northamptonshire Past & Present* 8/1 (1989–90), 35–38.

10. Shpayer-Makov, Haia. 'The making of a police labour force', *J. of Social History* 24 (1990), 109–34.

11. Sindall, Robin. *Street violence in the nineteenth century: media panic or real danger?* Leicester; Leicester UP; 1990. Pp 168.

12. Swift, Roger. 'Crime and the Irish in nineteenth-century Britain', Bc49, 163–82.

## (d) *External Affairs*

1. Cowles, Loyal. 'The failure to restrain Russia: Canning, Nesselrode, and the Greek question, 1825–1827', *International History R.* 12 (1990), 688–720.

2. Dawson, Frank Griffith. *The first Latin American debt crisis: the City of London and the 1822–1825 loan bubble.* London; Yale UP; 1990. Pp 294.

3. Gough, Barry M. 'The British reoccupation and colonization of the Falkland Islands, or Malvinas, 1832–1843', *Albion* 22 (1990), 261–87.

4. Hackler, Rhoda E.A. ' "My dear friend": letters of Queen Victoria and Queen Emma', *Hawaiian J. of History* 22 (1988), 101–30.

5. Hamilton, Keith A. *Bertie of Thame: Edwardian ambassador.* Woodbridge; Boydell (Royal Historical Soc. Studies in History 60); 1990. Pp 436.

6. Herrera, Luis Alberto de. *La Mision Ponsonby, 2: la diplomacia britanica y la independencia del Uruguay* [The Ponsonby mission, 2: British diplomacy and the independence of Uruguay]. Montevideo; Camara de Representantes; 1989. Pp 21, 370.

7. Ingram, Edward. 'Wellington and India', Bc13, 11–33.

8. King, John. 'Arms and the man: Abd el-Kader', *History Today* 40/8 (1990), 22–28.

9. McKercher, B.J.C. 'Diplomatic equipoise: the Lansdowne Foreign Office, the Russo-Japanese war of 1904–1905, and the global balance of power', *Canadian J. of History* 24 (1989), 299–339.

10. McLynn, Frank J. *Snow upon the desert: Sir Richard Burton, 1821–1890.* London; Murray; 1990. Pp xv, 428.

11. Moor, J.A. de. ' "A very unpleasant relationship": trade and strategy in

the eastern seas—Anglo-Dutch relations in the nineteenth century from a colonial perspective', Bc83, 49–69.

12. Muller, Harald. 'Der Streit um die Entsendung Clausewitz als preuss-ischer Gesandter nach London, 1819' [The controversy surrounding the despatch of Clausewitz as Prussian minister to London], *Militargesch-ichte* 29 (1990), 285–91.

13. Ngaosyvathn, Mayoury; Ngaosyvathn, Pheuiphanh. 'World super power and regional conflicts; the triangular game of Great Britain with Bangkok and the Lao during the embassies of John Crawfurd (1821–1822) and of Henry Burney (1825–1826)', *J. of the Siam Soc.* 76 (1988), 121–33.

14. Saunders, Graham. 'James Erskine Murray's expeditions to Kutei, 1843–1844', *Brunei Museum J.* 6/2 (1986), 91–115.

15. Stan, Valeriu. 'Diplomatic preliminaries to the union of the principalit-ies: two memoranda of Stratford Canning, British ambassador to Constantinople' [in Rumanian; French summary], *Revista de Istorie* 42 (1989), 31–44.

16. Waller, David. 'Northampton and the American Civil War', *Northamp-tonshire Past & Present* 8/2 (1990–91), 137–53.

17. Wrigley, W. David. 'The issue of Ionian neutrality in Anglo-Ottoman relations, 1821–1830', *Sudost-Forschungen* 47 (1988), 109–43.

## (e) *Religion*

1. Aspinwall, Bernard. 'Hands across the sea: the English speaking transatlantic religious world, 1820–1920', *Hispania Sacra* 40 (1988), 853–66.

2. Baxter, Rosemary A. *St Clement's parish Aberdeen, vol. 1: the people and places recorded by the Kirk Session, 1828–1851*. Aberdeen; Aberdeen & North-East Scotland Family History Soc.; 1989. Pp 54.

3. Bellenger, Dom Aidan. 'The English Benedictines: the search for monastic identity', Bc123, 299–321.

4. Binfield, Clyde. ' "We claim our part in the great inheritance": the message of four Congregational buildings', Bc115, 201–23.

5. Brecht, Martin. 'The relationship between the established Protestant Church and the Free Church: Hermann Gundert and Britain', Bc115, 135–51.

6. Bronner, Edwin B. 'Moderates in London Yearly Meeting, 1857–1873: precursors of Quaker liberals', *Church History* 59 (1990), 356–71.

7. Brown, Callum G. 'Faith in the city?', *History Today* 40/5 (1990), 41–47.

8. Brown, Callum G. 'Protest in the pews: interpreting Presbyterianism and society in fracture during the Scottish economic revolution', Bc55, 83–105.

9. Brown, Callum G. 'Religion, class and church growth', Bc58, 310–35.

10. Brown, David. 'Introduction' [Newman], Bc102, 1–18.

11. Brown, Neville. *Dissenting forebears: the maternal ancestors of J.M. Keynes*. Chichester; Phillimore; 1988. Pp xvii, 205.

12. Buckley, Jerome H. 'Newman's autobiography', Bc127, 93–110.
13. Chadwick, Henry. 'Newman's significance for the Anglican Church', Bc102, 52–74.
14. Chadwick, Henry. 'The *Lectures on justification*', Bc127, 287–308.
15. Chadwick, Owen. *The spirit of the Oxford movement*. Cambridge; Cambridge UP; 1990. Pp 324.
16. Cockshut, A.O.J. 'The literary and historical significance of the *Present position of Catholics*', Bc127, 111–27.
17. Cossiga, Francesco. 'Newman and Italy', Bc102, 19–23.
18. Crumb, Lawrence N. 'Publishing the *Oxford Movement*: Francis Rivington's letters to Newman', *Publishing History* 28 (1990), 5–53.
19. Darby, I.D. 'Colenso and baptism', *J. of Theology for Southern Africa* (Jun. 1989), 62–66.
20. d'Arcy, Eric. 'Newman's significance for the Roman Catholic Church', Bc102, 75–97.
21. Donaldson, Margaret. ' "The cultivation of the heart and the moulding of the will . . . ": the missionary contribution of the Society for Promoting Female Education in China, India, and the East', Bc128, 429–42.
22. Donovan, Grace. 'An American Catholic in Victorian England: Louisa, duchess of Leeds, and the Carroll family benefice', *Maryland Historical Magazine* 84 (1989), 223–34.
23. Dulles, Avery, SJ. 'The threefold office in Newman's ecclesiology', Bc127, 375–99.
24. Eisen, Sydney. 'Introduction' [Victorian faith], Bc145, 1–6.
25. Finnis, John. 'Conscience in the *Letter to the duke of Norfolk*', Bc127, 401–18.
26. Foister, Susan. *Cardinal Newman, 1801–1890: a centenary exhibition*. London; National Portrait Gallery; 1990. Pp 88.
27. Foster, Stewart. 'The life and death of a Victorian seminary: the English College, Bruges', *Recusant History* 20 (1990), 272–90.
28. Frappell, L.O. 'John Henry Newman: history and the two systems of providence', *J. of Religious History* 15 (1989), 470–87.
29. Gilley, Sheridan. *Newman and his age*. London; Darton, Longman & Todd; 1990. Pp x, 485.
30. Greenall, R.L. 'Parson as man of affairs: the Rev. Francis Litchfield of Farthinghoe (1792–1876)', *Northamptonshire Past & Present* 8/2 (1990–91), 121–35.
31. Griffiths, Eric. 'Newman: the foolishness of preaching', Bc127, 63–91.
32. Grubb, Mollie. 'Tensions in the Religious Society of Friends in England in the nineteenth century', *J. of the Friends' Historical Soc.* 56 (1990), 1–14.
33. Gunton, Colin. 'Newman's dialectic: dogma and reason in the seventy-third *Tract for the times*', Bc127, 309–22.
34. Helmstadter, Richard J. 'W.R. Greg: a Manchester creed', Bc145, 187–222.
35. Hill, Alan G. 'Originality and realism in Newman's novels', Bc127, 21–42.
36. Hill, Alan G.; Ker, Ian Turnbull. 'Newman as a letter-writer', Bc127, 129–51.

37. Hill, Myrtle. 'Ulster awakened: the '59 revival reconsidered', *J. of Ecclesiastical History* 41 (1990), 443–62.

38. Hillsman, Walter. 'Women in Victorian church music: their social, liturgical, and performing roles in Anglicanism', Bc128, 443–52.

39. Hutchison, William R. 'Religious liberty and the American impact abroad: William Cobbett on church and state', *Huntington Library Q.* 53 (1990), 1–13.

40. Jeremy, David J. *Capitalists and Christians: business leaders and the churches in Britain, 1900–1960.* Oxford; Oxford UP; 1990. Pp xviii, 492.

41. Kenny, Anthony. 'Newman as a philosopher of religion', Bc102, 98–122.

42. Kent, John. 'Anglican evangelicalism in the west of England, 1858–1900', Bc115, 179–200.

43. Ker, Ian Turnbull. 'Newman the satirist', Bc127, 1–20.

44. Ker, Ian Turnbull. *The achievement of John Henry Newman.* London; Collins; 1990. Pp x, 209.

45. Kowaleski-Wallace, Beth. 'Hannah and her sister: women and evangelicalism in early nineteenth-century England', *Nineteenth-Century Contexts* 12/2 (1988), 29–51.

46. Lash, Nicholas. 'Tides and twilight: Newman since Vatican II', Bc127, 447–64.

47. Leinster-Mackay, Donald. 'The continuing religious difficulty in late Victorian and Edwardian England: a case of gratuitous advice from the antipodes?', *History of Education* 19 (1990), 123–37.

48. Levine, George. 'Scientific discourse as an alternative to faith', Bc145, 225–61.

49. Lewis, Donald M. ' "Lights in dark places": women evangelists in early Victorian Britain, 1838–1857', Bc128, 415–27.

50. Lightman, Bernard. 'Ideology, evolution and late Victorian agnostic popularizers', Bc16, 285–310.

51. Lightman, Bernard. '*Robert Elsmere* and the agnostic crises of faith', Bc145, 283–311.

52. Lovegrove, Deryck W. 'Unity and separation: contrasting elements in the thought and practice of Robert and James Alexander Haldane', Bc115, 153–77.

53. Meynell, Hugo. 'Newman's vindication of faith in the *Grammar of assent*', Bc127, 247–61.

54. Mitchell, Basil. 'Newman as a philosopher', Bc127, 223–46.

55. Moore, James R. 'Of love and death: why Darwin "gave up Christianity" ', Bc16, 195–229.

56. Moore, James R. 'Theodicy and society: the crisis of the intelligentsia', Bc145, 153–86.

57. Munden, A.F. 'The first Palmerston bishop: Henry Montagu Villiers, bishop of Carlisle, 1856–1860, and bishop of Durham, 1860–1861', *Northern History* 26 (1990), 186–206.

58. Newsome, David. 'Newman and Oxford', Bc102, 35–51.

59. Norman, Edward. 'Newman's social and political thinking', Bc127, 153–73.

60. O'Brien, Susan. 'Lay-sisters and good mothers: working-class women in English convents, 1840–1910', Bc128, 453–65.

61. O'Collins, Gerald, SJ. 'Newman's seven notes: the case of the resurrection', Bc127, 337–52.

62. Quiney, Anthony. 'Treberfydd, the Raikes family, and their architect, John Loughborough Pearson', *Brycheiniog* 23 (1988–9), 65–74.

63. Quinn, John F. 'Newman, Faber and the Oratorian separation: a reappraisal', *Recusant History* 20 (1990), 106–26.

64. Rafferty, Oliver P. 'The Jesuit College, Manchester, 1875', *Recusant History* 20 (1990), 291–304.

65. Ramsey, Arthur Michael. 'John Henry Newman and the Oxford Movement', *Anglican & Episcopal History* 59 (1990), 330–44.

66. Roberts, J.M. '*The idea of a university* revisited', Bc127, 193–222.

67. Robson, John M. 'The *fiat* and finger of God: the Bridgewater Treatises', Bc145, 71–125.

68. Rodrigues-Pereira, Miriam. 'Relations of the Mahamad of the Spanish and Portuguese congregation of London with the Holy Land in the nineteenth century', *Jewish Historical Studies* 31 (1988–90), 197–229.

69. Rowlands, John Henry Lewis. *Church, state and society: the attitudes of John Keble, Richard Hurrell Froude and John Henry Newman, 1827–1845.* Worthing; Churchman; 1989. Pp xii, 262.

70. Sagovsky, Nicholas. *On God's side: the life of George Tyrrell.* Oxford; Oxford UP; 1990. Pp 276.

71. Seaborne, M.V.J. 'The religious census of 1851 and early chapel-building in north Wales: a sample survey', *National Library of Wales J.* 26 (1990), 281–310.

72. Sharrock, Roger. 'Newman's poetry', Bc127, 43–61.

73. Spencer-Silver, Patricia. 'George Myers [1803–1875], Pugin's builder', *Recusant History* 20 (1990), 262–71.

74. St John of Fawsley, lord. 'Newman: a portrait', Bc102, 24–34.

75. Stannard, Kevin P. 'Ideology, education, and social structure: elementary schooling in mid-Victorian England', *History of Education* 19 (1990), 105–22.

76. Stephen, M.D. ' "After thirty years": a note on Gladstone scholarship', *J. of Religious History* 15 (1989), 488–95.

77. Stewart, John V. 'Puller of Roath as a Christian apologist', *J. of Welsh Ecclesiastical History* 7 (1990), 55–67.

78. Strange, Roderick. 'Newman and the mystery of Christ', Bc127, 323–36.

79. Stuart, E.B. 'Unjustly condemned? Roman Catholic involvement in the APUC, 1857–1864' [Association for the Promotion of the Unity of Christendom], *J. of Ecclesiastical History* 41 (1990), 44–63.

80. Sullivan, Francis A., SJ. 'Newman on infallibility', Bc127, 419–46.

81. Sykes, S.W. 'Newman, Anglicanism, and the fundamentals', Bc127, 353–74.

82. Taylor, Brian. 'Founders and followers: leadership in Anglican religious communities', Bc123, 292–98.

83. Thompson, David M. 'The emergence of the nonconformist social gospel in England', Bc115, 255–80.
84. Tierney, David. 'The Catholic Apostolic Church: a study in Tory millenarianism', *Historical Research* 63 (1990), 289–315.
85. Turner, Frank. 'The Victorian crisis of faith and the faith that was lost', Bc145, 9–38.
86. von Arx, Jeffrey. 'The Victorian crisis of faith as a crisis of vocation', Bc145, 262–82.
87. Ward, Ted. 'Cornelia Churchill (1847–1927), 1st lady Wimborne, and the Church of England', *Hatcher Review* 3/29 (1990), 459–68.
88. Ward, W.R. 'Faith and fallacy: English and German perspectives in the nineteenth century', Bc145, 39–67.
89. Webb, R.K. 'The faith of nineteenth-century Unitarians: a curious incident', Bc145, 126–49.
90. Weidner, H.D (ed.). *The 'via media' of the Anglican Church: John Henry Newman.* Oxford; Oxford UP; 1990. Pp 416.
91. Williams, Rowan. 'Newman's *Arians* and the question of method in doctrinal history', Bc127, 263–85.
92. Wilson, A.N. 'Newman the writer', Bc102, 123–40.
93. Wolffe, John. 'The end of Victorian values? Women, religion, and the death of Queen Victoria', Bc128, 481–503.

## (f) *Economic Affairs*

1. Albert, Alice J. 'Fit work for women: sweated home-workers in Glasgow, *c.*1875–1914', Bc90, 158–77.
2. Alford, Bernard. 'Business enterprise and the growth of the commercial letterpress printing industry, 1850–1914', Bc24, 177–90.
3. Archer, John E. *'By a flash and a scare': incendiarism, animal maiming and poaching in East Anglia, 1815–1870.* Oxford; Oxford UP; 1990. Pp xi, 282.
4. Ballantine, Ishbel; *et al. The Singer strike, Clydebank, 1911.* Clydebank; Clydebank District Library; 1989. Pp 85.
5. Barker, Theodore Cardwell. 'Transport: the survival of the old beside the new', Bc25, 86–100.
6. Beaven, Bradley. 'Custom, culture and conflict: a study of the Coventry ribbon trade in the first half of the nineteenth century', *Midland History* 15 (1990), 83–99.
7. Benson, John. 'Black country history and labour history', *Midland History* 15 (1990), 100–10.
8. Berg, Maxine. 'Progress and providence in early nineteenth-century political economy' [review article], *Social History* 15 (1990), 365–75.
9. Broeze, Frank. ' "Our home is girt by sea": the passenger trade of Australia and New Zealand 1788–1914', Bc96, 441–65.
10. Brown, John C. 'The condition of England and the standard of living: cotton textiles in the northwest, 1806–1850', *J. of Economic History* 50 (1990), 591–614.

11. Brown, K.D. 'The children's toy industry in nineteenth-century Britain', *Business History* 32/2 (1990), 180–97.
12. Bruland, Kristine. 'The transformation of work in European industrialization', Bc25, 154–69.
13. Burt, Roger. 'The London Mining Exchange, 1850–1900', Bc24, 157–76.
14. Cain, P.J. 'Railways and price discrimination: the case of agriculture, 1880–1914', Bc24, 191–205.
15. Church, Roy A. 'Labour supply and innovation, 1800–1860: the boot and shoe industry', Bc24, 89–109.
16. Collins, Bruce. 'American enterprise and the British comparison', Bc144, 129–98.
17. Collins, Michael. 'English bank lending and the financial crisis of the 1870s', *Business History* 32/2 (1990), 198–224.
18. Cottrell, P.L. 'London financiers and Austria, 1863–1875: the Anglo-Austrian Bank', Bc24, 127–40.
19. Crafts, N.F.R.; Leybourne, S.J.; Mills, T.C. 'The climacteric in late Victorian Britain and France: a reappraisal of the evidence', *J. of Applied Econometrics* 4 (1989), 103–17.
20. Dawson, John. 'A mid-nineteenth century farm sales book', *T. of the Cumberland & Westmorland Antiq. & Arch. Soc.* 90 (1990), 287–93.
21. Dodd, J. Phillip. 'Agriculture in Sussex and the Corn Law lobby', *Southern History* 11 (1989), 53–68.
22. Drummond, Di. ' "Specifically designed"? Employers' labour strategies and worker responses in British railway workshops, 1838–1914', Bc43, 8–31.
23. Emmer, Piet C.; Kuijpers, A.J. 'The coolie ships: the transportation of indentured labourers between Calcutta and Paramaribo, 1873–1921', Bc96, 403–26.
24. Evans, Chris. 'Work, violence and community in early industrial Merthyr Tydfil', Bc27, 121–37.
25. Falkus, Malcolm. 'The development of municipal trading in the nineteenth century', Bc24, 61–88.
26. Feinstein, Charles H. 'Britain's overseas investments in 1913', *Economic History R.* 2nd ser. 43 (1990), 288–95.
27. Feinstein, Charles H. 'New estimates of average earnings in the United Kingdom, 1880–1913', *Economic History R.* 2nd ser. 43 (1990), 595–632.
28. Feinstein, Charles H. 'What really happened to real wages? Trends in wages, prices, and productivity in the United Kingdom, 1880–1913', *Economic History R.* 2nd ser. 43 (1990), 329–55.
29. FitzGerald, Robert. 'Employers' labour strategies, industrial welfare, and the response to new unionism at Bryant and May, 1888–1930', Bc43, 48–65.
30. Geary, Frank. 'Accounting for entrepreneurship in late Victorian Britain', *Economic History R.* 2nd ser. 43 (1990), 283–87.
31. Gemmell, Norman; Wardley, Peter. 'The contribution of services to British economic growth, 1856–1913', *Explorations in Economic History* 27 (1990), 299–321.

32. Green, E.H.H. 'The bimetallic controversy: empiricism belimed or the case for the issues', *English Historical R.* 105 (1990), 673–83.

33. Griffiths, Dennis. 'The early management of the *Standard*', Bc87, 120–32.

34. Harley, C. Knick. 'North Atlantic shipping in the late nineteenth-century: freight rates and the interrelationship of cargoes', Bc76, 147–71.

35. Harrison, A.E. 'Joint-stock company flotation in the cycle, motor-vehicle and related industries, 1882–1914', Bc24, 206–32.

36. Hartley, Charles W.S. *A biography of Sir Charles Hartley, civil engineer (1825–1915): the father of the Danube.* Lewiston (NY); Mellen; 1989. 2 vols. xiv, 399; 439.

37. Harvey, Charles; Press, Jon. 'The City and international mining, 1870–1914', *Business History* 32/3 (1990), 98–119.

38. Harvey, Charles; Press, Jon. 'William Morris and the marketing of art', Bc24, 22–40.

39. Harvey, Charles; Press, Jon. *Sir George White of Bristol, 1854–1916.* Bristol; Bristol Branch of the Historical Association; 1989. Pp 31.

40. Hatton, T.J. 'The demand for British exports, 1870–1913', *Economic History R.* 2nd ser. 43 (1990), 576–94.

41. Hetherington, Jill. 'Dairy-farming in Islington in the early nineteenth century: the career of Richard Laycock', *London & Middlesex Arch. Soc. T.* 38 (1987), 169–85.

42. Hickey, Joseph V. 'Welsh cattlemen of the Kansas Flint Hills: social and ideological dimensions of cattle entrepreneurship', *Agricultural History* 63/4 (1989), 56–71.

43. Huberman, Michael. 'Vertical disintegration in Lancashire: a comment on Temin' [with a reply by Peter Temin], *J. of Economic History* 50 (1990), 683–92.

44. Hyman, R. 'The sound of one hand clapping: a comment on the "rank and filism" debate', *International R. of Social History* 34 (1989), 309–26.

45. Irving, R.J. 'New industries for old? Some investment decisions of Sir W.G. Armstrong, Whitworth & Co. Ltd., 1900–1914', Bc24, 273–98.

46. James, Harold. 'The German experience and the myth of British cultural exceptionalism', Bc144, 91–128.

47. Jenkins, D.T.; Malin, J.C. 'European competition in woollen cloth, 1870–1914', *Business History* 32/4 (1990), 66–86.

48. Jeremy, David J. 'Anatomy of the British business elite, 1860–1980', Bc24, 341–61.

49. Jones, Francis I.W. 'The German challenge to British shipping, 1885–1914: its magnitude, nature and impact in China', *Mariner's Mirror* 76 (1990), 151–67.

50. Jones, S. 'The role of the shipping agent in migration: a study in business history', Bc96, 333–53.

51. Joyce, Patrick. 'Work', Bc46, 131–94.

52. Kershen, Anne J. 'Trade unionism among the Jewish tailoring workers of London and Leeds, 1872–1915', Bc38, 34–52.

53. Lane, Michael Ross. *Baron Marks of Woolwich: international*

*entrepreneur, engineer, patent agent and politician (1858–1938).*
London; Quiller; 1986. Pp xi, 146.

54. Lane, Michael Ross. *The Rendell connection: a dynasty of engineers.*
London; Quiller; 1989. Pp 208.

55. Lyons, J.S. 'Family response to economic decline: handloom weavers in
early nineteenth-century Lancashire', *Research in Economic History* 12
(1989), 45–91.

56. MacDougall, Philip. 'Granite and lime: the building of Chatham
dockyard's first stone dry dock', *Archaeologia Cantiana* 107 (1990 for
1989), 173–91.

57. Marx, Roland. 'Pleins feux sur la grandeur', Bc81, 22–37.

58. Mathias, Peter. 'Agriculture and industrialization', Bc25, 101–26.

59. Mathias, Peter. 'Financing the industrial revolution', Bc25, 69–85.

60. Matthew, H.C.G. 'Gladstonian finance', Bc70, 111–20.

61. McKeown, T.J. 'The politics of the Corn Law repeal and the theories of
commercial policy', *British J. of Political Science* 19 (1989), 353–80.

62. Morgan, Nicholas J. 'Enterprise and industry', *History Today* 40/5
(1990), 34–40.

63. Munro, J. Forbes. 'Suez and the shipowner: the response of the
MacKinnon shipping group to the opening of the canal, 1869–84',
Bc76, 97–117.

64. Musson, A.E. 'Joseph Whitworth and the growth of mass-production
engineering', Bc24, 232–72.

65. Newell, Edmund. ' "Copperopolis": the rise and fall of the copper
industry in the Swansea district, 1826–1931', *Business History* 32/3
(1990), 75–97.

66. Norris, John; Beale, Jerry; Lewis, John. *Edwardian enterprise: a review
of Great Western Railway development in the first decade of this
century.* Didcot; Wild Swan; 1987. Pp 202.

67. Payne, Peter. 'Entrepreneurship and British economic decline', Bc144,
25–58.

68. Peacock, A.J. *George Hudson, 1800–1871: the railway king*, vol. 2.
York; Peacock; 1989. Pp 353.

69. Peebles, H.B. 'A study in failure: J. & G. Thomson and shipbuilding at
Clydebank, 1871–1890', *Scottish Historical R.* 69 (1990), 22–48.

70. Pelzer, John D. 'Liverpool and the American Civil War', *History Today*
40/3 (1990), 46–52.

71. Perkins, Edwin J. 'Managing a dollar-sterling exchange account: Brown,
Shipley and Company in the 1850s', Bc24, 110–26.

72. Perren, Richard. 'Structural change and market growth in the food
industry: flour milling in Britain, Europe, and America, 1850–1914',
*Economic History R.* 2nd ser. 43 (1990), 420–37.

73. Pollard, Sidney. 'Reflections on entrepreneurship and culture in European societies', *T. of the Royal Historical Soc.* 5th ser. 40 (1990), 153–73.

74. Pollard, Sidney. *Britain's prime and Britain's decline: the British
economy, 1870–1914.* London; Arnold; new edn. 1989. Pp 336.

75. Ransom, Philip John Greer. *The Victorian railway and how it evolved.*
London; Heinemann; 1990. Pp 276.

76. Reisman, David. *Alfred Marshall's mission*. Basingstoke; Macmillan; 1990. Pp 309.
77. Robbins, Keith G. 'British culture versus British industry', Bc144, 1–24.
78. Robertson, Barbara W. 'In bondage: the female farm worker in south-east Scotland', Bc90, 117–35.
79. Rubinstein, W.D. 'Cultural explanations for Britain's economic decline: how true?', Bc144, 59–90.
80. Saul, S.B. 'The American impact on British industry, 1895–1914', Bc24, 321–40.
81. Saul, S.B. 'The machine tool industry in Britain to 1914', Bc24, 299–320.
82. Shaw, Gareth. 'Industrialization, urban growth and the city economy', Bc28, 55–79.
83. Shiells, Martha Ellen. 'Collective choice of working conditions: hours in British and US iron and steel, 1890–1923', *J. of Economic History* 50 (1990), 379–92.
84. Sutton, G.B. 'The marketing of ready made footwear in the nineteenth century: a study of the firm of C. & J. Clark', Bc24, 41–60.
85. Tucker, Gordon; Tucker, Mary. 'Slate working in north Cardiganshire with particular reference to Cwmerau', *Ceredigion* 11 (1988–9), 75–79.
86. Ville, Simon. 'Shipping in the port of Sunderland, 1815–1845', *Business History* 32/1 (1990), 32–51.
87. Warrington, Bernard. 'The bankruptcy of William Pickering in 1853: the hazards of publishing and bookselling in the first half of the nineteenth century', *Publishing History* 27 (1990), 5–25.
88. Williamson, Jeffrey G. 'The impact of the Corn Laws just prior to repeal', *Explorations in Economic History* 27 (1990), 123–56.
89. Williamson, Jeffrey G. 'The impact of the Irish on British labor markets during the industrial revolution', Bc49, 134–62.
90. Wykes, David L. ' "Trade flat, money scarce, spirits low": the journal of John Kirby of Leicester, 1813–1848', *Leicestershire Arch. and Historical Soc. T.* 64 (1990), 39–56.
91. Young, Craig. 'Computer-assisted mapping of the credit fields of nineteenth-century rural tradesmen in Scotland', *History & Computing* 1 (1989), 105–11.
92. Zeitlin, Jonathan. 'The meaning of managerial prerogative: industrial relations and the organisation of work in British engineering, 1880–1939', Bc43, 32–47.
93. Ziegler, Dieter. *Central bank, peripheral industry: the Bank of England in the provinces, 1826–1913*. London; Leicester UP; 1990. Pp 162.

## (g) *Social Structure and Population*

1. Anderson, Michael. 'The social implications of demographic change', Bc46, 1–70.
2. Anderson, Michael; Morse, D.J. 'The people' [of Scotland], Bc58, 8–45.
3. Bailey, Keith. 'Estate development in Victorian London: some examples

from Battersea', *London & Middlesex Arch. Soc. T.* 38 (1987), 187–202.

4. Baudemont, Suzanne. 'La gentry, sa saison, ses rites', Bc81, 93–108.
5. Burman, Rickie. 'Jewish women and the household economy in Manchester, *c.*1890–1920', Bc38, 55–75.
6. Campbell, R.H; Devine, Tom M. 'The rural experience' [Scotland], Bc58, 46–72.
7. Campbell, Roy H. 'Continuity and challenge: the perpetuation of the landed interest', Bc55, 122–35.
8. Cannadine, David. *The decline and fall of the British aristocracy.* Newhaven/London; Yale UP; 1990. Pp xiv, 813.
9. Cesarani, David. 'Introduction' [Anglo-Jewry], Bc38, 1–14.
10. Charlot, Monica; Marx, Roland. 'La société "duale" par excellence!', Bc81, 14–20.
11. Clarke, Norma. *Ambitious heights: writing, friendship, love—the Jewsbury sisters, Felicia Hemans and Jane Carlyle.* London; Routledge; 1990. Pp 256.
12. Davidoff, Leonore. 'The family in Britain', Bc46, 71–130.
13. Devine, Tom M. 'The emergence of the new elite in the Western Highlands and Islands, 1800–1860', Bc57, 108–35.
14. Dyck, Ian. 'Towards the "cottage charter": the expressive culture of farm workers in nineteenth-century England', *Rural History* 1 (1990), 95–111.
15. Fitzpatrick, David. 'A curious middle place: the Irish in Britain, 1871–1921', Bc49, 10–59.
16. Garrett, Eilidh M. 'The trials of labour: motherhood versus employment in a nineteenth-century textile centre', *Continuity & Change* 5 (1990), 121–54.
17. Garside, P.L. 'London and the Home Counties', Bc45, 471–539.
18. Gilley, Sheridan; Swift, Roger. 'Introduction' [Irish in Britain], Bc49, 1–9.
19. Glazier, Ira A.; Mageen, Deidre; Okeke, Barnabus. 'Socio-demographic characteristics of Irish immigrants, 1846–1851', Bc96, 243–78.
20. Gore, Keith. 'Shaftesbury Avenue, les feux de la rampe', Bc81, 129–43.
21. Hallas, Christine. 'Craft occupations in the late nineteenth century: some local considerations', *Local Population Studies* 44 (1990), 18–29.
22. Heath, Richard. *The Victorian peasant,* ed. Keith Dockray. Gloucester; Sutton; 1989. Pp xxvvii, 196.
23. Hendrick, Harry. *Images of youth: age, class and the male youth problem, 1880–1920.* Oxford; Oxford UP; 1990. Pp xii, 298.
24. Herson, John. 'Irish migration and settlement in Victorian England: a small-town perspective', Bc49, 84–103.
25. Hinde, P.R. Andrew. 'The marriage market in the nineteenth-century English countryside', *J. of European Economic History* 18 (1989), 383–92.
26. Howkins, Alun. 'Labour history and the rural poor, 1850–1980', *Rural History* 1 (1990), 113–22.
27. Ireson, Tony. 'Railway navvy to farmer: the memoirs of Thomas Henry

Masters of Catesby', *Northamptonshire Past & Present* 8/2 (1990–91), 161–66.

28. Israel, Kali A.K. 'Writing inside the kaleidoscope: re-presenting Victorian women public figures', *Gender & History* 2 (1990), 40–48.

29. Jamieson, Lynn. 'Rural and urban women in domestic service', Bc90, 137–57.

30. Kent, Susan Kingsley. *Sex and suffrage in Britain, 1860–1914*. London; Routledge; 1990. Pp 312.

31. Levine, Philippa. *Feminist lives in Victorian England: private lives and public commitment*. Oxford; Blackwell; 1990. Pp 256.

32. Livshin, Rosalyn. 'The acculturation of the children of immigrant Jews in Manchester, 1890–1930', Bc38, 79–96.

33. Mahood, Linda. 'The wages of sin: women, work and sexuality in the nineteenth century', Bc90, 29–48.

34. Meller, Helen. 'Planning theory and women's role in the city', *Urban History Yearbook* 17 (1990), 85–98.

35. Morris, R.J. 'Urbanisation and Scotland', Bc58, 73–102.

36. Oldham, Jean (ed.). *The diaries of Thomas Carleton Skarratt (1818–1909), draper of Kington, Herefordshire*. Kington; Kington History Soc.; 1987. Pp viii, 165.

37. Owen, Brian. 'The Newtown and Llanidloes Poor Law Union workhouse, Caersws, 1837–1847', *Montgomeryshire Collections* 78 (1990), 115–60.

38. Park, Peter B. *Guide to Liverpool's enumeration districts in the 1851 census*. Warrington; Liverpool & District Family History Soc.; 1989. Pp iii, 52.

39. Peterson, M. Jeanne. *Family, love, and work in the lives of Victorian gentlewomen*. Bloomington (In); Indiana UP; 1989. Pp xiv, 241.

40. Pooley, Colin. 'Segregation or integration? The residential experience of the Irish in mid-Victorian Britain', Bc49, 60–83.

41. Poovey, Mary. *Uneven developments: the ideological work of gender in mid-Victorian England*. Chicago; Chicago UP; 1989. Pp ix, 252.

42. Porter, Kevin; Weeks, Jeffrey. *Between the acts: lives of homosexual men, 1885–1967*. London; Routledge; 1990. Pp 176.

43. Postlethwaite, D. 'Mothering and mesmerism in the life of Harriet Martineau', *Signs* 14 (1989), 583–609.

44. Pretty, David. *The rural revolt that failed: farm workers' trade unions in Wales, 1880–1950*. Cardiff; Wales UP; 1989. Pp xiv, 291.

45. Price, Richard. *Labour in British society*. London; Routledge; 1990. Pp 272.

46. Ray, Michael. 'Who were the Brunswick Town commissioners? A study of a Victorian urban ruling elite, 1830–1873', *Sussex Arch. Collections* 127 (1989), 211–28.

47. Reay, Barry. 'Sexuality in nineteenth-century England: the social context of illegitimacy in rural Kent', *Rural History* 1 (1990), 219–47.

48. Reed, Mick. ' "Gnawing it out": a new look at economic relations in nineteenth-century rural England', *Rural History* 1 (1990), 83–94.

49. Reynolds, Sian. 'Women in the printing and paper trades in Edwardian Scotland', Bc90, 49–69.

50. Robbins, Keith G. 'La hierarchie des prostituées', Bc81, 144–56.
51. Robin, Jean. 'The relief of poverty in mid-nineteenth century Colyton', *Rural History* 1 (1990), 193–218.
52. Rowbotham, Judith. *Good girls make good wives: guidance for girls in Victorian fiction.* Oxford; Blackwell; 1989. viii, 301.
53. Rowlinson, Don D. 'An English settlement in Sheridan County, Kansas: the Cottonwood ranch', *Kansas History* 12 (1989), 160–65.
54. Ruggles, Steven. *Prolonged connections: the rise of the extended family in nineteenth-century England and America.* London; Wisconsin UP.; 1987. Pp xx, 282.
55. Smout, T.C. 'Scotland, 1850–1950', Bc45, 209–80.
56. Treble, James H. 'Skilled sectionalism, unemployment and class in Glasgow, 1880–1914', Bc104, 127–51.
57. Treble, James H. 'The occupied male labour force', Bc58, 167–205.
58. Wallis, Edmund Lamb. 'Mid-Victorian Finedon and Wellingborough: the memoirs of Edmund Lamb Wallis, [1848–1940]', *Northamptonshire Past & Present* 8/1 (1989–90), 39–51.
59. Williams, Bill. ' "East and West": class and community in Manchester Jewry, 1850–1914', Bc38, 15–33.
60. Woods, Robert. 'Population growth and economic change in the eighteenth and nineteenth centuries', Bc25, 127–53.

(h) *Social Policy*

1. Barnard, Sylvia M. *To prove I'm not forgot: living and dying in a Victorian city.* Manchester; Manchester UP; 1990. Pp xi, 212.
2. Bartrip, Peter W.J.; Fenn, P.T. 'The measurement of safety: factory accident statistics in Victorian and Edwardian Britain', *Historical Research* 63 (1990), 58–72.
3. Boot, H.M. 'Unemployment and Poor Law relief in Manchester, 1845–1850', *Social History* 15 (1990), 217–28.
4. Boyes, John H. 'Essex and the 1871 Fairs Act: "because Solon is virtuous there shall be no cream cakes and ale!" ', Bc65, 229–40.
5. Bradley, Ian Campbell. 'Titus Salt: enlightened entrepreneur', Bc70, 71–83.
6. Brayshay, Mark. 'The reform of urban management and the shaping of Plymouth's mid-Victorian landscape', Bc53, 105–30.
7. Briggs, Asa. 'Samuel Smiles: the gospel of self-help', Bc70, 85–96.
8. Brundage, Anthony; Eastwood, David; Mandler, Peter. 'The making of the New Poor Law *redivivus*', *Past & Present* 127 (1990), 183–201.
9. Cherry, Gordon E. 'Public policy and the morphology of western cities: the example of Britain in the nineteenth and twentieth centuries', Bc28, 32–44.
10. Childs, Michael J. 'Boy labour in late Victorian and Edwardian England and the remaking of the working class', *J. of Social History* 23 (1990), 783–802.
11. Craig, David. *On the crofter's trail: in search of the clearance Highlanders.* London; Cape; 1990. Pp 376.

12. Crowther, M.A. 'Poverty, health and welfare', Bc58, 265–89.
13. Daglish, N.D. 'Robert Morant's hidden agenda? The origins of the medical treatment of schoolchildren', *History of Education* 19 (1990), 139–48.
14. Darley, Gillian. *Octavia Hill*. London; Constable; 1990. Pp 399.
15. Daunton, M.J. 'Housing', Bc46, 195–250.
16. Davis, Graham. 'Little Irelands' [in the cities], Bc49, 104–33.
17. Dennis, R. 'The geography of Victorian values: philanthropic housing in London, 1840–1900', *J. of Historical Geography* 15 (1989), 40–54.
18. Dickie, Marie. 'Northampton's working-class homeowners: myth or reality?', *Northamptonshire Past & Present* 8/1 (1989–90), 69–72.
19. Driver, F. 'The historical geography of the workhouse system in England and Wales, 1834–1883', *J. of Historical Geography* 15 (1989), 269–86.
20. Eisenberg, Christiane. 'The comparative view in labour history: old and new interpretations of the English and German labour movements before 1914', *International R. of Social History* 34 (1989), 403–32.
21. Fraser, Derek. 'Joseph Chamberlain and the municipal ideal', Bc70, 135–46.
22. Fraser, W. Hamish. 'From civic gospel to municipal socialism', Bc104, 58–80.
23. Gaskell, S. Martin. 'Introduction' [slums], Bc48, 1–16.
24. Goodman, Judy. *'The unfortunate infants': an account of the Bermondsey Poor Law Institute for Children at the old Church House, Merton, 1820–1845*. London; John Innes Soc.; 1989. Pp 32.
25. Green, David R.; Parton, Alan G. 'Slums and slum life in Victorian England: London and Birmingham at mid-century', Bc48, 17–91.
26. Green, S.J.D. 'Religion and the rise of the common man: mutual improvement societies, religious associations and popular education in three industrial towns in the West Riding of Yorkshire, c.1850–1900', Bc104, 25–43.
27. Harrison, Brian. ' "Kindness and reason": William Lovett and education', Bc70, 13–28.
28. Klaus, Robert James. *The pope, the Protestants, and the Irish: papal aggression and anti-Catholicism in mid-nineteenth century England*. New York/London; Garland; 1987. Pp xii, 365.
29. Lacassagne, Claude-Laurence; Davie, Neil. 'Luxe, tintamarre et puanteur', Bc81, 57–74.
30. Lecaye, Alexis. 'L'homme qui riait la nuit', Bc81, 163–80.
31. Lown, Judy. *Women and industrialization: gender at work in nineteenth-century England*. Cambridge; Polity; 1990. Pp xi, 259.
32. MacMaster, Neil. 'The battle for Mousehold Heath, 1857–1884: "popular politics" and the Victorian public park', *Past & Present* 127 (1990), 117–54.
33. Mahood, Linda. *The Magdalenes: prostitution in the nineteenth century*. London; Routledge; 1989. Pp 205.
34. Mandler, Peter. 'Tories and paupers: Christian political economy and the making of the New Poor Law', *Historical J.* 33 (1990), 81–103.
35. Marx, Roland. 'Les trompettes de la charité', Bc81, 181–87.

36. Mingay, Gordon E. 'The rural slum', Bc48, 92–143.
37. Morris, Randall C. 'Whitehead and the new liberals on social progress', *J. of the History of Ideas* 51 (1990), 75–92.
38. Oddy, D.J. 'Food, drink and nutrition', Bc46, 251–78.
39. Pearson, Robin. 'Thrift or dissipation? The business of life assurance in the early nineteenth century', *Economic History R.* 2nd ser. 43 (1990), 236–54.
40. Phillips, John A. 'Working and moving in early nineteenth-century provincial towns', Bc27, 182–206.
41. Ridley, David. 'The Elemore colliery disaster, 1886, and its part in the debate on colliery explosions', *Archaeologia Aeliana* 5th ser. 18 (1990), 217–27.
42. Rodger, Richard. 'Crisis and confrontation in Scottish housing, 1880–1914', Bc59, 25–53.
43. Rodger, Richard. 'Introduction' [Scottish housing], Bc59, 1–24.
44. Tarn, John Nelson. 'New homes for barons and artisans', Bc92, 152–61.
45. Thompson, Francis M.L. 'Life after death: how successful nineteenth-century businessmen disposed of their fortunes', *Economic History R.* 2nd ser. 43 (1990), 40–61.
46. Tyack, Geoffrey. 'James Pennethorne and London street improvements, 1838–1855', *London J.* 15 (1990), 38–56.
47. Wilson, Ellen Gibson. *Thomas Clarkson: a biography.* Basingstoke; Macmillan; 1989. Pp 269.
48. Wrigley, Chris. 'May days and after', *History Today* 40/6 (1990), 35–41.

## (i) *Education*

1. Bartle, George F. 'The teaching manuals and lesson books of the British and Foreign School Society', *History of Education Soc. B.* 46 (1990), 22–33.
2. Berghoff, Hartmut. 'Public schools and the decline of the British economy, 1870–1914', *Past & Present* 129 (1990), 148–67.
3. Betts, Robin. 'A campaign for patriotism on the elementary school curriculum: lord Meath, 1892–1916', *History of Education Soc. B.* 46 (1990), 38–45.
4. Boucher, David. 'Practical Hegelianism: Henry Jones's lecture tour of Australia', *J. of the History of Ideas* 51 (1990), 423–52.
5. Corr, Helen. 'An exploration into Scottish education', Bc58, 290–309.
6. Evans, W. Gareth. 'The Welsh Intermediate and Technical Education Act, 1889: a centenary appreciation', *History of Education* 19 (1990), 195–210.
7. Evans, W. Gareth. 'The Welsh Intermediate and Technical Education Act 1889 and the education of girls', *Welsh History R.* 15 (1990–1), 183–217.
8. Evans, W. Gareth. *Education and female emancipation: the Welsh experience, 1847–1914.* Cardiff; Wales UP; 1990. Pp xii, 332.

9. Foden, Frank. *The examiner: James Booth and the origin of common examinations*. Leeds; School of Continuing Education, University of Leeds; 1989. Pp vii, 221.

10. Hansen, Volker. 'A note on Hugh J. Rose—a key figure in the British development of the theory of the teaching of English literature', *History of Education Soc. B.* 46 (1990), 34–37.

11. Jenkins, Roy. 'Newman and the idea of a university', Bc102, 141–58.

12. Kean, Hilda. *Challenging the state? The socialist and feminist educational experience, 1900–1930*. London; Falmer; 1990. Pp 217.

13. Osborne, Irving. *Jewish junior county awards in East London schools, 1893–1914: an interim report and guide to sources*. London; Centre for East London Studies; 1990. Pp 38.

14. Robertson, Pearl L. 'The development of an urban university: Glasgow, 1860–1914', *History of Education Q.* 30 (1990), 47–78.

15. Roderick, Gordon. 'Industry, technical manpower and education: South Wales in the nineteenth century', *History of Education* 19 (1990), 211–18.

16. Thomson, Christopher. 'Edwinstowe Artisans' Library', *Library History* 8 (1990), 140–44.

17. Turner, G. L'E. 'Experimental science in early nineteenth-century Oxford', *History of Universities* 8 (1989), 117–35.

18. Webster, Roger. 'Education in Wales and the rebirth of a nation', *History of Education* 19 (1990), 183–94.

19. York, B.A. 'Northamptonshire, the 1869 Endowed Schools Act and the reform of secondary education', *Northamptonshire Past & Present* 8/2 (1990–91), 155–59.

## (j) *Naval and Military*

1. Brown, D.K. *Before the ironclad: development of ship design, propulsion and armament in the Royal Navy, 1815–1860*. London; Conway Maritime; 1990. Pp 224.

2. Conacher, J.B. 'The Asian front in the Crimean War and the fall of Kars', *J. of the Soc. for Army Historical Research* 68 (1990), 169–87.

3. Gough, Barry M. 'Sea power and South America: the "Brazils" or South American station of the Royal Navy, 1808–1837', *American Neptune* 50 (1990), 26–34.

4. Henderson, Diana Mary. *Highland soldier: a social study of the Highland regiments, 1820–1920*. Edinburgh; Donald; 1989. Pp 336.

5. Lambert, Andrew D. *The Crimean war: British grand strategy against Russia, 1853–1856*. Manchester; Manchester UP; 1990. Pp xxi, 369.

6. Partridge, Michael S. 'Wellington and the defence of the realm, 1819–1852', Bc13, 238–62.

7. Robertson, Ian G. ' "Dear Betsey": reflections on two letters from the First Carlist War', Bc65, 185–98.

8. Sumida, Jon T. 'British naval administration and policy in the age of Fisher', *J. of Military History* 54 (1990), 1–26.

9. Sweetman, John. *Balaclava, 1854: the charge of the Light Brigade.* London; Osprey (Campaign ser. vol. 6); 1990. Pp 96.
10. Thompson, Neville. 'The uses of adversity', Bc13, 1–10.
11. Wood, Stephen. 'Thomas Carter and a manuscript history of the 26th (or Cameronian) Regiment', *J. of the Soc. for Army Historical Research* 68 (1990), 51–55; 120–27.

## (k) *Science and Medicine*

1. Alexander, Wendy. 'Early Glasgow women medical graduates', Bc90, 70–94.
2. Barton, Ruth. ' "An influential set of chaps": the X-Club and Royal Society politics, 1864–1885', *British J. for the History of Science* 23 (1990), 53–81.
3. Bartrip, Peter W.J. 'Quacks and cash', *History Today* 40/9 (1990), 45–51.
4. Bowler, Peter J. 'Holding your head up high: degeneration and orthogenesis in theories of human evolution', Bc16, 329–53.
5. Brock, W.H. 'The Cavendish Society's wonderful repertory of chemistry', *Annals of Science* 47 (1990), 77–80.
6. Brooke, John Hedley. 'Scientific thought and its meaning for religion: the impact of French science on British natural theology, 1827–1859', *Revue de Synthèse* 110 (1989), 33–60.
7. Browne, Janet. 'Spas and sensibilities: Darwin at Malvern', *Medical History*, Supplement 10 (1990), 102–13.
8. Bunting, Brian T. 'The turning of the worm: early nineteenth-century concepts of soil in Britain—the development of ideas and ideas of development, 1834–1843', Bc15, 85–107.
9. Collinson, Susan. 'Robert Knox's anatomy of race', *History Today* 40/12 (1990), 44–49.
10. Craig, Patricia Maureen. 'The changing public estimate of the medical profession in nineteenth-century Bristol', Bc126, 189–96.
11. Cunningham, Frank F. 'James Forbes on the Mer de Glace in 1842: early quantification in geomorphology', Bc15, 109–26.
12. Cunningham, Frank F. *James David Forbes, pioneer Scottish glaciologist.* Edinburgh; Scottish Academic Press; 1990. Pp 340.
13. Davidson, I. 'George Deacon (1843–1909) and the Vrynwy works', *Newcomen Soc. T.* 59 (1990 for 1987/8), 81–95.
14. Debruyn, John R. 'Journal of a plague year: Arthur Helps, Stephen Spring-Rice, John Simon and the Health Fund for London, 1853–1854', *B. of the John Rylands University Library of Manchester* 72/1 (1990), 171–86.
15. Elliott, Malcolm. 'John Buck [1816–1880]: pioneer of preventive medicine and the care of the mentally ill', *Leicestershire Arch. and Historical Soc. T.* 64 (1990), 57–61.
16. Emrys-Roberts, R. Meyrick. 'On the track of Woozles: where was the first cottage hospital?', Bc126, 29–38.

17. Geary, Laurence M. 'O'Connorite Bedlam: Feargus and his grand-nephew, Arthur', *Medical History* 34 (1990), 125–43.
18. Glaser, Sholem. 'Weaving a web around Dr Henry Harington', Bc126, 140–48.
19. Gooday, Graeme. 'Precision measurement and the genesis of physics teaching laboratories in Victorian Britain', *British J. for the History of Science* 23 (1990), 25–51.
20. Guy, Jean. 'Flying sparks: personalities in early south-western radiology', Bc126, 66–74.
21. Hamlin, Christopher. *A science of impurity: water analysis in nineteenth-century Britain.* Bristol; Hilger; 1990. Pp xiii, 342.
22. Helfand, William H. 'Samuel Solomon and the cordial balm of Gilead', *Pharmacy History* 31 (1989), 151–59.
23. Hillam, Christine. 'The dental profession in the provinces in the 1850s', Bc126, 83–89.
24. Jordan, D.W. 'The magnetic circuit model, 1850–1890: the resisted flow image in magnetostatics', *British J. for the History of Science* 23 (1990), 131–73.
25. Lycett, C.D.L. *Sir William Robert Smith, 1850–1932: a short biography.* London; Royal Inst. of Public Health & Hygiene; 1989. Pp 131.
26. Moscucci, Ornella. *The science of woman: gynaecology and gender in England, 1800–1929.* Cambridge; Cambridge UP (Cambridge History of Medicine); 1990. Pp 278.
27. Richards, Evelleen. 'Huxley and woman's place in science: the "woman question" and the control of Victorian anthropology', Bc16, 253–84.
28. Rupke, Nicolaas A. *Vivisection in historical perspective.* London; Routledge; 1990. Pp 384.
29. Schaffer, Simon. 'The nebular hypothesis and the science of progress', Bc16, 131–64.
30. Schweber, S.S. 'John Herschel and Charles Darwin: a study in parallel lives', *J. of the History of Biology* 22 (1989), 1–71.
31. Secord, James A. 'Behind the veil: Robert Chambers and *Vestiges*', Bc16, 165–94.
32. Summers, Anne. 'Ministering angels: Victorian ladies and nursing reform', Bc70, 121–33.
33. Vertinsky, Patricia. *The eternally wounded woman: women, doctors and exercise in the late nineteenth century.* Manchester; Manchester UP; 1990. Pp 279.
34. Wilson, David B. (ed.). *The correspondence between Sir George Gabriel Stokes and Sir William Thomson, Baron Kelvin of Largs*, vols 1–2. Cambridge; Cambridge UP; 1990. Pp 781.
35. Wood, J.L. 'The Sulzer steam engine comes to Britain', *Newcomen Soc. T.* 59 (1990 for 1987/8), 129–52.
36. Young, Anne. 'The nineteenth-century domestic medicine chest', Bc126, 169–79.

## (l) Intellectual and Cultural

1. Angelomatis-Tsougarakis, Helen. *The eve of the Greek revival: British travellers' perceptions of early nineteenth-century Greece*. London; Routledge; 1990. Pp 304.
2. Annan, Noel. 'The cult of homosexuality in England, 1850–1950', *Biography* 13 (1990), 189–202.
3. Armbrust, Crys. 'Nineteenth-century re-presentations of George Herbert: publishing history as critical embodiment', *Huntington Library Q.* 53 (1990), 131–51.
4. Arnold, A.J. 'The belated entry of professional soccer into the West Riding textile district of northern England: commercial imperatives and problems', *International J. of the History of Sport* 6 (1989), 319–34.
5. Ashplant, T.G. 'Northamptonshire's working-men's clubs, 1880–1914', *Northamptonshire Past & Present* 8/1 (1989–90), 53–68.
6. Bailey, Peter. 'Parasexuality and glamour: the Victorian barmaid as cultural prototype', *Gender & History* 2 (1990), 148–72.
7. Bain, Roly. 'Clowns and Augustes', Bc92, 297–305.
8. Barbour, Jane. 'Haywood Sumner—a very private person', *Hatcher Review* 3/29 (1990), 438–48.
9. Beer, John. 'The "civilization" of Bloomsbury', Bc93, 197–211.
10. Beetham, Margaret. 'Towards a theory of the periodical as a publishing genre', Bc87, 19–32.
11. Berthoud, Jacques. 'Literature and drama' [Edwardian], Bc93, 47–99.
12. Birkett, Dea. 'Mary Kingsley and West Africa', Bc70, 171–85.
13. Blain, Virginia. 'Rosina Bulwer Lytton and the rage of the unheard', *Huntington Library Q.* 53 (1990), 211–36.
14. Bowler, Peter J. *The invention of progress: the Victorians and the past.* Oxford; Blackwell; 1989. Pp 231.
15. Bradbury, David John. *Welbeck and the 5th duke of Portland.* Mansfield; Wheel; 1989. Pp 40.
16. Brandwood, G.K. 'To scrape or not to scrape? Plaster, stucco and Victorian church restorers in Leicestershire', *Leicestershire Arch. and Historical Soc. T.* 64 (1990), 73–77.
17. Bruckmuller-Genlot, Danielle. 'Le salon Rossetti: 16, Cheyne Walk, Chelsea', Bc81, 109–22.
18. Burkhauser, Jude. *'The Glasgow Girls': women in art and design, 1880–1920.* Edinburgh; Canongate; 1990. Pp 264.
19. Carré, Jacques. 'The public park' [later Victorian age], Bc92, 77–85.
20. Charlot, Claire. 'Harrod's, l'autel de la mode', Bc81, 76–84.
21. Charlot, Monica. 'Le spleen des exilés français', Bc81, 48–56.
22. Charlot, Monica. 'Mort et funérailles de la reine Victoria', Bc81, 220–28.
23. Cheyette, Bryan. 'The other self: Anglo-Jewish fiction and the representation of Jews in England, 1875–1905', Bc38, 97–111.
24. Colby, Robert A. 'Harnessing Pegasus: Walter Besant, *The Author* and the profession of authorship', *Victorian Periodicals R.* 23 (1990), 111–20.

25. Collins, Irene. 'Charles Dickens and the French revolution', *Literature & History* ns 1 (1990), 40–57.

26. Coote, Stephen. *The life and work of William Morris.* London; Garamond; 1990. Pp 224.

27. Cork, Richard. 'The visual arts' [Edwardian and later], Bc93, 157–95.

28. Crook, Paul. 'Peter Chalmers Mitchell and antiwar evolutionism in Britain during the Great War', *J. of the History of Biology* 22 (1989), 325–56.

29. Crosby, Christina. *The ends of history: Victorians and 'the women question'.* London; Routledge; 1990. Pp 240.

30. Crump, Jeremy. 'Athletics', Bc51, 44–77.

31. Cunningham, Hugh. 'Leisure and culture', Bc46, 279–340.

32. Curl, James Stevens. *Victorian architecture.* Newton Abbot; David & Charles; 1990. Pp 320.

33. Dearden, James Shackley. *John Ruskin's Camberwell.* St Albans; Brentham; 1990. Pp 52.

34. Dodd, Christopher. 'Rowing', Bc51, 276–307.

35. Donaldson, Islay Murray. *The life and work of Samuel Rutherford Crockett.* Aberdeen; Aberdeen UP; 1989. Pp 357.

36. Donnelly, Michael. 'Glasgow's glorious glass', *History Today* 40/5 (1990), 29–33.

37. Eadie, William. *Movements of modernity: the case of Glasgow and the art noveau.* London; Routledge; 1990. Pp viii, 292.

38. Edwards, Owen Dudley. 'Arthur Conan Doyle and the use of English provincial medicine in fiction', Bc126, 197–214.

39. Eisenberg, Christiane. 'The middle class and competition: some considerations of the beginnings of modern sport in England and Germany', *International J. of the History of Sport* 7 (1990), 265–82.

40. Fraser, W. Hamish. 'Developments in leisure', Bc58, 236–64.

41. Freeman, Gwendolen (ed.). *United family record: some late Victorians.* Studley; Brewin; 1989. Pp 128.

42. Fuller, Peter. 'Fine arts' [later Victorian], Bc92, 162–207.

43. Garrigan, Kristine Ottesen. 'Bearding the competition: John Ruskin's "Academy notes"', *Victorian Periodicals R.* 22 (1989), 148–56.

44. Germain, Lucienne. 'L'East End de Yaacov Revinski', Bc81, 85–92.

45. Gilbert, Cecil (ed.). *The studio diaries of Alfred Gilbert for 1900 and 1901.* Newcastle-upon-Tyne; Gilbert; 1990. Pp 178.

46. Gillett, Paula. *The Victorian painters' world.* Gloucester; Sutton; 1990. Pp xiii, 299.

47. Gomme, Andor. 'The city of Glasgow', Bc92, 208–21.

48. Gordon, Scott. 'Darwin and political economy: the connection reconsidered', *J. of the History of Biology* 22 (1989), 437–60.

49. Grandfield, Yvette. 'The holiday diary of Thomas Lott, 12–22 July 1815', *Archaeologia Cantiana* 107 (1990 for 1989), 63–82.

50. Hamilton, Vivien. *Joseph Crawhall, 1861–1913: one of the Glasgow Boys.* London; Murray; 1990. Pp xiv, 177.

51. Harrop, Josephine. *Victorian portable theatres.* London; Soc. for Theatre Research; 1989. Pp 145.

52. Harvie, Christopher; Walker, Graham. 'Community and culture', Bc58, 336–57.

53. Haskell, Francis. 'The growth of British art history and its debts to Europe', *P. of the British Academy* 74 (1989 for 1988), 203–24.

54. Haythornthwaite, J. 'Friendly encounters: a study of the relationship between the house of Blackwood and Margaret Oliphant in her role as literary critic', *Publishing History* 28 (1990), 79–88.

55. Hill, Alan. *One hundred years of libraries in Barking: a centenary report.* London; Borough of Barking and Dagenham; 1989. Pp vi, 31.

56. Holloway, John. 'Literature' [later Victorian], Bc92, 87–143.

57. Howarth, Thomas. *Charles Rennie Mackintosh and the modern movement.* London; Routledge; 1990. Pp 440.

58. Howson, James. *First in Essex: one hundred years of library service in Barking, 1889–1989.* London; Borough of Barking and Dagenham; 1989. Pp 30.

59. Huggins, M. 'The spread of Association Football in north-east England, 1876–1890: the pattern of diffusion', *International J. of the History of Sport* 6 (1989), 299–318.

60. Jenkins, Ray. 'Salvation for the fittest? A West African sportsman in Britain in the age of the new imperialism', *International J. of the History of Sport* 7 (1990), 23–60.

61. Jobey, George. 'The Society of Antiquaries of Newcastle-upon-Tyne', *Archaeologia Aeliana* 5th ser. 18 (1990), 197–216.

62. Johnson, Pam. 'Edith Simcox and heterosexism in biography: a lesbian-feminist exploration', Bc1, 55–76.

63. Jolliffe, John (ed.). *Neglected genius: the diaries of Benjamin Robert Haydon.* London; Hutchinson; 1990. Pp xii, 260.

64. Jones, Philip Henry. '*Yr Amserau*: the first decade, 1843–1852' [The Times], Bc87, 85–103.

65. Jones, Rosemary A.N. 'Popular culture, policing, and the "disappearance" of the ceffyl pren [wooden horse] in Cardigan, *c.*1837–1850', *Ceredigion* 11 (1988–9), 19–39.

66. Jones, Stephen. 'Attic attitudes: Leighton and aesthetic philosophy', Bc70, 187–97.

67. Kelley, Philip; Hudson, Ronald (ed.). *The Brownings' correspondence, vol. 7: March to October 1843.* London; Athlone; 1989. Pp 429.

68. Kennedy, Michael. 'Music' [Edwardian and later], Bc93, 116–54.

69. Kennedy, Michael. 'Music' [later Victorian], Bc92, 269–95.

70. Kramarae, Cheris; Rakow, Lana. *The revolution in words: righting women, 1868–1871.* London; Routledge; 1990. Pp 320.

71. Kramarae, Cheris; Russo, Ann (ed.). *The radical women's press of the 1850s.* London; Routledge; 1990. Pp 368.

72. Langley, Leanne. 'The musical press in nineteenth-century England', *Notes* 46 (1990), 583–92.

73. Layman, C.H. (ed.). *Man of letters: the early life and love letters of Robert Chambers.* Edinburgh; Edinburgh UP; 1990. Pp 200.

74. Lowerson, John. 'Angling', Bc51, 12–43.

75. Lowerson, John. 'Golf', Bc51, 187–214.

76. Lyons, J.B. 'Milton's Dublin editor: Edward Hill, MD', Bc126, 149–58.
77. MacKechnie, Aonghus. 'Walter Newall, architect in Dumfries', *Dumfriesshire & Galloway Natural History & Antiq. Soc. T.* 3rd ser. 62 (1988), 78–88.
78. Marsden, Gordon. 'Introduction' [Victorian values], Bc70, 1–12.
79. Marx, Roland. 'Sherlock Holmes et Baker Street', Bc81, 157–62.
80. Mason, Tony. 'Afterword' [sport], Bc51, 344–54.
81. Mason, Tony. 'Football', Bc51, 146–86.
82. Mason, Tony. 'Introduction' [sport], Bc51, 1–11.
83. Matthew, H.C.G. 'Noetics, Tractarians, and the reform of the university of Oxford in the nineteenth century', *History of Universities* 9 (1990), 195–225.
84. Mazlish, Bruce. 'Marx's historical understanding of the proletariat and class in nineteenth-century England', *History of European Ideas* 12 (1990), 731–47.
85. Metcalfe, Alan. ' "Potshare bowling" in the mining communities of east Northumberland, 1800–1914', Bc52, 29–44.
86. Miller, Elaine. 'Through all changes and through all chances: the relationship of Ellen Nussey and Charlotte Brontë', Bc1, 29–54.
87. Morgan, Joan; Richards, Alison. *A paradise out of a common field: the pleasures and plenty of the Victorian garden.* London; Century; 1990. Pp 256.
88. Mudge, Bradford Keyes. *Sara Coleridge, a Victorian daughter: her life and essays.* London; Yale UP; 1989. Pp 312.
89. Mulvey, Christopher. *Transatlantic manners: social patterns in nineteenth-century Anglo-American travel literature.* Cambridge; Cambridge UP; 1990. Pp 260.
90. Mumm, S.D. 'Writing for their lives: women applicants to the Royal Literary Fund, 1840–1880', *Publishing History* 27 (1990), 27–47.
91. Murphy, P.T. ' "Imagination flaps its sportive wings": views of fiction in British working-class periodicals, 1816–1858', *Victorian Studies* 32 (1989), 339–64.
92. Nacleod, Dianne Sachko. 'Private and public patronage in Victorian Newcastle', *J. of the Warburg & Courtauld Institutes* 52 (1989), 188–208.
93. Naylor, Gillian. 'Design and industry', Bc93, 255–93.
94. Naylor, Gillian. 'Design, craft and industry', Bc92, 223–59.
95. Nelson, C. 'Sex and the single boy: ideals of manliness and sexuality in Victorian literature for boys', *Victorian Studies* 32 (1989), 525–50.
96. Nenadic, Stana. 'Illegitimacy, insanity, and insolvency: Wilkie Collins and the Victorian nightmares', Bc61, 133–62.
97. Owen, J.S.W. 'Banbury and District Golf Club, 1894–1919', *Cake & Cockhorse* 11/7 (1990), 154–73.
98. Parratt, Catriona M. 'Athletic "womanhood": exploring sources for female sport in Victorian and Edwardian England', *J. of Sport History* 16 (1989), 140–57.
99. Paz, D.G. 'Bonfire night in mid-Victorian Northants: the politics of a popular revel', *Historical Research* 63 (1990), 316–28.

100. Port, M.H. 'The life of an architectural sinner: Thomas Wayland Fletcher, 1833–1901', *London J.* 15 (1990), 57–71.
101. Price, William. 'The Eisteddfod', Bc92, 261–67.
102. Pykett, Lyn. 'Reading the periodical press: text and context', Bc87, 3–18.
103. Reid, Douglas A. 'Beasts and brutes: popular blood sports, *c*.1780–1860', Bc52, 12–28.
104. Rich, Paul. 'The quest for Englishness', Bc70, 211–25.
105. Richards, Bernard. 'Écrivains, pubs et cafés', Bc81, 123–28.
106. Robbins, Keith G. 'On prophecy and politics: some pragmatic reflections', Bc115, 281–96.
107. Roberts, Brynley F. 'Welsh periodicals: a survey', Bc87, 71–84.
108. Robinson, Paul. 'Royal justice and folk justice: conflict arising over a skimmington in Potterne in 1857', *Wiltshire Arch. & Natural History Magazine* 83 (1990), 147–54.
109. Rowbotham, Sheila. ' "Commanding the heart": Edward Carpenter and friends', Bc70, 199–210.
110. Rowell, George. 'The drama of Wilde and Pinero', Bc92, 144–51.
111. Russell, David. *Popular music in England, 1840–1914: a social history.* Manchester; Manchester UP; 1989. Pp 303.
112. Scharff, Robert C. 'Mill's misreading of Comte on "interior observation" ', *J. of the History of Philosophy* 27 (1989), 559–72.
113. Scholfield, Philip (ed.). *Securities against misrule and other constitutional writings for Tripoli and Greece.* Oxford; Oxford UP (Collected works of Jeremy Bentham); 1990. Pp xvi, 558.
114. Scott, Patrick. 'Tennyson's *Maud* and its American publishers: a relationship reconsidered', *Papers of the Bibliographical Soc. of America* 83 (1989), 153–67.
115. Sharples, M.L. 'The Fawkes-Turner connection and the art collection at Farnley Hall, Otley, 1792–1937: a great estate enhanced and supported', *Northern History* 26 (1990), 131–59.
116. Shipley, Stan. 'Boxing', Bc51, 78–115.
117. Smith, David. 'George Frederick Cruchley, 1796–1880', *Map Collector* 49 (1989), 16–22.
118. Summerson, John. 'Architecture' [Edwardian], Bc93, 213–45.
119. Summerson, John. 'Architecture' [later Victorian], Bc92, 43–75.
120. Torrens, Hugh S. 'A Wiltshire pioneer in geology and his legacy—Henry Shorto III (1778–1864), cutler and fossil collector of Salisbury', *Wiltshire Arch. & Natural History Magazine* 83 (1990), 170–89.
121. Tranter, Neil L. 'Organised sport and the working classes of central Scotland, 1820-1900: the neglected sport of quoiting', Bc52, 45–66.
122. Tranter, Neil L. 'The chronology of organized sport in nineteenth-century Scotland: a regional study, I—patterns', *International J. of the History of Sport* 7 (1990), 188–203.
123. Trela, D.J. 'Carlyle, Bulwer and the *New Monthly Magazine*', *Victorian Periodicals R.* 22 (1989), 157–62.
124. Tyson, Blake. 'Some nineteenth-century inscriptions at Kirkby-in-Furness, Cumbria', *T. of the Ancient Monuments Soc.* 34 (1990), 133–50.

125. Vamplew, Wray. 'Horse-racing', Bc51, 215–44.
126. Walker, Helen. 'Lawn tennis', Bc51, 245–75.
127. Webster, E. 'Leisure and pleasure in nineteenth-century Halifax', *Halifax Antiq. Soc. T.* (1990 for 1989), 23–46.
128. Weinstein, D. 'Equal freedom, rights and utility in Spencer's moral philosophy', *History of Political Thought* 11 (1990), 119–42.
129. Williams, Gareth. 'Rugby Union', Bc51, 308–43.
130. Williams, Guy Richard. *Augustus Pugin versus Decimus Burton: a Victorian architectural duel.* London; Cassell; 1990. Pp 160.
131. Williams, Jack. 'Cricket', Bc51, 116–45.
132. Wolff, Janet; Arscott, Caroline. ' "Cultivated capital": patronage and art in nineteenth-century Manchester and Leeds', Bc70, 29–41.
133. Woodring, Carl. *Nature into art: cultural transformations in nineteenth-century Britain.* London; Harvard UP; 1989. Pp xvi, 326.
134. Yates, Nigel. 'Pugin and the medieval dream', Bc70, 59–70.
135. Young, Robert M. 'Herbert Spencer and "inevitable" progress', Bc70, 147–57.
136. Zimmer, Louis B. 'J.S. Mill and Bentham on liberty: the case of the unacknowledged mentor', *The Historian* [USA] 52 (1990), 375–93.

# I.  BRITAIN SINCE 1914

*See also*  Aa13,15,48,62,69,71,77,79,100,b3,c72;  Bc5,7–11,23,35,93,134; Ha2,8,17,b18,22,40,62,f92,g42,44,58,h9,i12,k25–26,l2,18,27–28,68,97, 115.

(a) *General*

1. Carswell, Jeanne; *et al.* (ed.). *Ours to defend: Leicestershire people remember the Home Front.* Coalville; Mantle Oral History Project; 1989. Pp 84.
2. Catterall, Peter. 'The state of literature on post-war British history', Bc35, 221–41.
3. Eglinton, Edmund; Greenhill, Basil (ed.). *The Mary Fletcher: seven days in the life of a west country coasting ketch.* Exeter; Exeter UP; 1990. Pp 96.
4. Ekstein, Morris. *Rites of spring: the Great War and the birth of the modern age.* Boston (Ma); Houghton Mifflin; 1989. Pp xvi, 396.
5. Laybourn, Keith. *Britain on the breadline: a social and political history of Britain between the wars.* Gloucester; Sutton; 1990. Pp 222.
6. Perrett, Bryan. *Liverpool: a city at war.* London; Hale; 1990. Pp 176.
7. Searle, Adrian. *The Isle of Wight at war, 1939–1945.* Wimborne; Dovecote; 1989. Pp 160.
8. Sinclair, Andrew. *War like a wasp: the lost decade of the forties.* London; Hamish Hamilton; 1989. Pp 326.
9. Smith, Malcolm. *British politics, society and the state since the late nineteenth century.* Basingstoke; Macmillan; 1990. Pp 264.

10. Stevenson, John. 'More light on World War One', *Historical J.* 33 (1990), 195–210.
11. Veysey, Arthur Geoffrey. *Clwyd a'r rhyfel* [Clwyd at war, 1939–1945]. Hawarden; Clwyd Record Office; 1989. Pp 72.


(b) *Politics*

1. Alderman, Geoffrey. 'M.H. Davis: the rise and fall of a communal upstart', *Jewish Historical Studies* 31 (1988–90), 249–68.
2. Amery, Julian. 'The Suez group: a retrospective on Suez', Bc7, 110–26.
3. Artis, Michael; Cobham, David (ed.). *Labour's economic policies, 1974–1979*. Manchester; Manchester UP; 1990. Pp 250.
4. Aughey, Arthur. 'The moderate Right: the Conservative tradition in America and Britain', Bc6, 99–123.
5. Ball, Stuart. 'The 1922 Committee: the formative years, 1922–1945', *Parliamentary History* 9 (1990), 129–57.
6. Ball, Stuart. 'The politics of appeasement: the fall of the duchess of Atholl and the Kinross and West Perth by-election, December 1938', *Scottish Historical R.* 69 (1990), 49–83.
7. Barnes, James; Barnes, Patricia. 'Oswald Mosley as entrepreneur', *History Today* 40/3 (1990), 11–16.
8. Billig, Michael. 'The extreme Right: continuities in anti-semitic conspiracy theory in post-war Europe', Bc6, 146–66.
9. Birkenhead, Frederick W.F.S., earl of. *Churchill, 1874–1922*, ed. Sir John Colville. London; Harrap; 1989. Pp 540.
10. Bourne, Richard. *Lords of Fleet Street: the Harmsworth dynasty.* London; Unwin Hyman; 1990. Pp 224.
11. Bowker, Mike; Shearman, Peter. 'The Soviet Union and the Left in Britain', Bc8, 147–67.
12. Callaghan, John. *Socialism in Britain since 1884.* Oxford; Blackwell; 1990. Pp viii, 279.
13. Cockett, Richard B. 'Ball, Chamberlain, and *Truth*', *Historical J.* 33 (1990), 131–42.
14. Cockett, Richard B. (ed.). *My dear Max: the letters of Brendan Bracken to lord Beaverbrook, 1925–1958.* London; Historians' Press; 1990. Pp viii, 218.
15. Coghlan, John F. *Sport and British politics since 1960.* London; Falmer; 1990. Pp 330.
16. Dalyell, Tam. *Dick Crossman: a portrait.* London; Weidenfeld & Nicolson; 1989. Pp x, 253.
17. Davidson, William Gordon. 'The Cairo Forces' Parliament' [1944], *Labour History R.* 55/3 (1990), 20–26.
18. Eatwell, Roger. 'Right or rights? The rise of the "New Right" ', Bc6, 3–17.
19. Garner, Robert W. *The ideological impact of the trade unions on the Labour Party, 1918–1931.* Manchester; Dept. of Government, University of Manchester; 1989. Pp 17.

20. Glazer, Nathan. 'Ideas and politics in Britain: an American view', Bc80, 13–31.

21. Hetherington, S.J. *Katharine Atholl, 1874–1960: against the tide.* Aberdeen; Aberdeen UP; 1990. Pp 234.

22. Holmes, Colin. 'Enemy aliens?', *History Today* 40/9 (1990), 25–31.

23. Hough, Richard. *Winston and Clementine: the triumph of the Churchills.* London; Bantam; 1990. Pp 480.

24. Jones, J. Graham. 'Socialism, devolution and a Secretary of State for Wales, 1940–1964', *Honourable Soc. of Cymmrodorion T.* (1989), 135–59.

25. King, Francis; Matthews, George (ed.). *About turn: the Communist Party and the outbreak of the Second World War (the verbatim record of the Central Committee meetings, 25 September and 2–3 October 1939).* London; Lawrence & Wishart; 1990. Pp 318.

26. Kushner, Tony. 'The impact of British anti-semitism, 1918–1945', Bc38, 191–208.

27. Leydesdorff, Selma. 'Politics, identification and the writing of women's history', Bc2, 9–20.

28. London, Louise. 'Jewish refugees, Anglo-Jewry and British government policy, 1930–1940', Bc38, 163–90.

29. Marquand, David. 'The decline of post-war consensus' [commentaries by Andrew Gamble, Peter Clarke, John Turner and Keith Middlemas], Bc35, 1–21.

30. Middlemas, Keith. *Power, competition and the state, vol. 2. Threats to the post-war settlement: Britain, 1961–1974.* Basingstoke; Macmillan; 1990. Pp x, 469.

31. Moore, Andrew. 'Sir Philip Game's "other life": the making of the 1936 Public Order Act in Britain', *Australian J. of Politics & History* 36 (1990), 62–72.

32. Morgan, Kenneth O. *The people's peace: British history, 1945–1989.* Oxford; Oxford UP; 1990. Pp xvi, 558.

33. O'Sullivan, Noel. 'The new Right: the quest for a civil philosophy in Europe and America', Bc6, 167–91.

34. Overy, Richard; Wheatcroft, Andrew (ed.). *The road to war.* London; Macmillan; 1989. Pp xiii, 365.

35. Panayi, Panikos. ' "The hidden hand": British myths about German control of Britain during the First World War', *Immigrants & Minorities* 7 (1988), 253–72.

36. Raison, Timothy. *Tories and the welfare state: a history of Conservative social policy since the Second World War.* Basingstoke; Macmillan; 1990. Pp xi, 218.

37. Rowthorn, Bob. 'The Thatcher revolution', Bc39, 281–98.

38. Rush, Michael. *The professionalization of the British member of parliament.* Exeter; Exeter UP; 1990. Pp 18.

39. Schneer, Jonathan. *Labour's conscience: the Labour left, 1945–1951.* Boston (Ma); Unwin Hyman; 1988. Pp xv, 249.

40. Seldon, Anthony (ed.). *UK political parties since 1945.* Hemel Hempstead; Allan; 1989. Pp ix, 159.

41. Sibley, Richard. 'The swing to Labour during the Second World War: when and why', *Labour History R*. 55/1 (1990), 23–34.
42. Smith, Adrian. 'Macmillan and Munich: the open conspirator', *Dalhousie R*. 68 (1988), 235–47.
43. Smith, Elaine R. 'Jews and politics in the East End of London, 1918–1939', Bc38, 141–62.
44. Smith, Justin Davis. 'The struggle for the control of the air waves: the Attlee governments, the BBC and industrial unrest, 1945–1951', Bc35, 53–67.
45. Smith, Justin Davis. *The Attlee and Churchill administrations and industrial unrest: a study in consensus*. London; Pinter; 1990. Pp 171.
46. Stevenson, John. 'The United Kingdom' [working class and politics], Bc5, 125–53.
47. Swerdlow, Amy. 'Female culture, pacifism and feminism: women strike for peace', Bc2, 109–30.
48. Thompson, J.A. 'The historians and the decline of the Liberal party', *Albion* 22 (1990), 65–83.
49. Thorpe, Andrew. 'J.H. Thomas and the rise of Labour in Derby, 1880–1945', *Midland History* 15 (1990), 111–28.
50. Tyler, David (ed.). *British opinion polls, 1960–1988*. Reading; Research Publications; 1990. 2 vols. Pp 320, 320.
51. Warde, Alan. 'Conditions of dependence: working-class quiescence in Lancaster in the twentieth century', *International R. of Social History* 35 (1990), 71–105.
52. Weiler, Peter. *British Labour and the Cold War*. Stanford; Stanford UP; 1988. Pp xiv, 431.
53. Wheen, Francis. *Tom Driberg*. London; Chatto & Windus; 1990. Pp 405.
54. Whitham, David. 'National policies and local tensions', Bc59, 89–103.
55. Whittaker, David J. *Fighter for peace: Philip Noel-Baker, 1889–1982*. York; Sessions; 1989. Pp 400.
56. Wood, Ian S. *John Wheatley*. Manchester; Manchester UP (Lives of the Left ser.); 1990. Pp vii, 152.
57. Wrigley, Christopher John. *Arthur Henderson*. Cardiff; Wales UP; 1990. Pp 224.

(c) *Constitution, Administration and Law*

1. Bloch, Michael. *The reign and abdication of Edward VIII*. London; Bantam; 1990. Pp 249.
2. Bradford, Sarah. *King George VI and the house of Windsor*. London; Weidenfeld & Nicolson; 1990. Pp 496.
3. Clark, Jonathan. 'The history of Britain: a composite state in a *Europe des patries*?', Bc80, 32–49.

(d) *External Affairs*

1. Abreu, Marcelo de Paiva. 'Brazil as a creditor: sterling balances, 1940–1952', *Economic History R.* 2nd ser. 43 (1990), 450–69.
2. Adamthwaite, Anthony. 'La France pendant la crise de Suez vue par la Grande-Bretagne', *Relations Internationales* 58 (1989), 187–94.
3. Anon. 'Discussion' [Anglo-Dutch relations], Bc9, 144–56.
4. Bell, Philip Michael Hett. *John Bull and the Bear: British public opinion, foreign policy and the Soviet Union.* London; Arnold; 1990. Pp 224.
5. Ben-Moshe, Tuvia. 'Winston Churchill and the "second front": a reappraisal', *J. of Modern History* 62 (1990), 503–37.
6. Blaut, Wieslaw. 'The problem of Anglo-American aid for the Home Army (AK)' [in Polish; English summary], *Studies in History* 32 (1989), 89–112.
7. Bluth, Christoph. 'The security dimension', Bc8, 92–119.
8. Boyle, Peter G. 'Oliver Franks and the Washington embassy, 1948–1952', Bc10, 189–211.
9. Brinkley, Douglas. 'Dean Acheson and the "special relationship": the West Point speech of December, 1962', *Historical J.* 33 (1990), 599–608.
10. Bullen, R.; Pelly, M.E. (ed.). *Documents on British policy overseas, ser. 2, vol. 3: German rearmament, 1950.* London; HMSO; 1989. Microfiche.
11. Clarke, Michael. 'British perspectives on the Soviet Union', Bc8, 68–91.
12. Cline, Catherine Ann. 'Ecumenism and appeasement: the bishops of the Church of England and the Treaty of Versailles', *J. of Modern History* 61 (1989), 683–703.
13. Cockett, Richard B. 'The Foreign Office news department and the struggle against appeasement', *Historical Research* 63 (1990), 73–85.
14. Danchev, Alex. *Establishing the alliance: the Second World War diaries of Brigadier Vivian Dykes.* Oxford; Brassey's Defence; 1990. Pp 250.
15. Deighton, Anne. 'Introduction' [Britain and the Cold War], Bc11, 1–8.
16. Deighton, Anne. 'Towards a "western strategy": the making of British policy towards Germany, 1945–1946', Bc11, 53–70.
17. Deighton, Anne. *The impossible peace: Britain, the German problem and the origins of the Cold War.* Oxford; Oxford UP; 1990. Pp 244.
18. Devereux, David R. 'Britain and the failure of collective defence in the Middle East, 1948–1953', Bc11, 237–52.
19. Dobson, Alan P. 'Labour or Conservative: does it matter in Anglo-American relations?', *J. of Contemporary History* 25 (1990), 387–407.
20. Drummond, Ian M.; Hillmer, Norman. *Negotiating freer trade: the United Kingdom, the United States, Canada, and the trade agreements of 1938.* Waterloo (Canada); Wilfrid Laurier UP; 1989. Pp x, 197.
21. Duncan, Peter J.S. 'Soviet perspectives on Britain and British foreign policy', Bc8, 47–67.
22. Edwards, Jill. 'Roger Makins: "Mr Atom"', Bc10, 8–38.
23. Fawcett, Louise L'Estrange. 'Invitations to Cold War: British policy in Iran, 1941–1947', Bc11, 184–200.

24. Foster, Alan. 'The British press and the coming of the Cold War', Bc11, 11–31.
25. Freedman, Lawrence; Gamba-Stonehouse, Virginia. *Signals of war: the Falklands conflict of 1982.* London; Faber & Faber; 1990. Pp 448.
26. Fuchs, Gerhard. 'Die britische Regierung und die volksdemokratische Revolution in der Tschechoslowakei (1945–1948)' [The British government and the people's democratic revolution in Czechoslovakia, 1945–1948], *Leipziger Beiträge für Revolutionsforschung* 23 (1988), 75–89.
27. Greenwood, Sean. 'Frank Roberts and the "other" long telegram: the view from the British embassy in Moscow, March 1946', *J. of Contemporary History* 25 (1990), 101–22.
28. Herzog, Chaim. 'The Suez-Sinai campaign: background', Bc7, 3–14.
29. James, Robert Rhodes. 'Eden', Bc7, 100–09.
30. Johnman, Lewis. 'Defending the pound: the economics of the Suez crisis, 1956', Bc35, 166–81.
31. Johnson, Edward. 'British proposals for a United Nations Force, 1946–1948', Bc11, 109–29.
32. Jones, Jill. 'Eradicating Nazism from the British zone of Germany: early policy and practice', *German History* 8 (1990), 145–62.
33. Jurgensen, Kurt. *Die Briten in Schleswig-Holstein, 1945–1949* [The British in Schleswig-Holstein, 1945–1949]. Neumunster; Wachholtz; 1989. Pp 167.
34. Kaser, Michael. 'Trade relations: patterns and prospects', Bc8, 193–214.
35. Keeble, Sir Curtis. 'The historical perspective' [Anglo-Soviet relations], Bc8, 17–46.
36. Keeble, Sir Curtis. *Britain and the Soviet Union, 1917–1989.* Basingstoke; Macmillan; 1990. Pp 387.
37. Kerr, Sheila. 'The secret hotline to Moscow: Donald Maclean and the Berlin crisis of 1948', Bc11, 71–87.
38. Kochavi, Arieh J. 'Anglo-American discord: Jewish refugees and United Nations Relief and Rehabilitation Administration policy, 1945–1947', *Diplomatic History* 14 (1990), 529–51.
39. Light, Margot. 'Anglo-Soviet relations: political and diplomatic', Bc8, 120–46.
40. Louis, W. 'L'imperialisme britannique et la fin du Mandat en Palestine', *Revue des Études Palestiniennes* 28 (1988), 37–63.
41. Lucas, W. Scott. 'Neustadt revisited: a new look at Suez and the Anglo-American "alliance" ', Bc35, 182–202.
42. Lucas, W. Scott. 'The path to Suez: Britain and the struggle for the Middle East, 1953–1956', Bc11, 253–72.
43. MacDonald, Callum. *Britain and the Korean War.* Oxford; Blackwell; 1990. Pp 160.
44. Miller, J.D.B.; Vincent, R.J. (ed.). *Order and violence: Hedley Bull and international relations.* Oxford; Oxford UP; 1990. Pp vii, 224.
45. Morgan, Roger. *Britain and Germany since 1945: two societies and two foreign policies.* London; German Historical Inst.; 1989. Pp 33.
46. Navias, Martin. 'Nuclear weapons and British alliance commitments, 1955–1956', Bc11, 146–61.

47. Olson, R. 'The second time around: British policy toward the Kurds (1921–1922)', *Welt Islams* 27 (1988), 91–102.
48. Orde, Anne. *British policy and European reconstruction after the First World War.* Cambridge; Cambridge UP; 1990. Pp ix, 357.
49. Ovendale, Ritchie. 'William Strang and the Permanent Under-Secretary's Committee', Bc10, 212–27.
50. Pappé, Ilán. 'Sir Alec Kirkbride and the Anglo-Transjordanian alliance, 1945–1950', Bc10, 121–55.
51. Parmar, Inderjeet. 'The FBI's foreign policy: the Anglo-American alliance, 1938–1945', *Business Archives* 60 (1990), 42–55.
52. Pelly, M.E.; Yasamee, H.J. (ed.). *Germany and western Europe, 11 August–31 December 1945.* London; HMSO; 1989. Pp xlv, 549.
53. Peter, Matthias. 'Britain, the Cold War and the economics of German rearmament, 1949–1951', Bc11, 273–90.
54. Petkova, Elena. 'The soldiers' revolt of 1918 and England's attitude toward the Bulgarian proposal for a truce' [in Bulgarian; English summary], *Istoricheski Pregled* 45 (1989), 53–65.
55. Pinder, John; Bosco, Andrea (ed.). *Pacificism is not enough: collected lectures and speeches of Philip Kerr, eleventh marquess of Lothian.* London; Lothian Foundation; 1990. Pp 320.
56. Rees, G. Wyn. 'Brothers in arms: Anglo-American defence co-operation in 1957', Bc35, 203–20.
57. Rothwell, Victor. 'Robin Hankey', Bc10, 156–88.
58. Sanders, David. *Losing an empire, finding a role: British foreign policy since 1945.* Basingstoke; Macmillan; 1990. Pp xi, 349.
59. Shemesh, Moshe (ed.). 'Abd al-Latif al-Bughdadi's memoirs', Bc7, 333–56.
60. Shemesh, Moshe (ed.). 'Sayyid Mar'i's political papers', Bc7, 357–69.
61. Shipley, Peter. *Hostile action: the KGB and secret Soviet operations in Britain.* Leicester; Pinter; 1989. Pp 200.
62. Smith, Raymond. 'Ernest Bevin, British officials and British Soviet policy, 1945–1947', Bc11, 32–52.
63. Smith, Raymond. 'Introduction' [officials and foreign policy], Bc10, 1–7.
64. Taylor, Peter J. *Britain and the Cold War: 1945 as geopolitical transition.* Leicester; Pinter; 1990. Pp xiii, 153.
65. Teague-Jones, Reginald. *The spy who disappeared: diary of a secret mission to Russian Central Asia in 1918*, ed. Peter Hopkirk. London; Gollancz; 1990. Pp 224.
66. Teitler, G. 'Anglo-Dutch relations, 1936–1988: colonial and European trends', Bc83, 70–83.
67. Thompson, Kenneth. *Foreign policy and arms control: Churchill's legacy.* Lanham; UP of America; 1990. Pp 148.
68. Troen, Selwyn Ilan (ed.). 'Ben-Gurion's diary: the Suez-Sinai campaign', Bc7, 289–332.
69. Tute, Warren. *The reluctant enemies: the war between Britain and France, 1940–1942.* London; Collins; 1990. Pp 288.
70. Wark, Wesley K. 'Development diplomacy: Sir John Troutbeck and the British Middle East Office, 1947–1950', Bc10, 228–49.

71. Watrin, Konrad W. *Machtwechsel im Nahen Osten: Grossbritanniens Niedergang und der Aufstieg der Vereinigten Staaten 1941–1947* [Power changes in the Near East: Great Britain's decline and the rise of the US]. Frankfurt; Campus; 1989. Pp 598.
72. Wheeler, Nicholas. 'The Attlee government's nuclear strategy, 1945–1951', Bc11, 130–45.
73. Williamson, David Graham. *The British in Germany, 1918–1930.* Oxford; Berg; 1990. Pp 256.
74. Wilson, Hugh. 'The best of friends: Britain, America and Thailand, 1945–1948', *Canadian J. of History* 25 (1990), 61–83.
75. Young, John W. 'Duff Cooper and the Paris Embassy, 1945–1947', Bc10, 98–120.
76. Zametica, John. 'Three letters to Bevin: Frank Roberts at the Moscow Embassy, 1945–1946', Bc10, 39–97.
77. Zweig, Ronald. 'Restitution and the problem of Jewish displaced persons in Anglo-American relations, 1944–1948', *American Jewish History* 78 (Sep. 1988), 54–78.

(e) *Religion*

1. Bebbington, D.W. 'Baptists and fundamentalists in inter-war Britain', Bc115, 297–326.
2. Campbell, Louise. *To build a cathedral: Coventry cathedral, 1945–1962.* Warwick; University of Warwick with A.H. Jolly; 1987. Pp 96.
3. Chadwick, Owen. *Michael Ramsey: a life.* Oxford; Oxford UP; 1990. Pp 416.
4. Darragh, James. 'The apostolic visitations of Scotland, 1912 and 1917', *Innes R.* 41 (1990), 7–118.
5. Hein, David. 'George Bell, bishop of Chichester, on the morality of war', *Anglican & Episcopal History* 58 (1989), 498–509.
6. James, Eric. *A life of Bishop John A.T. Robinson, scholar, pastor, prophet.* London; Fount; 1989. Pp xii, 356.
7. Kaye, Elaine. 'A turning-point in the ministry of women: the ordination of the first woman to the Christian Ministry in England in September 1917', Bc128, 505–12.
8. Obelkevich, James. 'Religion', Bc47, 311–56.

(f) *Economic Affairs*

1. Ashton, David; Green, Francis; Hoskins, Martin. 'The training system of British capitalism: changes and prospects', Bc39, 131–54.
2. Auerbach, Paul. 'Multinationals and the British economy', Bc39, 263–80.
3. Barker, Theodore Cardwell. 'Introduction: Francis Hyde, Harvard, Liverpool and the first 30 years of *Business History*', Bc24, 1–7.
4. Barker, Theodore Cardwell. *Moving millions: a pictorial history of London Transport.* London; London Transport Museum; 1990. Pp xii, 132.

5. Blackaby, David; Hunt, Lester. 'The manufacturing productivity "miracle": a sectoral analysis', Bc39, 122–30.

6. Blaug, Mark. *John Maynard Keynes: life, ideas, legacy.* London; Macmillan, for Inst. of Economic Affairs; 1990. Pp 112.

7. Bonsall, Penny. 'The Somerset coalfield, 1947–1973: attitudes and responses to pit closures in the post-nationalization era', *Southern History* 12 (1990), 114–30.

8. Bowden, Sue. 'Credit facilities and the growth of consumer demand for electric appliances in England in the 1930s', *Business History* 32/1 (1990), 52–75.

9. Bowen, David. *Shaking the iron universe: British industry in the 1980s.* London; Hodder & Stoughton; 1990. Pp 352.

10. Boyns, Trevor. 'Strategic responses to foreign competition: the British coal industry and the 1930 Coal Mines Act', *Business History* 32/3 (1990), 133–45.

11. Boyns, Trevor. 'The electricity industry in south Wales to 1949', *Welsh History R.* 15 (1990–1), 79–107.

12. Broadberry, S.N. 'The emergence of mass unemployment: explaining macroeconomic trends in Britain during the trans-World War I period', *Economic History R.* 2nd ser. 43 (1990), 271–82.

13. Burkitt, Brian; Baimbridge, Mark. 'The performance of British agriculture and the impact of the Common Agricultural Policy: an historical review', *Rural History* 1 (1990), 265–80.

14. Cairncross, Alec K. 'The United Kingdom' [government and economy], Bc23, 30–53.

15. Campbell, R.H. 'The North British Locomotive Company between the wars', Bc22, 172–205.

16. Chick, Martin (ed.). *Government, industries and markets: aspects of government/industry relations in Great Britain, Japan, West Germany and the United States of America since 1945.* Aldershot; Elgar; 1990. Pp 288.

17. Church, Roy A. 'Family firms and managerial capitalism: the case of the international motor industry', Bc22, 311–32.

18. Crafts, N.F.R. 'Long-term unemployment and the wage equation in Britain, 1925–1939', *Economica* 56 (1989), 247–54.

19. Crompton, Gerald. ' "Squeezing the pulpless orange": labour and capital on the railways in the inter-war years', Bc43, 66–83.

20. Davenport-Hines, Richard P.T. 'Vickers' Balkan conscience: aspects of Anglo-Romanian armaments, 1918–1939', Bc22, 253–85.

21. Dayer, Roberta A. *Finance and empire: Sir Charles Addis, 1861–1945.* London; Macmillan; 1989. Pp xxi, 431.

22. Dellheim, Charles. 'Utopia Ltd: Bournville and Port Sunlight', Bc104, 44–57.

23. Desai, Meghnad. 'Is Thatcherism the cure for the British disease?', Bc39, 299–312.

24. Dimsdale, N.H.; Nickell, S.J.; Horsewood, N. 'Real wages and unemployment in Britain during the 1930s', *Economic J.* 99 (1989), 271–92.

25. Donnelly, Tom. 'The British and American motor industries', *Business History* 32/2 (1990), 259–65.
26. Donnelly, Tom; Thomas, David. 'Trade unions, management and the search for production in the Coventry motor car industry, 1939–1975', Bc43, 98–113.
27. Downs, Laura Lee. 'Industrial decline, rationalization and equal pay: the Bedaux strike at Rover automobile company', *Social History* 15 (1990), 45–73.
28. Dudley, Geoffrey F.; Richardson, Jeremy John. *Politics and steel in Britain, 1967–1988: the life and times of the British Steel Corporation.* Aldershot; Dartmouth; 1990. Pp 314.
29. Dupree, Marguerite W. 'Struggling with destiny: the cotton industry, overseas trade policy and the Cotton Board, 1940–1959', *Business History* 32/4 (1990), 106–28.
30. Eaton, John Press; Haas, Charles A. *Falling Star: misadventures of White Star Line ships.* Wellingborough; Stephens; 1989. Pp 256.
31. Faulkner, Nicholas O.; et al. (comp.). *Allied Breweries: a long life— directory of ancestor breweries.* London; Allied Breweries; 1988. Pp 150.
32. Fearon, Peter. 'The vicissitudes of a British aircraft company: Handley Page Ltd. between the wars', Bc22, 148–71.
33. Fine, Ben. 'Denationalization', Bc39, 225–41.
34. Fine, Ben. 'Economies of scale and a featherbedding cartel? A reconsideration of the interwar British coal industry', *Economic History R.* 2nd ser. 43 (1990), 438–49.
35. Fitzpatrick, T.A. 'The Catholic Teachers' Union, 1917–1919', *Innes R.* 41 (1990), 132–35.
36. Foster, John. 'Strike action and working-class politics on Clydeside, 1914–1919', *International R. of Social History* 35 (1990), 33–70.
37. Freeman, Chris. 'R & D, technical change and investment in the UK', Bc39, 199–224.
38. Garside, William Redvers. *British unemployment, 1919–1939: a study in public policy.* Cambridge; Cambridge UP; 1990. Pp 430.
39. Gennard, John. *A history of the National Graphical Association.* London; Unwin Hyman; 1990. Pp 610.
40. George, A.D. 'A note on the demise of car manufacture at Crossley Motors of Manchester', [ c.1938], *Business Archives* 60 (1990), 61–64.
41. Glucksmann, Miriam. *Women assemble: women workers in the new industries in inter-war Britain.* London; Routledge; 1990. Pp 336.
42. Glyn, Andrew. 'The macro-anatomy of the Thatcher years', Bc39, 65–79.
43. Gospel, Howard F. 'Employers' labour policy: a study of the Mond-Turner talks, 1927–1933', Bc22, 206–23.
44. Gospel, Howard F. 'Product markets, labour markets, and industrial relations: the case of flour milling', Bc43, 84–97.
45. Green, Francis. 'Evaluating structural economic change: Britain in the 1980s', Bc39, 3–24.
46. Hannah, Leslie. 'Takeover bids in Britain before 1950: an exercise in business "pre-history" ', Bc22, 40–52.

47. Hare, Paul R. *The Royal Aircraft Factory*. London; Conway Maritime; 1990. Pp 352.

48. Harrison, Mark. 'A volume index of the total munitions output of the United Kingdom, 1939–1944', *Economic History R*. 2nd ser. 43 (1990), 657–66.

49. Harrison, Richard T. *Industrial organization and changing technology in United Kingdom shipbuilding: historical development and future implications*. Aldershot; Avebury; 1990. Pp 260.

50. Hillman, John. 'Bolivia and British tin policy, 1939–1945', *J. of Latin American Studies* 22 (1990), 289–315.

51. Howson, Susan. 'Cheap money versus cheaper money: a reply to Professor Wood', *Economic History R*. 2nd ser. 42 (1989), 401–05.

52. Howson, Susan; Moggridge, Donald (ed.). *The wartime diaries of Lionel Robbins and James Meade, 1943–1945*. Basingstoke; Macmillan; 1990. Pp 261.

53. Johnman, Lewis. 'The large manufacturing companies of 1935', Bc22, 20–39.

54. Jones, Geoffrey. 'Lombard Street on the Riviera: the British clearing banks and Europe, 1900–1960', Bc22, 286–310.

55. King, Peter. *The motor men: pioneers of the British car industry*. London; Quiller; 1989. Pp 168.

56. Kitson, Michael; Solomou, Solomos. *Protectionism and economic revival: the British inter-war economy*. Cambridge; Cambridge UP; 1990. Pp 180.

57. Legge, Ronald. *A man of trust: the life of J.M.S. Coates, 'financial advisor to the north of England'*. London; Coates; 1989. Pp xiv, 225.

58. Lewis, Colin A. 'Travelling stallions in and adjacent to Brycheiniog', *Brycheiniog* 23 (1988–9), 75–84.

59. Long, Brian. *The marques of Coventry: a history of the city's motor industry*. Warwickshire; Warwickshire Books; 1990. Pp 128.

60. Luckin, Bill. *Questions of power: electricity and environment in inter-war Britain*. Manchester; Manchester UP; 1990. Pp 190.

61. Lyth, Peter J. ' "A multiplicity of instruments": the 1946 decision to create a separate British European airline and its effect on civil aircraft production', *J. of Transport History* 3rd ser. 11 (1990), 1–18.

62. Marriner, Sheila. 'Cash and concrete: liquidity problems in the mass production of "homes for heroes" ', Bc22, 53–90.

63. Martin, Ron. 'Regional imbalance as consequence and constraint in national economic renewal', Bc39, 80–100.

64. Matthews, K.G.P. 'Could Lloyd George have done it?', *Oxford Economic Papers* 41 (1989), 374–407.

65. McCann, Neil Frank. *The story of the National Agricultural Advisory Service, 1946–1971*. Ely; Providence; 1989. Pp xi, 82.

66. McMillan, James. *The Dunlop story: the life, death and re-birth of a multi-national*. London; Weidenfeld & Nicolson; 1989. Pp vii, 215.

67. Melling, Joseph. 'Whatever happened to red Clydeside? Industrial conflict and the politics of skill in the First World War', *International R. of Social History* 35 (1990), 3–32.

68. Mennim, Eleanor Janet. *Reid's heirs: a biography of James Simms Wilson (1893–1976), optical instrument maker.* Braunton; Merlin; 1990. Pp 384.

69. Middleton, Roger. 'Keynes's legacy for postwar economic management', Bc35, 22–42.

70. Morrison, A.J. 'Businessmen, industries and tariff reform in Great Britain, 1903–1930', Bc22, 91–121.

71. Nolan, Peter. 'The productivity miracle?', Bc39, 101–21.

72. Nutter, Robert S. 'The Stone-Platt failure', *Business Archives* 60 (1990), 24–41.

73. Panayi, Panikos. 'German business interests in Britain during the First World War', *Business History* 32/2 (1990), 244–58.

74. Read, Donald. 'Sir Roderick Jones and Reuters: rise and fall of a news emperor', Bc104, 175–99.

75. Ritchie, Berry. *A touch of class: the story of Austin Reed.* London; James & James; 1990. Pp 160.

76. Ritchie, Berry. *The key to the door: the Abbey National story.* London; Abbey National; 1989. Pp 175.

77. Robertson, Alex J. 'Lancashire and the rise of Japan', *Business History* 32/4 (1990), 87–105.

78. Rubery, Jill. 'Labour market flexibility in Britain', Bc39, 155–76.

79. Shaw, Christine. 'The large manufacturing employers of 1907', Bc22, 1–19.

80. Singleton, John. 'Planning for cotton, 1945–1951', *Economic History R.* 2nd ser. 43 (1990), 62–78.

81. Singleton, John. 'Showing the white flag: the Lancashire cotton industry, 1945–1965', *Business History* 32/4 (1990), 129–49.

82. Slaven, Anthony. 'A shipyard in depression: John Brown's of Clydebank, 1919–1938', Bc22, 122–47.

83. Stark, Thomas. 'The changing distribution of income under Mrs Thatcher', Bc39, 177–98.

84. Tomlinson, Jim. 'Labour's management of the national economy, 1945–1951: survey and speculations', *Economy & Society* 18 (1989), 1–24.

85. Tomlinson, Jim. *Public policy and the economy since 1900.* Oxford; Oxford UP; 1990. Pp 380.

86. Toporowski, Jan. 'The financial system and capital accumulation in the 1980s', Bc39, 242–62.

87. Trounson, John H. *The Cornish mineral industry: past performance and future prospect—a personal view, 1937–1951.* Exeter; Exeter UP; 1989. Pp xxii, 198.

88. Turner, John. 'Labour and business in modern Britain', Bc43, 1–7.

89. Wainwright, David. *In the wake of disaster: the story of Toplis and Harding.* London; Quiller; 1990. Pp 160.

90. Wainwright, David. *Men of steel: a history of Richard Thomas and his family.* London; Quiller; 1986. Pp x, 149.

91. Wells, John. 'Uneven development and de-industrialization in the UK since 1979', Bc39, 25–64.

92. Whiting, R.C. 'Taxation and the working class, 1915–1924', *Historical J.* 33 (1990), 895–916.
93. Wood, G.E. 'A comment on "the origins of cheaper money" ', *Economic History R.* 2nd ser. 42 (1989), 396–400.

## (g) Social Structure and Population

1. Anon. *Images of a port: life and times on Preston Dock.* Preston; Lancashire Polytechnic; 1987. Pp 40.
2. Berridge, Virginia. 'Health and medicine', Bc47, 171–242.
3. Cesarani, David. 'The transformation of communal authority in Anglo-Jewry, 1914–1940', Bc38, 115–40.
4. Easton, Drew (ed.). *Water under the bridge: twentieth-century Tollcross, Fountainbridge and the West Port.* Aberdeen; Aberdeen UP; 1990. Pp 196.
5. Field, Geoffrey. 'Perspectives on the working-class family in wartime Britain, 1939–1945', *International Labor and Working-class History* 38 (1990), 3–28.
6. Fishwick, Nicholas. *English football and society, 1910–1950.* Manchester; Manchester UP; 1989. Pp xii, 164.
7. Gordon, Felicia. *The integral feminist: Madeleine Pelletier, 1874–1939.* Cambridge; Polity; 1990. Pp 240.
8. Haskell, Patricia. 'A changing city' [Portsmouth], Bc136, 169–76.
9. Hopkins, Eric. 'Working class life in Birmingham between the wars, 1918–1939', *Midland History* 15 (1990), 129–50.
10. Howarth, Olive (ed.). *Textile voices: mill life this century.* Bradford; Bradford Libraries & Information Service; 1989. Pp 72.
11. Jeffreys, Sheila. 'Butch and femme: now and then', Bc1, 158–87.
12. Jones, D.J.V. ' "Where did it all go wrong?" Crime in Swansea, 1938–1968', *Welsh History R.* 15 (1990–1), 240–74.
13. King, Peter. *The shooting field: with Holland and Holland since 1835.* London; Quiller; new edn. 1990. Pp 176.
14. Leneman, Leah. *Fit for heroes? Land settlement in Scotland after World War I.* Aberdeen; Aberdeen UP; 1989. Pp x, 244.
15. Mackenzie, Suzanne. *Visible histories, mobile geographies: women and environments in a post-war city.* Toronto; McGill/Queen's UP; 1990. Pp 240.
16. Macve, Jennifer. 'W.G. Tarrant: last squire of Hafod', *Ceredigion* 11 (1988–9), 59–73.
17. Matthews, Jill Julius. 'They had such a lot of fun: the Women's League of Health and Beauty between the wars', *History Workshop J.* 30 (1990), 22–54.
18. McCrone, David; Elliott Brian. 'The decline of landlordism: property rights and relationships in Edinburgh', Bc59, 214–35.
19. Miller, Mervyn. *Letchworth: the first garden city.* Chichester; Phillimore; 1989. Pp x, 244.
20. Morris, R.J. 'Clubs, societies and associations', Bc47, 395–443.

21. Newall, Venetia. 'The role of the seer within the Punjabi Asian minority of Britain', Bc103, 133–46.
22. Pedersen, Susan. 'Gender, welfare, and citizenship in Britain during the Great War', *American Historical R.* 95 (1990), 983–1006.
23. Phillips, Francis R. *Bishop Beck and English education, 1949–1959.* Lampeter; Mellen; 1990. Pp 304.
24. Ruffer, Jonathan Garnier. *The big shots: Edwardian shooting parties.* London; Quiller; new edn. 1989. Pp 160.
25. Rush, Christopher; Shaw, John. *With sharp compassion: Norman Dott, freeman surgeon of Edinburgh.* Aberdeen; Aberdeen UP; 1990. Pp 330.
26. Seccombe, Wally. 'Starting to stop: working-class fertility decline in Britain', *Past & Present* 126 (1990), 151–88.
27. Smyth, James J. ' "Ye never got a spell to think aboot it." Young women and employment in the inter-war period: a case study of a textile village', Bc90, 95–116.
28. Stephenson, Jayne D.; Brown, Callum G. 'The view from the workplace: women's memories of work in Stirling, *c*.1910–*c*.1950', Bc90, 7–28.
29. Thane, Pat M. 'The debate on the declining birth-rate in Britain: the "menace" of an ageing population, 1920s–1950s', *Continuity & Change* 5 (1990), 283–305.
30. Thompson, Francis M.L. 'English landed society in the twentieth century. Part 1, property: collapse and survival', *T. of the Royal Historical Soc.* 5th ser. 40 (1990), 1–24.
31. Tiratsoo, Nick. *Coventry, 1945–1960.* London; Routledge; 1990. Pp 240.
32. Twinch, Carol. *Women of the land: their story during two world wars.* Cambridge; Lutterworth; 1990. Pp 176.

## (h) *Social Policy*

1. Benner, Patrick. 'The early years of the National Health Service: an insider's view', Bc35, 43–52.
2. Carruthers, Susan L. ' "Manning the factories": propaganda and policy on the employment of women, 1939–1947', *History* 75 (1990), 232–56.
3. Edmund, J.D.G. 'Evacuation to Devon in the second half of 1939', *Devon Association Report and T.* 122 (1990), 17–24.
4. Fethney, Michael. *The absurd and the brave: CORB—the true account of the government's World War II evacuation of children overseas.* Lewes; Book Guild; 1990. Pp 333.
5. Gatrell, V.A.C. 'Crime, authority and the policeman-state', Bc47, 243–310.
6. Gibb, Andrew. 'Policy and politics in Scottish housing since 1945', Bc59, 155–83.
7. Gourlay, Teresa. 'Catholic schooling in Scotland since 1918', *Innes R.* 41 (1990), 119–31.
8. Grant, Mariel. 'The National Health campaigns of 1937–1938', Bc104, 216–33.
9. Harper, Sarah. 'The impact of the retirement debate on post-war retirement trends', Bc35, 95–108.

10. Harris, José. 'Enterprise and welfare states: a comparative perspective', *T. of the Royal Historical Soc.* 5th ser. 40 (1990), 175–95.

11. Harris, José. 'Society and the state in twentieth-century Britain', Bc47, 63–118.

12. Hill, Michael J. *Social security policy in Britain.* Aldershot; Elgar; 1990. Pp 224.

13. Jeans, D.N. 'Planning and the myth of the English countryside, in the interwar period', *Rural History* 1 (1990), 249–64.

14. Jones, Gareth Elwyn. '1944 and all that', *History of Education* 19 (1990), 235–50.

15. Jones, Gareth Elwyn. *Which nation's schools: direction and devolution in Welsh education in the twentieth century.* Cardiff; Wales UP; 1990. Pp xii, 232.

16. Knight, Christopher. *The making of Tory education policy in post-war Britain, 1950–1986.* London; Falmer; 1989. Pp 206.

17. Meller, Helen. *Patrick Geddes: social evolutionist and city planner.* London; Routledge; 1989. Pp 384.

18. Mellor, G. Hunt; Turner, J. 'Wretched, hatless and miserably clad: women and the inebriate reformatories from 1900–1913', *British J. of Sociology* 40 (1989), 144–70.

19. Minett, John. 'Government sponsorship of new towns: Gretna, 1915–1917 and its implications', Bc59, 104–24.

20. Morgan, Nicholas J. ' "£8 Cottages for Glasgow citizens": innovation in municipal house-building in Glasgow in the inter-war years', Bc59, 125–54.

21. Morris, Terence. *Crime and criminal justice since 1945.* Oxford; Blackwell; 1989. Pp x, 198.

22. Pepper, Simon. 'The Garden City', Bc93, 100–115.

23. Pigott, Daniel A. 'Agricultural scholarships for rural youth in England and Wales, 1922–1958', *History of Education Q.* 30 (1990), 17–45.

24. Prochaska, F.K. 'Philanthropy', Bc47, 357–94.

25. Rodger, Richard; Al-Qaddo, Hunain. 'The Scottish Special Housing Association and the implementation of housing policy, 1937–1987', Bc59, 184–213.

26. Silver, Harold. *A higher education: the Council for National Academic Awards and British higher education, 1964–1989.* London; Falmer; 1990. Pp x, 294.

27. Stevenson, Simon. 'Some social and political tides affecting the development of juvenile justice, 1938–1964', Bc35, 68–94.

28. Sutherland, Gillian. 'Education' [social agencies and institutions], Bc47, 119–70.

29. Webster, Charles. 'Doctors, public service and profit: general practitioners and the National Health Service', *T. of the Royal Historical Soc.* 5th ser. 40 (1990), 197–216.

30. Wooldridge, Adrian. 'Education: from Boyle to Baker', Bc80, 161–88.

31. Yelling, Jim. 'The metropolitan slum: London, 1918–1951', Bc48, 186–233.

32. Youngson, A.J. *Urban development and the Royal Fine Art Commissions*. Edinburgh; Edinburgh UP; 1989. Pp 224.

## (i) *Naval and Military*

1. Abbott, Patrick. *The British airship at war, 1914–1918*. Lavenham; Dalton; 1989. Pp ix, 142.
2. Adams, Jack. *The doomed expedition: the Norwegian campaign of 1940*. London; Mandarin; new edn. 1990. Pp 304.
3. Anon. 'Discussion' [Operation Market Garden], Bc9, 178–85.
4. Auckland, Reginald George (comp.). *British 'black' propaganda to Germany, 1941–1945*. Leeds; Psywar Soc.; 2nd rev. edn. 1989. Pp 43.
5. Barnett, Correlli. *Engage the enemy more closely*. London; Hodder & Stoughton; 1990. Pp 880.
6. Baylis, John. 'Britain and the formation of NATO', Bc134, 3–32.
7. Beaumont, Joan. 'Starving for democracy: Britain's blockade of and relief for occupied Europe, 1939–1945', *War & Soc.* 8 (1990), 57–82.
8. Bird, Antony (ed.). *Unversed in arms: subaltern on the Western Front*. Marlborough; Crowood; 1990. Pp 168.
9. Bloom, Cecil. 'Colonel [J.H.] Patterson, soldier and Zionist', *Jewish Historical Studies* 31 (1988–90), 231–48.
10. Bond, Brian; Robbins, Simon (ed.). *Staff officer: the diaries of Walter Guinness (first lord Moyne), 1914–1918*. London; Cooper; 1987. Pp 256.
11. Bowman, Martin W. *The Bedford triangle: United States undercover operations from Britain in World War II*. Wellingborough; Stephens; 1990. Pp 192.
12. Brooke, Justin. *The Volunteers: the full story of the British Volunteers in the Finnish winter war, 1939–1940*. Upton-upon-Severn; Self Publishing Association; 1990. Pp 256.
13. Brown, Raymond J. ' "Won by such as he" ' [Captain Frederick John Walker, R.N.], *US Naval Institute P.* 115 (1989), 43–48.
14. Caffrey, Kate. *Combat report: the Royal Air Force and the fall of France*. Marlborough; Crowood; 1990. Pp 128.
15. Clark, E.F. 'HMS Belfast: a central link in the Allen-Admiralty chain', *Newcomen Soc. T.* 59 (1990 for 1987/8), 97–128.
16. Crampton, Paul. *The blitz of Canterbury*. Rainham; Meresborough; 1989. Pp 48.
17. Dockrill, Michael. 'The changing shape of Britain's defence during the 1950s', Bc134, 49–64.
18. Ellis, John. *Brute force: Allied strategy and tactics in the Second World War*. London; Deutsch; 1990. Pp 544.
19. Farndale, Sir Martin. *History of the Royal Regiment of Artillery: the forgotten fronts and the home base, 1914–1918*. London; Royal Artillery Institution; 1988. Pp 508.
20. Farndale, Sir Martin. *History of the Royal Regiment of Artillery: Western Front, 1914–1918*. London; Royal Artillery Institution; 1986. Pp 10, 421.

21. Farquharson, John E. 'After Sealion: a German Channel Tunnel', *J. of Contemporary History* 25 (1990), 409–30.
22. Farquharson, John E. 'Hilfe für den Feind: die britische Debatte um Nahrungsmittellieferungen an Deutschland 1944/45' [Help for the enemy: the British debate on food supplies to Germany, 1944–1945], *Vierteljahrshäfte für Zeitgeschichte* 37 (1989), 253–78.
23. Folly, Martin H. 'The British military and the making of the North Atlantic Treaty', Bc134, 33–48.
24. Foot, Michael R.D. 'Stay-behind parties', *History Today* 40/8 (1990), 35–38.
25. Foot, Michael R.D. 'The Englandspiel' [Anglo-Dutch relations], Bc9, 120–30.
26. Fussell, Paul. *Wartime: understanding and behavior in the Second World War.* New York; Oxford UP; 1989. Pp xi, 331.
27. Gelb, Norman. *Dunkirk: the incredible escape.* London; Joseph; 1990. Pp 256.
28. Glover, Michael. *Invasion scare, 1940.* London; Cooper; 1990. Pp 196.
29. Gorst, Anthony. 'British military planning for postwar defence, 1943–1945', Bc11, 91–108.
30. Gough, Guy Francis. *Thirty days to Dunkirk: the Royal Irish Fusiliers, May 1940.* Wrexham; Bridge Books; 1990. Pp 212.
31. Gray, Edwyn. *Operation Pacific.* London; Cooper; 1990. Pp 256.
32. Grove, Eric J. 'British naval policy, 1945–1957', Bc35, 155–65.
33. Hackett, Sir John. 'Operation Market Garden', Bc9, 157–69.
34. Irvine, James W. *The waves are free: Shetland/Norway links, 1940 to 1945.* Lerwick; Shetland; 1988. Pp xiv, 257.
35. James, Lawrence. 'The roaring lions of the air', *History Today* 40/11 (1990), 20–25.
36. James, Lawrence. *T.E. Lawrence: the golden warrior.* London; Weidenfeld & Nicolson; 1990. Pp 384.
37. Kamphius, Piet. 'Operation Market Garden', Bc9, 170–77.
38. Kersaudy, Francois. *Norway, 1940.* London; Collins; 1990. Pp 266.
39. Leal, H.J.T. *Battle in the skies over the Isle of Wight.* Newport (IoW); Isle of Wight County Press; 1988. Pp 96.
40. Lowe, Peter. 'An ally and a recalcitrant general: Great Britain, Douglas MacArthur and the Korean War, 1950–1951', *English Historical R.* 105 (1990), 624–53.
41. MacKenzie, S.P. 'Morale and the cause: the campaign to shape the outlook of soldiers in the British Expeditionary Force, 1914–1918', *Canadian J. of History* 25 (1990), 215–32.
42. Marder, Arthur Jacob; Horsefield, John. *Old friends, new enemies: the Royal Navy and the Imperial Japanese Navy, 1936–1945, vol. 2: the Pacific war, 1942–1945.* Oxford; Oxford UP; 1990. Pp 650.
43. Marks, Leo. 'The Englandspiel' [Anglo-Dutch relations], Bc9, 131–38.
44. McBain, S.W. (ed.). *A regiment at war: the Royal Scots (the Royal Regiment), 1939–1945 (including the Canadian Scottish Regiment).* Edinburgh; Pentland; 1988. Pp 304.

45. Neillands, Robin. *The raiders: the army commandos, 1940–1946.* London; Fontana; 1990. Pp xiv, 370.
46. Nellemann, George. *For Danmarks frihed og Polens aere: den polsk-engelske efterretningstjeneste, 1940–1945* [For Denmark's freedom and Poland's honour: the Anglo-Polish intelligence services, 1940–1945]. [Place]; Frihedsmuseets Venner; 1989. Pp 109.
47. Paris, Michael. 'The Royal Air Force on screen, 1940–1942', *History Today* 40/8 (1990), 39–46.
48. Plummer, Russell. *Ships that saved an army: a comprehensive record of the one thousand three hundred little ships of Dunkirk.* Wellingborough; Stephens; 1990. Pp 240.
49. Pot, Leen. 'The Englandspiel' [Anglo-Dutch relations], Bc9, 139–43.
50. Powell, Geoffrey. *Plumer, the soldier's general: a life of viscount Plumer of Messines.* London; Cooper; 1990. Pp 350.
51. Powell, Geoffrey; Fullick, Roy. *Suez: the double war.* London; Cooper; 1990. Pp 240.
52. Reid, Brian Holden. *J.F.C. Fuller: military thinker.* London; Macmillan; new edn. 1990. Pp 304.
53. Richter, Heinz. 'General Lanz, Napoleon Zervas und die britischen Verbindungsoffiziere' [General Lanz, Napoleon Zervas and the British liaison officers], *Militargeschichtliche Mitteilungen* 45 (1989), 111–38.
54. Ridley, C.W. 'The battle of the "cauldron"' [1942], *J. of the Soc. for Army Historical Research* 68 (1990), 75–82.
55. Ruston, Roger. *A say in the end of the world: morals and British nuclear weapons policy, 1941–1987.* Oxford; Oxford UP; 1990. Pp ix, 272.
56. Sellers, J.A. 'Military lessons: the British perspective', Bc7, 17–53.
57. Slader, John. *The Red Duster at war: a history of the Merchant Navy during the Second World War.* London; Kimber; 1989. Pp 752.
58. Smithies, Edward. *War in the air: men and women, who built, serviced and flew warplanes remember the Second World War.* London; Viking; 1990. Pp 336.
59. Sonyel, Salahi R. 'The Mustafa Kemal-Lawrence interview according to British documents', *Belleten* 52 (1988), 1695–1706.
60. Stripp, Alan. *Codebreaker in the Far East.* London; Cass; 1989. Pp xiv, 208.
61. Sturtivant, Ray. *British naval aviation: the Fleet Air Arm, 1917–1990.* London; Arms & Armour; 1990. Pp 224.
62. Sweetman, John. *The dambusters' raid.* London; Arms & Armour; 1990. Pp 240.
63. Syrett, David. 'The battle for Convoy TM 1, January 1943', *American Neptune* 50 (1990), 42–50.
64. Thompson, Julian. *Ready for anything: the Parachute Regiment at war, 1940–1982.* London; Weidenfeld & Nicolson; 1989. Pp 400.
65. Whitehouse, Frank Edgar. *The poacher's brats: a social history of the Royal Air Force Cranwell Aircraft Apprentice.* Andover; RAF Cranwell Aircraft Apprentices' Association; 1989. Pp 212.
66. Wilt, Alan F. *War from the top: German and British military decision making during World War II.* London; Tauris; 1990. Pp 300.

67. Winter, J.M. *The experience of World War I.* Basingstoke; Macmillan; 1989. Pp 256.

## (j) *Intellectual and Cultural*

1. Aitken, Ian. *Film and reform: John Grierson and the documentary film movement.* London; Routledge; 1990. Pp 252.
2. Allsobrook, David. 'Two figures in the landscape of Welsh music education: W.H. Hadow and Walford Davies', *History of Education* 19 (1990), 219–34.
3. Anon. *From the first fifty years: an informal history of Blackwell Scientific Publications.* Oxford; Blackwell Scientific; 1989. Pp 32.
4. Arnold, A.J. ' "Not playing the game"? Leeds City in the Great War', *International J. of the History of Sport* 7 (1990), 111–19.
5. Auchmuty, Rosemary. ' "You're a dyke, Angela!" Elsie J. Oxenham and the rise and fall of the schoolgirl story', Bc1, 119–40.
6. Bergamasco, Lucia. 'Female education and spiritual life: the case of ministers' daughters', Bc2, 39–60.
7. Bishop, Alan; Bennett, Y. Aleksandra (ed.). *Wartime chronicle: diaries of Vera Brittain, 1939–1945.* London; Gollancz; 1989. Pp 352.
8. Blake, Lord Robert; Nicholls, Christine Stephanie. *The Dictionary of National Biography, 1981–1985, with an index covering the years 1901–1985.* Oxford; Oxford UP; 1990. Pp 608.
9. Bosch, Mineke. 'Gossipy letters in the context of international feminism', Bc2, 131–52.
10. Bowker, David. 'Parks and baths: sport, recreation and municipal government in Ashton-under-Lyne between the wars', Bc52, 84–100.
11. Callick, Eric Brian. *Metres to microwaves: British development of active components for radar systems.* Stevenage; Peregrinus; 1990. Pp 240.
12. Camporesi, Valeria. ' "We talk a different language": the impact of US broadcasting in Britain, 1922–1927', *Historical J. of Film, Radio and Television* 10 (1990), 257–74.
13. Cantor, David. 'The contradictions of specialization: rheumatism and the decline of the spa', *Medical History*, Supplement 10 (1990), 127–44.
14. Charlesby, A. 'A physicist intrudes into radiation chemistry', Bc19, 29–51.
15. Croarken, Mary. *Early scientific computing in Britain.* Oxford; Oxford UP; 1990. Pp 160.
16. Crook, Paul. 'War as genetic disaster? The First World War debate over the eugenics of warfare', *War & Soc.* 8 (1990), 47–70.
17. Cross, Gary. *Worktowners at Blackpool: mass-observation and popular leisure in the 1930s.* London; Routledge; 1990. Pp 288.
18. Douglas, Roy. *The World War, 1939–1945: the cartoonists' vision.* London; Routledge; 1990. Pp 320.
19. Durant, John R. 'Evolution, ideology and world view: Darwinian religion in the twentieth century', Bc16, 355–73.
20. Edwards, Ron. *Harrow College of Further Education: a short history.* Harrow; HCFE and London Borough of Harrow; 1987. Pp 96.

21. Ferris, Paul. *Sir Huge: a biography of Huw Wheldon*. London; Joseph; 1990. Pp 320.

22. Flavell, A.J. 'T.E. Lawrence, *The Seven Pillars of Wisdom* and the Bodleian', *Bodleian Library Record* 13 (1990), 300–13.

23. Freeden, Michael (ed.). *Reappraising J.A. Hobson: humanism and welfare*. London; Unwin Hyman; 1990. Pp xi, 185.

24. Grown, Peter C. 'An experiment in political education: "V.G.", "Slimy" and the Repton Sixth, 1914–1918', *History of Education* 19 (1990), 1–21.

25. Hargreaves, John Desmond; Fortes, Angela (ed.). *Aberdeen university, 1945–1981: quincentennial studies in the history of the university*. Aberdeen; Aberdeen UP; 1989.

26. Hart-Davis, Duff. *The house the Berrys built*. London; Hodder & Stoughton; 1990. Pp 299.

27. Hill, Jeffrey. 'League cricket in the north and midlands, 1900–1940', Bc52, 121–41.

28. Hobday, Charles. *Edgell Rickword: a poet at war*. Manchester; Carcanet; 1989. Pp 337.

29. Hopkin, Deian. 'Technology and the periodical press', Bc87, 184–97.

30. Hyde, Harford Montgomery. *The Lady Chatterley's Lover trial*. London; Bodley Head; 1990. Pp 336.

31. Hynes, Samuel. *A war imagined: the First World War and English culture*. London; Bodley Head; 1990. Pp 514.

32. Johnson, Pam. ' "The best friend whom life has given me": does Winifred Holtby have a place in lesbian history?', Bc1, 141–57.

33. Jones, Stephen G. 'Working-class sport in Manchester between the wars', Bc52, 67–83.

34. Kaye, Harvey J. 'E.P. Thompson, the British Marxist historical tradition and the contemporary crisis', Bc3, 252–75.

35. Keating, Peter. ' "Novels in nutshells": British novelists and the cinematograph', Bc104, 200–15.

36. Korr, Charles P. 'A different kind of success: West Ham United and the creation of tradition and community', Bc52, 142–58.

37. Lyte, Charles. *Frank Kingdon-Ward: the last of the great plant hunters*. London; Murray; 1989. Pp [256].

38. Manley, K.A.; Keeling, D.F. 'Sunshine in the gloom: the study of British literary history', *Libraries & Culture* 25 (1990), 80–85.

39. Marwick, Arthur. '*Room at the top*: the novel and the film', Bc61, 249–76.

40. Mason, Tony. 'Stanley Matthews', Bc52, 159–78.

41. McCrone, Kathleen E. 'Emancipation or recreation? The development of women's sport at the university of London', *International J. of the History of Sport* 7 (1990), 204–29.

42. Melling, Elizabeth. *Sir Gerrard Tyrwhitt-Drake and the Cobtree Estate, Maidstone*. Rainham; Meresborough; 1988. Pp 64.

43. Mellini, Peter. 'Gabriel's message', *History Today* 40/2 (1990), 46–52.

44. Mini, Piero V. *Keynes, Bloomsbury and 'The general theory'*. Basingstoke; Macmillan; 1990. Pp 300.

45. Moorhouse, H.F. 'Shooting stars: footballers and working-class culture in twentieth-century Scotland', Bc52, 179–97.

46. Morgan, Neil. 'The strategy of biological research programmes: reassessing the "dark age" of biochemistry, 1910–1930', *Annals of Science* 47 (1990), 139–50.

47. Morison, John. 'Anglo-Soviet cultural contacts since 1975', Bc8, 168–92.

48. Nelson, James G. *Elkin Mathews: publisher to Yeats, Joyce, Pound.* London; Wisconsin UP; 1989. Pp xiii, 299.

49. Oram, Alison. ' "Embittered, sexless or homosexual": attacks on spinster teachers, 1918–1939' [duplicated in Bc1], Bc2, 183–202.

50. Oram, Alison. ' "Embittered, sexless or homosexual": attacks on spinster teachers, 1918–1939' [duplicated in Bc2], Bc1, 99–118.

51. Pearson, Egon Sharpe. *'Student': a statistical biography of William Sealy Gosset,* ed. R.L. Plackett and G.A. Barnard. Oxford; Oxford UP; 1990. Pp viii, 142.

52. Potter, Jeremy. *Independent television in Britain, vol. 4: companies and programmes, 1968–1980.* Basingstoke; Macmillan; 1990. Pp 440.

53. Rees, Henry. *A university is born: the story of the foundation of the university of Warwick.* Coventry; Avalon; 1989. Pp 101.

54. Reynolds, David. 'The great Welsh education debate, 1980–1990', *History of Education* 19 (1990), 251–60.

55. Rose, Jonathan. 'The workers in the Workers' Educational Association, 1903–1950', *Albion* 21 (1989), 591–608.

56. Rowlands, Peter. *Oliver Lodge and the Liverpool Physical Society.* Liverpool; Liverpool UP; 1990. Pp 336.

57. Scholes, G. 'Radiation chemistry at Newcastle-upon-Tyne: J.J. Weiss', Bc19, 373–86.

58. Shepherd, Mary. *Heart of Harefield: the story of the hospital.* London; Quiller; 1990. Pp 224.

59. Sinyard, Neil. 'Grierson and the documentary film', Bc93, 246–53.

60. Smith, Dai. 'Focal heroes: a Welsh fighting class', Bc52, 198–217.

61. Smith, Harold L. *British feminism in the twentieth century.* Aldershot; Elgar; 1990. Pp 256.

62. Tansey, E.M. 'Sir Henry Dale's laboratory notebooks, 1914–1919, (from the Wellcome Institute Library)', *Medical History* 34 (1990), 199–209.

63. Taylor, Miles. 'Patriotism, history and the Left in twentieth-century Britain', *Historical J.* 33 (1990), 971–87.

64. Tylee, Claire M. *The Great War and women's consciousness: images of militarism and womanhood in women's writings, 1914–1964.* Basingstoke; Macmillan; 1990. Pp 293.

65. Wainwright, Milton. 'Besredka's "antivirus" in relation to Fleming's initial views on the nature of penicillin', *Medical History* 34 (1990), 79–85.

66. Willcox, Temple. 'Soviet films, censorship and the British government: a matter of the public interest', *Historical J. of Film, Radio and Television* 10 (1990), 275–92.

67. Williams, Jack. 'Recreational cricket in the Bolton area between the wars', Bc52, 101–20.
68. Williams, M.R.; Campbell-Kelly, Martin (ed.). *The early British computer conferences.* Cambridge (Ma); MIT Press; 1989. Pp xvi, 508.
69. Williams, Trevor I. *Robert Robinson: chemist extraordinary.* Oxford; Oxford UP; 1990. Pp 201.

# J. MEDIEVAL WALES

*See also* Aa2,65,94,b40–41; Bc75; Eh9.

(a) *General*

1. Brett, Caroline. 'John Leland, Wales, and early British history', *Welsh History R.* 15 (1990–1), 169–82.
2. Campbell, Ewan. 'A blue glass squat jar from Dinas Powys, south Wales', *B. of the Board of Celtic Studies* 36 (1989), 239–45.
3. Crouch, David. 'The earliest original charter of a Welsh king', *B. of the Board of Celtic Studies* 36 (1989), 125–31.
4. Evans, D. Simon (ed.). *A mediaeval prince of Wales: the 'Life' of Gruffudd ap Cynan.* Lampeter; Llanerch; 1990. Pp 138.
5. Pratt, Derrick. 'The Marcher lordship of Chirk, 1329–1330', *T. of the Denbighshire Historical Soc.* 39 (1990), 5–41.
6. Rees, Iorwerth (comp.). *A glossary of medieval and post-medieval terms relating to south Wales.* Cardiff; Glamorgan Archive Service; 1988. Pp ix, 143.
7. Suppe, Frederick. 'The cultural significance of decapitation in high medieval Wales and the Marches', *B. of the Board of Celtic Studies* 36 (1989), 146–60.
8. Walker, David. *Medieval Wales.* Cambridge; Cambridge UP; 1990. Pp x, 235.
9. Walker, R.F. 'Henry II's charter to Pembroke', *B. of the Board of Celtic Studies* 36 (1989), 132–46.

(b) *Politics*

1. Carr, A.D. 'Prydydd y Moch: ymateb hanesydd' [Prydydd y Moch: a historian's response], *Honourable Soc. of Cymmrodorion T.* (1989), 161–80.
2. Davies, Wendy. *Patterns of power in early Wales.* Oxford; Oxford UP; 1990. Pp viii, 103.
3. Given, James. *State and society in medieval Europe: Gwynedd and Languedoc under outside rule.* Ithaca (NY); Cornell UP; 1990. Pp xii, 302.

4. Lynch, Peredur. 'Llygad Gŵr: sylwebydd cyfoes' [Llygad Gŵr: a contemporary commentator], *Ysgrifau Beirniadol* 16 (1990), 31–51.
5. Turvey, R.K. 'The Marcher shire of Pembroke and the Glyndŵr rebellion', *Welsh History R.* 15 (1990–1), 151–68.

## (c) *Constitution, Administration and Law*

1. Pryce, Huw. 'Medieval Welsh law', *Newsletter of the School of Celtic Studies* (Dublin Inst. for Advanced Studies) 4 (1990), 30–34.
2. Richards, Melville (ed.). *Cyfreithiau Hywel Dda yn ôl Llawysgrif Coleg yr Iesu LVII Rhydychen* [The laws of Hywel the Good according to Jesus College, Oxford, MS LVII]. Cardiff; Wales UP; 2nd edn. 1990. Pp xxiv, 194.
3. Wiliam, Aled Rhys (ed.). *Llyfr Cynog: a medieval Welsh law digest.* Aberystwyth; Centre for Advanced Welsh and Celtic Studies; 1990. Pp xx, 77.

## (d) *External Affairs*

1. Evans, D. Simon. 'The Welsh and the Irish before the Normans— contact or impact', *P. of the British Academy* 75 (1990 for 1989), 143–61.
2. Siddons, Michael. 'Welsh seals in Paris: further additions', *B. of the Board of Celtic Studies* 36 (1989), 185–86.
3. Siddons, Michael. 'Welshmen in the service of France', *B. of the Board of Celtic Studies* 36 (1989), 161–84.

## (e) *Religion*

1. Baines, Michael E. 'An unrecorded early Christian stone at Llandeilo, Pembrokeshire', *Archaeologia Cambrensis* 138 (1990 for 1989), 110–11.
2. Fenn, R.W.D.; Sinclair, J.B. 'The Christian origins of Montgomery-shire', *Montgomeryshire Collections* 78 (1990), 47–64.
3. Graham, J.D.P. 'The treasures of Llanthony', *Brycheiniog* 23 (1988–9), 43–45.
4. Sharpe, Richard. 'Some medieval *miracula* from Llandegley (Lambeth Palace Library, MS. 94 fols. 153v–155r)', *B. of the Board of Celtic Studies* 37 (1990), 166–76.
5. Thomas, W. Gwyn. 'A cross-decorated stone at St Martin's Haven, Marloes, Pemb.', *Archaeologia Cambrensis* 138 (1990 for 1989), 113–14.
6. Thomas, W. Gwyn. 'An early sundial from the Towyn area', *Archaeologia Cambrensis* 138 (1990 for 1989), 111–13.
7. Williams, David H. 'Mapping Cistercian lands, with especial reference to Wales', Bc123, 58–63.
8. Williams, David H. *Atlas of Cistercian lands in Wales.* Cardiff; Wales UP; 1990. Pp xvi, 153.

## (f) *Economic Affairs*

1. Gruffydd, K. Lloyd. 'Y llong yn y canol oesoedd' [The ship in the middle ages], *Cymru a'r Môr/Maritime Wales* 13 (1990), 44–60.
2. James, Thomas B. 'Medieval Carmarthen and its burgesses: a study of town growth and burgess families in the later thirteenth century', *Carmarthenshire Antiquary* 25 (1989), 9–26.

## (g) *Social Structure and Population*

1. Campbell, Ewan. 'New finds of post-Roman imported pottery and glass from south Wales', *Archaeologia Cambrensis* 138 (1990 for 1989), 59–66.
2. Carr, A.D. 'Gwilym ap Gruffydd and the rise of the Penrhyn estate', *Welsh History R.* 15 (1990–1), 1–20.
3. Carter, Harold. 'Parallelism and disjunction: a study in the internal structure of Welsh towns', Bc26, 189–209.
4. Morgan, D.R. 'Towards a topography of early Brecon', *Brycheiniog* 23 (1988–9), 23–41.
5. Redknap, Mark; Campbell, Ewan; Lane, Alan. 'Llangorse crannog', *Archaeology in Wales* 29 (1989), 57–58.
6. Toorians, Lauran. 'Wizo Flandrensis and the Flemish settlement in Pembrokeshire', *Cambridge Medieval Celtic Studies* 20 (1990), 99–118.

## (h) *Naval and Military*

1. Arnold, C.J. 'Powis castle: the outer bailey', *Montgomeryshire Collections* 78 (1990), 65–71.
2. Butler, Lawrence. 'Dolforwyn Castle, Montgomery, Powys: first report, the excavations, 1981–1986', *Archaeologia Cambrensis* 138 (1990 for 1989), 78–98.
3. Dowdell, G.; Spurgeon, C.J.; Sell, S.H. 'Excavations at Sully Castle, 1963–1969', *B. of the Board of Celtic Studies* 37 (1990), 308–60.

## (i) *Intellectual and Cultural*

1. Bosco, M. 'Dafydd Benfras and his *Red Book* poems', *Studia Celtica* 22–23 (1987–8), 49–117.
2. Davies, Sioned. *Pedeir Keinc y Mabinogi* [The Four Branches of the Mabinogi]. Caernarfon; Gwasg Pantycelyn; 1989. Pp 77.
3. Fulton, Helen. *Dafydd ap Gwilym and the European context*. Cardiff; Wales UP; 1989. Pp xiv, 274.
4. Johnston, Dafydd. 'Tri chyfeiriad at Lywelyn ap Gruffudd' [Three references to Llywelyn ap Gruffudd], *B. of the Board of Celtic Studies* 36 (1989), 97–101.
5. Matonis, A.T.E. 'The concept of poetry in the middle ages: the Welsh evidence from the bardic grammars', *B. of the Board of Celtic Studies* 36 (1989), 1–12.

6. Rowland, Jenny. *Early Welsh saga poetry: a study and edition of the 'Englynion'*. Cambridge; Brewer; 1990. Pp ix, 688.
7. Slotkin, Edgar M. 'The fabula, story, and text of *Breuddwyd Rhonabwy*', *Cambridge Medieval Celtic Studies* 18 (1989), 89–111.
8. Tanguy, Bernard. 'De la vie de Saint Cadoc à celle de Saint Gurtiern', *Études Celtiques* 26 (1989), 159–85.
9. Welsh, Andrew. 'Doubling and incest in the *Mabinogi*', *Speculum* 65 (1990), 344–62.
10. Welsh, Andrew. 'Traditional tales and the harmonizing of story in *Pwyll Pendeuic Dyuet*', *Cambridge Medieval Celtic Studies* 17 (1989), 15–41.
11. Wood, Juliette. 'Prophecy in middle Welsh tradition', Bc103, 52–65.

# K. SCOTLAND BEFORE THE UNION

*See also* Aa51–52,108,b10,14,37–39,c35; Bc54,75,89; Fb6.

(a) *General*

1. Ash, Marinell. 'William Wallace and Robert the Bruce: the life and death of a national myth', Bc131, 83–94.
2. Buchanan, John Nyren. *Marginal Scotland*. New York; Lang (American University Studies 9th ser., vols. 64–65); 1989. 2 vols. Pp 275.
3. Kranel Heredia, Blanca. 'Sir James Douglas's death in Spain, 1330', *Scottish Historical R.* 69 (1990), 83–90.
4. Lynch, Michael. 'Queen Mary's triumph: the baptismal celebrations at Stirling in December 1566', *Scottish Historical R.* 69 (1990), 1–21.
5. Macinnes, Allan. 'Covenanting revolution and municipal enterprise' [in seventeenth-century Glasgow], *History Today* 40/5 (1990), 10–16.
6. Mair, Craig. *Stirling: the royal burgh*. Edinburgh; Donald; 1990. Pp 255.
7. Naismith, Robert J. *The story of Scotland's towns*. Edinburgh; Donald; 1989. Pp 181.
8. Reid, Norman H. (ed.). *Scotland in the reign of Alexander III*. Edinburgh; Donald; 1990. Pp 250.
9. Ross, Stewart. *The monarchs of Scotland*. Moffat; Lochar; 1990. Pp 192.
10. Stell, Geoffrey. 'Kings, nobles and buildings of the later middle ages: Scotland', Bc54, 60–72.

(b) *Politics*

1. Blake, William. *William Maitland of Lethington, 1528–1573: a study of the policy of moderation in the Scottish Reformation*. Lampeter; Mellen; 1990. Pp viii, 350.
2. Brims, John. 'From reformers to "Jacobins": the Scottish Association of the Friends of the People', Bc55, 31–50.

3. Brown, Keith M. 'In search of the godly magistrate in Reformation Scotland', *J. of Ecclesiastical History* 40 (1989), 553–87.
4. Cowan, Ian B. 'The reluctant revolutionaries: Scotland in 1688', Bc146, 65–81.
5. Donald, Peter H. *An uncounselled king: Charles I and the Scottish troubles, 1637–1641.* Cambridge; Cambridge UP; 1990. Pp 344.
6. Linklater, Magnus; Hesketh, Christian. *For king and conscience: John Graham of Claverhouse, viscount Dundee (1648–1689).* London; Weidenfeld & Nicolson; 1989. Pp xii, 244.
7. Macdougall, Norman. *James IV.* Edinburgh; Donald; 1989. Pp xi, 339.
8. McGladdery, Christine. *James II.* Edinburgh; Donald; 1990. Pp ix, 185.

## (c) *Constitution, Administration and Law*

1. Mason, Roger A. 'Kingship, nobility and Anglo-Scottish union: John Mair's *History of Greater Britain* (1521)', *Innes R.* 41 (1990), 182–222.
2. Morrill, John (ed.). *The National Covenant in its British context, 1638–1651.* Edinburgh; Edinburgh UP; 1990. Pp 240.
3. Smith, Brian. 'Shetland, Scandinavia, Scotland, 1300–1700: the changing nature of contact', Bc54, 25–37.
4. Stewart, Marion M. ' "A sober and peaceable deportment": court and council books of Dumfries, 1561–1661', Bc89, 143–54.

## (d) *External Affairs*

1. Badouin-Matuszek, M.-N. 'Mary Stewart's arrival in France in 1548', *Scottish Historical R.* 69 (1990), 90–95.
2. Dunlop, David. 'The *redresses and reparcons of attemptates*: Alexander Legh's instructions from Edward IV, March-April 1475', *Historical Research* 63 (1990), 340–53.

## (e) *Religion*

1. Adamson, Duncan. 'Kirkpatrick Fleming and the records of Middlebie presbytery, 1699–1743', *Dumfriesshire & Galloway Natural History & Antiq. Soc. T.* 3rd ser. 62 (1988), 48–77.
2. Atkinson, David W. 'Zachary Boyd as minister of the Barony parish: a commentator on the late Reformation church', *Scottish Church History Soc. Records* 24 (1990), 19–32.
3. Burns, J.H. 'John Ireland: theology and public affairs in the late fifteenth century', *Innes R.* 41 (1990), 151–81.
4. Clarke, Tristram. 'The Williamite Episcopalians and the Glorious revolution in Scotland', *Scottish Church History Soc. Records* 24 (1990), 33–51.
5. Dahlerup, Troels. 'Orkney bishops as suffragans in the Scandinavian-Baltic area: an aspect of the late medieval church in the north', Bc54, 38–47.

6. Finlay, Ian. *Columba*. Glasgow; Drew; new edn. 1990. Pp 256.
7. Hargreaves, Henry. 'An unnoticed manuscript pontifical in Scotland', *Innes R.* 41 (1990), 223–26.
8. Kyle, Richard. 'The major concepts in John Knox's baptismal thought', *Fides et Historia* xxl (1989), 20–30.
9. Leneman, Leah. ' "Prophaning" the Lord's Day: Sabbath breach in early modern Scotland', *History* 74 (1989), 217–31.
10. Macquarrie, Alan. 'Early Christian Govan: the historical context', *Scottish Church History Soc. Records* 24 (1990), 1–17.
11. MacQueen, John. 'The saint as seer: Adomnan's account of Columba', Bc103, 37–51.
12. Meckler, Michael. 'Colum Cille's ordination of Aedan mac Gabrain', *Innes R.* 41 (1990), 139–50.
13. Scott, J.G. 'Origins of Dundrennan and Soulseat abbeys', *Dumfriesshire & Galloway Natural History & Antiq. Soc. T.* 3rd ser. 62 (1988), 35–44.
14. Stones, J.A. (ed.). *Three Scottish Carmelite friaries: excavations at Aberdeen, Linlithgow, and Perth, 1980–1986*. Edinburgh; Oxbow for Soc. of Antiquaries of Scotland (Monograph ser. vol. 6); 1989. Pp 175.
15. Walker, G. 'Sir David Lindsay's *Ane satire of the Thrie Estaitis* and the politics of reformation', *Scottish Literary J.* xvi (1989), 5–17.

## (f) *Economic Affairs*

1. Ditchburn, David. 'A note on Scandinavian trade with Scotland in the later middle ages', Bc54, 73–89.
2. Ewan, Elizabeth. *Town life in fourteenth-century Scotland*. Edinburgh; Edinburgh UP; 1989. Pp 208.
3. Lillehammer, Arnvid. 'Boards, beans and barrel-hoops: contacts between Scotland and the Stavanger area in the seventeenth century', Bc54, 100–06.
4. Soltow, Lee. 'The distribution of private wealth in land in Scotland and Scandinavia in the seventeenth and eighteenth centuries', Bc54, 130–47.

## (g) *Social Structure and Population*

1. Cox, R.A.V. 'Place-name evidence in the west of Lewis: approaches and problems in establishing a profile of Norse settlement', *Scottish Arch. R.* vi (1989), 107–15.
2. Gordon, George. 'The morphological development of Scottish cities from Georgian to modern times', Bc26, 210–32.
3. Kelsall, Helen M.; Kelsall, Roger Keith (ed.). *An album of Scottish families, 1694–1696: being the first instalment of George Home's diary, supplemented by much further research into the Edinburgh and Border families forming his extensive social network*. Aberdeen; Aberdeen UP; 1990. Unpaginated.
4. Sanderson, M.H.B. 'The people of sixteenth-century Ayrshire', *Ayrshire Collections* 14 (1989), 298–343.

5. Sinclair, Cecil. *Tracing your Scottish ancestors: a guide to ancestry research in the Scottish Office.* Edinburgh; HMSO; 1990. Pp x, 153.
6. Whyte, Ian D. 'Urbanization in early modern Scotland: a preliminary analysis', *Social History* 14 (1989), 21–37.

## (h) *Naval and Military*

1. Aberg, Alf. 'Scottish soldiers in the Swedish armies in the sixteenth and seventeenth centuries', Bc54, 90–99.
2. Behre, Goran. 'Gothenburg in Stuart war strategy, 1649–1760', Bc54, 107–18.
3. McNamee, C.J. 'William Wallace's invasion of northern England in 1297', *Northern History* 26 (1990), 40–58.
4. Scott, Andrew Murray. *Bonnie Dundee: John Graham of Claverhouse.* Edinburgh; Donald; 1989. Pp vii, 220.

## (i) *Intellectual and Cultural*

1. Anon. *Inventory of the ancient monuments, vol. 6: Mid Argyll and Cowal (prehistoric and early historic).* London; HMSO (Royal Commission on the ancient and historical monuments of Scotland); 1988. Pp 228.
2. Broadie, Alexander. 'Thomas Reid and his pre-Reformation Scotttish precursors', Bc56, 6–19.
3. Cairns, John W.; Fergus, T. David; MacQueen, Hector L. 'Legal humanism in Renaissance Scotland', *J. of Legal History* 11 (1990), 40–69.
4. Gardener-Medwin, Alisoun. 'A ballad of the battle of Otterburn: Scottish folksong', Bc89, 81–95.
5. Houston, R.A. 'Scottish education and literacy, 1600–1800: an international perspective', Bc57, 43–61.
6. Huneycutt, Lois L. 'The idea of the perfect princess: the *Life of St Margaret* in the reign of Matilda II (1100–1118)', Bc72, 81–97.
7. Jones, Peter. 'Introduction' [Scottish Enlightenment], Bc56, 1–5.
8. Lyall, R.J. 'Books and book owners in fifteenth-century Scotland', Bc41, 239–56.
9. Macqueen, John. 'The Renaissance in Scotland', Bc75, 41–56.
10. MacQueen, John (ed.). *Humanism in Renaissance Scotland.* Edinburgh; Edinburgh UP; 1990. Pp ix, 199.
11. McClure, J. Derrick. ' "O'Phoenix Escossois": James VI as poet', Bc89, 96–111.
12. Moore, James R. 'Natural Law and the Pyrrhonian controversy', Bc56, 20–38.
13. Power, Rosemary. 'Scotland in the Norse Sagas', Bc54, 13–24.
14. Stevenson, David. *King's College, Aberdeen, 1560–1641: from protestant Reformation to covenanting revolution.* Aberdeen; Aberdeen UP; 1990. Pp 150.
15. Wood, Paul. 'Science and the Aberdeen Enlightenment', Bc56, 39–66.

# L. IRELAND TO c.1640

See also Ab34; Bc64,74–75,116,143,d33; Jd1; Mf1,j2.

## (a) General

1. Edwards, Nancy. *The archaeology of early medieval Ireland*. London; Batsford; 1990. Pp 256.
2. Lacy, Brian. *Siege city: the story of Derry and Londonderry*. Belfast; Blackstaff; 1990. Pp 293.
3. Raftery, Barry. 'Barbarians to the west', Bc141, 117–52.

## (b) Politics

1. Brady, Ciaran. 'The road to the *View*: on the decline of reform thought in Tudor Ireland', Bc88, 25–45.
2. Canny, Nicholas J. 'Introduction: Spenser and the reform of Ireland', Bc88, 9–24.
3. Carroll, D. Allen. ' "Rich and greene": Elizabethan beast fables and Ireland', *Eire–Ireland* 25 (1990), 106–13.
4. Ó Buachella, Breandán. 'Aodh Eangach and the Irish king-hero', Bc64, medieval Ireland', *Peritia* 6–7 (1990 for 1987–8), 307–20.
5. Smith, Brendan. 'The murder of Richard Gernon, sheriff of Louth, 1311', *J. of the County Louth Arch. and Historical Soc.* 21/4 (1988), 391–93.
6. Walshe, Helen Coburn. 'Enforcing the Elizabethan settlement: the vicissitudes of Hugh Brady, bishop of Meath, 1563–1584', *Irish Historical Studies* 26 (1989), 352–76.
7. Walshe, Helen Coburn. 'The rebellion of William Nugent, 1581', Bc85, 26–52; 297–302.

## (c) Constitution, Administration and Law

1. Blair, Claude; Delamer, Ida. 'The Dublin civic swords', *P. of the Royal Irish Academy* 88c (1988), 87–142.
2. Brand, Paul. 'The early history of the legal profession of the lordship of Ireland, 1250–1350', Bc143, 15–50.
3. Breatnach, Liam. 'Lawyers in early Ireland', Bc143, 1–14.
4. Clarke, John P. 'Notes on the devolution of title to the manors of Louth, Castlering and Ash, County Louth', *County Louth Arch. and Historical J.* 21/3 (1987), 257–73.
5. Hart, A.R. 'The king's serjeant at law in Tudor Ireland, 1485–1603', Bc143, 77–100.
6. Sheehan, Anthony. 'Irish revenues and English subventions, 1559–1622', *P. of the Royal Irish Academy* 90c (1990), 35–65.
7. Simms, Katherine. 'The brehons of later medieval Ireland', Bc143, 51–76.

(d) *External Affairs*

1. Enright, Michael J. 'Review article: medieval Ireland and the continent', *Irish Historical Studies* 27 (1990), 68–77.
2. Hays, L.; Jones, E.D. 'Policy on the run: Henry II and Irish Sea diplomacy', *J. of British Studies* 29 (1990), 293–316.

(e) *Religion*

1. Bitel, Lisa M. *Isle of the saints: monastic settlement and Christian community in early Ireland.* Ithaca (NY); Cornell UP; 1990. Pp 268.
2. Cosgrove, Art. 'The Armagh registers: an under-explored source for late medieval Ireland', *Peritia* 6–7 (1990 for 1987–8), 307–20.
3. Cottret, B. 'La conquête de l'Irlande. Religion et migration au xviiè siècle: notes critiques', *Revue de l'Histoire des Religions* 206 (1989), 55–66.
4. Ellis, Steven G. 'Economic problems of the church: why the Reformation failed in Ireland', *J. of Ecclesiastical History* 41 (1990), 239–65.
5. Fenning, Hugh. 'Irishmen ordained at Lisbon, 1587–1625, 1641–1660', *Collectanea Hibernica* 31–32 (1990), 103–17.
6. Herbert, Máire; Ó Riain, Padráig. *Betha Adamnain: the Irish life of Adomnan.* London; Irish Texts Soc. 54; 1988. Pp 110.
7. Herren, Michael. 'Mission and monasticism in the *Confessio* of Patrick', Bc64, 76–85.
8. Hurley, Maurice F. 'Excavations at an early ecclesiastical enclosure at Kilkieran, county Kilkenny', *Royal Soc. of Antiquaries of Ireland J.* 118 (1989 for 1988), 123–34.
9. Kiernan, Francis J. *The diocese of Kilmore: bishops and priests, 1136–1988.* Cavan; Breifne Historical Soc.; 1989. Pp 294.
10. Lennon, Colm. 'The chantries in the Irish Reformation; the case of St Anne's Guild, Dublin, 1550–1620', Bc85, 6–25; 293–97.
11. Lynch, Anthony. 'Documents of Franciscan interest from the episcopal archives of Armagh, 1265–1508', *Collectanea Hibernica* 31–32 (1990), 9–102.
12. Lynch, Anthony. 'Five documents of Drogheda interest from the registers of the archbishops of Armagh', *J. of the County Louth Arch. and Historical Soc.* 21/4 (1988), 407–14.
13. Murphy, Margaret. 'Ecclesiastical censures: an aspect of their use in thirteenth-century Dublin', *Archivium Hibernicum* 44 (1989), 89–97.
14. Ó Caoimh, Tomás. 'St Brendan sources: St Brendan and early Irish hagiography', Bc74, 17–24.
15. Ó Cróinín, Dáibhí. 'Cummianus Longus and the iconography of Christ and the apostles in early Irish literature', Bc64, 268–79.
16. Ó Cróinín, Dáibhí; McCarthy, Daniel. 'The "lost" Irish 84-year Easter table rediscovered', *Peritia* 6–7 (1990 for 1987–8), 227–42.
17. Ó Riain, Padráig. 'The saints and their amanuenses: early models and later issues', Bc116, 267–80.

18. Ó Riain, Padráig. 'The Tallaght martyrologies, redated', *Cambridge Medieval Celtic Studies* 20 (1990), 21–38.
19. Ó Riain-Raedel, Dagmar. 'Kalendare und Legende und ihre historische Auswertung' [Calendars and legends and their historical evaluation], Bc116, 241–66.
20. O'Dwyer, Peter. *Mary: a history of devotion in Ireland*. Dublin; Four Courts Press; 1988. Pp 331.
21. Picard, Jean-Michel; Pontfarcy, Yolande. *The vision of Tugnal*. Dublin; Four Courts Press; 1989. Pp 162.
22. Sharpe, Richard. '*Quatuor sanctissimi episcopi*: Irish saints before St Patrick', Bc64, 376–99.
23. Wiseman, W.G. 'Robert Dawson (1589–1643), bishop of Clonfert and Kilmacduagh', *T. of the Cumberland & Westmorland Antiq. & Arch. Soc.* 90 (1990), 205–15.

## (f) *Economic Affairs*

1. Brady, N.D.K. 'The plough pebbles of Ireland', *Tools & Tillage* vi (1988), 47–60.
2. Gillespie, Raymond. 'The small towns of Ulster, 1600–1700', *Ulster Folklife* 36 (1990), 23–31.
3. Maple, John T. 'Anglo-Norman conquest of Ireland and the Irish economy: stagnation or stimulation?', *The Historian* [USA] 52 (1990), 61–81.
4. O'Brien, A.F. 'The royal boroughs, the seaport towns and royal revenue in medieval Ireland', *Royal Soc. of Antiquaries of Ireland J.* 118 (1989 for 1988), 13–26.
5. Rynne, Colin. 'The introduction of the vertical watermill into Ireland: some recent archaeological evidence', *Medieval Archaeology* 33 (1989), 21–31.

## (g) *Social Structure and Population*

1. Bradley, John. 'The role of town-plan analysis in the study of medieval Irish town', Bc26, 39–59.
2. Cunningham, Bernadette; Gillespie, Raymond. 'Englishmen in sixteenth-century Irish annals', *Irish Economic & Social History* 17 (1990), 5–21.
3. Davies, Wendy. 'The place of healing in early Irish society', Bc64, 43–55.
4. Dungan, Thomas P. 'John Dongan of Dublin, an Elizabethan gentleman', *Royal Soc. of Antiquaries of Ireland J.* 118 (1989 for 1988), 101–17.
5. Dunleavy, Mairead. 'A classification of early Irish combs', *P. of the Royal Irish Academy* 88c (1988), 341–422.
6. Foley, Claire. 'Excavation at a medieval settlement site in Jerpoint church townland, County Kilkenny', *P. of the Royal Irish Academy* 89c (1989), 71–126.

7. Graham, B.J. 'Medieval settlement in County Roscommon', *P. of the Royal Irish Academy* 88c (1988), 19–38.
8. Stacey, Robin Chapman. 'Ties that bind: immunities in Irish and Welsh law', *Cambridge Medieval Celtic Studies* 20 (1990), 39–60.

## (h) Naval and Military

1. Henry, Grainne. 'The emerging identity of an Irish military group in the Spanish Netherlands', Bc85, 53–77; 302–09.
2. Ireland, John de Courcy. 'Maritime aspects of the Huguenot immigration into Ireland', Bc96, 145–63.
3. McGrail, Sean. 'Pilotage and navigation in the times of St Brendan', Bc74, 25–35.
4. McNeill, T.E. 'The great towers of early Irish castles', Bc72, 99–117.

## (i) Intellectual and Cultural

1. Boyer, Regis. 'The Vinland sagas and Brendan's *Navigatio*: a comparison', Bc74, 37–44.
2. ÓBreatnach, Pádraig A. 'Cú Chonnacht Dálaigh's poem before leaving Aodh Ruadh', Bc64, 32–42.
3. Breen, Aidan. 'The text of the Constantinopolitan creed in the Stowe missal', *P. of the Royal Irish Academy* 90c (1990), 107–21.
4. Breeze, Andrew. 'The Blessed Virgin's Joys and Sorrows', *Cambridge Medieval Celtic Studies* 19 (1990), 41–54.
5. Buckley, Ann. 'Musical instruments in Ireland from the ninth to the fourteenth centuries', *Irish Musical Studies*, ed. Gerard Gillan and Harry White (Dublin; Irish Academic Press; 1990), 13–57.
6. Devine, Kieran. *A computer-generated concordance to the 'Libri Epistolarum' of St Patrick*. Dublin; Royal Irish Academy; 1989. Pp 308.
7. Eames, Elizabeth S.; Fanning, Thomas. *Irish medieval tiles*. Dublin; Royal Irish Academy; 1988. Pp 144.
8. Esposito, Mario. *Irish books and learning in mediaeval Europe*, ed. Michael Lapidge. Aldershot; Variorum; 1990. Pp 332.
9. Grindle, W.H. *Irish cathedral music*. Belfast; Inst. of Irish Studies; 1989. Pp 261.
10. Herbert, Máire. 'The preface to *Amra Coluim Cille*', Bc64, 67–75.
11. Hofman, Rijcklof. 'Some new facts concerning the knowledge of Vergil in early medieval Ireland', *Études Celtiques* 25 (1988), 189–212.
12. Kelly, Dorothy. 'Cross-carved slabs from Latteragh, county Tipperary', *Royal Soc. of Antiquaries of Ireland J.* 118 (1989 for 1988), 92–100.
13. Kilbride-Jones, H.E. 'On some instances of Celtic art patterns inscribed on grave-slabs discovered at Carrowntemple, County Sligo, Ireland', *B. of the Board of Celtic Studies* 36 (1989), 230–38.
14. Lemarchand, M.J. '*Li Salt Brandan*: navigation and flight, a contribution to the study of the fantastic narrative in Benedeit's *Voyage of Saint Brendan*', Bc74, 45–50.

15. Mac Cana, Proinsias. 'The Voyage of St Brendan: literary and historical origins', Bc74, 3–16.
16. Mac Craith, Mícheál. 'Gaelic Ireland and the Renaissance', Bc75, 57–89.
17. McCone, Kim. 'A tale of two ditties: poet and satirist in Cath Maige Tuired', Bc64, 122–43.
18. McCone, Kim. Pagan past and Christian present in early Irish literature. Maynooth; Maynooth Monographs 3; 1990. Pp 277.
19. McNab, Susanne. 'Styles used in twelfth-century Irish figure sculpture', Peritia 6–7 (1990 for 1987–8), 265–97.
20. Newman, C. 'Fowler's type F3 early medieval penannular brooches', Medieval Archaeology 33 (1989), 7–20.
21. Ní Dhonnchadha, Máirín. 'An address to a student of law', Bc64, 159–77.
22. Ó Corraín, Donnchadh. 'Early Irish hermit poetry?', Bc64, 251–67.
23. Ó hUiginn, Ruairí. 'Tongu da dia toinges mo thuath [I swear by the God by whom my people swear] and related expressions', Bc64, 332–41.
24. Ó Murchadha, Domhnall; Ó Murchú, Giollamuire. 'Fragmentary inscripttions from the West Cross at Durrow, the South Cross at Clonmacnois, and the Cross of Kinnitty', Royal Soc. of Antiquaries of Ireland J. 118 (1989 for 1988), 53–66.
25. O'Dwyer, B.W. 'Celtic-Irish monasticism and early insular illuminated manuscripts', J. of Religious History 15 (1989), 425–35.
26. Picard, Jean-Michel. 'Eloquentiae Exuberantia: words and forms in Adomnan's Vita Columbae', Peritia 6–7 (1990 for 1987–8), 141–58.
27. Picard, Jean-Michel. 'The strange death of Guaire mac nedáin', Bc64, 367–75.
28. Ryan, Kathleen. 'Holes and flaws in medieval Irish manuscripts', Peritia 6–7 (1990 for 1987–8), 243–64.
29. Sayers, William. 'Warrior initiative and some short Celtic spears in the Irish and learned Latin traditions', Studies in Medieval and Renaissance History ns 11 (1989), 89–108.
30. Simms, Katherine. 'The poet as chieftain's widow: bardic elegies', Bc64, 400–11.
31. Stalley, Roger. 'European art and the Irish high crosses', P. of the Royal Irish Academy 90c (1990), 135–58.
32. Stalley, Roger. 'Gaelic friars and Gothic design', Bc71, 191–202.
33. Stevenson, Jane. 'Literacy in Ireland: the evidence of the Patrick dossier in the Book of Armagh', Bc121, 11–35.
34. Twohig, Dermot C. 'Excavation of three ringforts at Lisduggan North, county Cork', P. of the Royal Irish Academy 90c (1990), 1–33.
35. Vance, Norman. Irish literature: a social history. Oxford; Blackwell; 1990. Pp 315.
36. Zarnecki, George. 'Como and the Book of Durrow', Bc71, 35–45.

# M. IRELAND SINCE c.1640

See also Aa42,45,b34,c7; Bc49,60,63,84–85,88,113,125,143,d33; Fc23,i25; Hc12,g18–19,h16; La2,c1.

(a) *General*

1. Comerford, R.V. 'Ireland, 1850–1870: post-famine and mid-Victorian', Bc60, 372–95.
2. Connolly, S.J. 'Mass politics and sectarian conflict, 1823–1830', Bc60, 74–107.
3. Macdonagh, Oliver. 'Introduction: Ireland and the Union, 1801–1870', Bc60, xlvii-lxv.
4. Vaughan, W.E. 'Ireland, *c*.1870', Bc60, 726–800.
5. Woods, C.J. 'The historical writings of Patrick J. Corish to 1989', Bc85, 278–92.

(b) *Politics*

1. Bew, Paul. 'Varieties of Irishness? Some new explanations', *Historical J.* 33 (1990), 747–54.
2. Comerford, R.V. 'Churchmen, tenants and independent opposition, 1850–1856', Bc60, 396–414.
3. Comerford, R.V. 'Conspiring brotherhoods and contending elites, 1857–1863', Bc60, 415–30.
4. Comerford, R.V. 'Gladstone's first Irish enterprise, 1864–1870', Bc60, 431–50.
5. Connolly, S.J. 'Aftermath and adjustment', Bc60, 1–23.
6. Connolly, S.J. 'The Catholic question, 1801–1812', Bc60, 24–47.
7. Connolly, S.J. 'Union government, 1812–1823', Bc60, 48–73.
8. Cullen, Louis M. 'The political structures of the defenders', Bc63, 117–138.
9. Cummins, Seamus. 'Extra-parliamentary agitation in Dublin in the 1760s', Bc85, 118–134; 315–18.
10. Curtin, Nancy J. 'Symbols and rituals of united Irish mobilization', Bc63, 68–82.
11. Donnelly, James S., Jr. 'A famine in Irish politics', Bc60, 357–71.
12. Dooley, Terence. 'Monaghan Protestants in a time of crisis, 1919–1922', Bc85, 235–51; 339–42.
13. Dunne, Tom. 'Popular ballads, revolutionary rhetoric and politicization', Bc63, 139–155.
14. Dwyer, T. Ryle. *Michael Collins: the man who won the war*. Cork; Mercier; 1990. Pp 160.
15. English, Richard. 'Socialism and republican schism in Ireland: the emergence of the Republican Congress in 1934', *Irish Historical Studies* 27 (1990), 48–65.

16. Hempton, David. ' "For God and Ulster": evangelical Protestantism and the Home Rule crisis of 1886', Bc115, 225–54.

17. Hill, Jacqueline R. 'Religious toleration and the relaxation of the penal laws: an imperial perspective, 1763–1780', *Archivium Hibernicum* 44 (1989), 98–109.

18. Hill, Jacqueline R. 'The legal profession and the defence of the *ancien régime* in Ireland, 1790–1840', Bc143, 181–210.

19. Jackson, Alvin. 'The failure of unionism in Dublin, 1900', *Irish Historical Studies* 26 (1989), 377–95.

20. Jackson, Alvin. 'Unionist politics and protestant society in Edwardian Ireland', *Historical J.* 33 (1990), 839–66.

21. MacDonagh, Oliver. 'Politics, 1830–1845', Bc60, 169–92.

22. MacDonagh, Oliver. 'The age of O'Connell, 1830–1845', Bc60, 158–68.

23. Morgan, Austen. *Labour and partition: the Belfast working class, 1905–1923.* London; Pluto; 1990. Pp xxi, 358.

24. Newsinger, John. ' "A lamp to guide your feet": Jim Larkin, the Irish worker and the Dublin working class', *European History Q.* 20 (1990), 63–99.

25. O'Brien, Gerard. 'Francophobia in later eighteenth-century Irish history', Bc63, 40–51.

26. O'Connell, Maurice R. *Daniel O'Connell: the man and his politics.* Dublin; Irish Academic Press; 1989. Pp 158.

27. O'Flaherty, Eamon. 'Irish Catholics and the French revolution', Bc63, 52–67.

28. O'Grady, Joseph P. 'The Irish Free State passport and the question of citizenship, 1921–1924', *Irish Historical Studies* 26 (1989), 396–405.

29. Purdie, Bob. *Politics in the streets: the origins of the civil rights movement in Northern Ireland.* Belfast; Blackstaff; 1990. Pp 286.

30. Shepherd, Robert. *Ireland's fate: the Boyne and after.* London; Aurum; 1990. Pp xvi, 242.

31. Smyth, Jim. 'Popular politicization, defenderism and the Catholic question', Bc63, 109–116.

32. Stubbs, John O. 'The Unionists and Ireland, 1914–1918', *Historical J.* 33 (1990), 867–93.

33. Ward, Margaret. *Maud Gonne: Ireland's Joan of Arc.* London; Pandora; 1990. Pp xii, 211.

34. Whelan, Kevin. 'Politicization in county Wexford and the origins of the 1798 rebellion', Bc63, 156–178.

35. Whyte, John. *Interpreting Northern Ireland.* Oxford; Oxford UP; 1990. Pp 312.

36. Woods, C.J. 'The place of Thomas Russell in the United Irish movement', Bc63, 83–100.

(c) *Constitution, Administration and Law*

1. Barry, Colm. 'The police and protest in Dublin, 1786–1840', Bc113, 157–84.

2. Brady, J.C. 'Legal development, 1801–1879', Bc60, 451–81.
3. Brett, C.E.B. 'Two eighteenth-century provincial attorneys: Matthew Brett and Jack Brett', Bc143, 175–80.
4. Greer, D.S. 'The development of civil bill procedure in Ireland', Bc113, 27–59.
5. Griffin, Brian. 'Religion and opportunity in the Irish police forces, 1836–1914', Bc85, 219–34; 335–39.
6. Hogan, Daire. "Arrows too strangely pointed": the relations of Lord Justice Christian and lord O'Hagan, 1868–1874', Bc113, 61–83.
7. Hogan, Daire. ' "Vacancies for their friends": judicial appointments in Ireland, 1866–1867', Bc143, 211–30.
8. Jackson, Claire. 'Irish political opposition to the passage of criminal evidence reform at Westminster, 1883–1898', Bc113, 185–201.
9. Kenny, Colum. 'The records of King's Inns, Dublin', Bc143, 231–48.
10. MacDonagh, Oliver. 'Ideas and institutions, 1830–1845', Bc60, 193–217.
11. McDowell, R.B. 'Administration and the public services, 1800–1870', Bc60, 538–61.
12. McEldowney, J.F. 'Some aspects of law and policy in the administration of criminal justice in nineteenth-century Ireland', Bc113, 117–55.
13. McEldowney, J.F.; O'Higgins, Paul. 'Irish legal history and the nineteenth century', Bc113, 203–30.
14. McEldowney, J.F.; O'Higgins, Paul. 'The common law tradition in Irish legal history', Bc113, 13–25.
15. Osborough, W.N. 'Catholics, land and the popery acts of Anne', Bc84, 21–56.
16. Osborough, W.N. 'Executive failure to enforce judicial decrees: a neglected chapter in nineteenth-century constitutional history', Bc113, 85–116.
17. Osborough, W.N. 'The regulation of the admission of attorneys and solicitors in Ireland, 1600–1866', Bc143, 101–52.
18. Power, Thomas P. 'Conversions among the legal profession in Ireland in the eighteenth century', Bc143, 153–74.

(d) *External Affairs*

None

(e) *Religion*

1. Bartlett, Thomas. 'The origins and progress of the Catholic question in Ireland, 1690–1800', Bc84, 1–19.
2. Conlan, Patrick. 'The book of receptions and professions of the Franciscan novitiate in Drogheda, 1860–1877', *Collectanea Hibernica* 31–32 (1990), 220–28.
3. Dunlop, R. 'Dublin Baptists from 1650 onwards', *Irish Baptist History Soc. J.* 21 (1989), 5–16.

4. Fenning, Hugh (ed.). 'The library of the Augustinians of Galway in 1731', *Collectanea Hibernica* 31–32 (1990), 162–95.

5. Larkin, Emmet. *The Roman Catholic church and the Home Rule movement in Ireland, 1870–1874*. Dublin; Gill & Macmillan; 1990. Pp xi, 416.

6. Leighton, C.D.A. 'Gallicanism and the veto controversy: church, state and Catholic community in early nineteenth-century Ireland', Bc85, 135–58; 318–24.

7. Liechty, Joseph. 'The popular Reformation comes to Ireland: the case of John Walker and the foundation of the Church of God, 1804', Bc85, 159–87; 324–31.

8. Loupes, Philippe. 'The Irish clergy of the diocese of Bordeaux during the revolution', Bc63, 28–39.

9. Millett, Benignus. 'The community of St Isidore's College during the second French occupation of Rome, 1810–1814', *Collectanea Hibernica* 31–32 (1990), 196–99.

10. Millett, Benignus (ed.). 'Calendar of volume 14 of the *Fondo di Vienna* in Propaganda Archives: part 3, ff. 284–395', *Collectanea Hibernica* 31–32 (1990), 148–61.

11. Millett, Benignus (ed.). 'Correspondence of Irish interest in the *Lettere* in Propaganda Archives, vol. 38 (1657–1664)', *Collectanea Hibernica* 31–32 (1990), 118–47.

12. Mooney, Desmond. 'Popular religion and clerical influence in pre-famine Meath', Bc85, 188–218; 331–35.

13. Murphy, Celestine. 'The Wexford Catholic community in the later seventeenth century', Bc85, 78–98; 309–13.

14. Power, Thomas P. 'Converts', Bc84, 101–27.

15. Tierney, Mark (comp.). 'A short-title catalogue of the papers of Archbishop Michael Slattery in Archbishop's House, Thurles: part 2, 1840–1845', *Collectanea Hibernica* 31–32 (1990), 200–19.

16. Whelan, Kevin. 'The Catholic community in eighteenth-century county Wexford', Bc84, 129–70.

## (f) *Economic Affairs*

1. Crawford, W.H. 'The significance of landed estates in Ulster, 1600–1820', *Irish Economic & Social History* 17 (1990), 44–61.

2. Dickson, David J. 'Catholics and trade in eighteenth-century Ireland: an old debate revisited', Bc84, 85–100.

3. Donnelly, James S., Jr. 'Excess mortality and emigration', Bc60, 350–56.

4. Donnelly, James S., Jr. 'Famine and government response, 1845–1846', Bc60, 272–85.

5. Donnelly, James S., Jr. 'Landlords and tenants', Bc60, 332–49.

6. Donnelly, James S., Jr. 'Production, prices, and exports, 1846–1851', Bc60, 286–93.

7. Donnelly, James S., Jr. 'The administration of relief, 1846–1847', Bc60, 294–306.

8. Donnelly, James S., Jr. 'The administration of relief, 1847–1851', Bc60, 316–31.
9. Donnelly, James S., Jr. 'The soup kitchens', Bc60, 307–15.
10. Fitzpatrick, David. 'Emigration, 1801–1870', Bc60, 562–622.
11. Fitzpatrick, David. 'Was Ireland special? Recent writing on the Irish economy and society in the nineteenth century', *Historical J.* 33 (1990), 169–76.
12. Gahan, Daniel. 'Religion and land tenure in eighteenth-century Ireland: tenancy in the south-east', Bc85, 99–117; 313–15.
13. Grant, James. 'The Great Famine and the Poor Law in Ulster: the rate-in-aid issue of 1849', *Irish Historical Studies* 27 (1990), 30–47.
14. MacDonagh, Oliver. 'The economy and society, 1830–1845', Bc60, 218–41.
15. Marrinan, S. 'Limerick tokens of the seventeenth century', *North Munster Antiquarian J.* 29 (1989), 32–40.
16. O'Grada, Cormac. 'Industry and communications, 1801–1845', Bc60, 137–57.
17. O'Grada, Cormac. 'Poverty, population, and agriculture, 1801–1845', Bc60, 108–36.
18. Turner, Michael. 'Output and productivity in Irish agriculture from the famine to the Great War', *Irish Economic & Social History* 17 (1990), 62–78.
19. Vaughan, W.E. 'Potatoes and agricultural output', *Irish Economic & Social History* 17 (1990), 79–92.

## (g) *Social Structure and Population*

1. Beckles, Hilary McD. 'A "riotous and unruly lot": Irish indentured servants and freemen in the English West Indies, 1644–1713', *William & Mary Q.* 3rd ser. 47 (1990), 503–22.
2. Cullen, Louis M. 'Catholic social classes under the penal laws', Bc84, 57–84.
3. Doyle, David Noel. 'The Irish in north America, 1776–1845', Bc60, 682–725.
4. Fitzpatrick, David. ' "A peculiar tramping people": the Irish in Britain, 1801–1870', Bc60, 623–60.
5. Fitzpatrick, Rory. *God's frontiersmen: the Scots-Irish epic.* London; Weidenfeld & Nicolson; 1989. Pp vii, 296.
6. Freeman, T.W. 'Land and people, *c*.1841', Bc60, 242–71.
7. Harvey, Karen J. 'The family experience: the Bellews of Mount Bellew', Bc84, 171–97.
8. Hepburn, A.C. 'The Belfast riots of 1935', *Social History* 15 (1990), 75–96.
9. Nicholas, Stephen; Shergold, Peter R. 'Irish intercounty mobility before 1840', *Irish Economic & Social History* 17 (1990), 22–43.
10. O'Farrell, Patrick J. 'The Irish in Australia and New Zealand, 1791–1870', Bc60, 661–81.

(h) *Naval and Military*

1. Bartlett, Thomas. 'Army and society in eighteenth-century Ireland', Bc125, 173–82.
2. Bastlett, Thomas. 'Indiscipline and disaffection in the French and Irish armies during the revolutionary period', Bc63, 179–201.
3. Bertaud, Jean-Paul. 'Forgotten soldiers: the expedition of General Humbert to Ireland in 1798', Bc63, 220–28.
4. Burke, James. 'The New Model Army and the problems of siege warfare, 1648–1651', *Irish Historical Studies* 27 (1990), 1–29.
5. Elliott, Marianne. 'The role of Ireland in French war strategy, 1796–1798', Bc63, 202–219.
6. Ireland, John de Courcy. 'The contribution of seamen of Irish birth or descent to hydrography', Bc74, 189–98.
7. Ohlmeyer, Jane H. 'Irish privateers during the Civil War, 1642–1650', *Mariner's Mirror* 76 (1990), 119–33.
8. O'Sullivan, Harold. 'The plantation of the Cromwellian soldiers in the barony of Arda, 1652–1656', *J. of the County Louth Arch. and Historical Soc.* 21/4 (1988), 415–52.
9. Scott, Sam. 'The French revolution and the Irish regiments in France', Bc63, 14–27.
10. Walsh, P. 'Cromwell's barrack: a Commonwealth garrison fort on Inishbofin, Co. Galway', *J. of the Galway Arch. Soc.* 42 (1989), 31–71.

(i) *Intellectual and Cultural*

1. Akenson, D.H. 'Pre-university education, 1782–1870', Bc60, 523–37.
2. Barnard, T.C. 'Crises of identity among Irish protestants, 1641–1685', *Past & Present* 127 (1990), 39–83.
3. Bartlett, Thomas. ' "A people made rather for copies than originals": the Anglo-Irish, 1760–1800', *International History R.* 12 (1990), 11–25.
4. Brown, Barbara Traxler. 'Library history research in Ireland, 1918–1988', *Libraries & Culture* 25 (1990), 86–102.
5. Candy, Catherine. 'Canon Sheehan: the conflicts of the priest-author', Bc85, 252–77; 342–44.
6. Flanagan, Thomas. 'Literature in English, 1801–1891', Bc60, 482–522.
7. Kinane, Vincent; Benson, Charles. 'Some late 18th- and early 19th-century Dublin printers' account books: the Graisberry ledgers', Bc139, 139–50.
8. Knowlton, Steven R. 'The quarrel between Gavan Duffy and John Mitchel: implications for Ireland', *Albion* 21 (1989), 581–90.
9. McCann, Wesley. 'Patrick Neill and the origins of Belfast printing', Bc139, 125–38.
10. McCormack, W.J. 'French revolution . . . Anglo-Irish literature . . . Beginnings? The case of Maria Edgeworth', Bc63, 229–243.
11. Murphy, Brian. 'J.J. O'Kelly, the *Catholic Bulletin* and contemporary Irish cultural historians', *Archivium Hibernicum* 44 (1989), 71–88.
12. Ó Catháin, Diarmaid. 'John Fergus MD: eighteenth-century doctor, book

collector and Irish scholar', *Royal Soc. of Antiquaries of Ireland J.* 118 (1989 for 1988), 139–62.

13. O'Donoghue, Thomas A. 'Sources for the study of the history of the secondary school curriculum: a survey of the Irish scene, 1921–1962', *History of Education Soc. B.* 46 (1990), 46–55.

14. Osborough, W.N. 'The lawyers of the Irish novels of Anthony Trollope', Bc143, 249–65.

15. O'Sullivan, Patrick. 'A literary difficulty in explaining Ireland: Tom Moore and Captain Rock, 1824', Bc49, 239–74.

16. Walker, Graham. 'Irish nationalism and the uses of history', *Past & Present* 126 (1990), 203–14.

(j) *Local History*

1. Mac Neill, Máire. *Máire Rua: lady of Leamaneh*, ed. Maureen Murphy. Whitegate; Ballinkella; 1990. Pp xii, 122.

2. Power, Patrick C. *History of Waterford city and county.* Cork; Mercier; 1990. Pp xi, 359.

(k) *Science and Medicine*

1. Burnett, J.E.; Morrison-Low, A.D. *'Vulgar and mechanik': the scientific instrument trade in Ireland, 1650–1921.* Dublin; National Museums of Scotland and Royal Dublin Soc. (Royal Dublin Soc. Historical Studies in Irish Science and Technology, no. 8); 1989. Pp ix, 166.

2. Cassell, Ronald D. 'Lessons in medical politics: Thomas Wakley and the Irish medical charities, 1827–1839', *Medical History* 34 (1990), 412–23.

# N.  EMPIRE AND COMMONWEALTH POST 1783

*See also* Ac66; Bc68,79; Hb12,e21,f9,23,26,h11.

(a) *General*

1. Adamson, David. *The last empire: Britain and the Commonwealth.* London; Tauris; 1989. Pp 220.

2. Ansprenger, Franz. *The dissolution of the colonial empires.* London; Routledge; 1989. Pp 337.

3. Banana, Canaan S. *Turmoil and tenacity: Zimbabwe, 1890–1990.* Harare (Zimbabwe); College Press; 1989. Pp 376.

4. Barber, Laurie. *New Zealand: a short history.* London; Hutchinson; 1990. Pp 252.

5. Baring-Gould, S.; Bamfylde, C.A. *A history of Sarawak under its two white rajahs, 1839–1908.* Oxford; Oxford UP; 1989. Pp 464.

6. Beckles, Hilary McD. *A history of Barbados: from Amerindian society to nation state.* Cambridge; Cambridge UP; 1990. Pp 240.

7. Beinart, William. 'Empire, hunting and ecological change in southern and central Africa', *Past & Present* 128 (1990), 162–86.

8. Beukes, P. *The holistic Smuts: a study in personality.* Cape Town (S. Africa); Human & Rousseau; 1989. Pp 224.

9. Birkett, Dea. *Spinsters abroad: Victorian lady explorers.* Oxford; Blackwell; 1989. Pp xii, 300.

10. Blaut, J.M. 'Colonialism and the rise of capitalism', *Science & Society* 53 (1989), 260–96.

11. Bolton, Geoffrey. *The Oxford history of Australia, vol. 5: modern Australia, 1942–1986.* Sydney; Sydney UP/Oxford UP; 1990. Pp 360.

12. Bridge, Carl. *New perspectives on Australian history.* London; Sir Robert Menzies Centre for Australian Studies, Occasional Papers no. 5, University of London; 1990. Pp 201.

13. Bridge, Carl; Marshall, Peter J.; Williams, Glyndwr. 'A "British Empire"', *International History R.* 12 (1990), 2–10.

14. Bridge, Carl; Marshall, Peter J.; Williams, Glyndwr. *British colonial societies and the age of revolution, 1760–1830.* Burnaby (BC); Simon Fraser UP; 1990. Pp 220.

15. Chandavarkar, Rajnaryan. ' "Strangers in the land": India and the British since the late nineteenth century', Bc68, 368–79.

16. Cheyne, Sonia. 'Act of parliament or royal prerogative? James Stephen and the first New Zealand Constitution Bill', *New Zealand J. of History* 24 (1990), 182–89.

17. Delvoie, Louis A. 'The Commonwealth in Canadian foreign policy', *Round Table* 310 (1989), 137–143.

18. Gough, Barry M. '*Pax Britannica*: peace, force and world power', *Round Table* 314 (1990), 167–88.

19. Granatstein, J.L.; Irving, M. Arabella; Acheson, T.W.; Bercuson, David J.; Brown, R. Craig; Neatby, H. Blair. *Nation: Canada since confederation.* Toronto; McGraw-Hill Ryerson; 1990. Pp viii, 567.

20. Hopwood, Derek. *Tales of empire: the British in the Middle East, 1880–1952.* London; Tauris; 1989. Pp 256.

21. Kennedy, Paul. 'The costs and benefits of British imperialism, 1846–1914', *Past & Present* 125 (1990), 186–92.

22. Knight, Ian J. *The Zulus.* London; Osprey; 1989. Pp 64.

23. Majeed, J. 'James Mill's *The history of British India* and utilitarianism as a rhetoric of reform', *Modern Asian Studies* 24 (1990), 209–24.

24. O'Brien, Patrick Karl. 'The costs and benefits of British imperialism: reply', *Past & Present* 125 (1989), 192–99.

25. Rotberg, Robert I. *The founder: Cecil Rhodes and the pursuit of power.* Oxford; Oxford UP; 1989. Pp xxiv, 798.

26. Stafford, Robert A. *Scientist of empire: Sir Roderick Murchison, scientific exploration and Victorian imperialism.* Cambridge; Cambridge UP; 1990. Pp 293.

27. Tarling, Nicholas. 'Malaya in British history', *J. of the Malaysian Branch of the Royal Asiatic Soc.* 62/2 (1989), 11–20.

28. Thompson, Leonard. *A history of South Africa.* London; Yale UP; 1990. Pp 352.
29. Ufford, Letitia W. 'Imperialists at work and play: the papers of General Sir John and Lady Maxwell', *Princeton University Library Chronicle* 51 (1990), 141–82.
30. Woodiwiss, Audrey (ed.). *Lawrence of Lucknow: a story of love.* London; Hodder & Stoughton; 1990. Pp xx, 275.
31. Yearwood, Peter J. 'Great Britain and the repartition of Africa, 1914–1919', *J. of Imperial & Commonwealth History* 18 (1990), 316–41.

(b) *Politics*

1. Adjaye, Joseph K. 'Asantehene Agyeman Prempe I and British colonization of Asante: a reassessment', *International J. of African Historical Studies* 22 (1989), 223–49.
2. Akbar, M.J. *Nehru: the making of India.* Harmondsworth; Penguin; 1989. Pp 624.
3. Atkinson, Alan. 'The little revolution in New South Wales, 1808', *International History R.* 12 (1990), 65–75.
4. Bakshi, S.R. *Congress, the Muslim League and the partition of India.* New Delhi; Deep & Deep; 1990. Pp 319.
5. Barber, James; Barratt, John. *South Africa's foreign policy: the search for status and security, 1945–1988.* Cambridge; Cambridge UP; 1990. Pp 384.
6. Beaumont, Joan. *The evolution of Australian foreign policy, 1901–1945.* Geelong; Australian Inst. of International Affairs (Victorian Branch) & School of Social Sciences, Deakin University; 1989. Pp 29.
7. Berman, Bruce. *Control and crisis in colonial Kenya: the dialectics of domination.* London; Currey; 1990. Pp 479.
8. Birmingham, David. *Kwame Nkrumah.* London; Cardinal; 1990. Pp xiii, 129.
9. Bless, Roland. *'Divide et impera'? Britische Minderheitenpolitik in Burma, 1917–1948* ['Divide and rule'? British minority politics in Burma, 1917–1948]. Stuttgart; Steiner (Beiträge zur Kolonial- und Überseegeschichte, 45); 1990. Pp xx, 376.
10. Boyce, D. George (ed.). *The crisis of British power: the imperial and naval papers of the second earl of Selbourne, 1895–1910.* London; Historians' Press; 1990. pp viii, 456.
11. Brown, Judith Margaret. *Gandhi: prisoner of hope.* New Haven/London; Yale UP; 1989. Pp xii, 440.
12. Burgess, Michael D. *Canadian federalism: past, present and future.* Leicester; Leicester UP; 1990. Pp 211.
13. Burroughs, Peter. 'Liberal paternalist or Cassandra? Earl Grey as a critic of colonial self-government', *J. of Imperial & Commonwealth History* 18 (1990), 61–80.
14. Cain, Frank. 'An aspect of post-war Australian relations with the United Kingdom and the United States: missiles, spies and disharmony', *Australian Historical Studies* 23 (1989), 186–202.

15. Chandra, Bipra N. *India's struggle for independence, 1857–1947*. Harmondsworth; Penguin; 1989. Pp 600.

16. Charlton, Michael. *The last colony in Africa: diplomacy and independence of Rhodesia*. Oxford; Blackwell; 1990. Pp 224.

17. Cleary, A.S. 'The myth of Mau Mau in its international context', *African Affairs* 89 (1990), 227–45.

18. Clymer, Kenton J. 'Samuel Evans Stokes, Mahatma Gandhi and Indian nationalism', *Pacific Historical R.* 59 (1990), 51–76.

19. Cumpston, I. Mary. *Lord Bruce of Melbourne*. Melbourne; Longmans Cheshire; 1989. Pp 291.

20. Dignan, Don. 'British India in the souring of Anglo-Japanese relations, 1914–1922', *Australian J. of Politics & History* 35 (1989), 383–95.

21. Durrans, P.J. 'Beaconsfieldism', *Trivium* 24 (1989), 58–75.

22. Dutfield, Michael. *A marriage of inconvenience: the persecution of Ruth and Seretse Khama*. London; Unwin Hyman; 1990. Pp xiii, 223.

23. Edgerton, Robert B. *Mau Mau: an African crucible*. London; Tauris; 1990. Pp 310.

24. Goldsworthy, David. 'Keeping change within bounds: aspects of colonial policy during the Churchill and Eden governments', *J. of Imperial & Commonwealth History* 18 (1990), 81–108.

25. Kaplan, Thomas. 'Britain's Asian Cold War: Malaya', Bc11, 201–19.

26. Kawharu, Ian H. *Waitangi: Maōri and Pākehā—perspectives of the treaty of Waitangi*. Auckland (New Zealand); Oxford UP; 1989. Pp xxiv, 329.

27. Kent, John. 'Regionalism or territorial autonomy? The case of the British West African development, 1939–1949', *J. of Imperial & Commonwealth History* 18 (1990), 61–80.

28. Kent, John. 'The British Empire and the origins of the Cold War, 1944–1949', Bc11, 165–83.

29. Khosla, Gopal Das. *Stern reckoning: a survey of the events leading up to and including the partition of India*. Delhi; Oxford UP; 1990. Pp 358.

30. Landry, Connie. 'The war of 1812: the cornerstone of Canadian nationalism', *Concord R.* 1 (1989), 85–90.

31. Lonsdale, John. 'Constructing Mau Mau', *T. of the Royal Historical Soc.* 5th ser. 40 (1990), 239–60.

32. Lonsdale, John. 'Mau Maus of the mind: making Mau Mau and remaking Kenya', *J. of African History* 31 (1990), 393–421.

33. Low, Peter. 'Pompallier and the Treaty [of Waitangi]: a new discussion', *New Zealand J. of History* 24 (1990), 190–99.

34. Lynn, Martin. 'Britain's West African policy and the island of Fernando Po, 1821–1843', *J. of Imperial & Commonwealth History* 18 (1990), 191–207.

35. Martin, Ged W. (ed.). *The causes of Canadian confederation*. Fredericton (New Brunswick); Acadiensis; 1990. Pp 172.

36. McCabe, James Ian. *Ireland, the Commonwealth and NATO, 1948–1949*. Dublin; Irish Academic Press; 1990. Pp 240.

37. Milne, June. *Kwame Nkrumah: the Conakry years—his life and letters*. London; Panaf; 1990. Pp 432.

38. Nanda, B.R. *Gandhi: pan Islamism, imperialism and nationalism in India.* Bombay; Oxford UP; 1989. Pp 448.
39. Painchaud, Paul. *From Mackenzie King to Pierre Trudeau: forty years of Canadian diplomacy, 1945–1985.* Quebec; Les Presses de L'Université Laval; 1989. Pp 748.
40. Pradhan, G.P. *India's freedom struggle: an epic of sacrifice and suffering.* Bombay; Popular; 1990. Pp vii, 235.
41. Remme, Tillman. 'Britain, the 1947 Asian relations conference and regional cooperation in South East Asia', Bc35, 109–34.
42. Robinson, Francis. 'The Raj and nationalist movements, 1911–1947', Bc68, 350–60.
43. Roy, Asim. 'The high politics of Indian partition: the revisionist perspective', *Modern Asian Studies* 24 (1990), 385–415.
44. Royle, Trevor. *The last days of the raj.* London; Joseph; 1989. Pp xi, 291.
45. Shaikh, Farzana. *Community and consensus in Islam: Muslim representation in colonial India, 1860–1947.* Cambridge; Cambridge UP; 1989. Pp 250.
46. Singh, Anita Inder. 'Britain, India and the Asian Cold War, 1949–1954', Bc11, 220–36.
47. Tamarkin, M. *The making of Zimbabwe: decolonization in regional and international politics, 1974–1979.* London; Cass; 1990. Pp 326.
48. Vipond, Robert C. '1787 and 1867: the federal principle and Canadian confederation reconsidered', *Canadian J. of Political Science* 22 (1989), 3–25.
49. Whitehead, John. *Far frontiers: people and events in north-eastern India, 1857–1947.* London; BACSA; 1989. Pp xix, 204.
50. Worthington, E. Barton. 'Lord Hailey on the African survey: some comments', *African Affairs* 89 (1990), 579–83.
51. Yorke, Edmund. 'The spectre of a second Chilembwe: government, missions and social control in wartime Northern Rhodesia', *J. of African History* 31 (1990), 373–91.

## (c) *Constitution, Administration and Law*

1. Atkinson, Alan. 'The first plans for governing New South Wales, 1786–1787', *Australian Historical Studies* 24 (1990), 22–40.
2. Chun, Allen. 'Policing society: the "rational" practice of British colonial land administration in the new territories of Hong Kong, c.1900', *J. of Historical Sociology* 3 (1990), 401–22.
3. Donnelly, F.K. 'Clement Payne and the Barbados riots of 1937', *Labour History R.* 55/1 (1990), 35–43.
4. Foster, Hamar. 'Long-distance justice: the criminal jurisdiction of Canadian courts west of the Canadas, 1763–1859', *American J. of Legal History* 34 (1990), 1–48.
5. Hastings, W.K. 'The Wakefield colonization plan and constitutional development in South Australia, Canada and New Zealand', *J. of Legal History* 11 (1990), 279–99.

6. Kaplan, Martha. ' "Luve ni wai" [children of water] as the British saw it: constructions of custom and disorder in colonial Fiji', *Ethnohistory* 36 (1989), 349–71.

7. Kratoska, Paul H. 'The British Empire and the south-east Asian rice crisis of 1919–1921', *Modern Asian Studies* 24 (1990), 115–46.

8. Low, David A. 'What happened to Milner's young men: what of their successors?', *Round Table* 315 (1990), 257–67.

9. Machobane, L.B.B.J. *Government and change in Lesotho, 1800–1966.* Basingstoke; Macmillan; 1990. Pp 260.

10. McDonald, John; Shlomowitz, R. 'Morality on convict voyages to Australia, 1788–1868', *Social Science History* 13 (1989), 285–313.

11. Milobar, David. 'Conservative ideology, metropolitan government, and the reform of Quebec, 1782–1791', *International History R.* 12 (1990), 45–64.

12. Miners, Norman. 'The localization of the Hong Kong police force, 1842–1947', *J. of Imperial & Commonwealth History* 18 (1990), 296–315.

13. Ng'ong'ola, Clement. 'The state, settlers and indigenes in the evolution of land law and policy in colonial Malawi', *International J. of African Historical Studies* 23 (1990), 27–58.

14. Qalb-i-Abid. 'The working of the Montagu-Chelmsford reforms and communal antagonism in the Punjab', *J. of the Pakistan Historical Soc.* 37 (1989), 17–42.

15. Romney, Paul. 'From constitutionalism to legalism: trial by jury, responsible government, and the rule of law in the Canadian political culture', *Law & History R.* 7 (1989), 121–74.

16. Sethi, Kamla. *Administration of the Punjab: a study in British policy, 1875–1905.* Delhi; Renaissance; 1990. Pp vii, 336.

17. Sexton, Brendan. *Ireland and the crown, 1922–1936: the governor generalship of the Irish Free State.* Dublin; Irish Academic Press; 1989. Pp 238.

18. Staples, A.C. 'Memoirs of William Prinsep: Calcutta years, 1817–1842', *Indian Economic & Social History R.* 26 (1989), 61–79.

19. Stein, Burton. *Thomas Munro: the origins of the colonial state and his vision of empire.* Delhi; Oxford UP; 1990. Pp 384.

20. Swinfen, D.B. 'Lord Strickland, the *ultra vires* cases, and the Maltese constitution, 1934–1939', *J. of Imperial & Commonwealth History* 17 (1989), 413–32.

21. Thomas, Nicholas. 'Material culture and colonial power: ethnological collecting and the establishment of colonial rule in Fiji', *Man* 23 (1989), 41–59.

22. Thomas, Nicholas. 'Sanitation and seeing: the creation of state power in early colonial Fiji', *Comparative Studies in Soc. & History* 32 (1990), 149–70.

23. Tibenderana, Peter K. 'British administration and the decline of the patronage-clientage system in the northwestern Nigeria, 1900–1934', *African Studies R.* 31 (1989), 71–96.

24. Trapido, Stanley. 'From paternalism to liberalism: the Cape Colony, 1800–1834', *International History R.* 12 (1990), 76–104.

25. Wright, Ray. *The bureaucrats' domain: space and the public interest in Victoria, 1836–1884*. Melbourne; Oxford UP; 1990. Pp 366.
26. Zaffiro, James J. 'Twin births: African nationalism and government information management in the Bechuanaland protectorate, 1957–1966', *International J. of African Historical Studies* 22 (1989), 51–77.

## (d) *Religion*

1. Carson, Penelope. 'An imperial dilemma: the propagation of Christianity in early colonial India', *J. of Imperial & Commonwealth History* 18 (1990), 169–90.
2. Cox, Jeffrey. 'On redefining "crisis": the Victorian crisis of faith in the Punjab', Bc145, 315–42.
3. Grove, Richard. 'Scottish missionaries, evangelical discourses and the origins of conservation thinking in southern Africa, 1820–1900', *J. of South African Studies* 15 (1989), 163–87.
4. Hogan, Edmund M. 'Sir James Marshall [1829–1889] and Catholic missions to West Africa, 1873–1889', *Catholic Historical R.* 76 (1990), 212–34.
5. Johnson, Mark D. 'The crisis of faith and social Christianity: the ethical pilgrimage of James Shaver Woodsworth', Bc145, 343–79.
6. Minter, R.A. *Episcopacy without episcopate; the Church of England in Jamaica before 1824*. Upton-upon-Severn; Self Publishing Association Ltd; 1990. Pp 320.
7. Morrow, Sean. ' "On the side of the robbed": R.J.B. Moore, missionary on the Copperbelt, 1933–1941', *J. of Religion in Africa* 19 (1989), 244–63.
8. Panikkar, K.N. *Against lord and state: religion and peasant uprisings in Malabar, 1836–1921*. Delhi; Oxford UP; 1989. Pp 248.
9. Spencer, Leon P. 'Church and state in colonial Africa: influences governing the political activity of Christian missionaries in Kenya', *J. of Church and State* 31 (1989), 115–32.
10. Stanley, Brian. *The bible and the flag: Protestant missions and British imperialism in the nineteenth and twentieth centuries*. London; Apollos; 1990. Pp 224.
11. Studdert-Kennedy, Gerald. 'Gandhi and the Christian imperialists', *History Today* 40/10 (1990), 19–26.
12. Studdert-Kennedy, Gerald. 'The Christian imperialism of the die-hard defenders of the Raj, 1926–1962', *J. of Imperial & Commonwealth History* 18 (1990), 342–62.
13. Sykes, Marjorie. 'Unfinished pilgrimages: Geoffrey Maw and Jack Hayland in India', *J. of the Friends' Historical Soc.* 55 (1989), 220–37.

## (e) *Economic Affairs*

1. Attard, Bernard. 'Politics, finance and Anglo-Australian relations: Australian borrowing in London, 1914–1920', *Australian J. of Politics & History* 35 (1989), 142–63.

2. Bagchi, Amiya Kumar. *The presidency banks and the Indian economy, 1876–1914*. Delhi; Oxford UP; 1990. Pp 312.
3. Balachandran, G. *India and Britain's liquidity crisis: the stabilization of 1920*. London; School of Oriental & African Studies (University of London Occasional Papers in Third World Economic History); 1990. Pp vi, 34.
4. Cammack, Diana. *The Rand at war, 1899–1902: the Witwatersrand and the Anglo-Boer War*. London; Currey; 1990. Pp xiv, 222.
5. Davis, Lance E.; Huttenback, Robert A. 'Businessmen, the Raj, and the pattern of government expenditures: the British Empire, 1860–1912', Bc21, 190–230.
6. Fage, John D. 'African societies and the Atlantic slave trade', *Past & Present* 125 (1989), 97–115.
7. Henningham, Stephen. *A great estate and its landlords in colonial India: Darbhanga, 1860–1942*. Delhi; Oxford UP; 1990. Pp 180.
8. King, Frank H.H. *The Hong Kong Bank in the period of imperialism and war, 1895–1918: the forces of wealth—the history of the Hong Kong and Shanghai Banking Corporation*. Cambridge; Cambridge UP; 1989. Pp 800.
9. King, Frank H.H.; King, Catherine E.; King, David J.S. *The Hong Kong Bank between the wars and the bank interned, 1919–1945: return from grandeur—the history of the Hong Kong and Shanghai Banking Corporation*. Cambridge; Cambridge UP; 1989. Pp 744.
10. Manning, P. 'Slavery and the slave trade in colonial Africa', *J. of African History* 31 (1990), 135–40.
11. Nicholas, Stephen; Lewis, F.D. 'Australia: an economical prison?', *Economic History R.* 2nd ser. 43 (1990), 470–82.
12. Overton, John. 'War and economic underdevelopment? State exploitation and African response in Kenya, 1914–1918', *International J. of African Historical Studies* 22 (1989), 201–21.
13. Platt, D.C.M.; Adelman, Jeremy. 'London merchant bankers in the first phase of heavy borrowing: the Grand Trunk Railway of Canada', *J. of Imperial & Commonwealth History* 18 (1990), 208–27.
14. Porter, Andrew Neil. ' "Gentlemanly capitalism" and empire: the British experience since 1750', *J. of Imperial & Commonwealth History* 18 (1990), 265–95.
15. Robbins, Keith G. 'The imperial city: Glasgow, second city of the British empire', *History Today* 40/5 (1990), 48–54.
16. Schedvin, C.B. *Australia and the Great Depression*. Sydney; Sydney UP/ Oxford UP; 1989. Pp 436.
17. Shlomowitz, R. 'The Pacific labour trade and sugar exploitation', *J. of Pacific History* 24 (1989), 238–41.
18. Sutton, Inez. 'Colonial agricultural policy and the non-development of the northern territories of the Gold Coast', *International J. of African Historical Studies* 22 (1989), 637–69.
19. Wells, Andrew. *Constructing capitalism: an economic history of eastern Australia, 1788–1901*. Sydney; Allen & Unwin; 1989. Pp xvii, 198.

(f) *Social Structure and Population*

1. Bradlow, Edna. 'Empire settlement and South African immigration policy, 1910–1948', Bc79, 174–201.
2. Bradlow, Edna. 'The "great fear" at the Cape of Good Hope, 1851–1852', *International J. of African Historical Studies* 22 (1989), 401–21.
3. Breman, Jan. *Taming the coolie beast: plantation society and the colonial order in southeast Asia.* Delhi; Oxford UP; 1989. Pp xviii, 321.
4. Constantine, Stephen. 'Immigration and the making of New Zealand, 1918–1939', Bc79, 121–49.
5. Constantine, Stephen. 'Introduction: Empire migration and imperial harmony', Bc79, 1–21.
6. Ekechi, Felix K. *Tradition and transformation in eastern Nigeria: a socio-political history of Owerri and its hinterland, 1902–1947.* Kent (Oh); Kent State UP; 1989. Pp ix, 256.
7. Fedorowich, Kent. 'The assisted emigration of British ex-servicemen to the dominions, 1914–1922', Bc79, 45–71.
8. Gothard, Janice. ' "The healthy, wholesome British domestic girl": single female migration and the Empire Settlement Act, 1922–1930', Bc79, 72–95.
9. Gullick, J.M. *Malay society in the late nineteenth century: the beginnings of change.* Nairobi; Oxford UP; 1990. Pp 428.
10. Jolly, Margaret; Macintyre, Martha. *Family and gender in the Pacific: domestic contradictions and the colonial impact.* Melbourne; Cambridge UP; 1989. Pp xi, 296.
11. Marshall, Peter J. 'The whites of British India, 1780–1830: a failed colonial society?', *International History R.* 12 (1990), 26–44.
12. McGrath, Ann. 'The white man's looking glass: aboriginal-colonial gender relations at Port Jackson', *Australian Historical Studies* 24 (1990), 189–206.
13. Reece, Bob. 'The Welsh in Australian historical writing', *Australian Studies* 4 (1990), 88–104.
14. Roe, Michael. ' "We can die just as easy out here": Australia and British migration, 1916–1939', Bc79, 96–120.
15. Schultz, John A. ' "Leaven for the lump": Canada and Empire settlement, 1918–1939', Bc79, 150–73.
16. Vickery, Kenneth P. 'The Second World War revival of forced labour in the Rhodesias', *International J. of African Historical Studies* 22 (1989), 423–37.
17. Williams, Keith. ' "A way out of our troubles": the politics of Empire settlement, 1900–1922', Bc79, 22–44.

(g) *Naval and Military*

1. Bowie, John. *The Empire at war.* London; Batsford; 1989. Pp 127.
2. Butterfield, P.H. 'From monarch to monarch: Cetewayo's letters to Queen Victoria', *African Notes & News* 28 (1989), 197–203.

3. Crowell, Lorenzo M. 'Military professionalism in a colonial context: the Madras army, c.1832', *Modern Asian Studies* 24 (1990), 249–74.

4. Ellert, Henrik. *The Rhodesian Front war: counter insurgency and guerilla war in Rhodesia, 1962–1980.* Gweru (Zimbabwe); Mambo; 1989. Pp 214.

5. Farwell, Byron. *Armies of the Raj: from the great Indian mutiny to independence, 1858–1947.* London; Viking; 1990. Pp 320.

6. Fedorowich, Kent. ' "Society pets and morning coated farmers": Australian soldier settlement and the participation of British ex-servicemen, 1915–1929', *War & Soc.* 8 (1990), 38–56.

7. Follows, Roy; Popham, Hugh. *The jungle beat: fighting terrorists in Malaya, 1952–1961.* London; Blandford; 1990. Pp 192.

8. Furedi, Frank. 'Britain's colonial wars: playing the ethnic card', *J. of Commonwealth & Comparative Politics* 28 (1990), 70–89.

9. Grey, Jeffrey. *A military history of Australia.* Cambridge; Cambridge UP; 1990. Pp 300.

10. Haron, Nadzan. 'Colonial defence and the British approach to the problems in Malaya, 1874–1918', *Modern Asian Studies* 24 (1990), 275–95.

11. Hopkirk, Peter. *The great game: on secret service in high Asia.* London; Murray; 1990. Pp 256.

12. Jackson, F.W.D.; Whybra, Julian. 'Isandhlwana and the Durnford papers', *Soldiers of the Queen* 60 (1990), 18–31.

13. Jackson, Robert. *The Malayan emergency: the Commonwealth wars, 1948–1966.* London; Routledge; 1990. Pp 144.

14. Knight, Ian J. *Brave men's blood: the epic of the Zulu War, 1879.* London; Greenhill; 1990. Pp 199.

15. Knight, Ian J. *Queen Victoria's enemies: Asia, Australasia and the Americas.* London; Osprey; 1990. Pp 47.

16. Knight, Ian J. *Queen Victoria's enemies: India.* London; Osprey; 1990. Pp 47.

17. Knight, Ian J. *Queen Victoria's enemies: northern Africa.* London; Osprey; 1989. Pp 47.

18. Knight, Ian J. *Queen Victoria's enemies: southern Africa.* London; Osprey; 1990. Pp 48.

19. Kubicek, Robert V. 'The colonial steamer and the occupation of West Africa by the Victorian state', *J. of Imperial & Commonwealth History* 18 (1990), 9–32.

20. Marshall, David. *Breadfruit buccaneers and the Bounty bible: a fresh look at the mutiny on HMS Bounty and the story of the Pitcairn Island colony over two centuries.* Grantham; Stanborough; 1989.

21. McCormack, Robert. 'War and change: air transport in British Africa, 1939–1946', *Canadian J. of History* 24 (1989), 341–60.

22. Mockaitis, Thomas R. *British counter-insurgency, 1919–1960.* London; Macmillan; 1990. Pp 210.

23. Moorcroft, Paul. 'Rhodesia's war of independence', *History Today* 40/9 (1990), 11–17.

24. Moro, Rubén Oscar. *The history of the south Atlantic conflict; the war for the Malvinas.* Westport (Ct)/London; Praeger; 1989. Pp xvi, 360.

25. Mukherjee, Rudrangshu. ' "Satan let loose upon Earth": the Kanpur massacres in India in the revolt of 1857', *Past & Present* 128 (1990), 92–116.

26. Omissi, David Enrico. *Air power and colonial control: the Royal Air Force, 1919–1939.* Manchester; Manchester UP; 1990. Pp 260.

27. Paris, Michael. 'Air power and imperial defence, 1880–1919', *J. of Contemporary History* 24 (1989), 209–25.

28. Peers, Douglas M. 'Between Mars and Mammon: the East India Company and efforts to reform its army, 1796–1832', *Historical J.* 33 (1990), 385–401.

29. Perkins, Roger. *The Amritsar legacy: Golden Temple to Caxton Hall—the story of a killing.* Chippenham; Picton; 1989. Pp x, 233.

30. Porter, Andrew Neil. 'The South African war (1899–1902): context and motive reconsidered', *J. of African History* 31 (1990), 43–57.

31. Read, A.E. 'History of the Royal Naval Brigade and its role in the South African wars, 1880–1900', *Simon's Town Historical Soc. B.* 15 (1989), 127–40.

32. Richards, Donald Sydney. *The savage frontier: a history of the Anglo-Afghan wars.* Basingstoke; Macmillan; 1990. Pp 256.

33. Sarty, R.; Schurman, D.M. 'The Canadian navy from 1867 to 1945', *Guerres mondiales et conflits contemporains* 157 (1990), 25–48.

34. Smith, Ian R. 'The origins of the South African War (1899–1902): a reappraisal', *South African Historical J.* 22 (1990), 24–60.

35. Stearn, Roger T. 'Archibald Forbes and the British army', *Soldiers of the Queen* 61 (1990), 6–9.

36. Stockwell, Anthony J. 'Counter-insurgency and colonial defence', Bc35, 135–54.

37. Travers, Timothy H.E. 'Allies in conflict: the British and Canadian official historians and the real story of Second Ypres (1915)', *J. of Contemporary History* 24 (1989), 301–25.

38. White, Luise. 'Separating the men from the boys—constructions of gender, sexuality and terrorism in central Kenya, 1939–1959', *International J. of African Historical Studies* 23 (1990), 1–25.

## (h) *Intellectual and Cultural*

1. Arata, Stephen D. 'The occidental tourist: Dracula and the anxiety of reverse decolonization', *Victorian Studies* 33 (1990), 621–45.

2. Bayly, Christopher A. 'Exhibiting the imperial image', *History Today* 40/10 (1990), 12–18.

3. Bayly, Christopher A. 'From company to crown: nineteenth-century India and its visual representation', Bc68, 130–40.

4. Bradley, James. 'The MCC, society and empire: a portrait of cricket's ruling body, 1860–1914', *International J. of the History of Sport* 7 (1990), 3–22.

5. Brownfoot, Janice N. 'Emancipation, exercise and imperialism: girls and

the games ethic in colonial Malaya', *International J. of the History of Sport* 7 (1990), 61–84.

6. Cashman, Richard. 'Symbols of unity: Anglo-Australian cricketers, 1877–1900', *International J. of the History of Sport* 7 (1990), 97–110.

7. Chakravarty, Suhash. *The Raj syndrome—a study in imperial perceptions*. Delhi; Chanakya; 1989. Pp 325.

8. Checkland, Sydney George. *Voices across the water: an Anglo-Canadian boyhood*. Aberdeen; Aberdeen UP; 1989. Pp ix, 145.

9. Falconer, John. 'Photography in nineteenth-century India', Bc68, 264–77.

10. Fisher, Michael H. 'The Resident in court ritual, 1764–1858', *Modern Asian Studies* 24 (1990), 419–58.

11. Griffith, Kenneth. *The discovery of Nehru: an experience of India*. London; Joseph; 1989. Pp vii, 216.

12. Haggis, Jane. 'Gendering colonialism or colonising gender? Recent women's studies approaches to white women and the history of British colonialism', *Women's Studies International Forum* 13 (1990), 105–15.

13. Haynes, Douglas. 'Imperial ritual in a local setting: the ceremonial order in Surat, 1890–1939', *Modern Asian Studies* 24 (1990), 493–527.

14. Haynes, Edward S. 'Rajput ceremonial interactions as a mirror of a dying Indian state system, 1820–1947', *Modern Asian Studies* 24 (1990), 459–92.

15. Heath, J. 'A voluntary surrender: imperialism and imagination in *A Passage to India*', *University of Toronto Q.* 59 (1989–90), 287–309.

16. Hyam, Ronald. *Empire and sexuality: the British experience*. Manchester; Manchester UP; 1990. Pp 234.

17. Kelly, John D. 'Fear of culture: British regulation of Indian marriage in post-indenture Fiji', *Ethnohistory* 36 (1989), 372–91.

18. King, Hazel. *Elizabeth Macarthur and her world*. Sydney; Sydney UP/ Oxford UP; 1989. Pp 238.

19. Mackenzie, George A. (ed.). *From Aberdeen to Ottawa in 1845: the diary of Alexander Muir*. Aberdeen; Aberdeen UP; 1990. Pp 116.

20. Mackenzie, John M. *The empire of nature: hunting, conservation and British imperialism*. Manchester; Manchester UP; 1989. Pp 320.

21. Macmillan, Hugh; Marks, Shula (ed.). *Africa and empire: W.M. Macmillan, historian and social critic*. Aldershot; Temple Smith; 1989. Pp 353.

22. Mason, Tony. 'Football on the Maidan: cultural imperialism in Calcutta', *International J. of the History of Sport* 7 (1990), 85–96.

23. Mitter, Partha. 'Artistic responses to colonialism in India: an overview', Bc68, 360–67.

24. Mungazi, Dickson A. 'A strategy for power: commissions of enquiry into education and government control in colonial Zimbabwe', *International J. of African Historical Studies* 22 (1989), 267–85.

25. Nair, Janaki. 'Uncovering the zenana: visions of Indian womanhood in Englishwomen's writings, 1813–1940', *J. of Women's History* 2 (1990), 8–34.

26. Nuckolls, Charles W. 'The durbar incident', *Modern Asian Studies* 24 (1990), 529–59.
27. Patton, Adell, Jr. 'Dr John Farrell Easmon: medical professionalism and colonial racism in the Gold Coast, 1856–1900', *International J. of African Historical Studies* 22 (1989), 601–36.
28. Pinney, Christopher. 'Colonial anthropology in the "laboratory of mankind" ', Bc68, 252–63.
29. Searle, Christopher. 'Race before wicket: cricket, empire and the White Rose', *Race & Class* 31 (1990), 31–48.
30. Tidrick, Kathryn. *Empire and the English character*. London; Tauris; 1990. Pp 256.
31. Tillotson, G.H.R. 'The Indian picturesque: images of India in British landscape painting, 1780–1880', Bc68, 141–51.
32. Tinker, Hugh. 'Victorian colonial governors', *History Today* 40/12 (1990), 29–37.
33. Trevithick, Alan. 'Some structural and sequential aspects of the British imperial assemblages at Delhi, 1877–1911', *Modern Asian Studies* 24 (1990), 561–78.

# INDEX OF AUTHORS

# Index of Authors

Attard, Bernard, Ne1
Aubrey, Philip, Fb8
Auchmuty, Rosemary, Ha2; Ij5
Auckland, Clifford, Bb11
Auckland, Reginald George, Ii4
Audouy, Michel, Bb46
Auerbach, Paul, If2
Aughey, Arthur, Ib4
Aughton, Peter, Bb12
Awty, Brian G., Fi3–4
Ayers, B.S., Ek3
Aylmer, G.E., Ba5; Fc2
Ayton, Andrew, Ea1

Baber, C., Ha12
Babington, Anthony, Ba6
Bachrach, B.S., Bc122
Badouin-Matuszek, M.-N, Kd1
Baedecker, Karl, Ha24
Bagchi, Amiya Kumar, Ne2
Baggs, A.P., Bb13
Bailey, C.J., Bb14
Bailey, Keith, Hg3
Bailey, Mark, Ef5
Bailey, Peter, Hl6
Baimbridge, Mark, If13
Bain, Roly, Hl7
Baines, Michael E., Je1
Baker, Derek, Eh1
Baker-Smith, Dominic, Fk5
Bakshi, S.R., Nb4
Balachandran, G., Ne3
Baldwin, David, Ba7
Ball, R.M., Fc3; Gc1
Ball, Stuart, Ib5–6
Ballantine, Ishbel, Hf4
Ballard, Mark, Eh2
Bamfylde, C.A., Na5
Banana, Canaan S., Na3
Bangs, Jeremy Dupertuis, Bd4
Banks, Leslie, Bb15
Banks, Olive, Ab3
Barber, Bruno, Ca3
Barber, James, Nb5
Barber, Laurie, Na4
Barber, Sarah, Fb9
Barbour, Jane, Hl8
Bareham, Tony, Gd1
Baring-Gould, S., Na5
Barker, Felix, Ab4
Barker, Katherine, Bb16
Barker, Lynn K., Ei3
Barker, Nicolas, Fk6–7

Barker, Rosalin, Bb17
Barker, Theodore Cardwell, Hf5; If3–4
Barley, Maurice W., Ba8
Barnard, G.A., Ij47
Barnard, Leslie W., Ge1,2
Barnard, Sylvia M., Hh1
Barnard, T.C., Mi2
Barnes, James, Ib7
Barnes, June C.F., Gb1
Barnes, Patricia, Ib7
Barnett, Correlli, Ii5
Barnsby, George J., Bb18
Barr, Helen, Ei4
Barr, Marshall, Bb223
Barratt Brown, M., Ba9
Barratt, John, Nb5
Barrell, John, Gg3
Barrell, Rex A., Gi3
Barrett, John C., Bc141
Barrett, T.H., Ba10
Barroll, Leeds, Fk8
Barron, Caroline, Eb2,c1
Barrow, Julia, Ee4,i5
Barry, Colm, Mc1
Barry, Jonathan, Fe11,g2
Bartle, George F., Hi1
Bartlett, A., Ca22
Bartlett, Thomas, Me1,h1,i3
Barton, Ruth, Hk2
Bartrip, Peter W.J., Ba11; Hh2,k3
Bascombe, Kenneth, Db2
Baskerville, Stephen W., Gb2
Bass, Jeff D., Gb3
Bassett, David K., Gd2–3
Bastlett, Thomas, Mh2
Bately, J.M., De1
Bateman, D.I., Ba12
Bates, David, Ea2,b3
Batey, Mavis, Fk9
Bator, Paul G., Gi4
Baudemont, Suzanne, Hg4
Bauer, Frank, Gh1
Baxandall, Michael, Fk10
Baxter, Rosemary A., He2
Baylis, Audrey, Bb19
Baylis, John, Ii6
Bayly, Christopher A., Bc68; Nh2–3
Beacham, M.J.A., Ba13
Beale, Jerry, Hf66
Beamon, Sylvia P., Ba127
Beard, Geoffrey, Fk11
Beasley, Jerry C., Gd4
Beattie, Alastair G., Bd5

200

# Index of Authors

# Index of Authors

# Index of Authors

# Index of Authors

207

# Index of Authors

# Index of Authors

Hoskins, Martin, If1
Hough, Richard, Ib23
Houghton, John, Ek17
Houlding, J.A., Gh13
Houston, R.A., Bb141; Ki5
Howard, Maurice, Fg32
Howard, Peter, Ba78
Howard-Hill, T.H., Fk56
Howarth, David, Fk57
Howarth, Olive, Ig10
Howarth, Thomas, Hl57
Howe, A.C., Hb29
Howe, Nicholas, Da5
Howell, Brian, Hc5
Howell, D.W., Ha12
Howell, David, Aa62
Howell, R.L., Bb142
Howes, Audrey M., Eg19
Howkins, Alun, Hg26
Howson, James, Hl58
Howson, Susan, If51–52
Hoyle, Richard W., Fc17,f12
Hoyles, Martin, Ba79
Huberman, Michael, Hf43
Huddart, William, Ga12
Hudson, Ann, Ab20
Hudson, Anne, Ee41–42
Hudson, Helen, Bb143
Hudson, John, Eg20
Hudson, Pat, Bc42; Gf21–22
Hudson, Ronald, Hl67
Huffman, Joseph P., Ed5
Huggins, M., Hl59
Hughes, M., Ek18
Hughes, R. Elwyn, Ba80
Hull, Felix, Bb144
Hulton, Mary, Fh5
Hume, John Robert, Aa63
Hume, Robert D., Gi47
Humphreys, Anne, Hb30
Humphries, Jane, Gg11
Huneycutt, Lois L., Ea21; Ki6
Hunt, Edwin S., Eb15
Hunt, Lester, If5
Hunt, Tony, Ei25
Hunter, David, Gi32
Hunter, Michael, Fk58–59
Hurley, Maurice F., Le8
Hurst, John G., Bb24
Hurst, Norman, Ba81
Hutchings, Naomi, Ff13
Hutchison, William R., He39
Huttenback, Robert A., Ne5

Hutton, Ronald, Fb43
Hyam, Ronald, Nh16
Hybel, Nils, Ef21
Hyde, Harford Montgomery, Ij30
Hyde, Myrtle Stevens, Bd14
Hyman, R., Hf44
Hynes, Samuel, Ij31

Ide, Isabel, Gb38
Ingle, H. Larry, Fe50
Ingram, Edward, Hd7
Inikori, Joseph E., Ba82; Gf23
Innes, Joanna, Gb39,i33
Ireland, John de Courcy, Bc74; Lh2; Mh6
Ireson, Tony, Hg27
Irvine, James W., Ii34
Irvine, Susan E., De13
Irving, M. Arabella, Na19
Irving, R.J., Hf45
Isaac, Peter, Bc139; Gf34
Israel, Jonathan I., Fd14
Israel, Kali A.K., Hg28

Jackson, Alvin, Mb19,20
Jackson, Anthony R., Aa64
Jackson, Claire, Mc8
Jackson, F.W.D., Ng12
Jackson, Peter, Ab4
Jackson, R.V., Gf24
Jackson, Ralph, Ca23,b26
Jackson, Robert, Ng13
Jacobs, Norman, Bb145
Jacobs, Struan, Gc5
Jacobson, David L., Ge15
Jacques, D., Fk60
James, Eric, Ie6
James, Harold, Hf46
James, J.G., Gj12–13
James, Lawrence, Ii35–36
James, Robert Rhodes, Id29
James, S.A.L., Ea22
James, Susan E., Fg33
James, Thomas B., Ek19; Jf2
Jamieson, Lynn, Hg29
Jansen, Paule, Fe51
Jansen, Sharon L., Ei26
Jansen, Virginia, Ej20
Jardine, Lisa, Fk61
Jeans, D.N., Ih13
Jeffreys, Sheila, Ba83; Ig11
Jenkins, D.T., Hf47
Jenkins, David, Fh6
Jenkins, H.J.K., Ff14; Gh14

214

# Index of Authors

# Index of Authors

# Index of Authors

# Index of Authors

Lynch, Peredur, Jb4
Lynn, Martin, Nb34
Lyons, J.B., Hl76
Lyons, J.S., Hf55
Lyte, Charles, Ij37
Lyth, Peter J., If61

Mac Cana, Proinsias, Li15
Mac Craith, M!cheál, Li16
Mac Neill, Máire, Mj1
MacArthur, E. Mairi, Bb163
MacCaffrey, Wallace, Fd17
MacCulloch, Diarmaid, Fe62
Macdonagh, Oliver, Ma3,b21–22,c10,f14
MacDonald, Callum, Id43
Macdonald, Jessie, Bb164
MacDonald, Michael, Fg39–40; Gj16
MacDougall, Ian, Ga16
Macdougall, Norman, Kb7
MacDougall, Philip, Gh16; Hf56
MacGregor, Arthur, Bc34; Fb51,g41–42
Machobane, L.B.B.J., Nc9
Macinnes, Allan, Ka5
Macinnes, Lesley, Bc141; Ca29
Macintyre, Martha, Nf10
Mack, Peter, Bc129
Mackay, Angus, Bc29
Mackay, Donnie A., Bc142; Ca30; Ek31
Mackay, Ruddock F., Gh17
MacKechnie, Aonghus, Hl77
Mackenzie, George A., Nh19
Mackenzie, John M., Nh20
MacKenzie, S.P., Ii41
Mackenzie, Suzanne, Ig15
Maclean, Douglas, Bb165
Maclure, Stuart, Bb166
MacMaster, Neil, Hh32
Macmillan, Hugh, Nh21
Macquarrie, Alan, Ke10
MacQueen, Hector L., Ki3
MacQueen, John, Ke11,i9–10
Macve, Jennifer, Ig16
Madden, Lionel, Bc87
Maehle, Andreas-Holger, Gi41
Mageen, Deidre, Hg19
Maguire, William A., Bc125; Fc23
Mahoney, Dhira B., Eh16
Mahoney, Michael S., Fk79
Mahood, Linda, Hg33,h33
Maidment, B.E., Ac56
Maile, Ben, Hc4
Mainman, A.J., Df24

Mair, Craig, Ha16; Ka6
Mair, Douglas, Bb167
Majeed, J., Na23
Malin, J.C., Hf47
Mallalieu, Huon Lancelot, Ab22
Maloney, Catherine, Ca31
Manchester, Keith, Ba99; Eg21,j23,k11
Mandler, Peter, Hb36,h8,34
Manley, K.A., Ab23; Ij38
Manley, Lawrence, Fk80
Mann, J.C., Cb29–31
Manning, P., Ne10
Manning, Roger B., Fc24
Manning, W.H., Ca32
Maple, John T., Lf3
Marc'Hadour, Germain, Fe63
Marcombe, David, Ej23
Marder, Arthur Jacob, Ii42
Marius, Richard, Eb18
Markham, John, Bb168
Markley, R., Ge19
Marks, Gary, Ba100; Hb37
Marks, Lara, Bb169
Marks, Leo, Ii43
Marks, Shula, Nh21
Markus, Thomas A., Gg17,i42
Marquand, David, Ib29
Marr, L. James, Bb170
Marren, Peter, Bb171
Marrinan, S., Mf15
Marriner, Sheila, If62
Marsden, Gordon, Bc70; Hl78
Marsden, P., Ca33
Marsh, Christopher, Aa72
Marsh, Jan, Ba97
Marshall, David, Ng20
Marshall, John, Fe64
Marshall, John D., Gf26
Marshall, Peter J., Gd31–32; Na13–14,f11
Martel, Gordon, Ac57
Martin, C., Fi18
Martin, David, Ek24
Martin, G.H., Aa73–74; Bb172,c132; Ef26
Martin, Ged W., Nb35
Martin, Graham, Fi19
Martin, Janet D., Ek25
Martin, Judy, Ee45
Martin, Ron, If63
Marwick, Arthur, Ba101,c61; Ij39
Marx, Roland, Bc81; Hf57,g10,h35,l79
Mason, A. Stuart, Gc7

# Index of Authors

# Index of Authors

Mellers, Wilfrid, Fk83; Ha17
Melling, Elizabeth, Ij42
Melling, Joseph, Hb40; If67
Mellini, Peter, Ij43
Mellor, G. Hunt, Ih18
Melman, Billie, Ba105
Melton, Frank T., Ff15
Mendle, Michael, Fa11
Mendyk, Stan A.E., Fk84
Menefee, Samuel Pyeatt, Ba106
Mennim, Eleanor Janet, If68
Mercer, Eric, Ba107
Messick, Frederic M., Aa77
Metcalf, D.M., Dd6,7
Metcalfe, Alan, Hl85
Meynell, Geoffrey Guy, Aa78
Meynell, Hugo, He53
Michael, Emily, Fj31,k85; Gi45
Michael, Fred S., Fj31,k85; Gi45
Michael, M.A., Ei36
Middlemas, Keith, Ib30
Middleton, Richard, Gb44
Middleton, Roger, If69
Milburn, Geoffrey E., Bb185
Miles, A.E.W., Bb186
Miles, David, Cb36
Miles, Ellen G., Gi46
Milford, Elizabeth, Fi21
Milhous, Judith, Gi47
Miller, D.P., Gj17
Miller, Elaine, Hl86
Miller, F.J.W., Bb187
Miller, J.D.B., Id44
Miller, John, Fb55; Gb45
Miller, Mervyn, Ig19
Miller, Stuart Tindale, Bb185,188
Miller, Thomas P., Gi48
Millett, Benignus, Me9–11
Millett, Martin, Cb37
Mills, Anthony David, Ab28
Mills, T.C., Hf19
Milne, Gustav, Cb38; Dd8
Milne, June, Nb37
Milner, Lesley, Ej25
Milne-Tyte, Robert, Fc25
Milobar, David, Nc11
Miners, Norman, Nc12
Minett, John, Ih19
Mingay, Gordon E., Ba108; Gf28; Hh36
Mini, Piero V., Ij44
Minter, R.A., Nd6
Mirowski, Philip, Gf52
Mitchell, Alison, Bd17

Mitchell, Basil, He54
Mitchell, D.J., Bb189
Mitchell, D.M., Ej26
Mitchell, Karen Jane, Aa79
Mitchell, Leslie George, Gb46
Mitchell, Tessa, Ha18
Mitchison, Rosalind, Gg18–19
Mitter, Partha, Nh23
Mockaitis, Thomas R., Ng22
Moffat, Brian, Df25
Moggridge, Donald, If52
Moisan, Thomas, Fi22
Mokyr, Joel, Ba109
Moncreiff, Alison, Bb190
Moncreiff, Rhoderick, Bb190
Money, John, Gb47
Monnas, L., Ef28
Monod, Paul, Gb48
Montagu, Jennifer, Fe66
Moon, Marjorie, Aa80
Mooney, Desmond, Me12
Mooney, Linne R., Ei37
Moor, J.A. de, Hd11
Moorcroft, Paul, Ng23
Moore, Andrew, Ib31
Moore, James R., Bc16; He55–56; Ki12
Moore, John S., Eg22
Moore, M., Ca28
Moore, Pam, Bb191
Moore, W.F., Ca36
Moorhouse, H.F., Ij45
Moorhouse, Stephen, Ef29
Moreton, Charles E., Ec16; Fb56
Morgan, Austen, Mb23
Morgan, D. Densil, Ge23
Morgan, D.R., Jg4
Morgan, Joan, Hl87
Morgan, Kenneth O., Ib32
Morgan, Neil, Ij46
Morgan, Nicholas J., Bb192; Ha19,f62; Ih20
Morgan, Paul, Bb193; Fk86
Morgan, Raine, Aa81
Morgan, Roger, Fg44; Id45
Morison, John, Ij47
Moro, Rubén Oscar, Ng24
Morrill, John, Bc33; Fa12–13,b57–58; Kc2
Morris, J.N., Hb41
Morris, Janet, Ab29
Morris, Polly, Ba110
Morris, R.J., Ac61; Bc58; Ha20,b42,g35; Ig20

220

# Index of Authors

# Index of Authors

# Index of Authors

# Index of Authors

Postlethwaite, D., Hg43
Pot, Leen, Ii49
Potter, Jeremy, Ij52
Potter, Lois, Fk96
Potter, T.W., Cb39
Potts, Cassandra, Db13
Poulton, Rob, Df26
Pound, John F., Fa18
Pounds, N.J.G., Bb216; Eh20
Powell, Geoffrey, Ii50,51
Powell, R.F. Peter, Bb217
Powell, W. Raymond, Ac70; Eg24
Power, J.P., Ek7
Power, Michael J., Ff20
Power, Patrick C., Mj2
Power, Rosemary, Ki13
Power, Thomas P., Bc84; Mc18,e14
Pradhan, G.P., Nb40
Pratt, Derrick, Ja5
Pravda, Alex, Bc8
Prescott, Donald, Bb95
Press, Jon, Ac44; Hf37–39
Prest, John, Hb54
Prestwich, J.O., Ea35
Prestwich, Michael, Ea36,b23
Pretty, David, Hg44
Pretty, Jules N., Ef36
Price, David Trevor William, Bb218
Price, Helen, Aa93
Price, Richard, Ha22,g45
Price, William, Hl101
Prideaux, R.M., Bd25
Prior, Mary, Ac71; Fa19,g51
Prior, Roger, Fg52
Probert, Simon, Gf36
Prochaska, F.K., Ih24
Proctor, Molly Geraldine, Bb219
Pryce, Huw, Aa94; Jc1
Pugh, T.B., Eh21
Pugsley, Steven, Gi61
Pullan, Brian, Ac72
Purdie, Bob, Mb29
Pykett, Lyn, Hl102

Qalb-i-Abid, Nc14
Quail, Sarah, Bb220–222,c136
Quilligan, Maureen, Fb63
Quiney, Anthony, He62
Quinn, David Beers, Ba121
Quinn, John F., He63

Rack, Henry D., Ge26,27
Rafferty, Oliver P., He64

Raftery, Barry, La3
Raftis, J. Ambrose, Fg53
Railton, Margaret, Bb223
Raines, Robert, Fk97
Raison, Timothy, Ib36
Rakow, Lana, Hl70
Ramm, Agatha, Ha23,b55
Ramsay, Nigel, Ec20; Gi62
Ramsden, John, Ba176
Ramsey, Arthur Michael, He65
Randall, Adrian J., Gf37–39
Ranieri, F., Ba122
Ransom, Philip John Greer, Hf75
Ranson, Susan, Hc9
Raphael, D.D., Gi63
Ratcliffe, F.W., Aa95
Raven, G.J.A., Bc83
Raw, Barbara Catherine, De23
Rawcliffe, Carole, Ec21–22
Ray, Michael, Hg46
Raylor, Timothy, Fk112
Read, A.E., Ng31
Read, Donald, If74
Reay, Barry, Hb56,g47
Rebhorn, Wayne A., Fk98
Reclus, Elisee, Ha24
Redknap, Mark, Jg5
Redworth, Glyn, Fe70
Reece, Bob, Nf13
Reed, Michael, Ba123
Reed, Mick, Ac73; Ba124,c78; Hg48
Rees, Eiluned, Bb224
Rees, G. Wyn, Id56
Rees, Henry, Ij53
Rees, Iorwerth, Ja6
Refausse, Raymond, Aa96
Reid, Brian Holden, Ii52
Reid, Douglas A., Hl103
Reid, Norman H., Ka8
Reiffen, David, Gf33
Reisman, David, Hf76
Remme, Tillman, Nb41
Renzing, Rudiger, Gd36
Resnick, D.P., Ba125
Rexroth, Frank, Aa97
Reynolds, David, Ij54
Reynolds, Sian, Hg49
Rhodes, Dennis E., Fj34
Ribeiro, Alvaro, Gi64
Rich, Paul, Hl104
Richards, Alison, Hl87
Richards, Bernard, Hl105
Richards, Donald Sydney, Ng32

224

225

# Index of Authors

# Index of Authors

Smith, E.A., Hb60
Smith, Elaine R., Ib43
Smith, Godfrey, Ac89
Smith, Graham, Bk242
Smith, H.S.A., Fk110
Smith, Harold L., Ij61
Smith, Ian R., Ng34
Smith, J.E., Ac90
Smith, Joseph, Bc134
Smith, Julie A., Ee53
Smith, Justin Davis, Ib44–45
Smith, K.J., Aa112
Smith, Malcolm, Ia9
Smith, Peter, Ba141,b243; Fk111
Smith, Raymond, Id62–63
Smith, Robert, Bb244–245
Smith, William, Ei41
Smithies, Edward, Ii58
Smitten, Jeffrey R., Bc86; Gi72
Smoothy, Martyn, Cb14
Smout, T.C., Ga19; Hg55
Smyth, Charles, Fb25
Smyth, James J., Ig27
Smyth, Jim, Mb31
Smyth, Susan J.(ed.), Aa113
Snell, K.D.M., Ba142
Snetzler, M.F., Bb246
Snowden, Charmian, Ha8
Snowden, Keith, Bb247
Solomou, Solomos, If56
Soltow, Lee, Kf4
Somerville, C.J., Fe79
Sommerville, Johann, Fj39
Sonyel, Salahi R., Ii59
Soper, Kate, Ac91
Sotscheck, Ralf, Ab34
Southall, Humphrey, Ac92
Southern, P., Cb43
Southgate, B.C., Fg62
Spadafora, David, Gi73
Spalding, Frances, Ab36
Spalding, Ruth, Fb73–74
Sparrow, Elizabeth, Gc9
Spencer, Leon P., Nd9
Spencer-Silver, Patricia, He73
Spick, Bill, Bb248
Spiers, Sheila M., Ab37–39; Bd30
Spinks, Brian D., Fe80
Spring, Eileen, Ba143
Spufford, Margaret, Ba144
Spufford, Peter, Aa114–115; Bc132
Spurgeon, C.J., Jh3
Spurr, John, Fe81,j40

St John, John, Ba145
St John of Fawsley, lord, He74
Stacey, Robin Chapman, Lg8
Stafford, Pauline, Db15
Stafford, Robert A., Na26
Stagg, D.J., Bb249
Stagl, J., Fa21
Stalley, Roger, Li31–32
Stan, Valeriu, Hd15
Staniland, K., Ef41
Stanley, Brian, Nd10
Stanley, Christopher, Bb15
Stanley, Eric G., Bc31; Da13
Stanley, Liz, Ba146
Stanley, M.F., Bb250
Stannard, Kevin P., He75
Stansfield, Michael, Eh23
Staples, A.C., Nc18
Stapleton, Guy, Bb251
Stark, Thomas, If83
Starkey, Armstrong, Gh21
Starkey, David J., Fb75; Gh22–23
Statt, Daniel, Fb76
Staves, Susan, Ba147
Stearn, Roger T., Ng35
Stebbings, Chantal, Ba148
Steedman, Carolyn, Ha28
Steensgaard, Niels, Ff25
Stein, Burton, Nc19
Stell, Geoffrey, Ka10
Stenning, David F., Ek1
Stephen, M.D., He76
Stephens, G.R., Cb44
Stephenson, Jayne D., Ig28
Stevens, Douglas J., Fb77
Stevenson, David, Fb78; Ki14
Stevenson, David R., Ac93
Stevenson, Jane, Li33
Stevenson, John, Bc5; Gb53; Ia10,b46
Stevenson, Sara, Aa116
Stevenson, Simon, Ih27
Stevenson, Stephanie, Bb252
Stewart, John V., He77
Stewart, Marion M., Kc4
Stimson, Shannon G., Gc10
Stocker, David, Bb253
Stocker, Margarita, Fk112
Stockwell, Anthony J., Ng36
Stoker, David, Gi74
Stoljar, Samuel, Ba149
Stone, Lawrence, Ba150
Stoneman, William P., Fg1
Stones, J.A., Ke14

# Index of Authors

# Index of Authors

# Index of Authors

Wells, Roger A.E., Ac73; Bc78
Welsh, Andrew, Ji9–10
Wendorf, Richard, Ba171
Wenham, L.P., Ca56
Wenham, S.J., Df32
Wernham, Richard Bruce, Fd27
West, Edwin G., Ba172
Whatley, Christopher A., Ga20
Wheatcroft, Andrew, Ib34
Wheeler, Nicholas, Id72
Wheelwright, Julie, Ba18
Wheen, Francis, Ib53
Whelan, Kevin, Bc84; Mb34,e16
Whetter, James, Bb301
Whipp, Richard, Ba173
White, Adam, Ej39; Fk122
White, Bruce, Aa124
White, Eileen, Fa23
White, Graeme J., Ea44
White, Harry, Li32
White, Luise, Ng38
White, Paul Whitfield, Fk123
Whitehead, John, Nb49
Whitehouse, Frank Edgar, Ii65
Whitelock, Dorothy M., De29
Whitham, David, Ib54
Whiting, R.C., If92
Whitney, Charles E., Bb302
Whittaker, David J., Ib55
Whittaker, Ken, Ca3
Whittet, T. Douglas, Fg73
Whybra, Julian, Ng12
Whyte, Ian D., Bb303; Ga21,f53; Kg6
Whyte, John, Mb35
Whyte, Kathleen A., Ga21
Wiener, Joel H., Aa125
Wigram, Isolde, Eb30
Wildsmith, Osmond, Bb304
Wiliam, Aled Rhys, Jc3
Wilkes, J.J., Ac101
Willcox, Temple, Ij66
Willetts, Arthur, Bb305
Williams, Ann, Bc109–111,117–120;
  Db16
Williams, Barrie, Eb31
Williams, Bill, Hg59
Williams, C.L. Sinclair, Eh28
Williams, D.F., Ca40
Williams, Daniel, Bc32; Eg35
Williams, David H., Ab40,41; Je7–8
Williams, David Innes, Ba174
Williams, David M., Ba175
Williams, Gareth, Hl129

Williams, Glanmor, Bc75
Williams, Glyndwr, Na13–14
Williams, Glynn, Ba176
Williams, Guy Richard, Hl130
Williams, J. Gwynn, Fi36
Williams, Jack, Hl131; Ij67
Williams, James, Gg24
Williams, Janet Hadley, Bc89
Williams, Joanna M., Eb32
Williams, Keith, Nf17
Williams, Ken, Bb306
Williams, M.R., Ij68
Williams, Rowan, He91
Williams, Tim, Ca57
Williams, Trevor I., Ij69
Williamson, David Graham, Id73
Williamson, Jeffrey G., Ba177; Hf88–89
Wilson, A.N., He92
Wilson, Adrian, Ac102
Wilson, Christopher, Ee65
Wilson, Curtis, Bc18; Fk124
Wilson, David B., Hk34
Wilson, Ellen Gibson, Hh47
Wilson, Hugh, Id74
Wilson, Janet, Fe89
Wilson, Kathleen, Ga22
Wilson, P.R., Bc114
Wilson-North, W.R., Fk125
Wilt, Alan F., Ii66
Wilton, Robert, Bd32
Winkless, Doreen, Ee66
Winstanley, Michael J., Hb68
Winstone, Harry V.F., Ac103
Winter, J.M., Ii67
Winterbottom, S., Ca58
Wirdnam, Audrey, Bb307
Wiseman, W.G., Le23
Withers, C.W.J., Bb308; Gi79
Witney, K.P., Ef44–45
Wokler, Robert, Gi80
Wolff, Janet, Hl132
Wolffe, John, He93
Wong, Maria Lin, Bb309
Wood, Dennis, Gd43
Wood, Diana, Bc128
Wood, Ellen Meiksins, Ac104
Wood, G.E., If93
Wood, Ian N., Dc10,d9
Wood, Ian S., Ib56
Wood, J.L., Hk35
Wood, Jennifer, Aa126
Wood, Juliette, Ji11
Wood, Paul, Ki15

232

# Index of Authors

# INDEX OF PERSONAL NAMES

# Index of Personal Names

# Index of Personal Names

More, John (fl. 1511), Fj23
More, Sir Thomas, Fe45,63,i23,j12,34, 38,k21
Morgan, William, bishop of Llandaff, Fe54
Morgan, William (translator), Fe31
Morris, William, Aa70; Hf38,l26
Morrison, Colonel Joseph Wanton, Gh19
Mosley, Sir Oswald, Ib7
Mowlem, John (diarist), Ha15
Moyne, baron, *see* Guinness
Muir, Alexander (fl. 1845), Nh19
Munro, Sir Thomas (d. 1837), Nc19
Murchison, Sir Roderick (d. 1871), Na26
Muret, St Stephen, Ee45
Murphy, James, bishop of Clogher, Aa42
Murray, James Erskine, Hd14
Myers, George (d. 1875), He73

Nairn, Rev. James (d. 1678), Aa108
Napoleon I (emperor), Gd26
Natal, bishop of, *see* Colenso
Nehru, Jawaharlal, Nb2,h11
Neill, Patrick (printer), Mi9
Nesselrode, Charles (d. 1862), Hd1
Nettleton, John (d. 1553), Fk53
Neustadt, Richard (historian), Id41
Neville family, Ea34,b33
Newall, Walter (architect), Hl77
Newcastle, duchess of, *see* Cavendish; duke of, *see* Pelham-Holles
Newdigate, John (undergraduate), Fk70
Newdigate, Richard (undergraduate), Fk70
Newdigate, Robert (MP), Ff1
Newman, Cardinal John Henry, Bc102, 127; Ha26,b50,e10,12–14,16–18,20, 23,25–26,28–29,31,33,35–36,41,43– 44,46,53–54,58–59,61,63,65–66,69, 72,74,78,80–81,90–92,i11
Newton, Sir Isaac, Ac51; Ba179; Fk18, 119,124; Ge19
Nichol, John P. (astronomer), Hk29
Nkrumah, Kwame (d. 1972), Nb8,37
Noel-Baker, Philip (d. 1982), Ib55
North, Frederick, lord, Gb50
Northampton, earl of, *see* Howard; marquess of, *see* Parr
Northcliffe, viscount of, *see* Harmsworth
Northumberland, earl of, *see* Percy
Norton, Thomas (d. 1584), Fb28
Notcutt family, Bd18

Nowell, Laurence (d. 1576), Fk40
Nugent, William (d. 1625), Lb7
Nussey, Ellen, Hl86

Oakes family, Ba55
O'Brien, Máire Rua, Mj1
O'Conchobhair, Aodh O (king of Connacht), Lb4
O'Connell, Daniel, Ma2,b7,11,21–22,26
O'Connor, Arthur, Hk17
O'Connor, Feargus (d. 1855), Hk17
Odo, bishop of Bayeux, Eb7
O'Donnell, Red Hugh (d. 1602), Li2
Offa (king), Da6
Offley family, Bd19
Ogilby, John (b. 1600), Fk29
O'Hagan, Lord Chancellor Thomas, Mc6

O'Kelly, J.J. (author), Mi11
Olaf Tryggvason, Dc7
Oldacre family, Bd8
Oliphant, Margaret (critic), Hl54
Oliver, Isaac, the elder (d. 1617), Fk16,99
Orsini, Cardinal Hyacinth, Ee23
Osborne, Thomas, 1st earl of Danby, Fe40
Owain Lawgoch, Jd3
Oxenham, Elsie J. (author), Ij5
Oxford, bishop of, *see* Stubbs

Paine family, Bd21
Painter, William, Fc1
Palmer, J.J.N. (historian), Ed7
Palmer, William Waldegrave, 2nd earl of Selbourne, Nb10
Palmerston, Henry John, 3rd viscount, Hd8
Parker, Matthew, archbishop of Canterbury, Fk50
Parma, duke of, *see* Farnese
Parr, William, 1st marquess of Northampton, Fg33
Parry, William (d. 1585), Fk7
Paston family, Ea37,c16
Patrick, St, Le7,22,g3,i6,33
Patterson, Colonel J.H. (Zionist), Ii9
Payne, Clement (trade unionist), Nc3
Peake, Robert (d. 1612), Fk89
Pearson, J.L. (d. 1897), He62
Pedler family, Bd22
Peel, Sir Robert, Mb21
Pelham-Holles, Thomas, 1st duke of Newcastle, Gb44

# COUNTY ABBREVIATIONS

## ENGLAND

| | | | | | |
|---|---|---|---|---|---|
| Bedfordshire | Bdf | Berkshire | Brk |
| Buckinghamshire | Bkm | Cambridgeshire | Cam |
| Cheshire | Chs | Cornwall | Con |
| Cumberland | Cul | Derbyshire | Dby |
| Devon | Dev | Dorset | Dor |
| Durham | Dur | Essex | Ess |
| Gloucestershire | Gls | Hampshire | Ham |
| Herefordshire | Hef | Hertfordshire | Hrt |
| Huntingdonshire | Hun | Isle of Wight | IoW |
| Isles of Scilly | Ios | Kent | Ken |
| Lancashire | Lan | Leicestershire | Lec |
| Lincolnshire | Lin | Middlesex | Mdx |
| Norfolk | Nfk | Northamptonshire | Nth |
| Northumberland | Nbl | Nottinghamshire | Ntt |
| Oxfordshire | Oxf | Rutland | Rut |
| Shropshire | Shr | Somerset | Som |
| Staffordshire | Sts | Suffolk | Sfk |
| Surrey | Sry | Sussex | Ssx |
| Warwickshire | War | Westmorland | Wes |
| Wiltshire | Wil | Worcestershire | Wor |
| Yorkshire | Yks | | |
| | | | |
| Isle of Man | IoM | | |

## SCOTLAND

| | | | | | |
|---|---|---|---|---|---|
| Aberdeen | Abd | Angus | Ans |
| Argyll | Arl | Ayr | Ayr |
| Banff | Ban | Berwick | Bew |
| Bute | But | Caithness | Cai |
| Clackmannan | Clk | Dumfries | Dfs |
| Dunbarton | Dnb | East Lothian | Eln |
| Fife | Fif | Hebrides | Wis |
| Inverness | Inv | Kinross | Krs |
| Kincardine | Kcd | Kirkcudbright | Kkd |
| Lanark | Lks | Midlothian | Mln |
| Moray | Mor | Nairn | Nai |
| Orkney | Ork | Peebles | Pee |
| Perth | Per | Renfrew | Rfw |
| Ross & Cromarty | Roc | Roxburgh | Rox |
| Selkirk | Sel | Shetland Isles | Zet |
| Stirling | Sti | Sutherland | Sut |
| West Lothian | Wln | Wigtown | Wig |

# County Abbreviations

## WALES

| | | | |
|---|---|---|---|
| Anglesey | Agy | Brecknock | Bre |
| Caernarvon | Cae | Cardigan | Cgn |
| Carmarthen | Cmn | Denbigh | Den |
| Flint | Fln | Glamorgan | Gla |
| Merioneth | Mer | Monmouth | Mon |
| Montgomery | Mgy | Pembroke | Pem |
| Radnorshire | Rad | | |

## IRELAND

| | | | |
|---|---|---|---|
| Carlow | Car | Cavan | Cav |
| Clare | Cla | Cork | Cor |
| Donegal | Don | Dublin | Dub |
| Galway | Gal | Kerry | Ker |
| Kildare | Kid | Kilkenny | Kik |
| Laois | Las | Leitrim | Let |
| Limerick | Lim | Longford | Log |
| Louth | Lou | Mayo | May |
| Meath | Mea | Monaghan | Mog |
| Offaly | Off | Roscommon | Ros |
| Sligo | Sli | Tipperary | Tip |
| Waterford | Wat | Westmeath | Wem |
| Wexford | Wex | Wicklow | Wic |

## NORTHERN IRELAND

| | | | |
|---|---|---|---|
| Antrim | Ant | Armagh | Arm |
| Derry | Dry | Down | Dow |
| Fermanagh | Fer | Tyrone | Tyr |

# INDEX OF PLACES

# Index of Places

# INDEX OF SUBJECTS

# Index of Subjects

# Index of Subjects

Crown, Ea16,g36,h27; Gc3
Cryptography, Ii60
Culture, Ac28,60,93; Bc4,144; Gg5,i71;
  Ha27,f16,46,73,77,79; monastic, Li22;
  popular, Gi24; Hb30,67,g14–
  l5,65,108; Ij45; Mb13; provincial,
  Gi15; *and see* Industrial; Political;
  Urban
*Curiales*, Ea10,g30
Customs, Ba36,119,b264,c122; Lf4
*Daily Telegraph*, Ij26

Dance, Bb92
Danegeld, Db6,12,d6
'Dark earth' deposits, Ca59
Darwinism, Ij19
Databases, Ac4,9; Ee17,f18; *and see*
  Computing
*De consulatu Stiliconis*, Eb29
*De Re Militari*, Eh13
Death, Fg15; Hh1; literature, Li27; rates,
  Ba73; Fg20
Decapitation, Ja7
De-Christianization, Ge28
De-colonization, Id40; Nb16,47,h1
Decoys, duck, Bb80
Deer parks, Ek13
Defence, Ii17; coastal, Eh22; colonial,
  Ng36; imperial, Ng10,27; national,
  Hj6; planning, Ii29; urban, Ek22
Defenderism, Mb8,13,31
Degeneration, Hk4
De-industrialization, Ba138; If91
Democracy, Ib32
Demography, Ab27,c9,84; Ba109; Ef6;
  Fh6; Gg19; Hg1,38,54,60; Ig26,29
Demonology, Fg45,59
De-nationalization, If33
De-nazification, Id32–33
Dendrochronology, Ek21
Dentistry, Ba75; Hk23
Depression, Great, Ne16
Design, Hf38,l18,57,93–94
Devolution, Hc6; Ib24,h15
Diaries, Fb74; Gf28;
  Ha15,b32,g36,l49,63; Id65; Kg3;
  Nh19
Diet, Hh38
Diggers, Fi24,j26
Diocesan valuations, Le4
Diplomacy, Ab5,c38; Fd6; Nb39; *and see*
  Foreign Office; Foreign policy;
  Relations

Directories, Ab2; Hc9
Disasters, If89
Disease, Eg15,21; Fg19,29,54,i32; Gj5
Disobedience, civil, Fj20–21
Dispensaries, Bb187
Dissent, Fe49,90–91; He8; *and see*
  Nonconformity
Divorce, Ba150; Fg33; Gg20
Docks, Ig1
Dockyards, Fi5; Gh16; Hf56
Domesday Book, Ea1–2,4–6,17,22,28–
  29,33,38–41,c23–29,f44,g22,24
Domestic service, Hg29
Dovecotes, Ba13
Drama, Ei20; Fk1,15,22,63,117;
  Hl11,110; *and see* Theatre
Dress, Lg5
Druids, Cb15
Drunkenness, Ih18
Dunlop Ltd, If66

East India Company, Bb91; Gf25,29;
  Nd1,g28
Easter table, Le16
Eastern Question, Hd17
Ecclesiastical censures, Le13
Ecclesiology, Fe24
Econometrics, If8
Economic decline, Bc144;
  Hf16,46,67,77,79,i2; development,
  Gf14; enterprise, Hf73; geography,
  Hf82; growth, Gf24,31; Hf19; history,
  Aa35,c17,67; performance, If71;
  policy, Bc23; Hb29,f60; Ib3,29–
  30,37,f14,37–
  38,42,45,52,56,69,83,85,91; theory,
  Ac52–53; Gf32,46; If6,64,69,j44
Economics, Ba172; Hf76; Ij23
Economy, Bc39; Cb11,19,37; Mg6;
  domestic, Gg23; rural, Ba128; Ef14
Education: Aa26,c97;
  Ba125,139,b14,23,48,50,148,158,166,
  181,208,c106; Ei5,48;
  Fe17,64,g62,68,k26,70,115;
  Gf30,i6,22,27; Ha11,h26–27,i5,13,18;
  If1,35,g23,h7,14,23,28,j20,24,49–
  50,54–55; Ki5; Li8; Ma4,f14,i13;
  clerical, Ee31; colonial, Nh24; female,
  Hi7; Ij6; higher, Ac24; Ih26,j25,41,53;
  legal, Ec31; medical, Gj3; music, Ij2;
  policy, Ih16,28,30; primary, Mi1;
  religious, Ee2; scientific, Bb104; Hk19;
  secondary, Hi19; Mi1; technical, Hi7;

# Index of Subjects